CASES IN CONTEMPORARY STRATEGY ANALYSIS

CASES IN CONTEMPORARY STRATEGY ANALYSIS

SECOND EDITION

EDITED BY

Robert M. Grant
Georgetown University and City University

Kent E. Neupert
The Chinese University of Hong Kong

BLACKWELL *Business*

Copyright © Blackwell Publishers Ltd 1999
Editorial apparatus and arrangement copyright © Robert M. Grant and Kent E. Neupert 1999

First edition published 1996
Second edition published 1999

2 4 6 8 10 9 7 5 3 1

Blackwell Publishers Ltd
108 Cowley Road
Oxford OX4 1JF
UK

Blackwell Publishers Inc.
350 Main Street
Malden, Massachusetts 02148
USA

British Library Cataloguing in Publication Data

A CIP catalogue record for this book is available from the British Library.

Library of Congress Cataloging-in-Publication Data has been applied for.

ISBN 0-631-21359-7 (hbk)
ISBN 0-631-21360-0 (pbk)

Typeset in Photina 10/12 pt
by Best-set Typesetter Ltd., Hong Kong
Printed in Great Britain by TJ International, Padstow, Cornwall

This book is printed on acid-free paper.

CONTENTS

Against the backdrop of the largest auto merger in history, Daimler Chrysler, this case examines the sources of increasing price competition and declining profitability and looks ahead to the future of the industry.

Although the number of subscribers to both fixed-line and cellular telecommunications services in China had grown substantially, penetration rates in 1998 remained relatively low compared to other Asian and international markets. With the development of traditional services and enlarging of network size, many new value-added services, such as email, facsimile store and forward, and Internet service, had been introduced to and welcomed by subscribers, resulting in a high growth rate. These changes indicated a tremendous potential for further development in telecommunications in China. How the domestic and foreign companies maneuvered the industry forces would determine their success or failure in the market.

Eastman Kodak faced a dilemma as technology was changing within its core photographic market from chemical imaging to digital imaging. The company CEO, George Fisher, had staked the company's future on the critical decision to be an imaging company rather than a chemical/pharmaceutical company. However, it was still unclear how the market for digital imaging products would develop, and whether Kodak could build the capabilities needed to establish leadership against competitors such as Fuji, Hewlett-Packard, Canon, and Casio.

In 1998, the Royal Dutch/Shell Group of companies was emerging from one of the most ambitious and far-reaching organizational restructurings of its 91-year history. However, Shell remained a highly complex organization where lines of responsibility and authority were diffused, central direction remained weak, and a highly decentralized organization coexisted with a large corporate bureaucracy. Had enough been done to squeeze excess costs out of Shell and to turn its sprawling multinational empire into an enterprise capable of deploying its huge resources with speed and clear direction?

In 1995, meetings were held between Seagram Company Ltd. and Matsushita Industrial Electric Company Ltd. to discuss Seagram's possible acquisition of the entertainment company MCA Inc. Although Seagram's President and CEO saw huge potential in the entertainment industry, he was concerned that besides cash Seagram would bring little to the acquisition of MCA in terms of entertainment assets or management. Hollywood had a history of treating newcomers badly. Would Seagram fare any better in the unpredictable world of entertainment, where relationships in the Hollywood network were just as important as creativity, technology, and business experience?

Jack Welch's contribution as CEO of GE was to dismantle much of the organizational structure and the management systems he had inherited. In its place Welch created a corporation intended to mesh the strengths of enormous size and diversity with the agility and entrepreneurial drive of a series of small enterprises. In the process, Welch reformulated GE's business portfolio, pioneered global expansion, and pushed GE to unprecedented levels of profitability and shareholder return. After 16 years of Welch's leadership and two years away from retirement, the only question remaining for GE employees and the army of GE watchers in securities companies, business schools, and consulting companies was: "What next?"

AES was like no other company in the electricity-generation industry. It was committed to social responsibility and providing fun for employees. Its management system had been described as "empowerment gone mad." Yet the system worked well. It encouraged amazing loyalty, commitment, and initiative from employees, entrepreneurial drive at all levels, and unmatched levels of operational efficiency. However, international expansion and increasing industry competition presented challenges. Could its unique management system and organization structure survive increasing growth, internationalization, and growing competition?

PREFACE

Managers face complex business decisions. While the questions of which industries to invest in, what products or services to offer, and how to be competitive have long confronted managers, today's rapid technological changes and increasingly international markets compound the difficulties of decision-making. Our approach to sorting through challenges incorporates a recognition of the distinct resources and capabilities that firms command. This approach helps managers to better understand how to compete in today's changing marketplace.

This second edition of *Cases in Contemporary Strategy Analysis* represents a continuing commitment to examining current business theory in the context of real business situations. A reality of business practice is that strategy formulation and strategy implementation cannot be separated. A strategy that cannot be implemented is worthless, and strategy must be formulated with a view to its implementation. As a set of management situations, the cases in this collection focus on the implementation of strategy, forming a complementary resource to Robert Grant's *Contemporary Strategy Analysis, Third Edition*, also published by Blackwell.

The cases in this collection represent the challenges faced by managers at the close of the twentieth century. Most of the companies and their managers are well-known leaders in their industries. Others stand out for their unique approach to implementing strategy. In all, they represent 17 companies in 17 different industries doing business in various regions around the world. The international nature of the companies represents the increasingly global nature of business today.

A distinguishing feature of this casebook is that the cases present the reader with important management decision situations. This allows the reader to work through the situation as the manager has done. The casebook is suitable for MBA and under-graduate classes. The information in the cases is sufficient as to not require additional outside research before the issues can be discussed in class. All of the cases have been tested in MBA, executive, and undergraduate programs around the world.

ACKNOWLEDGMENTS

We would like to thank the colleagues who have contributed to this project:

Andoni Aguirreazaldegui	Kris Hammargren	Mike Novy
Paul W. Beamish	Bach Lien Ho	Andrew Nulman
Kimberly Bennett	Rene Houle	Lisa Paganini
Clara Chak	Andrew Inkpen	Polly Poon
Emer Dooley	Jay Jacobs	Mike Quitana
Roger Dunbar	Suresh Kotha	Melissa Schilling
Scott Duncan	Kristin Kraska	Michelle Shuey
Laura Estevez	Shalini Lal	Andrea Stueve
Joseph N. Fry	Adam Laux	Claudio Theirman
Henry Fu	Lui Sai Lung	Cynthia Varner
Jean Gibbons	Alex Ng	Ken Yeung
David Glass		

We also would like to thank Catriona King and the people at Blackwell Publishers for their encouragement and assistance. Without them, this book would not have been possible.

The editors and publishers gratefully acknowledge permission to reproduce copyright material:

Exhibit 1.2 ("Diver demographics: age of divers"), from Professional Association of Diving Instructors, *1991 Diver Survey Results and Analysis*, Preliminary Draft;

Excerpts on pages 27–9, 31–4, and 37–8 from "The Chief Executive's Statement," *Annual Reports*, 1996 and 1998, Laura Ashley Holdings plc, London;

Excerpts on pages 198, 206, 207, 210, 211, and 216 from "Who's writing the book on web business?" *Fast Company*, Oct.–Nov. 1996;

Exhibits 10.4a ("US consumption of coffee and other beverages") and 10.4b ("US specialty coffee consumption") from National Coffee Association of U.S.A., 1995 Report;

Exhibit 10.4c ("US consumption in gallons") from John C. Maxwell Jr., *Beverage Industry, Annual Manual*, 1995 and 1997;

Place of consumption data in Exhibit 10.6 ("Japan consumer preferences") from *Tea & Coffee Trade Journal*, Aug. 1995;

Figures 13.1 ("The Virgin companies") and 13.2 ("Financial performance of the Virgin Group") from *Financial Times*, Aug. 13, 1998;

Excerpts in Chapter 16 from "Speed, simplicity, and self confidence: an interview with Jack Welch" by Noel Tichy and Ram Charan, *Harvard Business Review*, Sept./Oct. 1989. Reprinted by permission of *Harvard Business Review*. Copyright © 1989 by the President and Fellows of Harvard College, all rights reserved;

Figure 16.3 ("GE's organization structure, 1994") from Noel Tichy and Stratford Sherman, *Control Your Destiny or Someone Else Will*. Copyright © 1993 by Noel M. Tichy and Stratford Sherman. Used by permission of Doubleday, a division of Random House, Inc.;

"Honeywell Inc. and Global Research & Development" case study (prepared by Professor Andrew C. Inkpen), Thunderbird, The American Graduate School of International Management, 1998;

"Seagram and MCA" case study (prepared by Professor Andrew Inkpen), Thunderbird, The American Graduate School of International Management, 1995.

Every effort has been made to trace copyright holders. We apologize for any apparent infringement of copyright and, if notified, we will be pleased to rectify any errors or omissions at the earliest opportunity.

Richard Ivey School of Business
The University of Western Ontario

CHAPTER ONE

CORAL DIVERS RESORT

Kent E. Neupert and Paul W. Beamish prepared this case solely to provide material for class discussion. The research assistance of Tara Hanna is gratefully acknowledged. The authors do not intend to illustrate either effective or ineffective handling of a managerial situation. The authors may have disguised certain names and other identifying information to protect confidentiality.

Jonathon Greywell locked the door on the equipment shed and began walking back along the boat dock to his office. He thought about the matters that had weighed heavily on his mind during the last few months. Over the years, Greywell had established a solid reputation for the Coral Divers Resort as a safe and knowledgeable scuba diving resort. It offered not only diving, but a beach front location. As a small but well regarded all-around dive resort in the Bahamas, many divers had come to prefer his resort to other, crowded tourist resorts in the Caribbean.

However, over the last three years, revenues had declined and, for 1995, bookings were flat for the first half of the year. Greywell felt he needed to do something to increase business before things got worse. He wondered if he should add some specialized features to the resort that would distinguish it from others. One approach was to focus on family outings. Rascals in Paradise, a travel company that specialized in family diving vacations, had offered to help him convert his resort to one which specialized in family diving vacations. They had shown him the industry demographics that indicated that families were a growing market segment (see Exhibit 1.1) and made suggestions about what changes would need to be made at the resort. They had even offered to create menus for children and to show the cook how to prepare the meals.

Another potential strategy for the Coral Divers Resort was adventure diving. Other resort operators in the Bahamas were offering adventure-oriented deep depth dives, shark dives, and night dives. The basic ingredients for adventure diving – reef sharks in the waters near New Providence and famous deep water coral walls – were already

EXHIBIT 1.1:
U.S. population demographics and income distribution

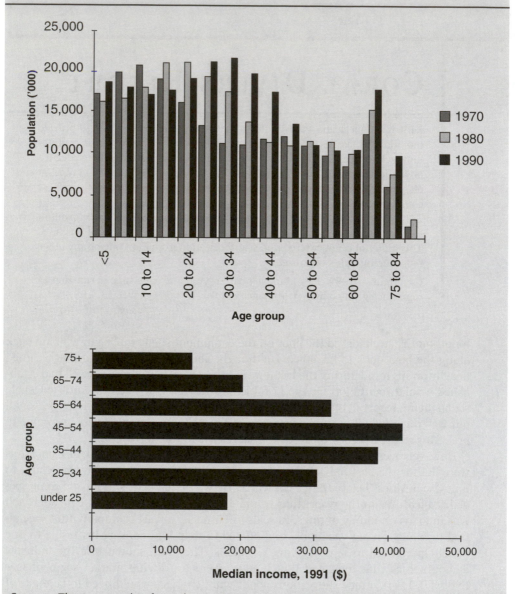

Sources: The top panel is from the *American Almanac, 1994–1995*, U.S. Bureau of Census; the lower panel is from *The Official Guide to the American Marketplace*, 1992.

in place. However, either of these strategies, family or adventure, would require changes and additions to his current operations. He was not sure whether any of the changes were worth the time and investment or whether he should instead try to improve upon what he was already doing.

A final option, and one which he had only recently thought about, was to leave New Providence and try to relocate elsewhere. At issue here was how much he might be able to recover if he sold Coral Divers and whether better opportunities existed elsewhere in the Bahamas or around the Caribbean.

SCUBA DIVING INDUSTRY OVERVIEW

Skin diving is an underwater activity of ancient origin in which a diver swims freely, unencumbered by lines or air hoses. Modern skin divers use three pieces of basic equipment: a face mask for vision, webbed rubber fins for propulsion, and a snorkel tube for breathing just below the water's surface. The snorkel is a plastic tube shaped like a J and fitted with a mouthpiece. When the opening of the snorkel is above water, a diver will be able to breathe. For diving to greater depths, the breath must be held; otherwise, water will enter the mouth through the snorkel.

Scuba diving provides divers with the gift of time to relax and explore the underwater world without having to surface for their next breath. Scuba is an acronym for Self-Contained Underwater Breathing Apparatus. While attempts to perfect this type of apparatus date from the early 20th century, it was not until 1943 that the most famous scuba, or Aqualung, was invented by the Frenchmen Jacques-Yves Cousteau and Emil Gagnan. The Aqualung made recreational diving possible for millions of nonprofessional divers. Scuba diving is also called free diving, because the diver has no physical connection with the surface. Although some specially trained commercial scuba divers descend below 100 m (328 ft) for various kinds of work, recreational divers rarely go below a depth of 40 m (130 ft) because of increased risk of nitrogen narcosis, a type of intoxication similar to drunkenness, or oxygen toxicity, which causes blackouts or convulsions.

The scuba diver wears a tank that carries a supply of pressurized breathing gas, either air or a mixture of oxygen and other gases. The heart of the breathing apparatus is the breathing regulator and the pressure-reducing mechanisms that deliver gas to the diver on each inhalation. In the common scuba used in recreational diving, the breathing medium is air. As the diver inhales, a slight negative pressure occurs in the mouthpiece, which signals the valve that delivers the air to open. The valve closes when the diver stops inhaling, and a one-way valve allows the exhaled breath to escape as bubbles into the water. When using a tank and regulator, a diver can make longer and deeper dives and still breathe comfortably.

Along with scuba gear and its tanks of compressed breathing gases, the scuba diver's essential equipment includes a soft rubber mask with a large faceplate, a soft rubber diving suit for protection from cold, long, flexible swimming slippers for the feet, buoyancy compensator device (known as a BC or BCD), weight belt, waterproof watch, wrist compass, and diver's knife. For protection from colder water, neoprene-coated foam rubber wet suits consisting of jacket, pants, hood, and gloves are worn.

Certification Organizations

There are several international and U.S.-based organizations that train and certify scuba divers.[1] PADI (Professional Association of Diving Instructors), NAUI (National Association of Underwater Instructors), SSI (Scuba Schools International), and NASDS (National Association of Scuba Diving Schools) are the most well known of these organizations. Of these, PADI is the largest certifying organization.

PADI is the largest recreational scuba diver training organization in the world. Founded in 1967, PADI has issued more than 5.5 million certifications since it began operation. Since 1985, seven of every ten American divers and an estimated 55 percent of all divers around the world have been trained by PADI instructors using PADI's instructional programs. At present PADI certifies well over half a million divers internationally each year and has averaged a 12 percent increase in certifications each year since 1985. In 1994, PADI International issued 625,000 certifications, more than in any other single year in company history.

PADI's main headquarters are in Santa Ana, California. Its distribution center is in the U.K. and it has seven local area offices in Australia, Canada, Japan, New Zealand, Norway, Sweden, and Switzerland, with professionals and member groups in 175 countries and territories. PADI is made up of four groups: PADI Retail Association, PADI International Resort Association, Professional Members, and PADI Alumni Association. The three association groups emphasize the "Three E's" of recreational diving: Education, Equipment, and Experience. By supporting each facet, PADI provides holistic leadership to advance recreational scuba diving and snorkel swimming to equal status with other major leisure activities, while maintaining and improving the excellent safety record PADI has experienced. PADI offers seven levels of instruction and certification ranging from entry-level to instructor.

NAUI first began operation in 1960. The organization was formed by a nationally recognized group of instructors in the U.S. that was known as the National Diving Patrol. Since its beginning, NAUI has been active worldwide, certifying sport divers in various levels of proficiency, from basic skin diver to instructor. In addition, NAUI regularly conducts specialty courses for cave diving, ice diving, wreck diving, underwater navigation, and search and recovery.

Industry Demographics

Scuba diving has grown steadily in popularity, especially in recent years.[2] For the period 1989–94, increases in the number of certifications averaged over 10 percent per year. The total number of certified divers worldwide is estimated to be over 10 million. Of these newly certified scuba divers, approximately 65 percent are male and 35 percent are female. Approximately half are married. Approximately 70 percent of them are between the ages of 18 and 34, while about 25 percent are between 35 and 49 (see Exhibit 1.2). They are generally well educated, with 80 percent having a college education. Overwhelmingly, they are employed in professional, managerial, and technical occupations. Their average annual household

EXHIBIT 1.2:
Diver demographics: age of divers

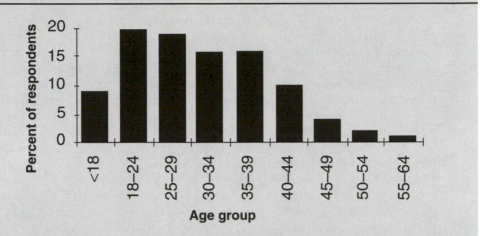

Sources: information taken from the PADI *1991 Diver Survey Results and Analysis*, Preliminary Draft.

income is $75,000. Forty-five percent of divers travel most often with their families. Another 40 percent travel with friends or informal groups.

Divers are attracted to diving for various reasons: seeking adventure and being with nature are the most often cited reasons (over 75 percent for each). Socializing, stress relief, and travel also are common motivations. Two-thirds of divers travel overseas on diving trips once every three years, while 60 percent travel domestically on dive trips each year. On average, divers spend $2,816 on dive trips annually, with an average equipment investment of $2,300. Aside from upgrades and replacements, the equipment purchase could be considered a one-time cost. Warm water diving locations are generally chosen 2 to 1 over cold water diving sites. Cozumel in Mexico, the Cayman Islands, and the Bahamas are the top three diving destinations outside the continental U.S. for Americans.

According to a consumer survey, the "strongest feelings" that divers associate with their scuba diving experiences are "excitement" and "peacefulness." In a 1991 survey, the two themes drew an equal number of responses. However, there seem to be very distinct differences in the two responses. One suggests a need for stimulation, while the other suggests relaxation and escape. Visual gratification ("beauty") is another strong motivation for divers. The feelings of "freedom, weightlessness, and flying" were also popular responses.

Under PADI regulations, 12 is the minimum age for certification by the majority of scuba training agencies. At the age of 12, the child can earn a Junior Diver certification. The Junior Diver meets the same standards as an Open Water Diver but generally must be accompanied on dives by a parent or other certified adult. At age

15, the Junior Diver certification can be upgraded to Open Water status by an instructor. This upgrade may require skills review and evaluation. Pre-dive waiver and release forms require the signature of a parent or guardian until the minor turns 18.

A cautious approach to young divers is based on the concept of readiness to dive. An individual's readiness to dive is determined by physical, mental, and emotional maturity. Physical readiness is the easiest to assess: Is the child large and strong enough to handle scuba equipment? An air tank and weight belt can weigh over 40 lbs., although most dive shops can provide equipment specially sized for smaller divers. Mental readiness refers to whether the child has the academic background and conceptual development to understand diving physics and perform the arithmetic required for certification. The arithmetic understanding focuses on allowable bottom time, which requires factoring in depth, number of dives, and length of dives. Emotional readiness is the greatest concern. Will the junior diver accept the responsibility of being a "dive buddy"? Divers never dive alone and dive buddies are supposed to look out for and rely on each other. Do they comprehend the safety rules of diving and willingly follow them? Most dive centers accept students from age 12, but the final determination of readiness to dive rests with the scuba instructor. Instructors are trained to evaluate the readiness of all students prior to completion of the course work and will only award a certification to those who earn it, regardless of age.

DIVING IN THE BAHAMAS [3]

New Providence Island, the Bahamas

New Providence Island is best known for its major population center, Nassau. Nassau's early development was based on its superb natural harbor. As the capital of the Bahamas, it is the seat of Government, also home to 400 banks, elegant homes, ancient forts, and a wide variety of duty-free shopping. It has the island's most developed tourist infrastructure, with elegant resort hotels, casinos, cabaret shows, and cruise ship docks. More than two-thirds of the population of the Bahamas live on New Providence and most of these 150,000 people live in or near Nassau, on the northeast corner of the island.

With thousands of vacationers taking resort courses (introductory scuba courses taught in resort pools), Nassau has become known as a destination that is as good for an exploratory first dive as it is for more advanced diving. There are many professional dive operations in the Nassau/Paradise Island area (see Exhibit 1.3). While all offer resort courses, many also offer a full menu of dive activities designed for the more advanced and experienced diver. Within a 30-minute boat ride of most operations are shipwrecks, beautiful shallow reefs, and huge schools of fish.

In contrast to the bustle of Nassau, the south side of New Providence Island is quieter and more laid back. Large tracts of pine trees and rolling hills dominate the central regions, while miles of white sand beach surround the island. At the west end of the island is Lyford Cay, an exclusive residential area. Nearby, the winding

EXHIBIT 1.3:
Names and location of diving operators in the Bahamas

Abaco
Brendal's Dive Shop
Dive Abaco
Walker's Cay Undersea
  Adventures

Andros
Small Hope Bay Lodge

Bimini
Bimini Undersea Adventures

Cat Island
Cat Island Dive Center

Eleuthera/Habour Island
Romora Bay Club
Valentine's Dive Center

Exuma
Exuma Fantasea

Long Island
Stella Maris Resort

*New Providence
  Island/Nassau*
Bahama Divers
Coral Divers Resort
Custom Aquatics
Dive Dive Dive
Diver's Haven
Nassau Scuba Center
Stuart Cove's Dive South
  Ocean

Sun Divers
Sunskiff Divers

San Salvador
Riding Rock Inn

Live-Aboard Dive Boats
Blackbeard's Cruises
Bottom Time Adventures
Nekton Diving Cruises
Out Island Voyages
Sea Dragon
Sea Fever Diving Cruises

Source: based on the Bahamas Diving Association membership.

canals of the Coral Harbor area offer easy access to the sea. While golf and tennis are available, the primary attraction is good scuba diving and top quality dive operations.

The southwest side of the island has been frequently used as an underwater movie/film set. The "Bond Wrecks" are popular diving destinations for divers and operators. The Vulcan Bomber used in *Thunderball* has aged into a framework draped with colorful gorgonians and sponges. The freighter, Tears of Allah, where James Bond eluded the Tiger Shark in *Never Say Never Again* remains a popular dive attraction in just 40 feet of water. The photogenic appeal of this wreck has improved with age, as more and more marine life congregates on this artificial reef.

There are also natural underwater attractions. Shark Wall and Shark Buoy are popular dive spots. Drop-off dives like Tunnel Wall feature a network of crevices and tunnels beginning in 30 feet of water and exiting along the vertical wall at 70 or 80 feet. Southwest Reef offers magnificent coral heads in only 15 to 30 feet of water, with schooling grunts, squirrelfish, and barracuda. A favorite of the shallow reef areas is Goulding Cay, where broad stands of elkhorn coral reach nearly to the surface.

Types of Diving

A wide array of diving activities are available in the Bahamas. These include shark dives, wreck dives, wall dives, reef dives, drift dives, night dives, and so forth. Illustrative examples follow.

Shark diving

The top three operators of shark dives in the Caribbean are in the Bahamas. While shark diving trips vary with the operators running them, there is at least one common factor in the Bahamas: the Caribbean Reef Shark (*Carcharhinus perezi*). When the dive boat reaches the site, the sound of the motor acts as a dinner bell. Even before the divers are in the water, the sharks gather for their handouts.

Long Island in the Bahamas was the first area to promote shark feed dives on a regular basis. This method began twenty years ago and has remained relatively unchanged. The feed is conducted as a feeding frenzy. Sharks circle as divers enter the water. After the divers position themselves with their backs to a coral wall, the feeder enters the water with a bucket of fish. This is placed in the sand in front of the divers and the action develops quickly. At Walker's Cay, in Abaco, the method is similar except for the number and variety of sharks in the feed. While Caribbean Reef Sharks make up the majority, Lemon Sharks, Bull Sharks, Hammerhead Sharks, and other species also appear.

The shark feed off Freeport, Grand Bahama, is a very organized event in which the sharks are fed either by hand or off the point of a polespear. The divers are arranged in a semi-circle with safety divers guarding the viewers as the feeder is positioned at the middle of the group. If the sharks become unruly, the food is withheld until they calm down. The sharks then go into a regular routine of circling, taking their place in line and advancing to receive the food. Although the sharks come within touching distance, most divers resist the temptation to reach out.

Shark Wall, on the southwest side of New Providence, is a pristine drop-off decorated with masses of colorful sponges along the deep water abyss known as the Tongue of the Ocean. Divers position themselves along sand patches among the coral heads in about 50 feet of water as Caribbean Reef Sharks and an occasional Bull or Lemon Shark cruise mid-water in anticipation of a free handout. During the feeding period, the bait is controlled and fed from a polespear by an experienced feeder. There are usually six to twelve sharks present, ranging from 4 to 8 feet in length. Some operators make two dives to this site, allowing divers to cruise the wall with the sharks in a more natural way before the feeding dive.

The Shark Buoy, also on the southwest side of New Providence, is tethered in 6,000 feet of water. Its floating surface mass attracts a wide variety of ocean marine life such as Dolphin fish, Jacks, Rainbow Runners, and Silky Sharks. The Silky Sharks are typically small, 3 to 5 feet long, but swarm in schools of six to twenty, with the sharks swimming up to the divemasters' hands to grab the bait.

From the operator's standpoint, the only special equipment needed for shark dives is a chain mail diving suit for the feeder's protection, some type of feeding apparatus, and intestinal fortitude. The thrill of diving among sharks is the main attraction for the divers. For the most part, the dives are safe, with only the feeder taking an occasional nick from an excited shark.

Divers participating in shark dives are required to sign waivers prior to the actual dive. As the fine print in most life insurance policies notes, claims for any scuba-related accidents are not payable. However, there do exist specialty insurers such as Divers Alert Network.

Wreck diving

Wreck diving is divided into three levels: non-penetration, limited penetration, and full penetration. Full penetration and deep wreck diving should be done only by divers who have completed rigorous training and have extensive diving experience. Non-penetration wreck diving refers to recreational diving on wrecks without entering an overhead environment that prevents direct access to the surface. Divers with Open Water certification are qualified for this type of diving without further training as long as they are comfortable with the diving conditions and the wreck's depth. Limited penetration wreck diving is defined as staying within ambient light and always in sight of an exit. Full penetration wreck diving involves an overhead environment away from ambient light and beyond sight of an exit. Safely and extensively exploring the insides of a wreck involves formal training and mental strength. On this type of dive, the first mistake could be the last.

Wall diving

In a few regions of the world, island chains, formed by volcanos and coral, have been altered by movements of the earth's crustal plates. Extending approximately due east–west across the central Caribbean Sea is the boundary between the North American and Caribbean crustal plates. The shifting of these plates has created some of the most spectacular diving environments in the world, characterized by enormous cliffs 2,000 to 6,000 feet high. At the cliffs, known as walls, the diver experiences the overwhelming scale and the dynamic forces that shape the ocean more than in any other underwater environment. It is on the walls that a diver is most likely to experience the feeling of free motion, or flying, in boundless space. Many of the dives in the Bahamas are wall dives.

Reef diving

Reefs generally are made up of three areas: a reef flat, a lagoon or bay, and a reef crest. The depth in the reef flat averages only a few feet, with an occasional deeper channel. The underwater life on a shallow reef flat may vary greatly in abundance and diversity within a short distance. The reef flat is generally a protected area, not exposed to strong winds or waves, making it ideal for novice or family snorkelers. The main feature distinguishing bay and lagoon environments from a reef flat is depth. Caribbean lagoons and bays may reach depths of 60 feet, but many provide teaming underwater ecosystems in as little as 15–20 feet. This is excellent for underwater photography and ideal for families or no decompression stop diving. The reef's crest is the outer boundary that shelters the bay and flats from the full force of the ocean's waves. Since the surging and pounding of the waves is too strong for all but the most advanced divers, most diving takes place in the protected bay waters.

FAMILY DIVING RESORTS

The current average age of new divers is 36. As the median age of new divers increased, families became a rapidly growing segment of the vacation travel industry. Many parents are busy and do not spend as much time with their children as they would prefer. Many parents who dive would like to have a vacation that would combine diving and spending time with their children. In response to increasing numbers of parents traveling with children, resort operators have added amenities ranging from babysitting services and kids' camps to dedicated family resorts with special facilities and rates. The resort operations available have greatly expanded in recent years. At all-inclusive self-contained resorts, one price includes everything: meals, accommodations, daytime and evening activities, and water sports. Many of these facilities offer special activities and facilities for children. Diving is included or available nearby.

For many divers, the most important part of the trip is the quality of the diving, not the quality of the accommodations. But for divers with families, the equation changes. Children, especially younger children, may find it difficult to do without a comfortable bed, television, or VCR, no matter how good the diving promises to be. Some resorts, not dedicated to family vacations, do make accommodations for divers with children. Condos and villas are an economical and convenient vacation option for divers with children. The additional space of this type of accommodation allows parents to bring along a babysitter. Having a kitchen on hand makes the task of feeding children simple and economical. Most diving destinations in the Bahamas, Çaribbean, and Pacific offer condo, villa, and hotel-type accommodations. Some hotels organize entertaining and educational activities for children while parents engage in their own activities.

As the number of families vacationing together has increased, some resorts and dive operators have started special promotions and programs. On Bonaire, part of the Netherlands Antilles, August has been designated Family Month. During this month, the island is devoted to families, with a special welcome kit for children and island-wide activities including "eco-walks" at a flamingo reserve, snorkeling lessons, and evening entertainment for all ages. In conjunction, individual resorts and restaurants offer family packages and discounts. Similarly, in Honduras, which has very good diving, a resort started a children's dolphin camp during summer months. While diving family members are out exploring the reefs, children between ages 8 and 14 spend their days learning about and interacting with a resident dolphin population. The program includes classroom and in-water time as well as horseback riding and paddle boating.

One travel company, Rascals in Paradise (1-800-U-RASCAL), specializes in family travel packages. The founders, Theresa Detchemendy and Deborah Baratta, are divers, mothers, and travel agents who have developed innovative packages for diving families. Theresa says, "The biggest concern for parents is their children's safety, and then what the kids will do while they're diving or enjoying an evening on the town." The Rascals people have worked with a number of family-run resorts all over the world to provide daily activities, responsible local nannies, and child-safe balconies, playgrounds, and children's pools.

They have also organized Family Weeks at popular dive destinations in Belize, Mexico, and the Cayman Islands. Family Week packages account for over 50 percent of Rascals' bookings each year. On these scheduled trips, groups of three to six families share a teacher/escort who brings along a fun program tailored for children and

EXHIBIT 1.4:
Rascals in Paradise pricing guide: Rascals Special Family Weeks, 1995

Destination	Duration	Price	Notes
Bahamas			
South Ocean Beach	7 nights	$3,120–$3,970	Lunch not included.
Small Hope Bay	7 nights	$3,504	Scuba diving included. Local host only.
Mexico			
Hotel Buena Vista	7 nights	$2,150–$2,470	
Hotel Club Akumal	7 nights	$2,080–$3,100	Lunch and airport transfer not included.

Prices are based on a family of four with two adults and two children aged 2–11. All packages include the following (except as noted): accommodations, Rascals escort, meals, babysitter, children's activities, airport transfers, taxes & services, and a $2,500 cancellation insurance per family booking. Airfares not included.

serves as activities director for the group. Rascals Special Family Weeks packages are priced based on a family of four (two adults and two children aged 2–11) and include a teacher/escort, one babysitter for each family, children's activities, meals, airport transfers, taxes, services, and cancellation insurance (see Exhibit 1.4). For example, in 1995, a 7-night family vacation at Hotel Club Akumal, on the Yucatan coast, was $2,080–3,100 per family. Rascals also packages independent family trips to 57 different condos, villas, resorts, and hotels which offer scuba diving. An independent family trip would not include a teacher/escort (see Exhibit 1.5). A 7-night independent family trip to Hotel Club Akumal ran $624–1,779.

Rascals' approach is unique in the travel industry because they personally select the resorts with which they work. "We try to work with small properties so our groups are pampered and looked after," says Detchemendy. "The owners are often parents and their kids are sometimes on the property. They understand the characteristics of kids." Typically, Detchemendy and Baratta visit each destination, often working with the government tourist board in identifying potential properties. If the physical structure is already in place, it is easy to add the resort to the Rascals booking list. If modifications are needed, the two sit down with the management and outline what needs to be in place so that the resort can be part of the Rascals program.

Rascals evaluate resorts according to several factors: (1) is the property friendly toward children and does it want them? (2) how does the property rate in terms of safety? (3) what are the facilities and is there a separate room to be used as a Rascals Room? (4) does the property provide babysitting and child care by individuals who are screened and locally known? A successful example of this approach is Hotel Club Akumal, in Akumal, Mexico. Detchemendy and Baratta helped the resort expand its market reach by building a family-oriented resort that became part of the Rascals program. Baratta explained, "In that case, we were looking for a place close to home,

EXHIBIT 1.5:
Rascals in Paradise pricing guide: independent family trips, 1995

Destination	Duration	Price	Notes
Bahamas			
South Ocean Beach	7 nights	$1,355–$1,771	
Small Hope Bay	7 nights	$2,860–$3,560	All meals, bar service, babysitter, and diving included.
Hope Town Harbour Lodge	7 nights	$962–$1,121	
Treasure Cay	7 nights	$875–$1,750	
Stella Maris, Long Island	7 nights	$1,547–$2,597	
Mexico			
Hotel Buena Vista	7 nights	$1,232–$1,548	All meals included.
Hotel Club Akumal	7 nights	$624–$1,779	
Hotel Presidente	7 nights	$1,120–$1,656	
La Concha	7 nights	$655–$963	
Plaza Las Glorias	7 nights	$632–$1,017	

Prices are based on a family of four with two adults and two children aged 2–11. Rates are per week (7 nights) and include accommodations and applicable taxes. These rates are to be used as a guide only. Each booking is quoted separately and will be dependent on season, type of accommodation, ages and number of children, meal and activity inclusions. All prices are subject to change. Some variations apply. Airfares not included.

with a multi-level range of accommodations, that offered something other than a beach, that was family friendly, and not in Cancun. We found Hotel Club Akumal, but they didn't have many elements in place, so we had to work with them. We established a meal plan, an all-inclusive product and designated activities for kids. We went into the kitchen and created a children's menu and we asked them to install a little kid's playground that's shaded." The resort became one of their most popular destinations.

Rascals offered two types of services to resort operators interested in creating family vacations. One was a consulting service. For a modest daily fee plus expenses, Baratta or Detchemendy, or both, would conduct an on-site assessment of the resort. This usually took one or two days. They would provide a written report to the resort regarding needed additions or modifications to the resort to make it safe and attractive for family vacations. Possible physical changes might include: the addition of a Rascals Room, child-safe play equipment, and modifications to existing buildings and structures, such as rooms, railings, and docks, to prevent child injuries. Rascals always tried to use existing equipment or equipment available nearby. Other, nonstructural changes could include: the addition of educational sessions, play-times, and other structured times for entertaining children while their parents were diving.

The report also included an implementation proposal. Then after implementation, the resort could decide whether or not to list with Rascals for bookings.

Under the second option, Rascals provided the consulting service at no charge to the resort. However, they asked that any requests for family bookings be referred back to Rascals. Rascals would then also list and actively promote the resort through their brochures and referrals. For resorts using the Rascals booking option, Rascals would provide premiums such as hats and T-shirts, in addition to the escorted activities. This attention to the family was what differentiated a Rascals resort from other resorts. Generally, companies who promoted packages received net rates from the resorts which were from 20 percent to 50 percent lower than "rack" rates. Rascals, in turn, promoted these special packages to the travel industry in general and paid a portion of their earnings out in commissions to other travel agencies.

Rascals tried to work with their resorts to provide packaged and prepaid vacations. This approach created a win–win situation for the resort managers and the vacationer. Packages or an all-inclusive vacation was a cruise ship approach. It allowed the inclusion of many activities in the package. For example, such a package might include seven nights' lodging, all meals, baby-sitting, children's activities, and scuba diving. This approach allowed the vacationer to know, up-front, what to expect. Moreover, the cost would be included in one set price, so that the family would not have to pay for each activity as it came along. The idea was to remove the surprises and make the stay enjoyable. It also allowed the resort operator to bundle activities together, providing more options than might otherwise be offered. As a result, the package approach was becoming popular with both resort owners and vacationers.

In their bookings, Rascals required prepayment of trips. This resulted in higher revenues for the resort since all activities were paid for in advance. Ordinarily, resorts on their own might only require a two- or three-night room deposit. Then, the family would pay for the rest of the room charge on leaving, after paying for other activities or services as they were used. While the vacationer might think they had a less expensive trip this way, in fact, prepaid activities were generally cheaper than à la carte activities. Moreover, à la carte activities potentially yielded lower revenues for the resort. Rascals promoted prepaid vacations as a win–win, low stress approach to travel. Rascals had been very successful with the resorts they listed. Fifty percent of their bookings were repeat business, and many inquiries were based on word-of-mouth referrals. All in all, Rascals provided a link to the family vacation market segment that the resort might not otherwise have. It was common for Rascals-listed resorts to average annual bookings of 90 percent.

CORAL DIVERS RESORT

Coral Divers Resort had been in operation ten years. Annual revenues had reached as high as $554,000. Profits generally had been in the 2 percent range, but for the past two years, losses had been experienced. The expected turnaround in profits in 1994 had never materialized (see Exhibit 1.6). While not making them rich, the business had provided an adequate income for Greywell and his wife, Margaret, and their two children, Allen, age 7, and Winifred, age 5. However, revenues had

EXHIBIT 1.6:
Comparative balance sheets as at June 30 (US$)

	1994	1993	1992
ASSETS			
Current assets:			
Cash	5,362	8,943	15,592
Accounts receivable	2,160	8,660	2,026
Inventories	5,519	6,861	9,013
Prepaid expenses	9,065	8,723	8,195
Total current assets	**22,106**	**33,187**	**34,826**
Fixed assets:			
Land	300,000	300,000	300,000
Building	200,000	200,000	200,000
Less: accumulated depreciation	(70,000)	(60,000)	(50,000)
Boats	225,000	225,000	225,000
Less: accumulated depreciation	(157,500)	(135,000)	(112,500)
Vehicles	54,000	54,000	54,000
Less: accumulated depreciation	(32,400)	(21,600)	(10,800)
Diving equipment	150,000	150,000	150,000
Less: accumulated depreciation	(90,000)	(60,000)	(30,000)
Total fixed assets	**579,100**	**652,400**	**725,700**
Total assets	**601,206**	**685,587**	**760,526**
LIABILITIES			
Current liabilities:			
Accounts payable	1,689	4,724	1,504
Bank loan	20,000	0	2,263
Mortgage payable, current portion	25,892	25,892	25,892
Note payable, current portion	40,895	40,895	40,895
Total current liabilities	**88,476**	**71,511**	**70,554**
Long-term liabilities:			
Mortgage payable, due in 1996	391,710	417,602	443,494
Note payable, 5-year	81,315	122,210	163,105
Total long-term liabilities	**473,025**	**539,812**	**606,599**
Total liabilities	**561,501**	**611,323**	**677,153**
SHAREHOLDERS' EQUITY			
Jonathan Greywell, capital	44,879	44,879	44,879
Retained earnings	(5,174)	29,385	38,494
Total shareholders' equity	**39,705**	**74,264**	**83,373**
Total liabilities and shareholders' equity	**601,206**	**685,587**	**760,526**

EXHIBIT 1.6: *Continued*

	1994	1993	1992
REVENUE			
Diving & lodging packages	482,160	507,670	529,820
Day diving	11,680	12,360	14,980
Certifications	5,165	5,740	7,120
Lodging	2,380	1,600	1,200
Miscellaneous	1,523	1,645	1,237
Total revenues	**502,908**	**529,015**	**554,357**
EXPENSES			
Advertising & promotion	15,708	15,240	13,648
Bank charges	1,326	1,015	975
Boat maintenance & fuel	29,565	31,024	29,234
Cost of goods sold	762	823	619
Depreciation	73,300	73,300	73,300
Dues & Fees	3,746	4,024	3,849
Duties & taxes	11,405	18,352	17,231
Insurance	36,260	34,890	32,780
Interest, mortgage, note & loan	40,544	40,797	41,174
Management salary	31,600	31,600	31,600
Office supplies	12,275	12,753	11,981
Professional fees	11,427	10,894	10,423
Repairs & maintenance, building	15,876	12,379	9,487
Salaries, wages & benefits	196,386	194,458	191,624
Telephone & fax	9,926	9,846	7,689
Trade shows	14,523	14,679	14,230
Utilities	20,085	19,986	17,970
Vehicles, maintenance & fuel	12,753	12,064	11,567
Total expenses	**537,467**	**538,124**	**519,381**
Net income	**(34,559)**	**(9,109)**	**34,976**
Retained earnings, beginning	**29,385**	**38,494**	**3,518**
Retained earnings, ending	**(5,174)**	**29,385**	**38,494**

Bahama$1 = US$1.

continued to decline. From talking with other operators, Greywell understood that resorts with strong identities and reputations for quality service were doing well. Greywell thought that the Coral Divers Resort had not distinguished itself in any particular aspect of diving or as a resort.

The Coral Divers Resort property was located on a deep water channel on the southwest coast of the island of New Providence in the Bahamas. The property occupied three acres and had beach access. There were six cottages on the property, each having a kitchenette, a full bath, a bedroom with two full-size beds, and a living room

EXHIBIT 1.7:
Coral Divers Resort pricing guide: family dive vacations, 1995

Destination	Duration	Price	Notes
Bahamas			
Coral Divers Resort	7 nights	$1,355–$1,455	Standard accommodations, continental breakfast, and daily two tank dive included.
Coral Divers Resort	7 nights	$1,800–$1,950	Deluxe accommodations, continental breakfast, and daily two tank dive included.

Prices are based on a family of four with two adults and two children aged 2–11. Rates are per week (7 nights) and include accommodations and applicable taxes. Rates will be dependent on season, type of accommodation, ages and number of children. All prices are subject to change. Airfares not included. Prices dropped to $600–700 per week for the standard package and $800–900 for deluxe accommodation if diving was excluded.

with two sleeper sofas. Four of the units had been renovated with new paint, tile floors, microwave, color TV, and VCR. The two other units ranged from "adequate" to "comfortable." Greywell tried to use the renovated units primarily for families and couples, while putting groups of single divers in the other units. Also on the property was a six-unit attached motel-type structure (see Exhibit 1.7 for prices and Exhibits 1.8 and 1.9 for comparison). Each of these units had two full-size beds, a pull-out sofa, sink, refrigerator, microwave, and TV. The resort had the space and facilities on the property for a kitchen and dining room, but they had not been used. However, there was a small family-run restaurant and bar within walking distance.

Greywell had three boats which could carry from eight to twenty passengers each. Two were 40-foot fiberglass V-hull boats powered by a single diesel inboard with a cruising speed of 18 knots and protective cabin, with dry storage space. The third was a 35-foot covered platform boat. Greywell also had facilities for air dispensing, equipment repair, rental and sale, and tank storage.

Coral Divers Resort, affiliated with PADI and NAUI, had a staff of eleven, which included four scuba diving instructors. Greywell, who worked full time at the resort, was a certified diving instructor by both PADI and NAUI. The three other diving instructors had various backgrounds. One was a former U.S. Navy SEAL working for Coral Divers to gain resort experience. One was a local Bahamian whom Greywell had known for many years. The third was a Canadian who had come to the Bahamas on a winter holiday and never left. There were two boat captains and two mates. Given the size of the operation, the staff was scheduled to provide overall coverage, all of the staff rarely working at the same time. In addition, there was a housekeeper, a groundskeeper, and a person who minded the office and store. Greywell's wife, Margaret, worked at the business on a part-time basis, taking care of administrative activities such as accounting and payroll. The rest of her time was spent looking after their two children and their home.

A typical diving day at Coral Divers for Greywell began around 7:30 a.m. He would open the office and review the activities list for the day. If there were any divers who needed to be picked up at the resorts in Nassau or elsewhere on the island, the van driver would need to leave by 7:30 a.m. to be back for the 9 a.m. departure. Most resort guests began to gather around the office and dock about 8:30. By 8:45, the day's captain and mate began loading the diving gear for the passengers.

The boat left at 9 a.m. Morning dives were usually "two tank dives," that is, two dives utilizing one tank of air each. The trip to the first dive site took about 20–30 minutes. Once there, the captain would explain the dive and the special attractions of the dive, and tell everyone when they were expected back on board. Most dives lasted 30–45 minutes, depending on depth. The deeper the dive, the faster the air consumption. A divemaster always accompanied the divers on the trip down. The divemaster's role was generally to supervise the dive. The divemaster was responsible for the safety and conduct of the divers while under water.

Once back on board, the boat would move to the next site. Greywell tried to plan dives at sites near each other. For example, the first dive might be a wall dive in 60 feet of water, while the second would be a nearby wreck 40 feet down. The second would also last about 40 minutes. If things went well, the boat would be back at the resort by noon. This allowed for lunch and sufficient surface time for divers who might be going back out in the afternoon. Two morning dives were part of the resort package. Whether the boat went out in the afternoon depended on whether enough non-resort guest divers had contracted for afternoon dives. If they had, Greywell was happy to let resort guests ride and dive along free of charge. If there were not enough outside paying divers, there were no afternoon dive trips and the guests were on their own to swim at the beach, go sightseeing, or just relax. When space was available it was possible for non-divers (either snorkelers or bubble-watchers) to join the boat trip for a fee of $15–25.

GREYWELL'S OPTIONS

Greywell's bookings ran 90 percent of capacity during the high season (December through May) and 50 percent during the low season (June through November). Ideally, he wanted to increase the number of bookings for the resort and dive businesses during both seasons. Adding additional diving attractions could increase both resort and dive revenues. Focusing on family vacations could increase revenues, since families would probably increase the number of paying guests per room. Break-even costs were calculated based on two adults sharing a room. Children provided an additional revenue source since the cost of the room had been covered by the adults, and children under 12 incurred no diving-related costs. However, either strategy, adding adventure diving to his current general offerings or adjusting the focus of the resort to encourage family diving vacations, would require some changes and cost money. The question became whether the changes would increase revenue enough to justify the costs and effort involved.

EXHIBIT 1.8:
A Canadian vacation comparison: diving in Nassau vs. skiing in Whistler/Banff, 1995

Nassau – 7 nights*

	January 5–11 (CAN$)			February 16–22 (CAN$)		
	Dbl/Person	Child	Family (3)	Dbl/Person	Child	Family (3)
Average cost for 12 packages	1,201	711	3,113	1,429	723	3,582
Range	919–1,377	667–737	2,575–3,461	1,217–1,687	707–737	3,157–4,081

* Includes quotes for select hotels only.
* Includes transportation and accommodation (some taxes may be additional) and estimated cost for five two-tank dives (CAN$337.50).

Ski Vacation – 7 Nights*

	January 5–11 (CAN$)			February 16–22 (CAN$)		
	Dbl/Person	Child	Family (3)	Dbl/Person	Child	Family (3)
Average cost for 20 packages	1,161	566	2,888	1,270	567	3,107
Range	757–1,645	454–1,166	2,087–3,845	824–1,739	454–1,172	2,221–4,031

* Incudes quotes for select hotels only.
* Includes transportation, accommodation, and lift passes, some taxes may be additional.
* Air Canada Vacations includes 4 lift passes/person, Cdn holidays includes 5 lift passes/person.
* Does not include airfare.

Emphasizing family diving vacations would probably require some changes to the physical property of the resort. Four of the cottages had already been renovated. The other two also would need to be upgraded. This would run $10,000 to $20,000 each, depending on the amenities added. The Bahamas had duties up to 50 percent, which caused renovation costs involving imported goods to be expensive. The attached motel-type units also would need to be refurbished at some point. He had the space and facilities for a kitchen and dining area, but had not done anything with them. The Rascals in Paradise people had offered to help set up a children's menu. He could hire a chef or cook and do it himself or offer the concession to the nearby restaurant or someone else. He would also need to build a play structure for children. There was an open area with shade trees between the office and the cottages that would be ideal for a play area. Rascals would provide the teacher/escort for the family vacation groups. It would be fairly easy to find babysitters for the children as needed. The people, particularly on this part of the island, were very family oriented and would welcome the opportunity for additional income. In asking around, it seemed that $5 per hour was the going rate for a sitter. Toys and other play items could be added gradually. The Rascals people had said that, once the program was in place, he could expect bookings to run 90 percent capacity annually from new and return bookings. While the package prices were competitive, the attraction was in group bookings and the prospect of a returning client base.

Adding adventure diving would be a relatively easy thing to do. Shark Wall and Shark Buoy were less than an hour away by boat. Both of these sites offered sharks that were already accustomed to being fed. The cost of shark food would be $10 per dive. None of Greywell's current staff were particularly excited about the prospect of adding shark feeding to their job description. But these staff could be relatively easily replaced. Greywell could probably find an experienced divemaster who would be willing to lead the shark dives. He would also have to purchase a special chain mail suit for the feeder at a cost of about $10,000. While there were few accidents during the feeds, Greywell would rather be safe than sorry. His current boats, especially the 40-footers, would be adequate for transporting divers to the sites. The other shark dive operators might not be happy about having him at the sites, but there was little they could do about it. Shark divers were charged a premium fee. For example, a shark dive would cost $100 for a two tank dive compared to $25–75 for a normal two tank dive. He figured that he could add shark dives to the schedule on Wednesdays and Saturdays without taking away from regular business. He needed a minimum of four divers on a trip at regular rates to cover the cost of taking out the boat. Ten or twelve divers were ideal. Greywell could usually count on at least eight divers for a normal dive, but he did not know how much additional new and return business he could expect from shark diving.

A third option was for Greywell to try to improve his current operations and not add any new diving attractions. This would require him to be much more cost efficient in his operations. Actions such as strictly adhering to the minimum required number of divers per boat policy, along with staff reductions, might improve the bottom line by 5–10 percent. He would need to be very attentive to materials ordering, fuel costs, and worker productivity in order to realize any gains with this approach. However, he was concerned that by continuing as he had, Coral Divers

EXHIBIT 1.9:
A US vacation comparison: diving in the Caymans/Cozumel vs. skiing in Vail/Breckenridge/Winter Park, 1995

7 nights*

	January 5–11 (US$)			April 16–22 (US$)		
	Dbl/Person	Child	Family (3)	Dbl/Person	Child	Family (3)
Cayman Islands						
7 Mile Beach Resort	1,099	free	1,998	949	free	1,689
Seaview Hotel	899	free	1,628	799	free	1,428
Hyatt Regency	1,499	free	2,856	1,299	free	2,198
Radisson	1,299	free	2,398	1,149	free	1,998
Cozumel						
Casa del Mar	899	free	1,648	799	free	1,248
Suites Colonia	799	free	1,538	719	free	1,278
Average cost	933	free	2,011	952	free	1,641

* Includes quotes for select hotels only.

Ski Vacation – 7 Nights*

	January 5–11 (US$)			February 16–22 (US$)		
	1 to a Room	2 to a Room	3 to a Room	1 to a Room	2 to a Room	3 to a Room
Average for 18 packages	945	678	659	1,250	880	821
Range	420–2,766	298–1,489	391–1,215	830–1,935	533–1,304	492–1,304

* Incudes quotes for select hotels only.
* Includes lodging and lift passes, some taxes may be additional.
* Mountain Vacations include rental cars.
* Does not include airfare.

Resort would not be distinguished as unique from other resorts in the Bahamas. He did not know what would be the long-term implications of this approach.

As Greywell reached the office, he turned to watch the sun sink into the ocean. Although it was a view he had come to love, a lingering thought was that perhaps it was time to relocate to a less crowded location.

NOTES

1. Information on certifying agencies is drawn from materials published by the various organizations.
2. This section draws from results of surveys conducted by scuba diving organizations and publications for the years 1991–3.
3. Based on information drawn from *The Islands of the Bahamas: 1994 Dive Guide*, published by the Bahamas Ministry of Tourism, Commonwealth of the Bahamas, in conjunction with the Bahamas Diving Association.

CHAPTER TWO

LAURA ASHLEY HOLDINGS plc: THE CRISIS OF 1998

Robert M. Grant prepared this case solely to provide material for class discussion. The author does not intend to illustrate either the effective or ineffective handling of a management situation. The author may have disguised certain names or other identifying information to protect confidentiality.

Copyright © 1999 Robert M. Grant

OCTOBER 1998

In June 1998, Victoria Z. Egan took over as Group Chief Executive of Laura Ashley Holdings plc. She was the company's sixth CEO since the death of Laura Ashley in 1985. Indeed, the life expectancy of Laura Ashley CEOs seemed to have shortened drastically. John James was CEO from 1976 to 1990. Jim Maxmin was CEO from 1991 to 1993. A. Schouten headed the company from 1993 to early 1995. In June 1995, Ann Iverson took over as CEO, only to be replaced by David Hoare in September 1997.

This top management turmoil coincided with a downward spiral for the company. In the financial year ended January 1998, a loss of 49 million pounds was reported (representing a return on sales of −14 percent and a return on equity of −133 percent).

In May 1998, MUI Group, a diversified Malaysian industrial and service corporation acquired 40 percent of Laura Ashley's equity and installed Mrs. Egan as Chief Executive. A marketing and management major from the University of the Philippines, Mrs. Egan had extensive experience of retail management in the Philippines. Prior to joining Laura Ashley she was President of MUI Resources Philippines Inc., President of Shangri-la Plaza Corporation, the leading up-scale shopping mall in the Philippines, and President of Yearsley Inc., a duty-free retailer.

However, little in her prior experience could have prepared her for the situation at Laura Ashley. Despite a succession of restructurings and strategy redirections since 1990, the company continued on its downhill trajectory. The half-yearly results announced on October 1, 1998 offered little basis for optimism. Sales revenue was down 17 percent on the year-ago period and the pre-tax loss before exceptional items had almost doubled. Many outside observers wondered whether there was any future for this icon of the 1970s, or whether Laura Ashley Holdings would follow its founder to the grave.

THE HISTORY

Development of the Business, 1953–1985

Bernard and Laura Ashley began designing and printing scarves and tablemats in their flat in Pimlico, London in 1953.[1] The products combined Laura's interest in color and design with Bernard's expertise in printing and dyeing. The product range was extended to include Victorian-styled aprons and linen kitchen towels. Laura's designs drew upon British traditional country styles, patterns, and colors. The designs were mainly floral, and the colors predominantly pastel. They sold mainly to department stores such as John Lewis, Heals, and Peter Jones. In 1957 the Ashleys opened a showroom in London, and in 1961 they transferred their production operations to a disused railway station at Carno, Wales with a retail shop at Machynlleth.

By 1966, the business employed 19 people and was using a flatbed printing process designed by Bernard with a capacity of 5,000 meters of fabric per week. The popularity of Laura's first dress designs encouraged the Ashleys to open a London retail store in Pelham Street, South Kensington in 1968. Although sales were initially slow, advertisements on the London Underground stimulated a surge of interest in Laura Ashley's dresses and fabrics. Throughout the early 1970s, the reaction against modernism, pop art, and other trends of the 1960s rekindled a strong interest in the rural English styles and traditions of the Victorian and Edwardian eras. Laura Ashley's positioning between English bourgeois tradition and hippie abandon, and her ability to evoke nostalgia for the comfort and simplicity of pre-industrial Britain placed her styles in the vanguard of contemporary fashion. During the early 1970s Laura Ashley expanded the company's product range from furnishing fabrics, clothes, and housewares into wallpaper and house paints. What Laura Ashley offered was a coordinated approach to home décor and clothing with a perfect matching of designs and colors across fabrics, wallpapers, paints, and ceramic tiles. The company expanded internationally too, with shops in Geneva, Paris, Amsterdam, and Dusseldorf. In Canada, Australia, and Japan licenses were sold to local companies to open Laura Ashley stores. In 1974 Laura Ashley entered the US, initially by licensing McCall's Patterns of New York to distribute its fabrics, and then with an office and retail store in San Francisco.

The company was highly vertically integrated. By the early 1980s, almost all products were designed by Laura Ashley and 85 percent of the products were manufactured either by the production facilities based in Wales or by subcontractors. The majority of sales were through Laura Ashley retail stores. The company became expert in the fast, flexible production of good quality fabrics manufactured in small runs. By the early 1980s there were eight garment making-up plants close to Carno in Wales, a fabric plant in Dublin, and two plants in England making home furnishing products and made-to-measure curtains and blinds. Distribution from plants and warehouses to retail stores was done by the company's own transport division. Products for the North American stores were airfreighted weekly; others were manufactured under contract at a plant in Kentucky.

The distinctive design of Laura Ashley products was extended to the retail stores. The dark-green Laura Ashley storefronts were clearly recognizable in the high street, and the interiors with their wooden fittings projected an image of quality and homeliness. The company was an early adopter of electronic point-of-sale systems, which linked retail sales to inventory planning, distribution, and production planning. Laura Ashley also offered mail order sales.

The family ownership and management of the group (in 1982 Nick Ashley took over from his mother, Laura, as director of design) was reflected in relationships with employees. The family atmosphere of the company was evident in a cooperative, non-hierarchical working environment with a high level of job security and generous employee benefits.

Continued growth (turnover reached 34 million pounds in 1981 and 96 million pounds in 1984) resulted in the adoption of a divisional structure. The six divisions were:

- *Laura Ashley Design Services* responsible for design and product development.
- *The Product Division* responsible for production, production contracting, and purchasing.
- *The UK Retail Division*, which included Laura Ashley shops, concession stores within Sainsbury Homebase stores, and the mail order operation.
- *The North America Division* with Laura Ashley stores mainly in shopping malls and mainly concentrating on clothing.
- *The Continental Europe Division* with 46 Laura Ashley stores mainly in Germany, Switzerland, the Netherlands, France, and Italy.
- *The Asia-Pacific Division* with Laura Ashley stores located in Australia, Japan, and Southeast Asia, together with a number of franchised stores in other countries.

In November 1985, the company went public. The offer for 23 percent of Laura Ashley Holdings plc was oversubscribed 34 times. Just one month before the public offering, Laura Ashley died after a fall in her home. *The Economist* wrote:

> Her popularity lay in the taste she stamped on her international empire, not so much for the elegance and smartness as for the prettiness and comfort. Nobody was intimidated by the look or price of a Laura Ashley design. Her home furnishings offered a cheap and feminine alternative to the drab, the posh, and the sternly post-war Habitat Scandinavian. She made it possible to look smart without paying Liberty prices.
>
> Her company's success has been the acceptable face of British capitalism in the past two decades. She was deputy chairman to her husband and her power has been considerable. She prized the loyalty of her staff and cared for their welfare. There was no smoking and no fried fish in the canteens, no night shift in the factories.

Expansion 1986–1989

Fuelled with capital from the public offering, Laura Ashley Holdings launched a new phase of its growth. Between 1986 and 1989 a series of acquisitions extended the product range and geographical scope of the company:

- In 1986 the acquisition of Sandringham Leather Goods Ltd. and Bryant of Scotland (a knitwear company) extended the product range and manufacturing capacity of the group.
- In 1987 Willis and Geiger a US outdoor clothing company with a strong brand name and with both production facilities and retail outlets was acquired. Also in 1987 Penhaligons, an old-established producer of perfumes and toiletries, was acquired. The plan was to expand Penhaligons by opening new Penhaligons retail stores and distributing the product range through Laura Ashley outlets.
- In 1989 Revman Industries, a US home furnishings company, was acquired.

The company also continued its internal expansion. In 1985 a 135,000 square foot textile factory in Wales was completed. This increased the company's production capacity by 50 percent. The new capacity was supported by heavy investment in a new computer-aided design system, computerized fabric-cutting equipment, and a computerized material-handling system.

In 1988 the company was organized into seven divisions, each with a divisional managing director, and each with profit and loss responsibility to the main board. The divisions were:

- Laura Ashley Group Services – head office functions;
- Laura Ashley Brand Management – design, sourcing, licensing;
- Laura Ashley Industries – manufacture and distribution;
- Laura Ashley UK Retail;
- Laura Ashley Inc. – retailing in North America;
- Laura Ashley Continental Europe;
- Laura Ashley Pacific Basin – retailing in Australia, Japan, and Asia.

Emerging Problems 1990–1991

Despite the expansion of the late 1980s, the bottom line deteriorated sharply. The 1989–92 recession in Britain combined with a series of internal problems within the company. (Table 2.1 summarizes financial performance over the period.) Problems included:

- massive overproduction of Laura Ashley catalogs in 1989;
- losses at the Willis and Geiger subsidiary;
- the 1989 autumn range arriving at the shops three months late;

TABLE 2.1
Laura Ashley Holdings plc: financial summary, 1989–1998 (£ million)

Financial year to January 31

	1998	1997	1996	1995	1994	1993	1992	1991	1990	1989
Turnover	344.9	327.6	336.6	322.6	300.4	247.8	262.8	328.1	296.6	252.4
Operating (loss)/profit	(23.6)	14.8	9.1	4.1	2.3	1.1	(0.6)	3.4	n.a.	n.a.
Exceptional operating costs	(12.4)	(0.4)	0.1	(33.4)	—	—	—	—	—	—
Operating (loss)/profit	(36.0)	14.4	9.2	(29.3)	2.3	1.1	(0.6)	3.4	6.1	23.6
Income from associated undertaking	0.5	2.1	2.0	1.5	1.8	1.5	1.9	0.1	(0.2)	42.0
Exceptional items	(11.4)	0.4	—	(1.0)	—	—	(8.1)	(2.6)	(3.1)	—
Net interest payable	(2.4)	(0.7)	(0.9)	(1.8)	(1.1)	(0.8)	(2.3)	(12.4)	(8.6)	(5.0)
(Loss)/profit before taxation	(49.3)	16.2	10.3	(30.6)	3.0	1.8	(9.1)	(11.5)	(4.7)	20.3
Taxation	—	(6.1)	(3.3)	(0.9)	(1.9)	(1.0)	—	2.5	(2.1)	(7.1)
(Loss)/profit after taxation	(49.3)	10.1	7.0	(31.5)	1.1	0.8	(9.1)	(9.0)	(6.8)	13.1
Dividends	—	(2.4)	(1.2)	—	(0.2)	(0.1)	(0.1)	(0.1)	(1.7)	(4.7)
Retained (loss)/profit for the year	(49.3)	7.7	5.8	(31.5)	0.9	0.7	(9.2)	(9.1)	(9.8)	8.4
Fixed assets	42.2	49.5	45.2	48.3	71.7	66.3	60.5	67.1	81.5	80.2
Net current assets	27.6	49.7	27.0	43.7	50.2	53.9	52.8	66.9	n.a.	n.a.
Long term creditors	(30.4)	(21.8)	(0.9)	(15.0)	(35.1)	(34.4)	(28.0)	(41.4)	3.5	44.7
Provisions for liabilities/charges	(19.7)	(7.3)	(8.3)	(21.3)	(0.7)	(0.3)	(0.5)	(0.4)	2.9	2.2
Net assets	19.7	70.1	63.0	55.7	86.1	85.5	84.8	92.2	72.9	79.8
Issued capital	11.9	11.9	11.8	11.7	11.7	11.7	11.7	11.7	10.0	10.0
Reserves	7.8	58.2	51.2	44.0	74.4	73.8	73.1	80.5	n.a.	n.a.
Equity shareholders' funds	19.7	70.1	63.0	55.7	86.1	85.5	84.8	92.2	72.9	79.8
Employees										
Total	3,657	4,104	4,173	4,430	n.a.	n.a.	n.a.	7,800	8,350	8,100
Manufacturing	617	859	1,019	1,010	n.a.	n.a.	n.a.	n.a.	n.a.	n.a.
Retail	2,415	2,592	2,459	2,639	n.a.	n.a.	n.a.	n.a.	n.a.	n.a.
Administrative	625	653	695	781	n.a.	n.a.	n.a.	n.a.	n.a.	n.a.

n.a. = not available.

Source: Laura Ashley Holdings plc, *Annual Reports.*

- high costs of producing in Britain due to the rising value of the pound sterling;
- higher interest expenses due to a rising cost of borrowing;
- exceptional charges resulting from the sale or closure of non-core businesses including Penhaligons, Bryant of Scotland, Sandringham Leather Goods, and the Units chain of stores;
- the closure or sale of several production plants.

Retrenchment was combined with the quest for a new design look that would be faithful to Laura Ashley values while appealing more to the 1990s consumer. In 1991, Jim Maxmin, formerly head of Thorn-EMI's US operations and with extensive marketing experience with Unilever and Volvo UK, was appointed Chief Executive of Laura Ashley Holdings.

THE IVERSON ERA

In June 1995, Ann Iverson, who had joined Laura Ashley as a non-executive director a year earlier, was invited by the Board to become Group Chief Executive. Iverson had had a long and successful career in retailing on both sides of the Atlantic. She had been a Vice President at Bloomindales, the US department store, a Senior Vice President at Bonwit Teller, and, most recently, CEO of Kay-Bee Toys, a subsidiary of the Melville Corporation of America. However, her reputation as a retailer was founded primarily upon her leadership of Mothercare, the highly successful British chain of mother and baby stores. For the first time, Laura Ashley was led by an experienced retailer.

Ann Iverson was joined by James Walsh, who took up the position of Group Finance Director. Walsh had previously been Finance Director of Harrods, CEO of Kurt Geiger Ltd., and Finance Director of House of Fraser. Both Iverson and Walsh were given service contracts with a minimum period of two years and signing-on bonuses of 350,000 pounds and 100,000 pounds respectively. In financial year 1995/96, Iverson received 883,000 pounds and Walsh 360,000 pounds.

Her first months at Laura Ashley saw a radical restructuring of the Group's manufacturing, purchasing, and merchandising. Processes were redesigned, decision-making was centralized, international procedures were standardized, unprofitable businesses sold, smaller shops closed, and cost controls tightened. In March 1996, Iverson outlined her strategy for the future:

> I was delighted to become Group Chief Executive in June 1995 because I saw a retail business that could be fixed and also a brilliant brand with great potential. However, it was a time of great unrest for the organization, as it was showing no signs of improvement or turnaround.
>
> The restructuring program announced last year was needed for the business. With that said, there were many business issues this program did not address. It only looked at overhead costs, it had no retail focus, it identified no change to our business processes and nothing was mentioned about sales growth and improving gross margins. All of

these elements are vital to the turnaround of this business and if not addressed could allow history to repeat itself.

When I joined the business I had many impressions that needed validation. I reacted from three different points of reference: as a customer, as a non-executive and finally as the new Group Chief Executive. I saw a business not led by a single point of view; we had multi-design, multi-buying, multi-merchandising and even multi-catalogues.

In other words, each market or business category was defining what they thought the Laura Ashley brand was all about. As you and I know, every successful brand has a single message consistently delivered to their customer. That was not the case at Laura Ashley.

I also found serious supply chain inefficiencies and, most importantly, shops that were too small to show the extensive range in garments and home furnishings. There were also no clear lines of accountability, which is an unproductive and demotivating culture to have. It doesn't allow hardworking people to really know what their job is, how they are going to be measured and where to go for answers.

So in my first three months we set about making things right. We consolidated design, buying and merchandising, the pivotal areas of our business, into our Fulham office.

We began the necessary changes in the buying process, reducing the width of the product ranges by 25% and also developing a common catalogue worldwide. We delivered the head count reduction that was identified in the restructuring program, changed and eliminated tasks and put the right structure in place. Simply said, we set about establishing a retail culture.

Additionally, I identified six key initiatives which were critical to the consolidation and turnaround of the Group. They have proved to be exactly the right priorities to have aggressively focused on for the second half of the financial year.

These initiatives are ongoing and I would like to describe them:

- *Product ranges and gross margins.* Improvement of product ranges and gross margins are the most important for topline growth. The key to this is modernizing the fashion offer in garments and expanding our strengths in home furnishings. The improved product offer in fashion will increase sales and reduce mark-downs and is absolutely essential for repositioning this international lifestyle brand. The home furnishings ranges are already very strong and offer the greatest opportunity for growth. They must be expanded, however, to reflect the developments in the market sector and realize the strength of the Laura Ashley brand.
- *Supply chain.* Development of efficient product sourcing is critical in achieving supply chain improvement. This will be accomplished by developing and working closely with our suppliers so they are more reactive to the needs of the business.
- *Manufacturing review.* A total review of manufacturing continues, within the context of the overall supply chain, focusing primarily on home furnishings where we produce 80% of our own product. It is essential that we ensure our factories are competitive as a supplier to a worldwide retailer.
- *Distribution.* In the area of distribution, our costs are well above industry standards. Work is being done to reduce these costs and we will begin to see these reductions coming through in the next financial year. We will strive to achieve best practice industry standards in this important supply chain category.
- *Shop portfolio.* The assessment of our shop portfolio with regard to both location and shop size is underway. Increasing the size of our shops is absolutely necessary to remain competitive in today's retail environment.

■ *The US market.* And lastly, determining the potential of the US market. This market should be our greatest vehicle for topline growth and profit improvement. Our brand values, reaffirmed through customer research, show a potential audience of over 19 million female shoppers. But our shops are too small to even begin presenting the width of the range that supports customer perception and demand. We have started to change this and have already opened the first of our new shops, much larger in format, positioned in premier locations.

The strategy of the Laura Ashley brand is already clearly defined. We are the quintessential English company with a timelessness and spirit understood and embraced worldwide. Our research supports the brand values our customer identifies with: love of flowers, family, romanticism, freedom and simplicity and the tradition which directly relates to the enduring brand qualities and its uniqueness.

In the past the business has talked too much about strategy and not about results. It is time we delivered to our customers and shareholders. As a retailer I see clearly what needs to be done and how to do it.

The way forward continues to be about focus and implementation of the key initiatives which are fundamental to the Company's turnaround. Additionally, we have identified two new initiatives, namely: to establish an appropriate infrastructure for licensing, franchising and wholesaling and to build a new mail order business.

I am pleased we were able to deliver profit improvement this year coming from hard work and focused efforts. We have a strong and highly experienced results driven team and working together we look forward to delivering the profits we know this brand is capable of generating.[2]

Under Iverson's leadership, Laura Ashley continued to impose tighter cost controls and increase the effectiveness of its management systems, while attempting to grow its sales through expanding its retail square footage, mainly through replacing smaller stores by bigger ones, especially in the US.

Iverson's first year at Laura Ashley was seen by both investors and industry observers as marking a turnaround in the fortunes of the beleaguered group. Even long-serving Laura Ashley executives were heartened by Iverson's turnaround strategy. Visiting the first new-style US Laura Ashley store in North Carolina, Sir Bernard Ashley commented, "I almost cried, it was so marvelous." *Business Week* reported:

Since becoming CEO of Laura Ashley Holdings, plc last July, Ann Iverson has replaced most of top management, cut the payroll, slashed costs, and unveiled an aggressive expansion plan in the US. "I'm the kind of person who has a steamroller behind her back," says Iverson, 52, who was recruited when shareholders were getting fed up. Now the market's applauding. On April 18, the company reported pretax income of $15.6 million for 1995, compared with a $46.5 million loss a year before. Since Iverson's appointment, Laura Ashley's stock has more than doubled . . . [but] no one knows yet if Iverson can solve the biggest problem: the apparel line with its signature floral prints and long, girlish dresses, is deeply unfashionable in the minimalist 1990s. . . . Iverson acknowledges that the company's Victorian look is dated, but cites recent research showing that the brand could appeal to 19 million women in America and Britain. She hopes the new designer she lured from Carole Little, Basha Cohen, will help freshen the line, but still keep the flowing romantic look. More important, she is betting that home

TABLE 2.2
Laura Ashley Holdings plc: sales by product group and by region (£ million)

	UK and Ireland	North America	Continental Europe
Year to 1.31.98			
Garments	85.9	57.0	23.0
Furnishings	90.0	34.5	24.7
Year to 1.31.97			
Garments	82.3	49.7	21.7
Furnishings	76.9	34.5	24.1
Year to 1.31.96			
Garments	80.8	60.1	28.6
Furnishings	67.4	35.9	31.9
Year to 1.31.95			
Garments	78.3	61.8	27.2
Furnishings	59.9	36.6	30.1

Source: Laura Ashley Holdings plc, Annual Reports 1996 and 1998.

furnishings will boost sales. The company's wallpaper, bedspreads, linens and curtains have proven much more resistant to fashion's whims than the frocks have.[3]

During 1996, the company's capital expenditures increased as the number of stores and their average size increased. Yet, any prospects of the new strategy delivering improved sale profit performance soon evaporated. Despite the emphasis on expansion in the US, North American sales fell during 1996. Then, in the spring of 1997, problems of poor coordination caused losses to mount. Overoptimistic sales projections for garments resulted in excessive levels of inventories, while in home furnishings demand was also weak. Clearance sales during spring and early summer devastated margins. Table 2.2 shows sales by product group and region.

In April 1996, John Thornton succeeded Lord Hooson as Chairman of the Board, and in September 1996, David Hoare, formerly a partner with management consultants Bain & Company and chief executive of the diversified holding company Cope Allman plc, became Chief Operating Officer. In November, Iverson and Walsh left the company. David Hoare became Chief Executive Officer, and Richard Pennycock became Finance Director.

RETRENCHMENT: SEPTEMBER 1996– JUNE 1998

The new team began undoing much of the previous strategy. Plans for further new store openings were radically pruned and several existing stores were closed both in the US and in Britain. (Table 2.3 shows the numbers of retail stores and retail square

TABLE 2.3
Laura Ashley Holdings plc: retail stores and floor space

Financial year to January 31:	Number of stores			Square footage (000s)		
	1998	1997	1996	1998	1997	1996
UK	237	189	174	561.5	441.8	394.1
North America	132	155	168	379.3	349.6	276.8
Continental Europe	72	74	76	114.1	115.9	117.7
Total	441	418	418	1055.2	907.3	788.6

Source: Laura Ashley Holdings plc, *Annual Reports* 1996 and 1998.

footage.) Top management's attention became focused on cost reduction, particularly on reducing levels of inventory. By the time 1997 drew to a close, Hoare and Pennycock were exploring opportunities to stanch losses and raise finance through disposing of non-core businesses. In January 1998, the company's remaining manufacturing plants were sold, and a 13 percent stake in Laura Ashley Japan Ltd. was sold to Laura Ashley's Japanese partner Jusco, for 9.5 million pounds.

In March 1998, David Hoare reported on his progress since September 1997 and on his plans for the future.

Introduction

I am pleased to have joined Laura Ashley in September 1997. I am well aware that over the past 12 years, since flotation, Laura Ashley's financial performance has been most disappointing. A number of serious problems face our business and need to be addressed. However, we have an opportunity to build a successful business on the back of a strong international brand.

Key problems facing Laura Ashley

- *Complexity of the Business*. Laura Ashley is too complex for a business of its size. We attempt to be experts in design, manufacturing, distribution, retailing in 13 countries, franchising, licensing and mail order. Our management information systems are outdated and our cost base is too high. We have not been sufficiently focused on our core competencies of brand management and retailing.
- *Garment Design*. Over the past three years, the garment range has been repositioned towards the High Street and a younger market. However, it has been taken too quickly and too far in this most competitive sector of the market. We have confused our loyal customers and not attracted sufficient new ones.
- *North American Expansion*. In 1996, we operated 168 stores in North America, with an average size of 1,600 sq. ft. This small-store format was not profitable. Over the past two years our North American store portfolio was restructured by closing 68 smaller stores and opening 32 larger stores (5,000 sq. ft.) in prestige

mall locations. Store merchandising was centralized in London. This program was implemented rapidly without sufficient planning and knowledge of market conditions and with an inadequate supply chain. Costs, particularly rents, have increased whilst sales have not grown significantly.

Overall, these problems led to a shortfall in sales against expectations and excess stocks in both garments and home furnishings, across all markets, which was cleared throughout the year with heavy discounting. As a result, gross profit margins reduced by 10% from 48% to 38% on sales of 345 million pounds, a 34 million pounds adverse gross profit variance. In addition, operating costs rose by 8% or 11.5 million pounds, principally due to a 16% increase in floor space in North America and the UK. As a result, we have reported an operating loss before exceptional items and tax of 25.5 million pounds for 1997/98 against 16.2 million pounds profit last year. In addition, exceptional charges of 23.8 million pounds have been taken mainly to restructure our North American and manufacturing business.

Recovery program

Whilst it is clear that we have had a number of significant problems at Laura Ashley, and that it will take time to fix them, it is also clear that there are great opportunities for our business. Laura Ashley is one of the best known international brand names, representing the quintessential English country lifestyle. We trade in 34 countries, in over 550 owned and franchised stores. We have a base of loyal customers who, though disappointed in the recent past, will return provided we can develop products and services that meet their aspirations.

In order to tackle our current problems and take advantage of the significant opportunities, we have put in place a three-phase recovery plan to be implemented over the next five years.

- *Phase I. Stabilize the Business*
    - –stop significant new store development
    - –rebuild the senior management team
    - –generate cash by reducing stocks and selling non-core assets
    - –raise additional finance
- *Phase II. Improve the Profitability of the Business*
    - –return to full price retailing
    - –redesign the product to meet the wishes of our core customers
    - –fix the North American retail business
    - –reduce business complexity and costs
    - –invest in systems
- *Phase III. Grow the Business*
    - –focus on core competence of brand management
    - –build our brand internationally with new products, new distribution channels and new partners

Phase I

In late 1997/98 good progress was made to stabilize the business. Store expansion was stopped, and we refocused on managing the existing business. We strengthened our senior management team by recruiting Richard Pennycock as our new Group Finance Director. A new Designer, and an interim Chief Executive Officer for our North American business, were also appointed.

Our worsening trading position in the autumn of 1997 required us to renegotiate with our banks. They supported us with a 15 month 170 million pound committed bank facility through to April 1999. Cash outflow was minimized by reducing year end stock by 32% from 93 million to 63 million pounds. In addition, following the year end, we announced the sale of part of our shareholding in our Japanese licensee, Laura Ashley Japan, to Jusco, the majority owner . . . in a transaction which realized aggregate gross proceeds of 9.5 million pounds. The transaction included a revision of the terms of the license agreement between us.

Phase II

Progress has also been made in improving the profits of the existing business. Following our January 1998 end of year sale, we returned to more normal full price retailing with occasional marketing promotions. As expected, sales have slowed. However, the key to maintaining satisfactory margins is having the right produce for our customers. We recognize that our garment range has moved too far towards the High Street and a younger market and has lost an element of its Laura Ashley signature. We are redesigning our product range, which, because of lead times, will be only partly evident in our Autumn/Winter 1998 collection. More substantial change will be seen in Spring/Summer 1999.

North America remains a major challenge. Our business there has suffered disproportionately from the problems affecting the Group. The product range was not right, the large-stores format did not work and the complexity of the business led to severe supply problems. Significant losses were incurred. However, research shows that there is a major opportunity in North America for lifestyle brands aimed at discerning 30–50 year old customers, and we believe that our quintessential English country brand can succeed in this market.

In order to fix our North American business we have strengthened the management team with the appointment of an interim Chief Executive Officer. They will be given the ability to select products from our global range and greater freedom in store merchandising. It has become clear to the Board that these management actions alone will be insufficient to turn around the business. Rather, a decisive program of restructuring, cost reduction, store closures and carefully targeted new investment will be required. As part of this program, we intend to close a number of larger stores while investing in information systems, store refurbishment and brand development.

Throughout the Group, our overheads are too high, partly as a result of the complexity of the business and partly due to the weakness of our systems which require significant investment. Some steps have been taken to reduce costs but greater progress will need to be made in 1998.

As a first step to simplifying our business we announced, in January 1998, our intention to sell our manufacturing operations with a continuing supply agreement. Our manufacturing operations in Wales and the Netherlands, although good businesses, are not part of our core. They will be better off owned and managed by a team whose primary focus is manufacturing. They will become a better supplier and we, with greater clarity, will become a better customer. The sale process is continuing.

Phase III

We have significant opportunities to expand our franchise, license and wholesale activities internationally. In 1997/98 we opened 22 new franchised stores. In addition, we continue to expand our range of licensed products. However, we will pursue this expansion program only once we are satisfied that we have the right product, service and infrastructure to give the required levels of support.

Current trading

Store sales, at constant exchange rates, in the first 10 weeks of the year were 13% below last year with substantially lower stock levels. However, last year excess garment stock was being cleared at very low margin.

Equity

In the light of last year's results, the investment need in North America, the opportunities in the rest of the business and the current levels of debt, we have added additional equity capital essential to improve the financial stability and operational health of the Group. On 17 April 1998 we announced that we intend to raise new equity of 43.7 million pounds net in a subscription by the Malayan United Industries Group. The Board believes that raising this new equity is essential in order to implement the recovery plan.

1998/99

We start the year with our Organization focused on stabilizing, simplifying and fixing our base business, without the pressure of an expansion program and excess stock. Although we recognize that an enormous amount of work needs to be done, and that it will take time, we are excited by the prospect of building the Laura Ashley brand worldwide to satisfy our customers, and to reap the rewards for our shareholders.

I would like to thank all our staff for their continued dedication, in what has been a very difficult year. With their support, we will make progress.[4]

Refinancing

In April 1998, the Board agreed to increase the issued equity of Laura Ashley Holdings and to sell the new equity to the MUI Group, a Malaysian internationally diversified group with interests in retailing, hotels and resorts, food and confectionery, cement and building materials, real estate, and financial services. After the equity sale, MUI would own 40 percent of Laura Ashley's equity and would appoint four board members:

- Mr. Ng Kwan Cheong, managing director of Metrojaya, a Malaysian retail chain, would become non-executive director.
- Mr. David Walton Masters, managing director of Kerry Investment Management, a Hong Kong financial services group, would become non-executive director.

TABLE 2.4
Laura Ashley Holdings plc: retail sales and contribution by geographical segment (£ million)

	UK and Ireland	North America	Continental Europe	Total retail
Turnover				
26 weeks to 8.1.98	76.0	34.6	19.4	130.0
26 weeks to 7.26.97	89.1	48.5	23.8	161.4
Year to 1.31.98	175.9	91.5	47.7	315.1
Year to 1.31.97	159.2	84.2	45.8	289.2
Contribution				
26 weeks to 8.1.98	8.6	(4.0)	3.2	7.8
26 weeks to 7.26.97	8.0	(2.4)	4.4	10.0
Year to 1.31.98	14.9	(12.9)	7.3	9.3
Year to 1.31.97	24.5	7.6	10.7	42.8

Source: Laura Ashley Holdings plc, *Annual Reports* 1996 and 1998, and interim results for six months to August 1, 1998.

■ Mrs. Victoria Egan, president of MUI's retail subsidiary in the Philippines, would become Deputy Chief Executive of Laura Ashley Holdings, with a view to her taking over as Chief Executive.
■ Mr. Paul Ng Tuan Tee, executive director of Metrojaya, would become President of Laura Ashley North America.

The sale of 40 percent of the company to MUI was a result of two factors. First, debt had increased steeply from 16.8 million pounds at the end of January 1997 to 30.6 million pounds at the end of January 1998, and up to 38.7 million pounds by the beginning of April 1998. By the end of 1997, Laura Ashley had been forced to renegotiate its bank facility, and during 1998, the group's bankers became increasingly concerned. After discussions with its bankers, Laura Ashley was permitted to retain for use within the business the 9.5 million pounds received from the sale of shares in Laura Ashley Japan, but Laura Ashley was not permitted to draw further on its banking facility, nor could it use funds available from outside of North America to fund continued losses within North America.

Looking longer term, the group believed that the extensive restructuring and repositioning that were needed, especially in North America, would require significant capital investment in the future. Tables 2.4 and 2.5 show the deteriorating financial performance of the North American business, while Table 2.6 shows performance by business segment.

Of the 43.7 million pounds that the equity sale would raise (net of expenses), 20 million pounds was to be used for the North America recovery program – in particular, for closing up to six large-format stores, while investing in IT, store refurbishment, and a new merchandising approach that would allow North American

TABLE 2.5
Laura Ashley Holdings plc: sales, profit, and net assets by geographical segment (£ million)

	Year to 1.31.98	Year to 1.31.97	Year to 1.31.96	Year to 1.31.95
Sale:				
UK and Ireland	197.2	175.1	160.0	145.2
North America	96.4	92.7	104.6	107.0
Continental Europe	50.2	57.7	65.8	57.4
Other	1.1	1.1	1.3	0.9
Profit before tax (after exceptionals):				
UK and Ireland	(12.6)	8.6	(0.5)	(29.5)
North America	(29.4)	3.3	1.7	(1.2)
Continental Europe	(7.8)	1.4	5.6	(0.8)
Other	0.5	3.2	3.5	1.6
Net assets:				
UK and Ireland	16.0	25.7	15.4	14.1
North America	(18.6)	11.4	13.3	14.3
Continental Europe	19.9	29.2	32.5	26.4
Other	2.4	2.3	1.8	0.9

Source: Laura Ashley Holdings plc, Annual Reports 1996 and 1998.

TABLE 2.6
Laura Ashley Holdings plc: sales, contribution, and net assets by business segment (£ million)

	26 weeks to 8.1.98	26 weeks to 7.26.97	Year to 1.31.98	Year to 1.31.97
Turnover:				
Retail	130.0	161.3	315.1	289.2
Non-retail	14.2	13.2	29.8	22.9
Contribution:				
Retail	7.8	10.0	9.3	42.8
Non-retail	4.5	5.4	7.6	12.1
Net assets:				
Retail	40.8	43.0	(0.6)	40.7
Non-retail	19.7	21.7	20.3	27.9

Retail includes Laura Ashley managed retail stores and mail order. Non-retail includes wholesale, licensing, franchising, and manufacturing.

Source: Laura Ashely Holdings plc, Annual Reports 1996 and 1998, and interim results for six months to August 1, 1998.

management the freedom to select from the Laura Ashley global product range. The funds would also be needed to cover losses in North America.

The expenditures on IT in North America were part of a global upgrading of Laura Ashley's logistics and information systems. This would require investing some 6.5 million pounds outside of North America.

The Board agreed with its banks to reduce its existing 50 million pounds revolving credit facility to 35 million pounds by the end of 1998. It was intended to reduce bank borrowings through both cash flow from operations and proceeds from asset disposal.

Summer 1998

Soon after MUI acquired its 40 percent interest in Laura Ashley, Victoria Egan took over as Group Chief Executive from David Hoare. Her approach was to continue with the three-phase strategy already in place, with its emphasis on reducing losses, restructuring the North American business, and disposing of assets. In August 1998, a reorganization plan was announced involving creating three profit centers: Europe, North America, and Franchising. A 2.5 million pounds provision was made to cover the redundancy costs associated with this reorganization.

The half-yearly results announced at the beginning of October showed that, even if cost-cutting measures were stabilizing margins, sales were sharply lower than the year-ago period (see Appendix for details.) Reporting on Laura Ashley's results for the six months ended August 1, 1998, Egan emphasized continuity of the strategy of the previous management team:

> The current management team is continuing the three phase approach to tackling Laura Ashley's problems: stabilizing the business, improving profitability, and then growing the business. Over the last several months, the Group has substantially completed Phase I, stabilizing the business. The Group's performance has improved and the half year results are in line with management's expectations. In addition to margin improvement, the Group now has net cash, and stock levels are down 23% year on year to 59 million pounds and down 7% since the beginning of the financial year.
>
> The North American recovery program is proceeding. The Group closed five large-format stores after the half year and expects to close an additional five by the end of the year. This is more than the six the Group announced in April 1998, but the closure costs have been lower than expected and remain within the 9 million pound provision taken last year. While the Group does not expect significant, additional large-format store closures in North America, it will continue to make adjustments to the store portfolio there, closing and relocating stores where appropriate.
>
> Although the Group continues to incur losses in North America, it is profitable outside that region. The UK store business increased its year-on-year performance in what has become an increasingly tough market, with branch contribution up 7%. The performance in Europe was acceptable given the strength of the pound. Franchising and licensing remain profitable businesses.
>
> As announced on 15 August, the Group is devolving considerable responsibility and accountability to three profit-center markets – Europe, North America and Franchising. This will allow decisions to be taken much closer to markets. This reorganization will

lead to significant savings of 3 million pounds per year beginning in February 1999. The Group took a provision this half for the 2.5 million pounds redundancy costs to be incurred in the future.

The Group is also proceeding ahead with its asset disposal program. Shareholders gave their approval to the sale of one third of the Group's stake in Laura Ashley Japan for 9.5 million pounds in March 1998. The Group recently exchanged contracts to sell and lease back its Bagleys Lane headquarters premises for 4.5 million pounds, a price that includes a rent free period for the next 12 months. The Group is also continuing its efforts to sell its manufacturing facilities.

APPENDIX
LAURA ASHLEY HOLDINGS PLC FINANCIAL INFORMATION

TABLE 2.A1
Laura Ashley Holdings plc: profit and loss statement (£ million)

	26 weeks to 8.1.98	26 weeks to 7.26.97	Year to 1.31.98	Year to 1.31.97
Turnover	144.2	174.6	344.9	327.6
Cost of sales	(79.4)	(103.8)	(214.0)	(168.9)
Gross profit	64.8	70.8	130.9	158.7
Operating expenses	(74.1)	(74.9)	(166.9)	(144.3)
Other operating income	1.5	—	—	—
Operating profit/(loss)	(7.8)	(4.1)	(36.0)	(14.4)
Share of operating (loss)/profit of associate cos.	(0.1)	0.6	0.5	2.1
Profit on sale of investment in associate cos.	7.5	—	—	—
Amounts written-off investment	—	—	(2.4)	—
Provision for disposal of manufacturing business	—	—	(9.0)	—
(Loss)/profit on ordinary activities before interest	(0.4)	(3.5)	(46.9)	16.9
Net interest payable	(1.3)	(1.0)	(2.4)	(0.7)
(Loss)/profit on ordinary activities before taxation	(1.7)	(4.5)	(49.3)	16.2
Taxation on (loss)/profit on ordinary activities	(0.9)	0.1	—	6.1
(Loss)/profit on ordinary activities after tax	(2.6)	(4.4)	(49.3)	16.2
Dividend	—	—	—	(2.4)
Retained (loss)/profit for the period	(2.6)	(4.4)	(49.3)	7.7

TABLE 2.A2
Laura Ashley Holdings plc: balance sheet (£ million)

	At 8.1.98	At 7.26.97	At 1.31.98	At 1.31.98
Fixed assets				
Tangible fixed assets	36.3	43.3	38.9	44.0
Investment in associated undertaking	1.4	2.6	2.5	2.2
Own shares	0.8	3.3	0.8	3.3
Total	38.5	49.2	42.2	49.5
Current assets				
Stocks (inventories)	59.0	76.8	63.2	93.1
Debtors	20.1	27.7	21.2	24.4
Short-term deposits and cash	12.0	6.3	10.2	6.2
Total	91.1	110.8	94.6	123.7
Creditors: amounts due within one year				
Borrowings	0.1	—	9.9	—
Trade and other creditors	46.7	66.7	57.1	72.6
Total	46.8	66.7	67.0	74.0
Net current assets	44.3	44.1	27.6	49.7
Total assets less current liabilities	82.8	93.3	69.8	99.2
Creditors: amounts due after 1 year				
Borrowings	—	22.0	29.2	21.0
Trade and other creditors	0.9	0.9	1.2	0.8
Total	0.9	22.9	30.4	21.8
Provisions for liabilities and charges	21.4	5.7	19.7	7.3
Net assets	60.5	64.7	19.7	70.1
Capital and reserves				
Share capital	19.9	11.9	11.9	11.9
Share premium account	87.3	51.6	51.6	51.5
Profit and loss account	(46.7)	1.2	(43.8)	6.7
Equity shareholders' funds	60.5	64.7	19.7	70.1
Ordinary shares issued (millions)	292	236	236	236

TABLE 2.A3
Laura Ashley Holdings plc: cash flow statement (£ million)

	26 weeks to 8.1.98	26 weeks to 7.26.97	Year to 1.31.98	Year to 1.31.97
Net cash flow from operating activities	(7.0)	4.9	5.2	(0.7)
Returns on investments and servicing of finance:				
Interest received	0.3	0.4	1.2	0.8
Interest paid	(1.5)	(1.2)	(3.3)	(1.2)
Interest element of lease payments	(0.1)	(0.1)	(0.3)	(0.3)
Dividends received from associates	0.1	0.2	0.2	0.1
Net cash outflow for returns on investments and the servicing of finance	(1.2)	(0.7)	(2.2)	(0.6)
Tax paid	(0.6)	(0.5)	(5.5)	(1.6)
Capital expenditure and financial investment:				
Acquisition of tangible fixed assets	(1.6)	(4.0)	(9.6)	(14.2)
Disposal of tangible fixed assets	—	0.2	0.1	0.2
Net cash flow for investment	(1.6)	(3.8)	(9.5)	(14.0)
Acquisitions and disposals	7.9	—	—	—
Equity dividends paid	—	(1.4)	(1.4)	(2.1)
Cash outflow before financing	(2.5)	(1.5)	(13.4)	(18.8)
Financing:				
Issue of ordinary share capital	43.7	0.1	0.1	1.4
Settlement of currency swaps	—	1.6	0.5	4.0
Loans taken out	—	1.0	18.1	21.0
Repayment of loans	(39.0)	—	—	(5.0)
Capital element of lease payments	(0.6)	(0.6)	(0.9)	(1.2)
Net cash inflow from financing	4.1	2.1	17.8	20.2
Increase in cash	1.6	0.6	4.4	1.4

NOTES

1. This section draws upon "Laura Ashley: History," Laura Ashley Holdings plc; and J. L. Heath, *Laura Ashley Holdings PLC (A) and (B)*, European Case Clearing House, 1991.

2. "Chief Executive's Statement," *Laura Ashley Holdings plc Annual Report 1996*, London 1996.

3. "Giving Laura Ashley a Yank," *Business Week*, May 27, 1997, p. 147.

4. "Chief Executive's Statement," *Laura Ashley Holdings plc Annual Report 1998*, London 1998.

CHAPTER THREE

DAIMLER CHRYSLER AND THE WORLD AUTOMOBILE INDUSTRY

Robert M. Grant prepared this case with the assistance of Andoni Aguir-reazaldegui, Laura Estevez, Andrew Nulman, Michele Shuey, and Claudio Thiermann solely to provide material for class discussion. The author does not intend to illustrate either the effective or ineffective handling of a management situation. The author may have disguised certain names or other identifying information to protect confidentiality.

THE MERGER

The merger between Daimler Benz and Chrysler Corporation announced at the beginning of May 1998 was the biggest industrial merger in history. The merger, to be consummated at end of 1998, would create the world's third largest automotive company (after GM and Ford) with sales of about $130 billion (in 1997) and 421,000 employees worldwide.[1]

During the summer of 1998, a series of meetings took place between the two chairmen, Jürgen Schrempp and Robert Eaton, to iron out the details of the merger. Meanwhile, discussions were initiated between executives and corporate staff members of the two companies on a variety of topics. Among the strategic planning staffs at the two companies, discussions took place over coordinating the strategic plans and capital expenditure budgets of the two corporations. A critical issue in these discussions was the likely future of the world automobile industry.

Both companies recognized that the world automobile industry was at a critical stage of its development. At the end of the 1990s, a number of uncertainties were converging. These included overcapacity, the financial crisis affecting Asia and many emerging-market countries, and the environment. Even before the merger was consummated, the new company needed to establish a consensus concerning the future of the industry, including the potential for profit over the next five years, and which markets and product segments would be favored by the trends reshaping the industry.

THE MARKET

Trends in Market Demand

From its beginnings in Europe and the United States during the 1890s, the automobile industry had grown almost continuously until the mid-1980s. However, market growth has followed different time-paths in different parts of the world. The US market entered its period of rapid growth during 1910–28. In Europe, the growth phase was both later and more subdued. By the late 1950s and early 1960s, the US market had reached maturity, though in Europe and Japan, market penetration of the automobile continued during the 1960s and 1970s. However, the advanced industrial world of North America, Europe, and Japan has seen little growth in automobile demand over the past two decades. Although sales in these nations have been subject to strong cyclical influences, there has been little in the way of overall growth. Thus, despite the strong upturn in car sales in the US during 1992–5, sales were heading downhill in 1998, and even during cyclical peaks, total sales and production have yet to surpass the peak reached in 1973 (see Table 3.1).

Market growth has been strongest in those countries with strong economic growth and with comparatively low levels of automobile ownership. During the 1980s and 1990s it has been the newly industrializing countries Korea, Malaysia, Taiwan, Thailand, Turkey, Brazil, and Argentina where the most rapid growth in automobile demand has occurred. As these markets became increasingly saturated, so China, India, and the former Soviet Union were seen as the "next wave" of attractive markets. In the next decade it seems likely that the major opportunities for market growth will be among the emerging market economies of Eastern Europe and the former Soviet Union, China, and India, together with Latin America. Table 3.2 shows world production.

The slowing demand growth was also caused by the tendency for cars to last longer. Table 3.3 shows the increase in the average age of cars in use in the US during the 1980s and 1990s.

The Evolution of the Automobile

The early years of the industry were characterized by considerable uncertainty over the design and technology of the motor car. Early "horseless carriages" were precisely that – they followed design features of existing horse-drawn carriages and buggies. Early motor cars demonstrated a bewildering variety of technologies. During the early years, the internal-combustion engine vied with the steam engine. Among internal-combustion engines there was a wide variety of cylinder configurations. Transmission systems, steering systems, and brakes all displayed a remarkable variety of technologies and designs, as well as considerable ingenuity.

Over the years the technologies and designs of different manufactured parts tended to converge as many approaches (and their manufacturers) were eliminated through competition. The Ford Model T represented the first "dominant design" in automobiles – the technologies and design features of the Model T set a standard

TABLE 3.1
US motor vehicle production

	Passenger cars	Trucks and buses	Total
1900	4,192	n.a.	4,192
1905	24,250	750	25,000
1910	181,000	6,000	187,000
1915	895,930	74,000	969,930
1920	1,905,560	321,789	2,227,349
1925	3,735,171	530,659	4,265,830
1930	2,787,456	575,364	3,362,820
1935	3,273,874	697,367	3,971,241
1940	3,717,385	754,901	4,472,286
1945	69,532	655,683	725,215
1950	6,665,863	1,337,193	8,003,056
1955	7,920,186	1,249,105	9,169,292
1960	6,674,796	1,194,475	7,869,271
1965	9,305,561	1,751,805	11,057,366
1967	7,436,764	1,539,462	8,976,226
1970	6,546,817	1,692,442	8,239,257
1975	6,712,852	2,272,160	8,985,012
1977	9,200,849	3,411,521	12,642,370
1980	6,400,026	1,667,283	8,067,309
1985	8,002,259	3,464,327	11,466,586
1990	6,049,749	3,718,781	9,768,530
1991	5,407,120	3,375,422	8,782,542
1992	5,684,221	4,042,486	9,726,689
1993	5,981,046	4,883,157	10,864,203
1994	6,601,223	5,648,767	12,249,990
1995	6,350,367	5,634,742	11,985,091
1996	6,083,000	5,749,000	11,832,000
1997	5,927,000	6,169,000	12,096,000

Source: Ward's Automotive Yearbook.

for other manufacturers to imitate. During the 1920s, the process of development continued, especially in car bodies with the general adoption of the enclosed, all-steel body.

During the post-war period, technological and design convergence continued. During the 1970s and 1980s, most of the models which were "outliers" in terms of distinctively different design disappeared: the VW Beetle with its rear, air-cooled engine, the Citroen 2-CV and its idiosyncratic braking and suspension system, Daf with its "Variomatic" transmission. The fall of the Berlin Wall was followed by the disappearance of other automotive idiosyncrasies, such as the 3-cylinder Wartburg and the 2-cycle Trabant. Engines became more similar: typically 4 or 6 cylinders,

TABLE 3.2
World motor vehicle production (passenger cars and commercial vehicles)

	Total (mil.)	US and Canada as % of total		Total (mil.)	US and Canada as % of total
1950	10.58	79.4	1988	48.21	27.3
1955	13.63	70.9	1989	49.10	26.2
1960	16.49	50.4	1990	48.35	24.2
1965	24.27	49.4	1991	46.50	23.0
1970	29.40	32.1	1992	47.69	24.5
1975	33.00	31.4	1993	46.40	28.3
1980	38.51	24.8	1994	49.69	29.4
1985	44.81	30.3	1995	49.93	28.8
1986	45.30	29.1	1996	52.50	28.2
1987	45.90	27.4	1997	54.15	28.0

Source: American Automobile Manufacturers Association (AAMA).

TABLE 3.3
Average age of passenger cars in the US (years)

	Mean	Median
1996	8.5	7.4
1994	8.4	7.4
1992	8.1	7.0
1990	7.8	6.5
1988	7.6	6.8
1984	7.5	6.7
1980	6.6	6.0
1976	6.2	5.5
1972	5.7	5.1
1968	5.6	4.7
1962	6.0	5.7
1958	5.6	5.1
1952	6.8	4.5
1948	8.8	8.0
1941	5.5	4.9

Source: R.L. Polk & Co.

usually in-line (although V-6 and V-8 configurations are common in larger engines) with overhead camshafts. Front-wheel drive and disc, anti-lock brakes became standard; suspension and steering systems became more standard; body shapes became increasingly alike. Although the automobile continued to evolve, changes tended

TABLE 3.4
Pounds of material in a typical family automobile

	1978	1997
Steel	2,128	1,790
Iron	512	378
Plastic and plastic composites	180	242
Aluminum	112	206
Copper and brass	37	46
Zinc castings	31	14
Glass	86	96
Rubber	146	138
Other	337	338
Total	3,569	3,248

Source: *Ward's Automotive Yearbook.*

to be incremental; for the most part these took the form of new accessories and features (safety features such as air bags and rear seat belts, and various electronic features). Major design innovations of the 1990s include "cab forward" design (pioneered by Honda), which has increased the passenger space within cars by the length of the engine compartment, and the introduction of engines with multi-valve cylinders. The quest for fuel economy has resulted in the substitution of lighter materials (aluminum, plastics, ceramics, and composites) for iron and steel (see Table 3.4).

During the 1990s, electronic components accounted for an increasing proportion of the value of cars. A 1950 Mercedes had about 10 meters of wiring. A 1995 SL 500 with full options has 3,000 meters of wiring and 48 different microcomputers. The current Ford Taurus embodies more computing power than was used in the 1969 moon landing. Current development, including satellite navigation systems, communications technology, emergency signaling, collision-avoidance radar, and intelligent monitoring systems, will only increase the importance of electronic technology within cars. Despite the adoption of new, technology-based accessories and design improvements, there is little in today's family cars that is radically new (see Table 3.5).

Also apparent is increased convergence of designs and technologies between manufacturers. While different types of vehicle (family cars, sports cars, passenger minivans, sport-utility vehicles) retain distinctive design features, within each of these categories manufacturers' product offerings have tended to become increasingly similar. By the 1990s, multi-story car parks were increasingly populated by bewildered motorists unable to locate their own cars among a multitude of similar-looking vehicles.

Convergence of automobile design also occurred across countries. In particular, family cars were becoming increasingly similar in size – while US cars downsized, Japanese and Italian cars became larger. Although the automobile market remained

TABLE 3.5
From option to standard: convergence in automobile features

Feature	Introduction	General adoption
Speedometer	1901 by Oldsmobile	Circa 1915
Automatic transmission	First installed 1904	Introduced by Packard as an option 1938. Standard on Cadillacs and other luxury cars early 1950s
Electric headlamps	GM introduced 1908	Standard equipment by 1916
All-steel body	Adopted by GM 1912	Becomes standard early 1920s
Steel enclosed body	Dodge 1923	Becomes standard late 1920s
Radio	Optional extra 1923	Standard equipment 1946
Four-wheel drive	Appeared 1924	Only limited availability by 1994
Hydraulic brakes	Introduced 1924	Become standard 1939
Shatterproof glass	First used in cars 1927	Standard feature in Fords 1938
Power steering	Introduced 1952	Standard equipment by 1969
Anti-lock brakes	Introduced 1972	Standard on GM cars in 1991
Air bags	Introduced by GM 1974	Standard in most new cars by 1994

Source: Washington Post.

highly segmented, the increased convergence of national markets was evident from the tendency for the same market segments to emerge in different countries. Thus, Mercedes, BMW, Jaguar, and the up-market brands of the Japanese (Lexus, Infiniti, etc.) dominated the luxury segment throughout most of the world. Toyota, Land Rover, Chrysler (Jeep), Suzuki, and a few other manufacturers led the worldwide sport-utility segment (4-wheel drive vehicles designed for off-road use). The passenger minivan segment established by the Chrysler Caravan in North America appeared in Europe as the "multi-purpose vehicle" (MPV) segment led by the Renault Espace. The major differences between countries were in the *sizes* of the various segments. Thus, in the US, the "mid-size" family sedan was the largest segment, with the Ford Taurus, Honda Accord, and Toyota Camry the leading models. In Europe and Asia, small family cars ("subcompacts") formed the largest market segment. Other national differences were also apparent. In North America, pickup trucks, used as commercial vehicles in most of the world, were used widely as two-seater passenger cars.

The Evolution of Manufacturing Technology

At the beginning of the twentieth century, car manufacture, like carriage-making, was a craft industry. Cars were built to order according to individual customers' preferences and specifications. In Europe and North America there were hundreds of companies producing cars, few with annual production exceeding 1,000 vehicles. When Henry Ford began production in 1903, he used a similar approach. Even with fairly long runs of a single model (the first version of the Model T, for example), each car was individually built. The development of more precise machine tools permitted interchangeable parts, which in turn permitted mass production: batch or continuous production of components which are then assembled on moving assembly lines by semi-skilled workers. The productivity gains were enormous. In 1912 it took 23 man-hours to assemble a Model T, just 14 months later it took only 4. The productivity gains achieved through Henry Ford's system reduced the price of cars by more than two-thirds over a 10-year period, opening up a new era of popular motoring. Soon, the leading automobile manufacturers were emerging among the ranks of the world's biggest industrial enterprises.

If "Fordism" was the first major revolution in process technology, then Toyota's "lean production" was the second. The system was developed by Toyota in post-war Japan at a time when shortages of key materials encouraged extreme parsimony and a need to avoid inventories and waste through defects. Key elements of the system were statistical process control, just-in-time scheduling, quality circles, teamwork, and flexible production (more than one model manufactured on a single production line). Central to the new manufacturing was the transition from static concepts of efficiency optimization towards continuous improvement to which every employee contributed. During the 1980s and 1990s all the world's car manufacturers redesigned their manufacturing processes to incorporate variants of Toyota's lean production.

New manufacturing methods required heavy investments by the companies in both capital equipment and training. The 1980s were a period of unprecedentedly high investment expenditures. However, as GM was to learn after spending more than $10 billion in upgrading its plants, the essence of the Toyota system was not robotics, computer-integrated manufacturing, and other elements of manufacturing "hardware." The critical elements were the "software" – the development of new employee skills, new methods of shop-floor organization, redefining the role of managers, and new relationships with suppliers.

One consequence of the new manufacturing technology was that increased flexibility permitted high levels of efficiency in medium-sized plants. During the 1960s and 1970s it was generally believed that efficiency required giant assembly plants with outputs of at least 400,000 units a year. During the 1990s, most of the new plants established had output capacities of between 150,000 and 300,000 units.

New Product Development

The declining importance of scale economies in automobile manufacture has done little to assist the competitiveness of the smaller firms the industry. The critical scale economy issue of the 1980s and 1990s related to the escalating costs of new product development.

TABLE 3.6
New car development costs during the 1990s

Ford Mondeo/Contour	$6 billion
GM Saturn	$5 billion
Ford Taurus (1996 model)	$2.8 billion
Ford Escort (new model)	$2 billion
Chrysler Neon	$1.3 billion
Renault Clio (1999 model)	$1.3 billion
Honda Accord (1997 model)	$0.6 billion
Rolls Royce Silver Seraph	$0.33 billion

Source: Assembled from various newspaper reports.

Despite the convergence of technologies and design among different manufacturers, the costs of new model development rose steeply between 1975 and 1995. Rising development costs were a result of increasing complexity of the product, the application of new technologies (including electronics and new materials), the upgrading of safety requirements, quality improvements, new environmental standards, the need for increased fuel efficiency, and rising costs of tooling new production lines. By the late 1980s the cost of creating an entirely new, mass-production passenger car from drawing board to production line was about $1.25 billion. By the early 1990s, the costs of major new models had escalated substantially above this level (see Table 3.6).

For smaller manufacturers, the costs of developing entirely new models were entirely beyond their means. One way for smaller producers to remain competitive was to avoid new model changes: at the time of its acquisition by Ford, Jaguar's two models the XJ-6 and XJ-S were almost two decades old and almost no investment had been made in developing a new model. The tiny Morgan car company economized on product development costs by building the same model from the late 1930s on. The alternative was to license designs from larger manufacturers. Thus, prior to its acquisition by BMW, Rover Cars licensed designs from Honda. Similarly, smaller manufacturers in Asia and Eastern Europe have traditionally licensed designs from leading US, European, and Japanese manufacturers (Proton of Malaysia builds Mitsubishi-designed cars, Maruti of India builds Suzuki-designed cars).

The high cost of new product development has been the major source of the cost-uncompetitiveness of smaller car producers. The result has been mergers between smaller manufacturers, and the acquisition of smaller producers by bigger ones (see Table 3.7). The desire to share development costs also results in increased collaboration and joint ventures: Renault and PSA established joint engine manufacturing, GM collaborated with Daewoo to build small cars, in China and India most new auto plants were joint ventures between local and overseas companies.

During the 1990s, new product development emerged as the critical organizational capability differentiating car manufacturers. Designing, developing, and putting into production a completely new automobile is a hugely complex process

TABLE 3.7

Mergers and acquisitions among automobile manufacturers

1998	Daimler Benz (Germany)	Chrysler (US)
	VW (Germany)	Rolls Royce Motors (UK)
	Hyundai (S. Korea)	Kia (S. Korea)
1997	Proton (Malaysia)	Lotus (UK)
	BMW (Germany)	Rover (UK)
1996	Daewoo (S. Korea)	FSO (Poland)
	Daewoo (S. Korea)	FS Lublin (Poland)
1995	Fiat (Italy)	FSM (Poland)
	Ford (US)	Mazda (Japan)
1994	Daewoo (S. Korea)	Oltcit/Rodae (Romania)
1991	VW (Germany)	Skoda (Czech Republic)
1990	GM (US)	Saab-Scandia (Sweden)
	Ford (US)	Jaguar (UK)
1987	Ford (US)	Aston Martin (UK)
	Chrysler (US)	Lamborghini (Italy)
1986	VW (Germany)	Seat (Spain)

involving every function of the firm, up to 3,000 engineers, close collaboration with several hundred suppliers, and up to five years from drawing board to market launch. If the primary competitive advantage of the Japanese manufacturers during the 1970s was low production cost, and during the 1980s was superior quality, by the 1990s the critical Japanese advantage was shorter new product development times and lower development costs. By the early 1990s, US and European carmakers were studying the Japanese companies' use of product development teams as a means of achieving improved functional integration and accelerated product development cycles. Chrysler's benchmarking of Honda resulted in Chrysler restructuring its product development system around a team-based system.

Manufacturers also looked to new technology to lower the costs and increase the speed of new model development. A key development was the adoption of "virtual prototyping" – the use of 3D computer graphics to design and test prototypes. Boeing's use of virtual prototyping to design and engineer its 777 jetliner and save an estimated $100 million in development is widely seen as a model for the auto industry.

THE INDUSTRY

The Manufacturers

The major automobile manufacturers are shown in Table 3.8. The ranks of the leading producers are dominated by US, Japanese, and European companies.

TABLE 3.8
The world's leading auto manufacturers

		Production ('000s of autos + CVs)					Revenues ($bill.)					
		1992	1994	1995	1996	1997	1992	1993	1994	1995	1996	1997
GM	US	6,764	8,254	8,619	8,176	8,310	133	133	154	160	164	178
Ford	US	5,742	6,679	6,462	6,611	6,943	101	109	128	137	147	154
Toyota	Japan	4,249	4,565	4,465	4,794	4,850	80	85	88	100	99	84
Volkswagen	Germany	3,286	2,436	3,299	3,977	4,325	57	46	49	53	61	64
Nissan	Japan	2,963	2,702	2,839	2,712	2,801	50	54	69	55	54	47
Peugeot	France	2,437	2,027	1,890	1,975	1,146	29	26	30	53	61	31
Chrysler	US	1,983	2,880	2,808	3,080	3,051	44	44	52	53	61	61
Renault	France	1,929	1,881	1,761	1,755	1,868	34	30	32	33	33	35
Fiat	Italy	1,800	1,967	2,143	2,545	2,486	48	35	41	47	49	51
Honda	Japan	1,762	1,725	1,765	2,021	2,269	33	36	40	40	43	43
Mitsubishi	Japan	1,599	1,504	1,529	1,452	1,529	25	27	34	35	33	29
Mazda	Japan	1,248	1,215	974	984	1,052	21	20	22	17	16	15
Suzuki	Japan	888	1,076	510	1,387	1,458	10	11	13	12	13	11
Hyundai	S. Korea	874	1,153	1,255	1,402	1,370	9	9	12	16	n.a.	n.a.
Daimler-Benz	Germany	799	884	930	1,002	1,149	63	59	64	64	62	70
VAZ	Russia	674	528	585	562	575	n.a.	n.a.	n.a.	n.a.	n.a.	n.a.
Fuji	Japan	648	434	419	525	542	8	9	11	n.a.	12	n.a.
Daihatsu	Japan	610	554	606	691	683	n.a.	12	n.a.	n.a.	n.a.	n.a.
BMW	Germany	598	573	563	641	672	21	18	26	27	31	34
Kia	S. Korea	502	675	691	847	750	4	5	7	n.a.	n.a.	n.a.
Isuzu	Japan	473	487	456	462	481	12	14	15	n.a.	n.a.	n.a.
Rover	UK	405	485	503	510	479	18	14	20	—	—	—
Volvo	Sweden	365	439	448	446	466	15	31	36	24	20	23
Daewoo	S. Korea	179	419	523	710	819	n.a.	28	n.a.	50	n.a.	n.a.
FSM	Poland	143	n.a.	n.a.	n.a.	n.a.	n.a.	n.a.	n.a.	n.a.	n.a.	n.a.
Tofas	Turkey	142	n.a.	128	n.a.	n.a.	n.a.	n.a.	n.a.	n.a.	n.a.	n.a.
Maruti	India	128	n.a.	n.a.	n.a.	346	1	n.a.	2	n.a.	n.a.	n.a.
Proton	Malaysia	99	118	160	n.a.	n.a.	1	n.a.	2	2.5	n.a.	n.a.

Volkswagen's production for 1996 and 1997 includes Skoda and Seat.

Sources: Ward's Automotive Yearbook, Fortune.

However, despite the relative decline of the United States as an auto-producing nation, GM and Ford have maintained their positions as the world's largest motor vehicle manufacturers because of the importance of their overseas production: both GM and Ford produce more cars outside the US than within it.

New Entry

Despite the pressures on smaller automobile firms and a tendency for them to be absorbed by their bigger competitors, a number of newcomers have entered the industry since the 1960s. The Japanese companies Honda, Suzuki, and Daihatsu entered auto manufacture in the 1960s. They were followed by the Koreans: Hyundai, Daewoo, and Kia entered during the 1970s and 1980s, while Samsung and Ssangyong began car production in 1996. Most of the new auto manufacturers of the 1990s have been set up within protected markets with considerable government support (e.g., Proton in Malaysia, Maruti in India). These companies all have licensing agreements with large overseas automobile companies which give them access to technology and modern automobile designs. Such partnerships often involve equity stakes.

Outsourcing and the Growing Role of Suppliers

Henry Ford's system of mass production tended to be supported by heavy backward integration. In Ford's giant River Rouge plant, iron ore entered at one end, Model Ts emerged at the other. Ford even owned rubber plantations in the Amazon basin. The trend of the past 20 years has been towards less vertical integration with increasing outsourcing of materials, components, and subassemblies. This has been led primarily by the desire for lower costs and increased flexibility. The Japanese example has been influential: Japanese car manufacturers have traditionally been much less backward integrated than their US or European counterparts.

Moreover, the Japanese companies' relationships with their suppliers were much different. In contrast to the US model of arms-length relationships and written contracts, the Japanese manufacturers developed close, collaborative long-run relationships with their "first-tier" suppliers. During the 1980s and 1990s, all the world's auto manufacturers moved towards the Japanese model and in the process greatly reduced the number of their suppliers while becoming increasingly dependent upon suppliers for technology and design.

The result has been growing size and power of the components manufacturers, especially those which develop and supply sophisticated subassemblies such as transmissions, braking systems, and electrical and electronic equipment. By the 1990s companies such as Bosch, TRW, Lucas-Varity, Eaton, and GKN were major global players in the automotive sector with size and geographical scope similar to many of the automobile manufacturers (see Table 3.9).

TABLE 3.9
Leading suppliers of automotive components ($ billion)

	Revenues		
	1994	1996	1997
Robert Bosch (Germany)	19.6	16.3	17.8
Denso Corp. (Japan)	11.0	13.9	11.7
Johnson Controls (US)	7.1	6.3	11.1
TRW (US)	7.9	6.5	10.8
Dana (US)	5.5	7.7	8.3
Eaton (US)	4.4	7.0	7.6
Lucas-Varity (UK–US)	3.9	7.2	7.6
Aisin Seiki (Japan)	7.3	7.8	6.5
Lear Corp (US)	3.1	6.2	n.a.
Valeo SA (France)	3.8	5.0	5.7
Toyoda Auto Loom Works	4.6	4.8	4.1

Sources: Ward's Automotive Yearbook, Business Week "Global 1000."

The Quest for Cost Reduction

Increasing competition in the industry has intensified the quest for cost reduction among automobile manufacturers. Cost-reduction strategies have included the following:

- Worldwide outsourcing. The tendency for increased outsourcing of components has been referred to above. In addition, auto firms have developed OEM supply arrangements amongst themselves: Daewoo supplies several of GM's models, Mitsubishi supplies engines and complete cars to Chrysler, BMW supplies engines to Rolls Royce.
- Just-in-time scheduling has been used to reduce levels of inventory and work-in-progress.
- In high-cost locations (North America, Western Europe, and Japan) increased automation has reduced labor input.
- Component production and some assembly activities have been shifted to lower-cost locations: VW's North American production is based in Mexico and the company has also shifted production from Germany to the Czech Republic, Spain, and Hungary; the Japanese companies have moved more and more production to lower-cost locations in Southeast Asia; Daimler Benz and BMW have developed greenfield plants in the Deep South of the US.

TABLE 3.10
US motor vehicle manufacturers' investment in plant and equipment ($ billion)

1996	13.82	1991	10.20	1984	10.17	1972	3.00
1995	12.60	1990	11.28	1982	7.13	1968	2.67
1993	10.56	1988	9.75	1980	8.54	1960	1.47
1992	8.69	1986	12.79	1976	3.60	1950	0.78

Source: Dept. of Commerce.

Different companies have faced different cost issues. While European manufacturers were constrained by rigid working conditions, restrictions on layoffs, and generous benefits, US companies were hit by increased provisions for pensions and health care. In Japan the critical issue for most of the 1990s was the escalating value of the yen.

The quest for economies of scale and scope in relation to product development meant that companies sought to spread rising development costs over larger production and sales volumes. Increasingly during the 1990s the auto manufacturers attempted to introduce single global products. After failing to get agreement between its European and US designers over a common Escort model, Ford's Mondeo/Contour was the company's first truly global model.

This desire for scale economies in development, manufacture, and purchasing also resulted in the standardization of designs and components across the different models of each manufacturer. By 2000, GM will have as many different models as it had in 1990, but will have only half the number of platforms compared to 1990. Similar standardization is apparent in engines.

Excess Capacity

While plant closures continued at an unprecedented rate during the 1980s and early 1990s, especially in the US, a key factor exacerbating competitive pressures in the industry was the enormous overhang of excess capacity. During the 1980s and early 1990s, Japanese companies were the main investors in new capacity with a number of greenfield "transplants" in North America and Europe. During the 1990s all the world's major car companies responded to the quest for globalization with new plants (many of them joint ventures) in the growth markets of Southeast Asia, China, India, South America, and Eastern Europe. During 1992–7, the Korean car companies were especially aggressive investors in new capacity. Meanwhile, US and European manufacturers were continuing to upgrade their plants at home. Table 3.10 shows the trend of capital investment in US motor vehicle manufacturing. Despite strong economic growth in the US during the 1990s, it was clear by the late 1990s that the growth in new production capacity was greatly outstripping

TABLE 3.11
Capacity utilization in US motor vehicle manufacturing (%)

	1998 (est.)	1996	1994	1992	1990
United States	70.8	72.4	83.5	69.9	71.6
Western Europe	71.5	72.0	69.8	75.8	77.8
Asia	61.2	68.5	69.8	75.1	76.7

Sources: AAMA, *The Economist*.

the growth of demand for new cars. Table 3.11 shows excess capacity in the industry.

Internationalization

The most important force transforming the structure of the world auto industry during the past quarter-century has been the internationalization strategies of the manufacturers. Although international growth extends back to 1920s, when Ford and General Motors established their European subsidiaries, until the 1970s the world auto industry was made up of fairly separate national markets. Each of the larger national markets was supplied primarily by domestic production, and indigenous manufacturers tended to be market leaders. For example in 1970, the Big Three (GM, Ford, and Chrysler) held close to 85 percent of the US market, VW and Daimler Benz dominated the market in Germany, as did Fiat in Italy, British Leyland (later Rover) in the UK, Seat in Spain, and Renault, Peugeot, and Citroen in France. By 1998, the industry was global in scope: in almost every significant national market, all the world's leading manufacturers had established themselves.

Internationalization has occurred through *trade* and *foreign direct investment*. Despite the efforts by the US and Europe to protect their markets against Japanese imports by means of quotas, growth in trade has been stimulated by declining tariffs and the convergence of national preferences. Total world motor vehicle trade has grown substantially over time. (See Table 3.12.)

If GM and Ford were the pioneers of international expansion in the auto industry, during the 1970s and 1980s it was Japanese car manufacturers who became the main drivers of internationalization. The patterns of international expansion were also different. While Ford and GM had established self-sufficient, fully integrated subsidiaries in overseas countries, the Japanese companies preferred to export from their home plants. The Japanese companies' transfer of production outside of Japan was initially the result of import barriers imposed by the US and Europe, and subsequently the result of the rising value of the yen. Table 3.13 shows some of the North American auto plants established by Japanese companies. By contrast, the Europeans internationalized within Europe and into the developing world. VW

TABLE 3.12
International trade in motor vehicles

	1970	1980	1990	1992	1994	1996	1997
World motor vehicle exports (millions)	8.7	15.2	18.3	20.3	19.8	22.9	23.5
US exports of motor vehicles & parts ($ bill.)	7.1	17.4	36.5	47.0	57.8	64.2	74.0
US imports of motor vehicles & parts ($ bill.)	7.4	28.3	88.5	91.8	98.3	130.1	140.8

Source: AAMA.

TABLE 3.13
Japanese "transplants" in North America

Company	Parent(s)	Location	Production of cars and lt. trucks 1997
NUMMI	Toyota and GM	Fremont, CA	357,809
CAMI Automotive	Suzuki and GM	Ontario	99,770
Toyota USA	Toyota	Georgetown, KY	431,881
Toyota Canada	Toyota	Ontario	108,952
Honda of America	Honda	E. Liberty and Marysville, OH	648,300
Honda of Canada	Honda	Ontario	165,181
Diamond-Star Motors	Mitsubishi and Chrysler	Normal, IL	189,086
Subaru-Isuzu Auto	Fuji and Isuzu	Lafayette, IN	186,891
Nissan Motor Mfr. USA	Nissan	Sryrna, TN	398,308
BMW	BMW	Spartanburg, NC	62,943
Mercedes-Benz	Mercedes-Benz	Vance, AL	19,462

Source: Ward's Automotive Yearbook.

expanded heavily into the rest of Europe during the 1980s; Fiat, PSA, and VW established plants in Latin America, Africa, and Asia; Renault (which acquired AMC) and VW both established production within the US, only to withdraw at the end of the 1980s. BMW and Daimler Benz concentrated production in their home bases and exported worldwide. However, in 1994, both companies opened plants in the US. During the mid-to-late 1990s some of the most aggressive overseas expansion has been by the Korean auto producers. Kia is most recent to establish dealerships in Europe and North America and in August 1996 announced a $1 billion plant in

Russia. Daewoo has also moved rapidly into Eastern Europe with plants in Poland, Romania, and Uzbekistan, as well as starting joint ventures in India and elsewhere. The global growth strategies of the Korean companies have been severely dented by the Asian economic crisis of 1997–8.

During the 1990s, some of the main opportunities for new investment have been in the emerging market economies of Eastern Europe and Asia. Following the collapse of the "Iron Curtain" there was a rush by the major auto companies to acquire interests in struggling Eastern European producers. For example:

- Volkswagen acquired 70 percent of Skoda (Czech Republic) with its annual production volume of 200,000 for $5.6 billion. It also began work on a $420 million assembly plant in Hungary.
- Fiat paid $2 billion for 90 percent of Tychy/FSM (Poland) with its annual production of 200,000 Fiat-designed cars.
- GM-Opel bought the Eisenach assembly plant in former East Germany for $587 million, and in Hungary acquired 67 percent of the Szentgotthard factory (producing 10,000 Opel Astras a year) for $300 million.
- Suzuki acquired 60 percent of a Hungarian plant producing 8,000 Suzuki Swifts a year for $250 million.[2]

The biggest magnet for the world's auto producers has been Asia. Here the attractions have been, first, projections of rapid market growth, and second, increased economic liberalization. In India, most of the leading auto companies have established a presence, mostly through joint ventures. The most successful has been the Maruti–Suzuki joint venture. Once a failing indigenous producer, Maruti's Suzuki-designed small cars and light trucks have been outstandingly successful, and the company is now market leader. By 1996, PSA (Peugeot), Mercedes, Daewoo, Fiat, Ford, GM, Honda, and Hyundai had all invested in manufacturing facilities in India.

In China, Chrysler has a long-established position through Beijing Jeep (begun in 1984 by AMC). VW has a 50:50 joint venture in Shanghai. GM closed its joint venture truck plant at Shenyang, but in November 1995 formed a new $1.1 billion joint venture. The main winner in China appears to be Mercedes Benz, which, after several years of building trucks and buses in China, was selected to build a $1 billion minivan plant. Meanwhile, Ford's joint venture with Jiangling Motors is expanding its output of Ford Transit vans and Isuzu trucks above 100,000 units per year. Throughout the 1990s, Beijing continued to carefully plan the development of the country's motor vehicle industry with tight restrictions on inward foreign investment.[3] Table 3.14 shows the leading manufacturers in China.

Despite the tremendous internationalization of the auto industry since 1970, national producers still retain leadership in their home markets. For example, Fiat is market leader in Italy, VW in Germany, Renault and PSA in France, Hyundai and Daewoo in Korea (see Table 3.15). This is partly due to import protection (France and Italy only recently dismantled their national restrictions on Japanese auto imports; Korea still maintains significant import barriers), partly due to nationalism among domestic consumers (especially in Japan), and partly due to the strong local dealership networks and intimate local knowledge of domestic manufacturers.

TABLE 3.14
Major auto manufacturers in China, 1997

Manufacturer	Production	Notes
Shanghai Automotive Industry Corp.	178,042	Production included 35,000 VW/Audi models assembled under joint venture and license agreements. Joint venture with GM agreed 1995.
First Auto	221,000	Includes 46,000 vehicles produced by First Auto–VW joint venture.
Dongfeng Automobile Co. Ltd	142,335	Includes Dongfeng-Citroen joint venture producing Citroen ZX under "Fukang" badge.
Beijing Automobile	128,000	Includes joint venture with Chrysler to build Jeep Cherokees.
Tianjin Automobile	158,581	License agreement with Daihatsu. Capacity in 2000 to increase to 150,000
Shanghai-VW Automotive	230,443	Includes 110,000 VW Santanas. Capacity in 2000 to increase to 300,000
Nanjing Motor Corp.	74,074	Includes 5,000 light trucks under license agreement with Iveco-Fiat.
Guangzhou-Peugeot Automobile Co.	8,052	Produces Peugeot 505s. Capacity in 2000: 150,000.

Source: Ward's Automotive Yearbook, Financial Times.

Although a large domestic market share is a source of strength, lack of international diversity makes nationally focused companies vulnerable to competition from global rivals. As a result, nationally focused car companies have tended to be acquired by larger groups (e.g., the acquisition of Seat and Skoda by VW, BMW's purchase of Rover). Among the small firms, Proton (Malaysia) and Maruti (India) used alliances and joint ventures to access the strengths of bigger competitors.

Probably the best known example of market dominance by domestic manufacturers is that of Japan. Despite low tariff rates, an absence of quotas, and a rising currency (which should make Japan a profitable export market), Japan's import penetration ratio remains the lowest of any of the advanced nations. Yet, despite the tortuous and acrimonious US–Japanese negotiations over the access of US companies to the Japanese auto and auto parts market, the reasons for Japan's seemingly impenetrable market are still not well understood. While Japan's system of distribution imposes difficulties on overseas companies, some observers allege that US companies' dismal market performance in Japan also results from failure to address the needs of the Japanese consumer in such basic features as providing cars with steering wheels on the right-hand side (see Table 3.16).

TABLE 3.15
Automobile market shares in individual countries (%)

Japan	1997	1994	1992	1988	France	1997	1994	1992	1988
Toyota	30.6	33.7	35.3	43.9	Renault	27.4	30.0	29.4	29.1
Nissan	—	18.0	19.9	23.2	Peugeot	28.8	31.1	30.1	34.2
Honda	10.1	8.5	10.5	10.8	VW	11.4	8.0	9.7	9.2
Mitsubishi	7.9	9.2	7.5	4.9	Ford	8.0	8.1	8.2	7.1
Mazda	4.3	6.3	7.3	6.7					
Suzuki	8.6	n.a.	n.a.	n.a.					

Korea*	1997	1994	1992	1988	Italy	1997	1994	1992	1988
Hyundai	46.6	46.5	46.7	55.9	Fiat	43.0	46.0	43.0	59.9
Kia	23.0	26.5	25.8	25.0	VW	9.9	10.4	14.8	11.7
Daewoo	30.2	16.0	15.5	19.1	Ford	9.3	9.6	10.8	3.7
					Renault	6.8	7.0	7.6	7.1

Australia	1997	1995	1992	1988	UK	1997	1994	1992	1988
Ford	19.6	24.4	23.3	28.1	Ford	18.7	22.2	22.5	26.3
GM	17.7	21.3	19.6	20.9	GM	14.3	16.9	17.6	13.7
Toyota	13.4	19.0	15.5	15.3	BMW/Rover	12.9	12.8	13.5	15.0
Nissan	3.6	3.8	11.5	9.9	Peugeot	11.4	12.1	11.8	8.7
Mitsubishi	11.9	10.1	11.5	12.2					
Hyundai	11.1	8.9	n.a.	n.a.					

Taiwan	1997	1994	1992	1988	Germany	1997	1994	1992	1988
Ford	16.2	17.8	23.0	25.7	VW	25.0	20.9	26.4	28.3
Toyota	18.1	20.0	15.9	0.0	GM	15.6	16.5	16.7	16.1
Yulon/Honda	17.3	11.8	14.5	0.0	Ford	11.0	9.9	9.3	10.1
					Mercedes	8.5	8.2	6.5	9.2
					Japanese	12.3	12.5	13.4	15.2

* Excludes imports.

Source: Ward's Automotive Yearbook.

Industry Location

In view of the changes affecting the world auto market – maturity in North America and Europe, growth in Southeast Asia, falling tariff barriers, changing patterns of national competitive advantage, and increased flows of direct investment – it might be expected that the geographical distribution of the industry would have changed substantially over the past quarter-century. However, compared to some other man-ufacturing industries, such as apparel, consumer electronics, and footwear, such

TABLE 3.16
Adapting to the local market: Japan and the US

	No. of models	Total no. of versions	No. of sales outlets
Availability of American cars with right-hand drive in Japan			
GM	0	0	249
Ford	1	1	310
Chrysler	1	2	1,917
Availability of Japanese cars with left-hand drive in the US			
Toyota/Lexus	15	37	1,359
Honda/Acura	16	49	1,285
Nissan/Infiniti	12	31	1,250
Mazda	9	19	906
Mitsubishi	6	16	514
Others	10	27	1,586

Source: The Economist.

TABLE 3.17
World motor vehicle production by region (% of world total)

	1960	1989	1991	1992	1994	1995	1997
United States	52.0	23.8	19.8	20.6	24.5	23.8	22.0
Western Europe	38.0	31.7	30.7	32.5	31.2	32.4	32.6
Russia and E. Europe	2.0	4.8	—	—	4.3	4.6	5.6
Japan	1.0	18.2	29.7	26.7	21.2	20.1	20.5
Korea	—	1.8	3.4	3.7	4.6	4.8	4.8
Other	7.0	19.7	16.4	16.4	14.4	14.4	14.5
Total units (millions)	12.8	49.5	44.6	47.5	50.0	50.2	55.0

Products for E. Europe and USSR included in "Other" for 1991 and 1992.
Source: AAMA, *Automotive News*.

changes have been less than might have been expected. The main feature of the post-war period was the growth of production in Japan and a corresponding decline within the US. Since 1980, the changes have been slight. The key feature of industry location has been the dominance of the three major manufacturing regions: Western Europe, North America, and Japan, each accounting for close to 30 percent of world production. The continuing dominance of this triad is despite the attempts of newly industrializing countries to develop their domestic industries, either by protecting domestic manufacturers or by encouraging inward investment. (Table 3.17 shows car production by different regions and Table 3.18 shows car production by different countries in recent years.)

TABLE 3.18
Car production by country (thousands of cars)

	1997	1995	1994	1992	1990	1987
US	5,884	6,338	6,601	5,664	6,077	7,099
Canada	1,374	1,339	1,215	1,020	1,072	810
Mexico	833	710	840	778	346	266
Total N. America	8,091	8,387	8,657	7,463	7,496	8,176
Germany	4,678	4,360	4,040	4,864	4,805	4,604
France	3,326	3,051	3,175	3,320	3,295	3,052
Italy	1,580	1,422	1,341	1,477	1,874	1,701
UK	1,868	1,532	1,467	1,292	1,296	1,143
Spain	1,961	1,959	1,822	1,799	1,679	1,403
Sweden	373	390	353	294	336	432
Total W. Europe	14,687	14,350	13,844	13,520	13,672	13,471
Japan	8,494	7,664	7,801	9,379	9,948	7,891
Korea	2,088	1,893	1,805	1,307	987	793
Australia	323	284	286	270	361	225
China	543	356	313	208	n.a.	n.a.
Taiwan	258	271	263	283	277	175
Former USSR	1,066	834	798	1,050	1,260	1,329
Poland	426	260	250	212	256	301
E. Germany	—	—	—	—	144	230
Brazil	1,680	1,312	1,249	816	663	789

Sources: Japan Automobile Manufacturers Association, Korean Automobile Manufacturers Association, Marketing Systems.

The advantages of these countries lie primarily in labor costs, which are often a fraction of those in the older industrialized countries (see Table 3.19). Nevertheless, with the exception of Korea, none of the new auto-manufacturing countries has emerged as a major auto-producing locality. The ability of the established auto-manufacturing countries to sustain their leadership points to the importance of factors other than wage rates in driving international competitiveness in the auto industry. Table 3.20 shows that, although wage costs are much lower in Mexico than in the US, this cost advantage is outweighed by other factors.

Market Segments and Market Positioning

Despite the globalization of the leading automakers, the world still lacks a single global market. The need for manufacturers to build extensive dealership chains in the markets they supply, differences in national regulations and customer preferences, differences in affluence and infrastructure, and trade restrictions all continue

TABLE 3.19
Hourly compensation for motor vehicle workers (US$ per hour including benefits)

	1975	1981	1984	1986	1988	1990	1992	1994
US	9.55	17.03	19.02	20.09	20.80	22.48	25.12	26.56
Mexico	2.94	5.27	2.55	2.03	1.96	2.79	4.35	4.05
Brazil	1.29	2.53	1.79	—	—	—	—	—
Japan	3.56	7.61	7.90	11.80	16.36	15.77	19.97	26.36
Korea	0.45	1.33	1.74	1.84	3.20	5.78	7.05	—
Taiwan	0.64	1.86	2.09	2.23	3.50	5.72	6.57	6.76
France	5.10	9.11	8.20	11.06	13.54	15.94	17.42	17.66
Germany	7.89	3.34	11.92	16.96	23.05	27.58	32.61	36.10
Italy	5.16	8.21	8.00	11.03	14.51	17.97	20.48	16.74
Spain	—	7.03	5.35	7.74	10.85	15.00	17.52	15.17
UK	4.12	8.10	7.44	9.22	11.95	13.87	16.80	15.07

Source: US Dept. of Labor.

TABLE 3.20
The cost of producing a compact automobile, US and Mexico, 1992 ($)

	US	Mexico
Parts and components	7,750	8,000
Labor	700	140
Shipping costs	300	1,000
Inventory	20	40
Total	8,770	9,180

Source: US Office of Technology Assessment, October 1992.

to segment the world market. The world market is also segmented by types of product. The US market has traditionally been segmented by sizes of automobile: full size, medium size, compact, subcompact, and so on. At the top end of the market are "luxury cars" distinguished primarily by their price. There are also specific types of vehicle: sports cars, sport-utility vehicles, small passenger vans ("minivans"), and light pickup trucks, for example.

Margins vary considerably between product segments. During the 1980s, Chrysler's dominant position in the rapidly growing and high-margin minivan segment as a result of its Dodge Caravan and Plymouth Voyager models was largely responsible for saving the company from bankruptcy. Traditionally, the luxury car segment, world wide, has been associated with high margins. However, the 1990s saw a reversal of that situation. The recession of the early 1990s, a luxury car tax in the US, and increased competition within the segment resulted in dismal financial performance by Jaguar, Rolls Royce, Daimler Benz, and BMW.

Economies of scope in technology, dealership networks, marketing, and corporate overhead encouraged the auto manufacturers to broaden their range of models, resulting in the entry of the major mass-manufacturing car producers into specialist segments of the market. For example, the luxury car segment had traditionally been dominated by specialist producers such as Mercedes, Jaguar, Rolls Royce, and BMW. Among the mass manufacturers, only GM has a major position, with its Cadillac division. By 1990, many of the major manufacturers had entered the luxury segment, either through the creation of new divisions and models (e.g., Honda Acura, Toyota Lexus, Nissan Infinity) or through acquisition (Ford–Jaguar, VW–Audi and Rolls Royce, Fiat–Lancia and Alfa-Romeo). Similarly, most of the mass manufacturers had entered the minivan and sport-utility segments. The Japanese companies in particular had proliferated their model range: Toyota had entered sports cars, pickup trucks, passenger vans, luxury cars (Lexus), and four-wheel-drive sport-utility cars.

THE OUTLOOK

The discussions between the corporate planners and staff economists of Daimler Benz and Chrysler produced both consensus and dissent. It was agreed that, for the next two or three years, the critical issue facing the industry was the continuing growth in new capacity from plants already under construction against a weak market background. Whether the world economy would move into recession was still uncertain. What was clear was that demand was likely to fall in Japan and Southeast Asia, and was likely to weaken in North America.

Looking further ahead into the next millennium, a number of key factors would determine the prosperity of the industry and its evolution. Most critical to the industry was whether demand would revive and absorb the overhang of manufacturing capacity that was currently building up. The ability of the industry to control excess capacity and limit the tendency towards price competition which it stimulated would depend to a great extent on whether the industry was about to enter a new phase of consolidation. It was felt that the Daimler–Chrysler merger might trigger a new round of consolidation in the industry. The Korean industry had already been reduced from five to two players with the acquisition of Kia and the exit of Samsung and Ssangyong. By the beginning of 1999 there would be 13 companies producing over a million cars a year.[4] Behind these were seven companies producing between 300,000 and one million units a year.[5] Several of the smaller Japanese producers looked vulnerable, while within Europe Volvo, Renault, Peugeot, and Fiat were all seen as lacking size, international scope, or both. The pressure for continued consolidation would come primarily from economies of size in new product development. However, if the industry could find ways of drastically reducing development costs, this could transform the competitive positions of the smaller manufacturers.

On the technology front, the key issue was whether automotive technology would continue to evolve in a linear, incremental fashion, or whether the industry would be subject to radical, discontinuous change. The major threat to the gradual, continuous evolution was the impact of environmental concerns, in particular the challenge from electrically powered cars. With the State of California suspending its requirement for manufacturers to introduce zero-emission automobiles, the carmakers had breathed a collective sigh of relief. However, it was inevitable that environmental factors would have a continuing influence on technology and demand. In Europe, government policies encouraged the substitution of electrically powered vehicles for gasoline-powered vehicles, and in Sweden electric vehicles were required for public sector use. Although electrically powered vehicles remained overpriced and underpowered, fuel-cell technology was fast emerging as the preferred mode of power for electric-engine cars. However, the major threat to the internal-combustion engine appeared to be government restrictions on emissions and car use rather than motorists' demand for a superior technology. While GM had been investing heavily in battery-powered electric cars, Daimler Chrysler believed itself to have a clear lead in cars powered by fuel cells.

Interesting developments were also occurring within the value chain. The increase in the value added contributed by component suppliers seemed likely to continue. Many manufacturers seemed to be unconcerned about losing control over production and technology so long as they could control marketing and distribution. But here too some disturbing developments were occurring. The auto companies controlled their markets through their networks of franchised dealers, through which they supplied not only new cars but also consumer finance and spare parts. By the late 1990s, established dealer networks were being threatened by the emergence of new automobile "megastores." In the US, Republic Industries' AutoNation stores combined car sales with rentals, leasing, and repair; Circuit City's CarMax group was also introducing concepts of mass retailing into selling cars. As *Business Week* observed, "Retailers have historically been the apparatus auto makers use to find homes for all the new cars they crank out. Powerful new buyers could be a threat, the relationship could change to where the retailer tells the auto maker what to do and what price to sell at."[6]

The factors which would drive success during the coming decade seemed to be similar to those in the past. The critical issue would again be cost. Being a low-cost supplier would depend upon exploiting the economies of size in product development and purchasing, while shifting production to those countries benefiting from the advantages of low labor costs and a depreciating currency. At the same time, it seemed possible that in the more affluent markets, customers might be giving greater emphasis to considerations of safety and design. Daimler Chrysler was well aware of the higher margins that could be earned through product differentiation: Mercedes cars and Chrysler minivans and Jeep sport-utility vehicles had all benefited from their niche positions. Now, the desire for unique styling was driving the small-car segment: in Europe, the Ford *Ka*, the Renault *Twingo*, and the Mercedes A-class had all created strong consumer interest. Flexible exploitation of emerging market trends would be heavily dependent on speeding new product development cycles.

APPENDIX

TABLE 3.A1
Sales revenue ($ billion) and return on equity (%)

	1980		1981		1982		1983		1984	
	Rev.	ROE	Rev.	ROE	Rev.	ROE	Rev.	ROE	Rev.	ROE
GM	58	(4.2)	63	19.5	60	5.3	75	17.9	84	18.7
Ford	37	(18.1)	38	(14.3)	37	(10.8)	44	24.7	53	20.5
Toyota	14	13.7	16	12.7	16	11.7	20	11.6	24	13.3
Benz	17	23.5	16	53.5	16	14.2	16	15.0	15	15.4
Fiat	25	n.a.	20	n.a.	15	n.a.	14	n.a.	14	10.9
VW	18	5.8	17	3.7	15	(3.8)	16	(2.2)	16	4.4
Nissan	14	15.1	16	11.7	16	10.5	16	8.7	18	5.7
Honda	6	13.7	8	28.0	8	18.2	9	14.3	10	16.4
Renault	19	7.6	16	6.9	16	(12.3)	14	(15.4)	12	(749)
Chrysler	9	n.a.	11	n.a.	10	n.a.	13	61.0	20	72.0
Peugeot	17	(13.1)	13	20.6	12	(27.0)	11	(49.6)	10	(7.1)
Mitsubishi	11	9.8	12	7.7	13	8.3	12	7.0	14	17.3
Mazda	n.a.	n.a.	n.a.	n.a.	n.a.	n.a.	n.a.	n.a.	n.a.	n.a.
BMW	4	15.3	4	11.8	4	12.6	6	14.4	5	20.1

	1985		1986		1987		1988		1989	
	Rev.	ROE	Rev.	ROE	Rev.	ROE	Rev.	ROE	Rev.	ROE
GM	96	13.5	103	9.6	102	10.1	121	13.6	127	12.1
Ford	53	20.5	70	8.7	72	38.1	92	24.6	97	16.9
Toyota	26	15.3	32	9.8	41	8.2	50	9.4	60	10.2
Benz	18	7.9	30	14.7	38	16.2	42	15.8	41	36.9
Fiat	14	15.9	20	17.3	30	18.6	34	22.4	37	19.1
VW	18	7.9	24	5.3	30	3.7	34	6.9	35	7.7
Nissan	18	6.2	20	2.1	26	3.9	29	4.0	36	7.2
Honda	11	19.0	12	15.2	17	10.5	22	13.0	26	11.2
Renault	14	loss	16	loss	25	loss	27	64.7	27	37.5
Chrysler	21	39.2	23	26.3	26	19.8	35	13.8	36	5.0
Peugeot	11	67.9	15	31.4	20	29.0	23	30.8	24	24.2
Mitsubishi	14	10.7	16	11.2	11	4.7	13	4.5	17	8.5
Mazda	7	11.3	n.a.	n.a.	11	1.3	15	2.9	16	3.8
BMW	5	12.9	7	11.5	11	7.2	12	11.0	14	9.4

TABLE 3.A1 *Continued*

	1990		1991		1992		1993	
	Rev.	*ROE*	*Rev.*	*ROE*	*Rev.*	*ROE*	*Rev.*	*ROE*
GM	125	(6.6)	124	(16.3)	113	(46.0)	134	44.1
Ford	98	3.7	89	(10.0)	100	2.6	109	16.2
Toyota	65	10.8	78	9.5	95	5.0	85	3.3
Benz	54	9.0	57	9.4	62	7.7	59	3.6
Fiat	48	9.1	47	4.8	40	3.5	35	10.6
VW	44	7.2	46	7.2	54	1.2	46	(19.0)
Nissan	40	7.2	43	2.7	58	3.1	54	(5.2)
Honda	27	8.3	31	7.0	39	3.5	36	2.3
Renault	31	6.7	29	8.5			30	3.3
Chrysler	31	1.0	29	(12.9)	37	18.1	44	(37.3)
Peugeot	29	18.4	28	9.8	29	6.6	26	18.4
Mitsubishi	17	6.9	19	10.3	26	10.4	27	1.3
Mazda	17	6.6	19	6.4	25	2.2	20	(12.9)
BMW	17	11.0	18	11.1	20	14.4	18	8.0

	1994		1995		1996		1997	
	Rev.	*ROE*	*Rev.*	*ROE*	*Rev.*	*ROE*	*Rev.*	*ROE*
GM	155	39.2	169	29.5	168	21.2	178	37.1
Ford	128	24.5	137	16.9	147	16.6	154	22.9
Toyota	88	2.4	111	5.4	109	7.5	84	8.0
Benz	64	5.0	72	(43.8)	72	10.5	70	12.0
Fiat	41	5.1	46	9.7	51	9.7	51	10.6
VW	50	1.3	61	3.4	67	5.9	64	21.6
Nissan	59	(10.2)	63	(7.2)	59	6.3	47	(8.0)
Honda	40	5.3	44	6.8	47	17.5	43	18.8
Renault	32	8.2	37	4.8	36	(14.2)	35	12.6
Chrysler	52	34.7	53	18.5	61	30.5	61	24.6
Peugeot	30	5.6	33	3.1	34	1.3	31	(4.7)
Mitsubishi	34	2.3	37	2.9	33	2.6	n.a.	n.a.
Mazda	22	(11.2)	19	(4.3)	17	(5.6)	15	(1.0)
BMW	30	8.5	32	8.5	35	9.4	34	14.1
Daewoo					65	4.4	n.a.	n.a.

NOTES

1. "Merger agreement signed: Daimler-Benz and Chrysler combine to form leading global automotive company," Press Release, Chrysler Corporation, May 1998.

2. "East Europe's car makers feel sting of capitalism," *New York Times*, April 28, 1994, p. D1.

3. *The Economist*, July 15, 1995, p. 47.

4. GM, Ford, Daimler Chrysler, Toyota, VW, Nissan, Peugeot, Renault, Fiat, Honda, Mitsubishi, Hyundai, and BMW/Rover.

5. Daewoo, Suzuki, Daihatsu, VAZ, Fuji (Subaru), Isuzu, and Volvo.

6. *Business Week*, February 24, 1997, p. 89.

CHAPTER FOUR

The Telecommunications Industry in China in 1998

Kent E. Neupert, Clara Chak, Henry Fu, Lui Sai Lung, Alex Ng, Polly Poon, and Ken Yeung prepared this case solely to provide material for class discussion. The authors do not intend to illustrate either effective or ineffective handling of a management situation. The authors may have disguised certain names or identifying information to protect confidentiality.

Introduction

With the transformation of the Chinese economy from a planned to a more market-oriented economy, in 1998 the telecommunications industry in China had come to be characterized by rapid growth in investment and improvements in technology and service quality. The total turnover of telecommunications had been developing on an exponential curve, reaching RMB163.37 billion (US$19.75 billion) in 1997, increasing 15 times from RMB10.95 billion (US$1.32 billion) in 1990.[1] (See Exhibit 4.1.) While the number of subscribers to both fixed-line and cellular telecommunications services in China had grown substantially in the last five years, penetration rates remained relatively low compared to other Asian and international markets. With the development of traditional services and the enlarging of network size, many new value-added services, such as email, facsimile store and forward, and Internet service, were being introduced to and welcomed by subscribers, resulting in a high growth rate (see Exhibit 4.2). All these developments indicated a tremendous potential for further development in telecommunications in China.

Industry Structure

In China's telecommunications industry there were essentially two markets or relationships – the first between equipment suppliers (most of them foreign investors) and service providers, the second between service providers and end-users (nearly

EXHIBIT 4.1:
Developing trend in total turnover of telecommunications in China, 1990–1997 (in billion RMB)

	1990	1991	1992	1993	1994	1995	1996	1997
Total turnover	10.95	13.41	20.05	33.85	52.69	87.33	120.88	163.37

Source: Liang, X., Zhang, X., and Yang, X., "The development of telecommunications in China," IEEE Communications Magazine, November 1998, pp. 54–8.

EXHIBIT 4.2:
The development of new value-added services, 1994–1997

Service	Subscribers ('000)				Annual growth rate (%)
	1994	1995	1996	1997	
Packet switching	8.5	28.0	56.4	84.6	115.1
DDN	—	17.0	51.4	111.7	156.3
Email	2.329	5.932	9.888	14.726	151.4
EDI	1.083	2.495	1.987	2.247	27.5
Videotext	—	0.132	0.113	0.216	27.9
Facsimile storage transfer	—	0.495	1.217	2.914	142.6
Internet	—	7	34	159.803	377.8
Frame relay	—	—	—	3.084	—
N-ISDN	—	—	—	0.319	—

Source: See Exhibit 4.1.

monopolized by China Telecom).[2] The Appendix contains a glossary of terms relating to the industry.

Equipment Suppliers

More than 90 percent of telecommunications equipment in China was imported over the past decade, and about 80 percent of the market share of major telecommunications products was occupied by foreign companies.[3] The market for products in this industry sector had been comprehensively developed, and China was home to no fewer than 16 foreign-invested manufacturers of digital switching or syn-

EXHIBIT 4.3:
Switching equipment shipped by vendor, 1993–1997 (millions of lines)

	1993	1994	1995	1996	1997
Chinese suppliers	0.8	1.2	3	5	7.3
Foreign suppliers	10.3	18.3	19	19	10.4
Total	11.1	19.5	22	24	17.7

Source: "Who needs competition," *Business China*, October 1998, pp. 4–5.

chronous digital hierarchy (SDH) transmission equipment.[4] As a result, competition was intense between the players who supplied the Ministry of Posts and Telecommunications (MPT), the provincial and municipal posts and telecommunications authorities (PTAs and PTBs), Unicom, and other private network operators.

Although much progress had been made in the last few years, China's own development in telecommunications equipment lagged behind the more advanced international level. China had over 100 telecommunications plants, which produced several hundred thousand mobile telephones, but only ten of them were able to make cellular mobile telephone equipment. Of these, one manufacturer was solely funded by foreign investors and eight were joint ventures with foreign companies.[5] Chinese experts criticized that this was a result of MPT policies that focused only on earning more profits by taking advantage of its status as a state monopoly and neglecting the technical competition for improving equipment that required much more time and energy. As a result, Chinese-made telecommunications equipment was losing the domestic market to the foreign producer companies.[6]

With the establishment of the Ministry of Information Industry early in 1998, the Chinese government had realized that problems existed and was determined to put a buy-local policy into effect, particularly in the relatively lower-technology infrastructure segments such as switching and basic cabling.[7] This unspoken policy has essentially three tiers:

1. Purchase from local vendors provided their equipment is up to standard.
2. If not, buy from foreign-investment joint ventures.
3. And when all else fails, buy imported.

As a result, domestic suppliers such as Huawei, Datang, and Zhongxing were able to increase their market share in the switching business from 7 percent in 1993 to around 42 percent in 1997.[8] (See Exhibit 4.3.) The rise in the number of domestic competitors drove down the prices China Telecom had to pay for the equipment. Success in the switching equipment market emboldened the Chinese manufacturers to attempt to repeat their performance in other industry segments. Huawei and other companies were already active in cellular switching and transmission markets, and were starting to produce data communications equipment. In response, foreign vendors swiftly diversified their product lines. Although no longer profitable, they were still captivated by the market's size and promise, and many foreign equipment suppliers intended to stay in the market to compete.

Service Suppliers

Prior to 1993, the MPT was the sole provider of all public telecommunications services in China. This was done through the provincial PTAs and municipal and county PTBs under the MPT's control.[9] In 1993, the State Council issued regulations permitting other domestic companies to be licensed by the MPT to provide to the public certain non-basic telecommunications services, such as radio paging, domestic VSAT, and EDI.[10] In 1994, Unicom was established to operate all types of telecommunications services. Since then, the monopoly in the telecommunications service market has been broken in China.[11]

Until 1994, China Telecom had a monopoly on the national public telecommunications network under the jurisdiction of the MPT. Separated from the MPT in early 1994, China Telecom became an enterprise with autonomy in its accounting and personnel hiring.[12] As the biggest telecommunications carrier in China, China Telecom was empowered to manage, operate, and build a nationwide telecommunications network and to provide basic and value-added services with the obligation of universal service. To get ready for competition and in order to get access to foreign capital, some restructuring had taken place, and its cellular services in Guangdong and Zheijiang were listed in Hong Kong under the name of China Telecom (Hong Kong) Limited.

China Unicom was a consortium formed by the Ministry of Electric Industries (MEI), the Ministry of Railways (MOR), the Ministry of Electric Power (MEP), and 12 other state-owned firms. Its goals were twofold: to build a national trunk network based on the private-network infrastructure of its two parents, MOR and MEP, and to build up its fixed-line subscriber base.[13] To generate cash flow, Unicom initially focused on cellular services based on the global system for mobile communications (GSM) standard. This allowed it to generate sizable profits in a relatively short period of time. The company also pioneered revenue-sharing agreements that would allow foreign investors to earn income on cellular services without taking a direct stake in a deal. The foreign investor put up 100 percent of the capital to form a joint venture and received most of the profits by acting as a consultant to the project. However, the foreign investor had to relinquish control over how the project proceeded.[14]

To protect its dominant position in the market, the MPT quickly put up defenses by slashing prices, increasing cross-subsidization, and delaying interconnect agreements. Finally, the MPT created a "competitor" of its own in cooperation with the People's Liberation Army. The joint venture, called Great Wall, received very different treatment from the MPT than was received by Unicom. Great Wall was able to share MPT base-station sites and network together with China Telecom to develop CDMA and different cellular systems.[15]

GOVERNMENT REGULATIONS AND POLICIES

Historically, the MPT System had exclusive responsibility for providing, operating, and regulating all public telecommunications services in China. In March 1998, the ninth National People's Congress in China made the long-anticipated merger of the communications-related ministries (i.e., MPT, MEI, and the Ministry of Radio, Film, and Television (MFRT)) to form the Ministry of Information Industry (MII). The previous system is explained below, followed by a more detailed description of the present system.

MPT System

Within the MPT System there were 33 provincial PTAs and more than 2,385 municipal and county-level PTBs established with the approval of and under the administrative authority of the MPT. The PTAs and PTBs provided telecommunications services under the name of China Telecom within their respective provinces, municipalities, and counties and exercised day-to-day operational responsibilities over the MPT System's networks. The PTAs exercised regulatory responsibilities over posts and telecommunications at the provincial level as well as administrative responsibilities over telecommunications services provided by the PTBs within their respective jurisdictions. The PTBs did not generally assume any regulatory functions over the telecommunications industry.[16]

In early 1994, the MPT began an internal reorganization designed to stimulate the growth of the telecommunications sector. As part of this reorganization, the Directorate General of Telegraph (DGT) was established as a state-owned enterprise with primary responsibility for the construction, maintenance, and operational management of the public telecommunications networks in China, still under the name of China Telecom. In addition, the DGT provided a full range of telecommunications services, including domestic and international telephone, telegraph, data, facsimile, Internet access, and email services, as well as mobile and satellite communications. The goal of the reorganization was to achieve a separation of roles between the MPT, as the industry regulator, and the DGT, as operator of the MPT System's telecommunications services. The DGT was then responsible for determining operational goals and policies for the MPT System. Telecommunications services continued to be provided at the provincial, city, and county levels by the PTAs and PTBs within the MPT System.[17]

The Ministry of Information Industry

The main functions of this new ministry were to plan, regulate, harmonize, and macro-control the development of the information industry.[18] The three rival ministries were combined together in the hope of effectively controlling and planning for the development of proprietary telecommunications, data communications, and broadcast networks. The MII could then focus on building one multimedia network incorporating all these technologies. It was also hoped that it would bring clarity and impartiality to the governance of communications services.[19] The favoritism that the old showed its operator, China Telecom, would be eliminated. The conflicts between the MPT, which owned China Telecom, and the MEI, which was a major shareholder in Unicom, would be resolved with the separation between China Telecom and the regulatory body. Following the central policy, *Zhenqi Fenkai* or the separation of political functions from industrial functions in the telecom sector, would not only increase efficiency and promote the development of a market economy, but also foster the development of the MII as an independent arbitrator for the telecom sector.[20] Arguments for the disaffiliation of the former MPT's long-distance trunks from China Telecom were advanced in Beijing, with the likely outcome being the formation of numerous "China Telecom" companies separated by function, such as long-distance and mobile service. Signs of such a restructuring began to emerge, as announcements were made that a "China Telecom Paging Co." would be formed.[21]

However, the MII remained under the strong influence of the former MPT. Former MPT officials, led by the former MPT minister and then current MII minister Wu Jichuan, led the way in designing the structure of the new ministry. Observers found it difficult to imagine that the long-developed ties between MPT officials and China Telecom would dissolve simply as a result of government decree. Moreover, there was virtually no discussion of promulgating a telecom law in the context of the restructuring, despite the fact that a telecom law or other form of legislation should be the centerpiece of any effort to introduce a fair and level playing-field for services competition.[22] The merger was actually more a result of a policy aimed at trimming down the size of the national government bureaucracy.[23] The number of officials at the MII was to be reduced from 870 to 320. The full impact of the formation of the MII was not yet clear.

Not surprisingly, telecommunications remained one of China's key infrastructure industries. Rapid network expansion in China was not pushed by domestic industry competition but did serve to boost China's economy. The government was struggling to meet its 8 percent GDP growth target for 1998, and spending on telecommunications infrastructure was used to prop up growth. In 1998, US$15.5 billion had been spent on network infrastructure and the ministry planned to increase the industry's fixed assets to US$32.3 billion by the end of the century.[24] (See Exhibit 4.4 for telecommunications infrastructure spending.) Moreover, they planned to add 20 million new switching lines, 7.5 million new cellular users, and 8 million new paging users in 1998.

Fixed Line

A local wired telephone network is an infrastructure that requires a large initial investment but provides low returns, especially for undeveloped areas. In most situations, to build up such a foundation, government support and low competition are essential.

EXHIBIT 4.4:
Telecoms network infrastructure spending, 1994–2002 (US$ million)

	1994	1995	1996	1997	1998	1999	2000	2001	2002
Switching	3,297	2,944	2,159	1,264	1,503	1,544	1,517	1,440	1,413
Transmission	3,651	3,294	3,076	2,590	2,899	2,957	2,920	1,852	2,749
Access network	1,272	1,156	1,266	1,209	1,271	1,325	1,325	1,283	1,235
WLL[a] system	0	0	0	0	91	97	130	153	176
Local cable/ outside plant	6,548	5,958	6,526	6,335	6,836	7,019	6,974	6,831	6,555
Public data network	14	40	266	104	218	243	319	395	433
Terminal equipment	945	1,426	993	1,628	1,578	1,697	1,860	1,927	2,003
Other	1,258	1,185	1,143	1,050	1,152	1,191	1,204	1,191	1,165
Total	16,985	16,004	15,429	14,179	15,547	16,073	16,250	16,073	15,729

[a] Wireless local loop.
Figures for 1998–2002 are forecasts.
Source: See Exhibit 4.3.

EXHIBIT 4.5:
Development of telecommunications in China, 1991–2000

	1991–1995 Target	1991–1995 Actual	1996–2000 Target
Total investment (RMB billion)	50	241.4	500
Switching capacity (million lines)	48	85.1	170
National teledensity (%)	2.5	4.66	10
Urban teledensity (%)	n.a.	17	35

Source: "Still out in the cold," *Business China*, June 1998, p. 7.

In China, the local telephone network was primarily constructed by the MPT. Over the past two decades, the MPT ran an impressive industrial rollout in China. Yearly targets consistently were met or exceeded and the expansion of China's fixed-line infrastructure corresponded with the construction of mobile and data communication networks. (See Exhibit 4.7.) As a state-owned corporate, China Telecom's goal was getting more customers. Its network planning, based on five-year plans rather than customer demand, continued to focus resources on increasing customer numbers and not customer service. Main-line additions were expected to average 10

EXHIBIT 4.6:
Main lines and penetration rate, 1994–2003

	1994	1995	1996	1997	1998	1999	2000	2001	2002	2003
Main lines (millions)	27.3	40.1	54.9	70.3	87.4	105.5	123.9	142.1	160.0	176.8
Penetration rate (%)	2.3	3.3	4.5	5.7	7.0	8.4	9.8	11.1	12.3	13.5

Figures for 1998–2003 are forecasts
Source: See Exhibit 4.3.

EXHIBIT 4.7:
Shanghai's telecom service income, January–September 1998 (million RMB)

Service	Service income in Sept. 1998	Total income in Jan.–Sept. period
Local telephone	3,590.8	25,365.4
Long-distance telephony	1,562.1	12,743.3

Source: "Provincial – Shanghai," *CTC News*, April 1998, p. 4.

million annually over the next five years, giving China a teledensity of 13.5 lines per hundred people by 2003. (See Exhibit 4.8.) The public telecommunication networks had absorbed almost 80 million local phone subscribers by the end of June 1998. Almost 15 million phone subscribers registered in the January–June period of 1998, with the daily increase in fixed phone subscribers averaging 83,200.[25] Despite this rapid growth, the penetration rate of 5.7 percent in 1997 was low in comparison to other countries.

Uneven development
The development of fixed-line telecommunications in China was uneven. The coastal provinces and cities grew much faster than inland areas. Major cities, such as Shanghai, Beijing, Tianjin, Guangdong, and Liaoning, shared most of the GNP growth and the resources for development. Likewise, the expansion was strongest in urban areas rather than in rural areas. For example, the fixed development rate in Guangdong was 100 times faster than in Tibet.

The relatively small investment in rural telephone networks is due to several factors. One factor is that there is a perception that telecommunications investment in rural areas directly benefits only as relatively narrow and privileged portion of the population. Another is the difficulty presented by China's geographic terrain. For example, development of rural telephony in middle-western provinces is not as easy as along the eastern coast of the country. The PTAs pointed out that the biggest problem faced in building a telephone network is the mountainous geography and dispersed population.[26]

Pricing

China Telecom, as the industry leader, maintains a high installation charge for telephones. This adds to the uneven development and distribution of services. For instance, the charge for having a telephone in Shenzhen is RMB4,000 (US$484), in addition to a charge of RMB0.6 (US$0.07) for a three-minute call. The installation charge was set high to recover the cost of setting up the network. However, indications were that China Telecom had no intention of reducing it. The situation of long-distance service is similar. In June 1998, a one-minute call to Japan from Shenzhen or Shanghai cost RMB12.70, while the same call from Hong Kong cost only about RMB8.20. Given its position in the market, China Telecom was able to price its services as it wanted. Although income is not the primary motivation for network development, both local telephone and long-distance telephone services generated a fair amount of revenue for providers. Also, long-distance telephone service was much more profitable than local telephony. In Shanghai, these two services together generated more than RMB5 million in September 1998. (See Exhibit 4.7.)

Equipment

As China increased construction of telecommunications facilities, an aggregate investment of RMB50.8 billion was put into fixed assets in the first half of 1998. This was a 78.6 percent increase over the investment of the previous year, which had shown only a 12.9 percent growth rate. For 1998, total investments in fixed assets were expected to reach RMB160 billion.[27]

The installation of fiber-optic trunks had a good foundation on which to build. The former MPT had installed about 820,000 kilometers of fiber-optic backbones, including national long-distance, intra-provincial, and urban-access backbones. The long-distance cables had been extended to 155,000 kilometers, 1.31 million lines, including 164,000 newly added lines.[28]

Unlike the telephone service providers, network equipment suppliers were primarily joint ventures in vigorous competition. At least seven foreign firms had set up their equipment manufacturing operations as joint ventures. Many investing companies had been attracted to China because its domestic industry was huge and rapidly expanding. No other country boasted the potential of the China telecommunications market. While China relied on foreign technology, and although there was no formal decree to the effect, it was clear to foreign equipment manufacturers that a "buy-local" policy was operating. The potential profit squeeze of this policy and the traditional monopoly made many foreign investors uneasy.

As one of the seven big Chinese switching manufacturers, Beijing International Switching System Corp (BISC) had run since 1991 a widely publicized and fast-growing plant in Beijing producing telecommunication switches for public networks.[29] Siemens of Germany held 40 percent of BISC, which sold 90 percent of its switches to the MPT and the remaining 10 percent to China Unicom (Liangtong), a

EXHIBIT 4.8:
Shares of different services in the telecommunications service market in 1997

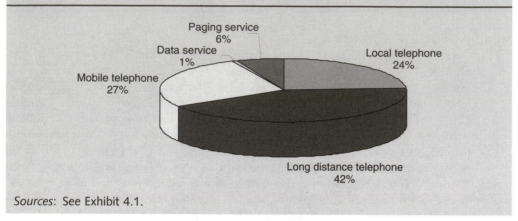

Sources: See Exhibit 4.1.

rival of the MPT. This caused problems because, from the MPT perspective, BISC was working with the competition. As a result, the MPT put BISC at the bottom of its list of approved switching vendors.[30] Analysts suspected that such traditional-minded bureaucratic behavior could be a deterrent to foreign investors.

Cellular Phones

With long-distance service representing the largest segment in the telecommunications market (42 percent), cellular service was the second largest segment (27 percent) in China. (See Exhibit 4.8.) In terms of size, China had the third largest mobile network in the world.[31] According to the MPT, the number of new subscribers to mobile phone services increased by an average 188 percent annually, reaching 13.23 million subscribers in 1997.[32] Although the growth rate for mobile service was slowing, the number of subscribers increased by 6 million in 1997. (See Exhibit 4.9.) It was projected that by 2000, the mobile network capacity would surpass 50 million, the number of mobile subscribers would reach 38 million, and the penetration rate would be over 3 percent, compared to 1 percent in 1997.[33]

Mobile attractiveness
China's mobile network capacities' continued expansion provided a needed outlet for demand as the fixed-lined infrastructure grew more slowly. Compared to fixed-line networks, cellular networks are cheaper, easier to construct, and pay for themselves quicker. This helps explain why the inaugural networks launched by China Unicom in the four major markets of Beijing, Tianjin, Shanghai, and Guangzhou were cellular.

EXHIBIT 4.9:
Growth rates of subscribers to mobile phone service, 1991–1997 (%)

	1991	1992	1993	1994	1995	1996	1997
Growth rate	166.70	268.80	260.40	145.80	131.40	88.78	93.00

Source: See Exhibit 4.1.

For Chinese subscribers, mobile phones were a more than adequate interim service in a country where fixed-line penetration was less than 5 percent. At about RMB10,000 for the first year, including the cost of the handset, mobile phones were beyond the reach of the 65–70 percent of the population who lived in the rural areas. Therefore, major urban centers with increasing personal incomes were attractive target markets. For these people, mobile phones combined two irresistible features: efficiency and status. Also, the increasing availability of roaming service allowed China's growing mobile business class to use their phones throughout the country.[34]

Network technologies
GSM 900/1800 was the dominant technology, having the largest coverage area and the largest number of subscribers. This digital system was expected to see sustained and rapid development over the coming years. The analog TAC System was expected to be maintained, although some bands will gradually move to GSM. The plan to develop a new 800 MHz code division multiple access (CDMA) system was terminated in order to meet the requirement from the World Trade Organization (WTO) for a standardized wireless telecommunications system. The government had decided to focus resources on developing the GSM network. (See Exhibit 4.10 for Chinese mobile networks.)

Cellular teledensity
Cellular teledensity, like fixed lines, has experienced more growth in the eastern/coastal regions of China. Mobile teledensity in the eastern/coastal regions was 6 times and 2.5 times higher than that of western and central China, respectively.[35] (See Exhibit 4.11 for teledensity comparisons.) Beijing was the top-ranked city for teledensity in 1997, followed by Shanghai and Guangdong.[36] Except for Heilongjiang, all the top ten provinces/cities were in the eastern regions of the country.

Competition among operators
There were three mobile operators in China: China Telecom, China Unicom, and China Telecom Great Wall Network. Nationwide, China Telecom holds over 97 percent of the mobile market, while China Unicom holds about 3 percent of the market (see Exhibit 4.12). In 1998, China Telecom Great Wall Network had commercial trial systems in four cities, yielding a negligible subscriber base.[37]

EXHIBIT 4.10:
Chinese mobile operators in 1998

System operator	Analog TACS	Digital GSM 900/1800	Digital 800MHz CDMA
China Telecom	Deployed in 1987. Covers 238 cities and 1,588 counties. The network capacity has reached 11.44 million. There are 7,545 base stations and 279,000 channels. The number of subscribers is 6.4 million.	Deployed in 1995. Covers 304 cities and 1,731 counties. The network capacity has reached 15.95 million. There are 13,000 base stations and 533,000 channels. The number of subscribers is 9.37 million. Dual-band trials started in 1996.	Three trials in Tianjin, Shanghai, and Guangzhou since early 1998.
China Unicom		Deployed in 1995. Covers more than 80 cities. The network capacity has reached 1.5 million. The number of subscribers is about 600,000.	
China Telecom Great Wall Network			Four trials in Beijing, Shanghai, Guangzhou, and Xian since 1996.

Source: Caos, R., "Current development of IMT-2000 in China," *IEEE Communications Magazine*, September 1998, p. 158.

EXHIBIT 4.11:
Cellular teledensity in China

Region	Mobile teledensity (%)
National	1.07
Eastern China	2.34
Central China	0.9
Western China	0.37
Top ten provinces/cities in 1997	
Beijing	5.54
Shanghai	5.24
Guangdong	3.36
Tianjin	2.94
Fujian	2.4
Zheijiang	2.03
Liaoning	1.96
Hainan	1.86
Heilongjiang	1.65
Jiangsu	1.27

Source: "Huge imbalance among regional markets," *CTC News*, March 5, 1998, p. 2.

EXHIBIT 4.12:
Cellular market share in 1997 (%)

Region	China Telecom	Unicom
National	97.4	2.6
Eastern China	96.62	3.38
Central China	99.29	0.71
Western China	99.03	0.97

Source: See Exhibit 4.11.

China Unicom had been handicapped in terms of market access, bandwidth, economies of scale, and fund-raising.[38] MPT reacted to competition by improving the range and quality of its services. For instance, the former MPT, together with China Telecom Great Wall, planned to adopt CDMA together when they realized the limitation of GSM capacity. To stay competitive in the marketplace, China Unicom had no choice but to develop its own CDMA network. Unfortunately, the efforts were in vain given the termination of the CDMA network in response to WTO requirements.

The MPT also had used its considerable power to hinder the development of its competitors, principally by delaying interconnection of China Unicom's mobile networks with its national backbone infrastructure. Although China Unicom was independent from the MPT, it relied on the MPT's existing network to connect with the rest of China. Without the interconnection, China Unicom could not offer national roaming services and risked losing subscribers to the MPT and its affiliated provincial and municipal posts and telecommunication groups.[39]

China Telecom also undermined Unicom on pricing. MPT slashed the cost of both handsets and monthly charges in order to create a demand surge, allowing it to secure customers while Unicom was still building its networks. Once connected, customers are unlikely to drift away, as China's pricing structure tended to lock customers in for the long term. While handset and connection charges were high, monthly and user charges were low.[40] Great Wall received very different treatment from the MPT. Great Wall was able to share MPT base-station sites and networks. Interestingly, its presence allowed the MPT to argue that it was actively fostering competition.

The rules imposed by the MPT that prevented foreign telecom operators from holding ownership in operations limited foreign investors' control over their investments. This resulted in foreign companies withdrawing from China. For example, BellSouth Corp backed out on its deal to provide cellular service in Tianjin, and McCaw International sold its 30 percent stake in its Shanghai joint venture to Hong Kong-based CCT Telecom.[41] The termination of "Chinese–Chinese–Foreign," or CCF, joint ventures in telecommunications services was a major blow to China Unicom and to global investors seeking access to the lucrative network services market in China.

Given China's ban on foreign ownership and operation of telecom networks, the only significant players are the major multinational equipment operators. However, a few foreign companies such as Hong Kong Telecom and SmarTone have sold stakes in their Chinese operations to the MPT.

Equipment and handset supplier competition

China's regulatory provisions forbid foreign direct investment in providing telecommunication services. Therefore, the only way for foreign firms to enter the China market is through the handset and network transmission markets. Previously Motorola had dominated this market, with more than 70 percent of the mobile phone market. This strong position also allowed it to earn high profits. However, with the introduction of the GSM system in late 1994, Motorola started to lose market share. In 1997, Sweden's Ericsson displaced the US company as China's dominant supplier of mobile telephony. Similarly, Finland's Nokia secured a large portion of the handset and transmission markets. (Exhibits 4.13, 4.14, and 4.15, respectively, show market shares in the handset segment, cellular transmission capacity segment, and cellular switching capacity segment.) Ericsson and Nokia were full-range manufacturers, while Motorola manufactured only GSM phones and transmission systems. Therefore, Ericsson and Nokia were able to offer one-stop shopping to the

EXHIBIT 4.13:
Market share of handsets in 1997

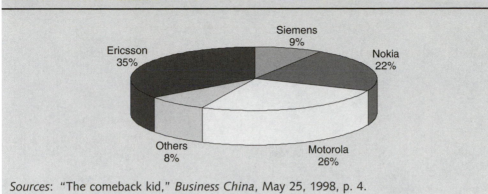

Ericsson
35%

Siemens
9%

Nokia
22%

Others
8%

Motorola
26%

Sources: "The comeback kid," *Business China*, May 25, 1998, p. 4.

EXHIBIT 4.14:
Market share of cellular transmission installed capacity in 1997

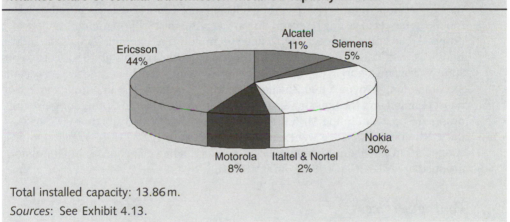

Ericsson
44%

Alcatel
11%

Siemens
5%

Nokia
30%

Motorola
8%

Italtel & Nortel
2%

Total installed capacity: 13.86 m.

Sources: See Exhibit 4.13.

PTAs while Motorola had to team up with Siemens to provide switches. This allowed Ericsson and Nokia to lock up many more exclusive supplier relationships with the PTAs.

Despite the attractive growth of cellular subscription, many industry observers predicted that it would not be easy to make money on these deals. Investment bank Deutsche Morgan Grenfell estimated that many foreign companies would not see a payback for 20 years.[42] Realizing this, US-based Ameritech Corp decided that after two years, it had waited long enough and pulled out of its deal to build a cellular system with China Unicom.[43]

EXHIBIT 4.15:
Market share of cellular switching installed capacity in 1997

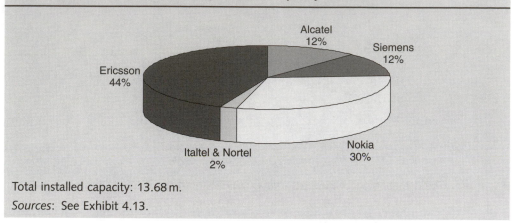

Total installed capacity: 13.68 m.

Sources: See Exhibit 4.13.

Dropping prices

In 1997, competition between China Telecom and China Unicom caused prices of mobile handsets to go down several times. Likewise, the tariff on mobile services also dropped, causing mobile service to develop rapidly. For example, prices on mobile handsets went down three times in Beijing during the first half of 1997.[44] The constantly dropping charges for both connection fees and monthly usage fees, especially in Guangdong province and Zheijiang province, became the dynamic catalyst to boost demand and the industry as a whole. Connection fees in Guangdong province dropped 67 percent from RMB6,000 in 1994 to RMB2,000–3,000 in 1997. In Zheijiang, the connection fee went from RMB11,000 to RMB2,000–3,000. Monthly usage fees in Zheijiang remained flat at RMB62, while the charges in Guangdong dropped to RMB100 in 1997 from RMB150.[45]

Paging Services

In China, as in other countries, the way into the public telecommunications network business lies in radio-based services. The first area of entry, and the point of least resistance, was in paging. From 1984, China operated paging networks, originally through the provincial PTAs. But in recent years, other organizations entered the market. They followed a cautious approach, since they were mostly dependent on the MPT and PTAs for leased circuits and there had been cases where the local PTBs simply cut their lines.

Lowered growth rates

With the rapid development of cellular services, the growth of paging services declined, but it remained a market with strong potential. By June 1998, paging had

EXHIBIT 4.16:
Nationwide paging customer base, 1993–2000

Year	Subscriber count (million)	Annual net increase (million)	Annual growth rate (%)
1993	5.60	3.38	152
1994	11.20	5.60	100
1995	25.00	14.00	125
1996	39.00	14.00	56
1997	51.03	12.03	31
1998	63.00	11.97	23
1999	72.00	9.00	14
2000	80.00	8.00	11

Figures for 1998–2000 are forecasts.

Source: "Restructuring becomes key to survival," CTC News, July 5, 1998, p. 2.

EXHIBIT 4.17:
Paging market share in 1997 (%)

Region	China Telecom	Other operations
National	67.68	32.32
Eastern China	63.66	36.34
Central China	80.58	19.42
Western China	61.17	38.83

Source: See Exhibit 4.11.

achieved a 4.5 percent penetration and a user count of 61 million people, making it one of the largest paging markets in the world.[46] (See Exhibits 4.16 and 4.17 for paging network statistics.)

Competition
Unlike the sectors of local telephony and cellular services, the paging market was comprised of more than 2,000 operators. However, only 20 of the paging operators provided cross-regional service. The biggest paging networks included China Telecom's high-speed paging network, Unicom's paging network, and Asia-Pacific paging network. China Telecom had 34.19 million paging subscribers by the end of 1997, up 34.8 percent over 1996. Its total market share was only 67.68 percent, while other paging operators held the remaining third of the market. The extent of competition was more evident when analyzed on a province-by-province basis. In

some provinces, China Telecom's market share was less than 50 percent, especially in Beijing, where it held only 14.4 percent.[47]

With the development of radio paging services, competition developed on a different level. Service competition replaced price competition among paging service operators as they tried to enlarge the size of their paging networks and provide better services, such as providing nationwide networks and email services for subscribers.

Restructuring through mergers, alliances, and acquisitions
In 1998, the MII announced that it would spin off its paging business as part of the plan to reorrganize the Chinese telecommunications industry. The paging division of China Telecom was to be registered and reorganized into a nationwide publicly listed company. Paging divisions of the PTAs also would have to become independent before July 1998. Mergers or alliances among non-China Telecom operators were expected as a response to the decision to restructure China Telecom. It was expected that using an alliance strategy to provide better service to subscribers instead of competing against each other would encourage standardization and bring more benefits to subscribers.[48]

Network development
China Telecom set up two paging networks. One ran on the 150 MHz frequency band and the other on the 280 MHz frequency band. The first phase of the FLEX-based 280 MHz high-speed paging network was completed and began operations in 1997. China Telecom expected to extend coverage of high-speed paging services to more than 100 cities and bring the network capacity up to 5 million subscribers by the end of 1998.[49]

China Unicom also ran its own high-speed paging system, known as 191/192 network, to compete directly with China Telecom. It was reported that China Unicom's 191/192 paging user base had surpassed the 1 million subscribers mark with service to over 100 cities. The company's goal was to have 2 million paging customers by the end of 1998.[50]

Internet Services

As with other sectors of the telecommunications industry, the development of data services in China exhibited rapid growth. Since 1994, most new data services developed at growth rates of over 100 percent. In particular, since 1995, Internet subscribers increased at an annual rate of 377.8 percent. With data services holding only 1.2 percent of the market, there was strong potential for developing the market in the future.

Growing demand for Internet services
According to statistical information provided by the China Network Information Center (CNNIC), the main purposes for using the Internet in China were academic, business, leisure, and sports information. With 70 percent of domain names registered in the commercial sector, the Internet seemed to be the business person's tool.

The rapid growth of Internet users closely matched the rapid economic growth in China. The Internet was widely used for academic purposes, and the Chinese government established many web sites to provide general information for both Chinese citizens and foreign Internet users. The expected trend is that the Internet will become more popular in the future.

As the Chinese economy continues to grow, on-line advertisement, shopping, and commercial activities will become more popular. The number of Internet users had reached 620,000 by the end of 1997. By June 1998, that figure had doubled, reaching 1.18 million users or 10 times the number of users at the end of 1996. It is estimated that the number of Internet users will reach 4–5 million by the end of 1999.

Competition and restricted control

With strong growth potential in the market, many companies entered the Chinese Internet sector. In 1998, there were four network operators and about 100 ISPs (Internet Service Providers) offering service in China. According to CNNIC, the Chinese government allocated most of the resources to CHINANET, which was the state-owned ISP in China. CHINANET provided Internet service in most of the major cities in China including Beijing, Tianjin, and Shanghai. In some cities, CHINANET was the only ISP, and most Internet users in China used CHINANET. Therefore, CHINANET captured the majority of the market share early in the sector's development. Some analysts suggested that even though competition had been introduced, CHINANET still had an advantage over other ISPs because it had established its position in the market first.

As with other telecommunication services in China, foreign participation in providing Internet services had been very restricted. For example, if a foreign company wanted to set up an ISP in China, a joint venture with a Chinese company holding more than 51 percent had to be formed. In other words, the controlling interest in the joint venture had to be in the hands of the Chinese company, not the foreign company. The first government-authorized commercial ISP, called "Computerworld," was formed in 1996 by a US company consisting of a group of research institutes in the US, Canada, and Chengdu Net. In 1998, more than 10 similar joint ventures had been established. However, after the year 2000, a new regulation will be adopted which restricts foreign companies to forming joint ventures with only the MPT or the recently formed MII.

Apart from requiring foreign investors to set up joint ventures, there are regulations controlling citizens' use of the Internet. For example, the government has stated that all Internet links will run through its own computers and was also planning to extend the law to all territories, including Hong Kong.[51] Put bluntly, all information will pass through MPT before it can flow into China.

Pricing

A lack of competition resulted in high prices and low quality. According to CNNIC, 61.2 percent of Internet users in China think that Internet services are too expensive and that they cannot afford the service as their incomes are low compared to those of people in other developed countries. In fact, many people in China, especially students, access the Internet via computers in universities. Therefore, very few of the users have a line connection from an ISP, resulting in low revenue generation for ISPs.

Quality

Despite the growing importance of using the Internet in China, the quality of Internet services provided is not satisfactory. Many users complained that the speed of data transfer is slow. This is attributed to the lack of advanced softwsre in China. By contrast, Hong Kong ISPs provide the latest versions of navigators and browsers, while such software cannot be found in China.

SUMMARY

The opening of China's telecommunications market suggested tremendous business opportunities to domestic and foreign companies. The expansion in the market segments of fixed lines, cellular phones and service, paging service, and Internet service was expected to continue into the future. However, the overall industry was still subject to the control of various governmental agencies. How the domestic and foreign companies negotiated the industry forces would determine their success or failure in this market.

APPENDIX
GLOSSARY

Analog: Communications by transmission of continuously varying representations of the input signal, as compared to binary coding of words in **digital** transmission.

Base station: Transmitter and receiver, which serve as a bridge between all mobile users in a **cell** and connect mobile calls to the mobile switching center.

Base-station controller: Equipment that monitors and controls one or more base stations (message exchange and frequency administration).

CDMA: Code Division Multiple Access technology, a continuous digital transmission technology that accommodates higher throughput by using various coding sequences to mix and separate voice and data signals for wireless transmission.

Cell: Coverage area of whole or part of a **base station**.

Cell site: The entire infrastructure and radio equipment associated with a cellular transmitting and receiving station, including the land, building tower, antennae, and electrical equipment.

Cell splitting: The process of dividing a single cell into a number of calls that can be handled in a given area.

Cellular system: A telephone system based on a grid of cells deployed at a specified frequency.

Channel: Communication path for transmitting voice or non-voice signals.

DCS 1800: Digital Cellular System for 1,800 MHz, a European digital cellular standard based on **GSM** technology that operates in the 1,800 MHz frequency band.

DGT: The Directorate General of Telecommunications, a state-owned enterprise established by and under the control of the MPT.

Digital: A method of storing, processing, and transmitting information through the use of electronic or optical pulses that represent the binary digits 0 or 1. Digital transmission and switching technologies employ a sequence of discrete, distinct pulses to represent information, as opposed to the continuously variable **analog** signal.

Dual-band handset: A mobile or portable telephone which is capable of operating in two frequency bands, such as GSM 900 and DCS 1800.

Frequency: The number of cycles per second, measured in hertz, of a periodic oscillation or wave in radio propagation.

GSM: Global System for Mobile Communications, the pan-European mobile telephone system operating in the 900 MHz frequency band based on digital transmission and cellular network architecture with **roaming**. GSM is the standard accepted in most of Europe, the Middle East, Africa, Australia, and Asia (with the exception of Japan, South Korea, and some other countries).

GSM 900: A GSM network in the 900 MHz frequency range.

Interconnect: Any variety of hardware arrangements that permit the connection of telecommunications equipment to a communications common carrier network such as a public switched telephone network.

MHz: Megahertz, a unit of measure of frequency; 1 MHz is equal to one million cycles per second.

MII: Ministry of Information Industry.

Mobile switching center: A central switching point to which each call is connected, which controls the routing of calls. A mobile switching center allows cellular telephone users to move freely from cell to cell while continuing their calls.

MPT: The Ministry of Posts and Telecommunications of the PRC.

Network infrastructure: Fixed infrastructure equipment consisting of a base transceiver station, base station, controllers, antennae, switch, management information system, and other equipment that receives, transmits, and processes signals from and to subscriber equipment and/or between wireless systems and the public switched phone network.

Penetration: Number of subscribers per 100 of population.

Penetration rate: Total market subscribers divided by population of the service area.

PSTN: Public switched telephone network, which comprises the network infrastructure necessary for providing basic telephone services.

PTA: Provincial-level Posts and Telecommunications Administrations established by and under the administrative authority of the MPT.

PTB: Posts and Telecommunications Bureaus at the municipal and county levels under the control of the PTAs.

RMB: The official currency of the PRC; US$1 = RMB8.27.

Roaming: A service offered by mobile network operators, which allows a subscriber to use his or her handset while in the service area of another carrier. Roaming requires an agreement between operators in different individual markets to permit customers to access the other's system.

Switch: A mechanical, electrical, or electronic device which opens or closes a circuit and completes or breaks an electrical path, or selects paths or circuits used to route traffic between the mobile system and the **PSTN**.

TACS: Total Access Multiple Access or digital wireless transmissions in the 800 MHz and 900 MHz frequency bands.

Transmission line: Dedicated telecommunications transmission line linking one fixed point to another.

NOTES

1. Liang, X., Zhang, X., and Yang, X., "The development of telecommunications in China," *IEEE Communications Magazine*. November 1998, pp. 54–8.
2. "Tilting the playing field," *Business China*, May 12, 1998, pp. 3–5.
3. "Development trend of China's telecommunications market," Xinhua Electronics News, Xinhua News Agency, (www.idgchina.com/xinhua/trend/htm).
4. "Tilting the playing field," *Business China*.
5. "Development trend of China's telecommunications market," Xinhua Electronics News.
6. Ibid.
7. "Who needs competition," *Business China*, October 1998, pp. 4–5.
8. Ibid.
9. China Telecom Hong Kong IPO Prospectus, 1997.
10. Liang, et al., "The development of telecommunications in China."
11. Ibid.
12. Ibid.
13. "Cunning," *Business China*, September 29, 1997, pp. 8–9.
14. Ibid.
15. Ibid.
16. China Telecom Hong Kong IPO Prospectus, 1997.
17. Ibid.
18. Wallerstein, D., "Industry Shake-up," *China Trade Report*, September 1998, pp. 8–10.
19. "Super ministry brings rivals together," *CTC News*, April 1998, pp. 1–3.
20. Wallerstein, "Industry shake-up."
21. Ibid.
22. Ibid.
23. "Super ministry brings rivals together," *CTC News*.
24. "Who needs competition," *Business China*.
25. "Development trend of China's telecommunications market," Xinhua Electronics News.
26. Lee, S. N., *Telecommunications and Development in China*, Hampton Press, 1997, pp. 113–30, 201–23, 245–63.
27. "Still out in the cold," *Business China*, June 8, 1998, p. 7.
28. *CTC News*, 1998.
29. "Cunning," *Business China*.
30. Ibid.
31. Liang et al., "The development of telecommunications in China."

32. Ritt, C. S., "Current developments of IMT-2000 in China", *IEEE Communications.*

33. Liang et al., "The development of telecommunications in China."

34. "Cunning," *Business China.*

35. "Huge imbalance among regional markets," *CTC News*, March 5, 1998, pp. 1–2.

36. Ibid.

37. Ritt, "Current developments of IMT-2000 in China," and *Business China*, 1998.

38. Chae, Y. H., "An epic future?" *China Trade Report*, November 1997, pp. 6–7.

39. "Cunning," *Business China.*

40. Ibid.

41. Zita, K., "China closes the door," *Far Eastern Economic Review*, October 22, 1998, p. 32.

42. "Cunning," *Business China.*

43. Zita, "China closes the door."

44. Ritt, "Current developments of IMT-2000 in China," and *Business China*, 1998.

45. Chae, "An epic future?"

46. "Restructuring becomes key to survival," *CTC News*, July 1998, pp. 1–2.

47. Liang et al., "The development of telecommunications in China," and *CTC News.*

48. "Restructuring becomes key to survival," *CTC News*; Liang et al., "The development of telecommunications in China."

49. "Restructuring becomes key to survival," *CTC News.*

50. Ibid.

51. Williams, M., "China issues regulations to control Internet." 1996 (http://nb.pacifica.com/reg/chinaissuesregulation_494.shtml).

CHAPTER FIVE

EASTMAN KODAK: MEETING THE DIGITAL CHALLENGE

Scott Duncan, Jean Gibbons, Scott Haenni, Adam Laux, and Cynthia Varner under the supervision of Robert M. Grant. This case was prepared solely to provide material for class discussion. The authors do not intend to illustrate either the effective or ineffective handling of a management situation. The authors may have disguised certain names or other identifying information to protect confidentiality.

Soon after his arrival at Kodak's Rochester, New York, headquarters in November 1993, newly appointed CEO George Fisher began to be referred to as "George the Second." Fisher did not discourage comparisons with Kodak's founder, George Eastman. If George Eastman had created Eastman Kodak, George Fisher's mission was to recreate it in a new era of digital imaging.

However, by the fall of 1998, the journey ahead for Kodak looked as long and perilous as it had when he had first arrived. Despite huge efforts to cut costs, develop digital technologies, launch new products, and revitalize the staid Kodak culture, the long-awaited revitalization of this giant multinational remained but a promise. Kodak was still in the midst of a perilous transition. Its traditional photography business was subject to increasing competition and declining profit and margins, while its new digital and hybrid products had yet to fill the gap. The release of Kodak's third quarter results on October 13, 1998 was met by a 12 percent dive in the price of Kodak shares. Although cost cutting and other belt-tightening measures had been successful in boosting earnings for the first nine months of 1998 by 49 percent above 1997, what shocked the market was the continuing decline in Kodak's sales – down 9 percent from 1997. Tables 5.1 and 5.2 show recent financial performance.

The next few years would present huge challenges to Kodak. Fisher had staked the future of Kodak on leadership in the emerging field of digital imaging. Yet, it was still unclear how the market for digital imaging products would develop, and whether Kodak could build the capabilities needed to establish leadership against competitors such as Fuji, Sony, Hewlett-Packard, Canon, and Casio.

TABLE 5.1

Eastman Kodak: revenues and earnings for first three quarters of 1997 and 1998 ($ million, unless otherwise stated)

	Jan.–Sept. 1998	Jan.–Sept. 1997
Revenues	10,084	10,879
Costs:		
Cost of goods sold	5,193	5,703
Selling, general, and admin.	2,348	2,905
R&D costs	671	782
Purchased R&D	—	186
Interest expense	96	69
Other costs	82	99
Total costs	8,390	9,744
Earnings before income taxes	1,694	1,135
Provision for income taxes	576	386
Net earnings	1,118	749
Capital expenditures	619	1,024
Sales by industry segment		
Consumer imaging (total)	5,289	5,698
Inside the US	2,422	2,556
Outside the US	2,867	3,142
Commercial imaging (total)	4,576	5,084
Inside the US	2,194	2,462
Outside the US	2,382	2,622
Operating earnings by segment		
Consumer imaging	858	806
Percentage of sales	16.2%	14.1%
Commercial imaging	776	378
Percentage of sales	17.0%	7.4%

Source: Eastman Kodak *10K Report* (www.sec.gov/Archives/edgar).

HISTORY OF EASTMAN KODAK

When George Eastman told a co-worker at the Rochester Savings Bank that he had made plans for a vacation to Santo Domingo, the co-worker suggested that Eastman take photographs to remember it by. Eastman heeded the advice and purchased a state-of-the-art 3 × 4-foot camera, along with all of the developing plates, glass tanks, developing tents, chemicals, jugs of distilled water, tripods, phosphoric flashes, and photographic emulsions he would need. Eastman never made it to Santo Domingo with his heavy load, but he did fall in love with photography and set about the challenge of creating amateur photography as a more convenient and affordable pastime.

TABLE 5.2
Selected financial data, 1995–1997 ($ million)

	1997	1996	1995
From income statement			
Revenues	14,713	16,244	15,269
Costs			
Cost of goods sold	7,979	8,326	7,962
Selling, general, and admin.	3,912	4,410	4,158
R&D costs	1,044	1,028	935
Purchased R&D	186	—	—
Interest expense	98	83	78
Restructuring costs and asset impairments	1,290	358	—
Other costs	151	483	210
Total costs	14,660	14,688	13,343
Earnings before income taxes	53	1,556	1,926
Provision for income taxes	48	545	674
Gain on sale of discontinued operations	—	277	—
Net earnings	5	1,288	1,252
From balance sheet	*1997*	*1996*	
Current assets			
Cash and cash equivalents	728	1,777	
Receivables	2,271	2,738	
Inventories	1,252	1,575	
Total current assets	5,475	6,965	
Land, buildings, and equipment (net)	5,509	5,422	
Long-term receivables and other noncurrent assets	1,231	1,238	
Total Assets	13,145	14,438	
Current liabilities			
Payables	3,832	4,116	
Short-term borrowings	611	541	
Total current liabilities	5,177	5,417	
Other liabilities			
Long-term borrowings	585	559	
Post employment liabilities	3,075	2,967	
Other long-term liabilities	1,083	659	
Deferred income tax credits	64	102	
Total liabilities	9,984	9,704	
Shareholders' equity	3,161	4,734	
Total liabilities and shareholders' equity	13,145	14,438	
From cash flow statement	*1997*	*1996*	*1995*
Cash flows from operating activities			
Earnings from continuing operations	5	1,011	1,252
Adjustments for non-cash items	2,075	1,473	1,378
Net cash provided by operating activities	2,080	2,484	2,630

TABLE 5.2 *Continued*

	1997	1996	1995
Cash flows from investing activities			
Additions to properties	(1,485)	(1,341)	(1,034)
Proceeds from sale of properties	109	124	121
Cash flows from sale of Office Imaging business	(129)	688	—
Acquisitions, net of cash acquired	(341)	(128)	—
Cash flows from sale of non-imaging health businesses	(65)	(7)	(1,411)
Net cash used in investing activities	(1,896)	(636)	(2,380)
Cash flows from financing activities	(1,198)	(1,833)	(512)

Source: Eastman Kodak *Annual Report 1997*.

Eastman began the commercial manufacture of a new type of dry photographic plate in 1880 and established the Eastman Dry Plate Company with his friend Henry Strong in 1881. In 1884, Eastman developed silver halide paper-based photographic film, followed by the first fully portable camera in 1888. With these two products, and the processes to develop and print the new silver halide film, photography became a leisure activity for the masses. The company changed its name to the Eastman Kodak Company and was incorporated on October 24, 1901. Kodak's strategy was to provide a fully integrated photographic service supplying the camera and film through to processing and printing. Its first advertising slogan was "You push the button, we do the rest." George Eastman remained chairman until his death in 1932, during which period Eastman Kodak came to dominate the world market for photographic film, photographic paper and chemicals, and low-cost cameras.

Eastman established seven basic business principles for Kodak that he felt were vital to the company's future success. Kodak claims that these remain its guiding principles.

- Mass production at low cost
- International distribution
- Extensive advertising
- A focus on the customer
- Fostering growth and development through continuing research
- Treating employees in a fair, self-respecting way
- Reinvesting profits to build and extend the business

After Eastman's death, Kodak continued to build upon its dominant position in the world photographic market. Its approach was one of vertical integration combined with continuous innovation and product development. New product introductions and events included:

- 1939 – KODACHROME film for professional and leisure photography
- 1942 – KODACOLOR, the world's first true color negative film
- 1951 – The first home movie camera, the BROWNIE 8 mm
- 1959 – EKTACHROME commercial high-speed film
- 1963 – INSTAMATIC cameras and film for amateur photography
- 1969 – Kodak cameras and film accompany Aldrich and Armstrong to the moon
- 1972 – 110 Film Cartridge for amateur photography

THE 1980s: STORM CLOUDS AND NEW HORIZONS

As the 1970s drew to a close, a series of new challenges and market reversals threatened Kodak's dominance of the world photographic market. These included:

- The entry of Fuji Photo Film Company on to the world stage. Fuji's combination of cost leadership, high quality, and market aggressiveness forced Kodak to retaliate through price cuts and bigger advertising budgets, severely denting Kodak's margins. Fuji's sponsorship of the 1984 Los Angeles Olympic games proclaimed its presence in Kodak's backyard
- Kodak's withdrawal from instant photography as Polaroid won a patent infringement suit in 1986
- The failure of Kodak's disk camera introduced in 1982
- The loss of market share in cameras as Japanese 35 mm cameras came to dominate the world market

In July 1983, amidst declining earnings and a falling share price, Colby Chandler took over as Chairman and CEO with Kay Whitmore as President. Under the guidance of these two executives, Kodak embarked upon a decade of diversification and technology-driven business development. Chandler and Whitmore's initiatives were concentrated in two main areas: imaging and life sciences.

Imaging and data storage products

The 1980s and early 1990s were a period of rapid development in imaging technologies and new printing and reprographic products. Chastened by its having passed up the opportunity to acquire Chester Carlson's xerography patents (these were bought by Haliod Corp., which renamed itself Xerox Corp.), Kodak was determined not to be sidelined by new technological opportunities. Kay Whitmore took a leading role in broadening Kodak's imaging interests beyond its traditional area of chemical-based photographic imaging and into electrostatic imaging, electromagnetic imaging, and electronic imaging and thermal printing. Whitmore invested heavily in electronic data storage and data processing products and systems including:

- The KAR4000 Information System, providing advanced capabilities for computer-assisted storage and retrieval of film images (1983)

- Kodak floppy disks for PCs (1984), followed by the acquisition of the floppy disk manufacturer Verbatim
- The Ektaprint Electronic Publishing System and Kodak Image Management System to edit, store, retrieve, and print text and graphics (1985)
- Supralife batteries (1986)
- Joint ventures with Matsushita for producing videocassettes and batteries
- The world's first electronic image sensor with 1.4 million pixels (1986). This was followed by a number of new products for electronic publishing, scanning, and editing for the printing and publishing industry, including Imagelink for document imaging and Optistar for micrographic or digital capture of images (1989)
- A 14-inch optical disk capable of storing 6.8 billion bytes of information (1986)
- A new family of document management products under the Kodak Lionheart brand to provide high-speed printing capability for centralized duplicating departments (1990)
- Announcement of the Photo CD system (1990), which was followed by the launch of a number of Photo CD products (1992–3)
- Development of writable CDs for MCI (1992)

Life sciences

The second area of development built upon Kodak's capabilities in chemical technology. Eastman Chemicals had been established in the 1920s to supply photographic chemicals both to Kodak's film and processing division and to third-party customers. By the 1980s Eastman was a major international supplier of photographic chemicals, fibers, plastics (especially for soft drink packaging), printing inks, and nutrition supplements. Building upon its capabilities in chemicals and biotechnology, and on its existing healthcare activities (e.g., nutritional supplements and diagnostic equipment), Kodak established its Life Sciences Division in 1984. In 1986 Kodak established Eastman Pharmaceuticals, and greatly expanded its pharmaceutical interests with the acquisition of Sterling Drug in 1988 and a series of joint ventures with Sanofi during 1991–2. In addition, Kodak expanded its range of medical imaging products including its Insight Thoracic Imaging System and X-Omatic RA cassette for pediatric patients.

Organizational changes

Chandler and Whitmore did much to change Kodak's internal organization. After almost a century of dominating the world photographic industry, Kodak was perceived as centralized, bureaucratic, slow-moving, and risk averse. Kodak's system of lifetime employment engendered strong employee loyalty but insulated the company from external influences. Pressured by falling profits, Chandler and Whitmore cut costs and reshaped the organizational structure. Employment was cut from 136,500 in 1982 to 110,000 in 1992. To decentralize and increase profit orientation, divisions were subdivided into business units with clear bottom-line responsibilities. To promote entrepreneurship, an internal venturing fund that supported new business proposals was established.

To systematize and accelerate product development and improve product-launch quality, Kodak introduced a new product development methodology called the "Manufacturability Assurance Process" (MAP), which was based upon phases and gates.[1] MAP consisted of six phases, each accessed through a "gate." This resulted in clear project direction and improved control but did little to reduce product development cycle time (typical project duration was 24–40 months).

Despite the many initiatives of the late 1980s and early 1990s, the deluge of new products and new ventures added little to Kodak's revenue or profit growth. Two main criticisms of Whitmore's strategy were prevalent: lack of focus and inadequate attention to cost cutting. With regard to the former, the efforts to push Kodak into the future by pioneering computer-based, digital technologies had been dissipated among too many technologies, too many projects, and by the expansion into healthcare. Whitmore was undeterred: "We are not interested in doing more new things. We've got all the new things we need; it's making a success of each of those areas. [Silver halide] photography is successful. Our chemical company has a very solid base; it's successful. The thing we need to do is to make a success of the commercial applications of [digital] imaging and make a success of our health strategies."[2] Whitmore was firmly committed to the view that, with increasing competition in its core film manufacturing market, Kodak had to take an active role in developing the digital photographic technology that would eventually replace its core market. However, the effectiveness of Kodak's digital strategy had been undermined by a lack of integration between Kodak's different digital products and projects, and by spreading its resources too thinly.

With regard to costs, Whitmore's commitment to growth had meant lack of attention to overheads and productivity. Faced with deteriorating financial performance, in February 1993 Whitmore hired Chris Steffens as Chief Financial Officer, the first outsider ever to hold that post. To the dismay of analysts and shareholders, Steffens' tenure at Kodak lasted less than 11 weeks. "Change was the reason we brought Chris Steffens to Kodak, and we are fundamentally changing the way we run the company," said Whitmore. "[He left] not because we disagreed on what needs to change, but because we could not agree on the process for making that change happen."[3]

Kodak's Board of Directors became increasingly skeptical of Whitmore's ability to deliver results. Kodak's stock had trailed the S&P 500 by 50 percent. In the marketplace, Kodak's leadership was being eroded by Fuji Photo Film, in the US as well as overseas. Kodak had already been through five restructurings with little to show but big write-offs and debt totaling 69 percent of total capital. Kodak was earning only 6 percent on capital that cost more than 14 percent.[4] Frustrated with Kodak's dismal performance and concerned about the threat of competition in the future, the Board fired Whitmore in 1993 and replaced him with George Fisher, then CEO of Motorola.

GEORGE FISHER TAKES THE HELM

George Fisher was one of the most highly regarded CEOs in America. He was viewed as one of the leaders of America's resurgence in high technology and was on every headhunter's list. He had already turned down the opportunity to become IBM's CEO (IBM's Board subsequently turned to Lou Gerstener). Fisher was unique among CEOs: with a doctorate in applied mathematics from Brown University and ten years of R&D experience at Bell Labs, he had a scientist's grasp of electronic technology. "He really does understand all those 1s and 0s in the digital world."[5] Fisher was one of America's leading exponents of total quality management. Motorola's "Six Sigma" program had revolutionized every aspect of its operations.[6] He had driven Motorola's wireless analog and digital technology into a multibillion-dollar business, establishing Motorola as the world leader in cellular technology and among *Fortune*'s ten most admired companies.[7]

Nevertheless, skeptics abounded. "[If Fisher succeeds] it will be one of the greatest feats in business annals," an industry analyst remarked. Another said, "Growth [at Kodak]? I don't think so. Making Kodak grow is not like teaching an elephant to dance. It's like cloning an elephant into a mouse."[8] Compared to IBM or AT&T, Kodak was viewed as a much tougher candidate for turnaround.

Refocusing on Imaging

From the outset, Fisher's strategic vision for Kodak was as an imaging company: "We are not in the photographic film business or in the electronics business, we are in the picture business."[9] In order to focus Kodak's efforts and lower debt, Fisher immediately approved proposals to spin off Eastman Chemical Company. This was followed by a string of other divestments. In 1994 the divestment of all healthcare businesses (other than medical imaging) was announced, the most important being the Sterling Winthrop pharmaceutical company. Sterling had been acquired at a cost of $5.1 billion in 1988; it was sold to SmithKline Beecham for $2.9 billion. The funds generated were used mainly to pay off debt.

Developing a Digital Imaging Strategy

The intention of the divestments was to enable Kodak to focus all of its resources on its core imaging business. However, developing a coherent strategy for digital imaging business was not easy. After reviewing the company's financials, Fisher was shocked to learn that Kodak had poured $5 billion into digital imaging research since the mid-1980s and had little to show for it in terms of world-beating products.

Fisher's digital strategy was to create greater coherence among Kodak's multiple digital projects, in part through creating a single digital projects division headed by newly hired Carl Gustin (previously with Apple Computer and DEC). Fisher emphasized an incremental approach: "The future is not some harebrained scheme of the digital Information Highway or something. It is a step-by-step progression of enhancing photography using digital technology."[10]

This approach involved the introduction of new products that represented modest technological advances, but could be introduced quickly, with no defects, with modest development costs, and strongly supported by marketing. During 1994 and

1995, Kodak introduced a number of products embodying digital technology, and joint venture agreements with leading computer companies including Microsoft, IBM, and Hewlett-Packard. Kodak's new products included the following:

- Kodak developed digital cameras for both the top end and the bottom end of the market. In January 1994, Kodak launched a Professional Digital Camera (the camera alone costing $8,500) and the Apple Quicktake computer camera (manufactured by Kodak, marketed by Apple Computer), which, at $75, was the cheapest digital camera available at the time. In March 1995, Kodak introduced the first full-featured digital camera priced at under $1,000.
- In 1994, Kodak introduced its CopyPrint Station, a walk-up, self-service system allowing customers to make copies and enlargements of existing photographs. The system takes a digital copy of the picture that can then be enlarged or otherwise manipulated before thermal printing. The machines initially cost $27,000 and were sold mainly to film processing and camera retailers.
- In November 1994, the more sophisticated $40,000 Digital Enhancement Station went on sale. It was intended primarily for photo retailers and permits more complex photo manipulation (e.g., eliminating red-eye).
- After the failure of its initial launch of the Photo CD system, based upon a Photo CD player that could store digital images of photographs on floppy disk, in February 1995 Kodak introduced the next-generation Photo CD imaging workstation, which targeted commercial laboratories, photo processors, and PC users. The system also permits commercial users to offer copyright infringement protection for digital images.
- In March 1995, Kodak introduced its Kodak Digital Science brand name, to help bring attention to its strengths in science and technology. The trademark would be used for the company's digital imaging hardware, software, and service products.
- In August 1995, Kodak's Ektascan Imagelink system included the capability of converting medical images to digital images, which could then be transmitted via phone lines to local hospitals. At the same time, the Kodak Color Management System was used to set color standards in 80 percent of the desktop imaging software market.
- In February 1996, Kodak unveiled the Advantix brand, to be used on all the company's advanced photo system films, cameras, and related products. Advanced photo system is the result of agreement between Kodak and Fuji on technical standards for cameras and film that store both chemical film images and data that can be downloaded electronically. The system combines the resolution of conventional film with the versatility and communicability of digital imaging.
- In August 1996, Kodak produced the Ektascan laser printer, making it the world leader in medical laser imaging.
- In February 1997, Kodak introduced five new Advantix cameras, offering features such as three picture-size formats and messages and annotations in five languages.

■ In April 1997, Kodak unveiled its DC120 Zoom Digital Camera, the first point-and-shoot digital camera.

Among Kodak's collaborations with computer companies, that with Microsoft took on particular importance. Kodak collaborated with Microsoft on the walk-up imaging kiosks that produced Photo CDs. The two companies co-branded to endorse computer applications that supported digital images. Kodak also assisted with the launch of Windows 95 to illustrate the use of pictures in desktop systems.[11]

Organizational Changes

Some of Fisher's biggest challenges were in improving organizational structure and management processes, increasing accountability, and building morale among Kodak's demoralized employees. Fisher worked hard to engender a positive attitude in all parts of the business. Growth should occur not just in the new digital technologies, but also in the basic film business: "Half the people in the world have yet to take their first picture," noted Fisher in January 1995. "The opportunity is huge, and it's nothing fancy. We just have to sell yellow boxes of film."

Fisher's style as CEO was a strong contrast to the bureaucratic, autocratic approach that had traditionally been associated with Kodak. His approach was informal and communicative, dropping in on various parts of the company, and encouraging direct email communication from employees.

The essence of his management approach has been to enforce accountability. On coming to Kodak, Fisher found that: "It was so hierarchically orientated that everybody looked to the guy above him for what needed to be done . . . How can you hold a person accountable if you've had three overrides on his decision?" Accountability has required simplifying Kodak's matrix structure, which tended to diffuse individual responsibility. Organizational changes also created the opportunity to bring in outsiders. These included a new CFO (Harry Kavetas, former CEO of IBM Credit Corporation), a new Treasurer (Jesse Greene, also from IBM), a new head of Digital and Applied Imaging (Gustin), and a new marketing advisor (John Sculley, former CEO of Apple Computer).

A key benefit of increased decentralization and accountability was faster decision-making. Fisher himself set the standard with his quick decisions to divest all Kodak's non-imaging businesses. Speed also required cutting cycle times in manufacturing and product development. Under Fisher, Kodak developed a systematic approach to the front end of product development: rather than starting with a product idea and moving directly into the "phases and gates" process, the company selects an opportunity, designs models and plans, and only then does it begin the subsequent phases of development.

Most of the changes that Fisher introduced into Kodak's product development process were practices that had worked well at Motorola. The product development approach of Motorola employed cross-functional teams, which improved integration and lowered costs. Most importantly, it permitted short product development cycles, with a typical project lasting only 18–30 months.[12] Such speed was essential in the fast-moving wireless communication equipment markets where Motorola competed.

1997 – A Difficult Year

During his first three years at Kodak, George Fisher confounded the skeptics who had predicted doom and gloom. His style and strategic and operating changes won him support both within the company and on Wall Street. Return on equity increased from 14.8 percent in 1994 to 27.1 percent in 1995, and to 28.2 percent in 1996. However, during 1997 Fisher's strategy appeared to be unraveling. Losses in digital imaging of $400 million for the year coincided with a downturn in revenues and profits from photography products as Fuji cut prices in the US market and made big inroads into the professional market. Once restructuring costs were included, net income fell to almost nothing in 1997.

At meetings with securities analysts, institutional investors, and news reporters in New York on November 11, 1997, Fisher, COO Dan Carp, and CFO Harry Kavetas announced changes in strategy designed to "get the company's four-year-old turn-around back on track." The changes focused on two areas:

- Cutting costs. Fisher announced that Kodak would cut $1 billion from its cost structure during 1998 and 1999
- Greater selectivity in investments in digital imaging

On the digital front, Fisher explained that this would mean focusing on areas that are strategic, such as investments in digitization and image network services, where Kodak can provide advantages its electronic competitors cannot. In addition, Kodak would prioritize its investments in strategic products such as digital cameras and scanners, which have not yet delivered adequate returns. Finally, the company would scrutinize its non-strategic product and service portfolios, such as writable CDs and 14-inch optical disks.

Commenting on the $400 million loss from digital products and services for 1997, Fisher stated:

> In those categories that are not providing an acceptable return, we will do what is necessary to move them to a level of adequate return – including buy, sell, or partner if necessary.
>
> Four years ago, when we talked about the possibilities of digital photography, people laughed. Today, the high-tech world is stampeding to get a piece of the action, calling digital imaging perhaps the greatest growth opportunity in the computer world. And, it may be. We surely see it as the greatest future enabler for people to truly "Take Pictures. Further."
>
> We start at retail, our distribution stronghold. Here consumers are at the peak moment of satisfaction, when they open their photofinishing envelopes. We believe the widespread photo-retailing infrastructure will continue to be the principal avenue by

which people obtain their pictures. Our strategy is to build on and extend this existing market strength which is available to us, and at the same time be prepared to serve the rapidly growing, but relatively small, pure digital market that is developing. Kodak will network its rapidly expanding installed base of *Image Magic* stations and kiosks, essentially turning these into nodes on a massive, global network. The company will allow retailers to use these work stations to bring digital capability to the average snapshooter, extending the value of these images for the consumers and retailers alike, while creating a lucrative consumable business for Kodak.[13]

Despite the determined and up-beat tone of the meeting, the bad news for 1997 was not over. In December, the World Trade Organization rejected claims by Kodak and the Clinton Administration that Fuji had conspired with the Japanese government to impede Kodak's sales to Japanese consumers.

In reporting on Kodak's 1997 performance, Fisher acknowledged the company's difficulties, but concentrated upon the task ahead and his commitment to a successful future for Kodak.

I look forward to striving for continuous improvement at Kodak, for our work here is far from complete. With the kind of intelligence, skill, creativity, and dedication we have at Kodak, that work should be fun. My commitment to our work here is so important to me, in fact, that the Kodak Board recently agreed to extend my five-year management contract by two years, which takes us at least through the year 2000. I'm immensely proud to be associated with this great company, its terrific heritage, its bright future, its thousands of energetic and dedicated employees, and I thank you for putting your trust and confidence in us.

We really believe we are at the beginning of perhaps the most exciting chapter in our history as we help people understand how they can truly realize the Kodak slogan: Take Pictures. Further.[14]

DIGITAL IMAGING IN 1998

The Technology

Digital imaging covers a wide variety of technologies. At its simplest, digitalization is the process of describing something in binary code, the 0 s and 1 s that form the language that all electronic devices use to communicate.

The converse of digital is analog. Most people know that a record or tape is analog, but a compact disc (CD) is digital. In some ways, analog is better because it is an exact replica of the sound recorded. A CD, no matter how much data is put onto it, is still only a finite approximation of the original sound. For most listeners, though, the difference is imperceptible. For them, the advantages of digital recordings – no imperfections and ease of editing – outweigh the loss of fidelity to the original.

In much the same way, film-based photography is analog. It provides a true copy of the original, but it is subject to imperfections and is difficult to edit. Digital imaging is not the de facto winner, however. It, too, has advantages and disadvantages:

Pros
- Infinite ability to manipulate an image
- Images are easily stored/transmitted
- No disposable media (i.e., film) required
- No wasted media (unwanted images are simply erased)

Cons
- Not a true reproduction of the original
- Complex/expensive equipment required for editing
- Lack of standards for storing/processing images
- Storage is memory-intensive

The memory-intensive nature of digital imaging is worth considering further. The technology to store images digitally is nothing new. In fact, even before VCRs became popular, firms were considering using CDs to store videos. Unfortunately, those firms soon discovered that storing images takes much more space than storing sound does. At that time in the early 1970s, a music album could be stored on a single CD, but a full-length feature film would have taken 360 CDs!

The Development of Digital Imaging

As with most technologies, digital imaging has migrated from high-end users to consumers. The first users were governments and hospitals. Governments use digital imaging for military purposes, including spy satellites. Hospitals turned to digital storage for CT scans and MRIs (Magnetic Resonance Imaging). Digital imaging is also used in weather forecasting. Increasingly, companies are using digital imaging to store and search for data. Newspaper and magazine publishers are also becoming interested in the technology. Digital imaging allows photographers to transmit pictures instantly to the publisher from anywhere in the world. It also allows the contents of periodicals to be transmitted to publishing locations worldwide.

In the early 1990s, digital imaging finally came to individual users. Initially, those users were primarily business users and professional photographers because of the high cost of digital cameras and scanners. With the rapid growth of Internet use and the explosion in demand for digital images for web sites, commercial demand increased, to be followed by increasing consumer demand. By 1997, more than forty companies were producing digital cameras and scanners. The cost of the least expensive digital camera had fallen to $200 and scanners could be had for $100.

Nevertheless, the divide in the digital imaging industry between the professional and the consumer segments remains huge. While some features are beginning to trickle down to consumers, most manufacturers – especially Kodak – have a clearly differentiated product range for each segment, which is reflected in prices. Price multiples between professional and consumer models can be as much as 150 times for cameras ($30,000 vs. $200), 100 times for scanners ($10,000 vs. $100), and 15 times for color laser printers ($30,000 vs. $2,000).

Product Applications of Digital Imaging

Digital imaging encompasses numerous media and industries. The equipment required to operate this technology, even in its most basic form, is substantial. At its simplest, though, digital imaging involves acquiring an image, processing it, and then outputting it. To achieve that end, the following technologies are involved:

- *PCs.* Computers form the skeleton required to manipulate images. Not only are the processor speed, RAM, and hard disk capacity important factors, but increasingly enhancements aimed specifically at image handling (such as Intel's MMX technology) play a crucial role.
- *Monitors.* Monitors represent the most basic way to display a digital image. Since the quality of a digital image is only as good as the weakest link in the chain, however, monitors remain an important component. Small monitors and low-resolution monitors make viewing digital images unpleasant, and editing them impossible.
- *Cameras.* Digital cameras look identical to film-based cameras. Functionally, however, they are quite different. The images are stored in internal memory, on removable FlashROM cards, or on floppy disks. While the price has fallen, features that users take for granted on a regular camera have also disappeared. The Kodak DC20 sells for around $200, but lacks zoom, shutter speed control, and even a flash! Also, picture quality is clearly lacking. At the other end of the spectrum, there is Minolta's RD-175, which claims it has "The quality of film in a digital camera!" At $5,600, it should. Of course, true professionals require Kodak's EOS*DCS1c, which retails for a mere $30,000.
- *Scanners.* Scanners take something that exists as a hardcopy and translate the image into a digital version. Flatbed scanners look like a photocopier and work like a fax machine. Photo/slide scanners are built specifically for scanning photos and/or slides. Scanners became common as the popularity of desktop publishing grew. While HP has historically dominated the market, UMAX and Microtek have made inroads, especially at the low end.
- *Graphics cards.* The part of the computer most directly related to image handling performance is the graphics card. All computer signals routed to the monitor will pass through this component.
- *Software.* Software can be divided into four broad categories: editing, color control, conversion, and filing. Editing software allows the user to manipulate images. Basic software, such as Microsoft's Picture It ($50), can crop, lighten/darken, and sometimes eliminate red-eye. High-end software, such as Adobe's Photoshop ($550), can manipulate the image almost infinitely. Color control software attempts to keep the color consistent from the point of capture, through manipulation, up until the point of display. Conversion software allows the user to read and write files in a variety of image formats. This is necessary because there are more than a dozen image formats widely used. Filing software provides a system for storing, indexing, and searching one's images.

- *Video boards.* Another way to get images into a computer is through a video board. These devices allow you to hook your video camera up to your computer. The board translates the analog videotaped recording to digital signals, and then passes it to the computer for storage. Most video boards also allow the reverse: recording computer activity on videotape.

- *Storage devices.* Keeping digital images in quantities comparable to film-based photographs could quickly devour a computer's hard disk. The smallest file size is more than 100 kilobytes, whereas high-end models use 6 megabytes per image and professional models can use up to 18 megabytes. Thus, a way to store images outside the computer is necessary. Storage is comprised of removable and on-line categories. In the removable category, there are two types: camera-based and computer-based. Camera-based storage is primarily centered around FlashROM cards. (These memory cards are about the size of a credit card and can be inserted into slots on some digital cameras.) One problem is that each company has a proprietary format for storing images on FlashROM cards. Once transmitted into the computer, though, the image can be stored in another format. Sony's Mavica camera has tried to make things easier by creating a camera that uses $3\frac{1}{2}$-inch floppy disks. As for computer-based storage, since digital images tend to be large, the same $3\frac{1}{2}$-inch floppy disks are not suitable for archiving numerous images. The growth in high-capacity removable storage media's popularity is exemplified by the ubiquitous Iomega Zip drive. Some firms, including Kodak, have taken a different route, offering customers the ability to store pictures on their server for a fee. The images are transmitted via the Internet.

- *Printers.* The ultimate irony, of course, is printing the digital image. Despite the move towards a paperless world, printing remains prevalent. Otherwise, images can only be shared among people who have the equipment necessary to view them. Even the cheapest color laser printers used to be out of the reach of most users (priced at $10,000 or more), but recently units for $2,000 are becoming widely available. Color inkjet printers have also fallen in price, from about $1,000 down to $250. Photo printers are relatively new and are specifically designed to print digital images. The output looks and feels like a film-based photograph. Consequently, special paper must be used.

Digital Imaging Standards

A true standard for imaging, while critical to bringing the pieces of the digital industry together, remains elusive. One attempt, FlashPix, was developed by a consortium of firms, including Kodak, Microsoft, Intel, Adobe, Canon, Fuji, HP, and IBM.[15] Its acceptance is not universal, however, for a number of reasons: a variety of widely used formats already exist, companies are hesitant to limit themselves to one format, and each company has incentives to develop a new, technologically superior standard. Even Kodak, a strong proponent of FlashPix, has developed another standard (EXIF) in partnership with Fuji for use within digital cameras. Additionally, a consortium of Japanese camera makers has created its own standard (CIFF).[16]

Competitors in Digital Imaging

Digital photography has quickly become a crowded marketplace, with 45 manufacturers in 1997 offering more than 100 digital camera models below $1,000.[17] With the emergence of Intel's "just-add-water" digital camera kit, a number of low-cost entrants have been able to flood the market with low-priced digital cameras – despite the fact that the market itself is so young.[18]

The industry – led by Kodak, Hewlett-Packard, Fuji, Intel, and Microsoft – has attempted to establish FlashPix as the standard to avoid the complexity of differing product standards and platforms.[19] Given so many diverse competitors in the marketplace, however, it will be very difficult for firms to avoid price competition at the early stages of market growth as they attempt to build a customer base and to establish brand equity.

Industry analysts expect price competition to be the norm until significant product innovations and quality improvements can be made, and competitors can successfully differentiate themselves. Without significant product innovation, they believe, the market itself will never overtake film photography. The fierceness of this price competition will depend mostly on the growth rate of the industry and rivals' ability to forecast it.

As of April 1998, the top three companies – Kodak (20 percent market share), Casio (20 percent), and Sony (11 percent) – accounted for over 50 percent of all digital camera sales.[20] Several powerful companies, ranging from traditional camera manufacturers to consumer electronics firms, loom in the background, however.

Casio

When digital photography was in its infancy, Casio was the unchallenged world leader. After obtaining a market share of over 50 percent between 1985 and 1996, Casio watched its market share fall to 20 percent in 1997.[21] Casio's President, Kazuo Kashio, has vowed that his company will respond "to the challenge by investing in and developing technologies that will maintain Casio as a leader in this field."[22] Casio knows how to be successful in a high-tech market; it honed its skills in the highly competitive world of calculators and digital watches.[23] With a much stronger marketing presence, Kashio hopes to halt his company's downward slide in digital imaging market share, and to be able to build on his company's expertise in technologies, such as LCDs, that are key to digital imaging.

Sony

As one of the world's largest consumer electronics manufacturers, Sony prides itself on understanding what consumers want. In late 1997, the company introduced a major breakthrough in digital photography – the Mavica. The Mavica was the first camera to store pictures directly on a standard $3\frac{1}{2}$-inch diskette, allowing for simple downloading to a computer. Since the introduction of the Mavica, more than one-third of all digital still cameras sold in the US have been a Sony model.[24] With a powerful brand name and expertise in high-technology and miniaturization, Sony has the consumer-savvy to be successful in the digital photography market.

Olympus

A traditional camera company, Olympus seems poised for significant movement and growth in the digital market. Once seen as "dangerously late to the party" in digital photography, Olympus has suddenly become an emerging force in the market with its introduction of two high-resolution, low-price digital cameras.[25] Unlike most of the other companies in the digital photography market, Olympus has significant experience in camera design and ergonomics. It does not, however, have significant experience with electronics.

Hewlett-Packard

Despite its lack of expertise in photography, HP is a high-tech juggernaut that poses a significant challenge to conventional photography companies in this newly evolving market. In spite of its relative lack of mass-marketing experience, HP has a good track record of responding to consumer needs – and even exceeding their expectations – and branching off into new product markets. HP's highly successful venture into printers is a good example of this tangential approach to new product development. Today, HP gets roughly $15 billion in revenue annually from its laser and inkjet printers.[26] HP's expertise in inkjet printing and desktop scanning, in particular, and high-tech equipment, in general, gives it the competence to succeed in the digital imaging industry. Additionally, given the shorter life-cycles of its products[27] and experience fighting off heavy foreign competition, along with its strong financial foundation and brand image, HP seems primed for the fight ahead. Indeed, it might even be at an advantage in this emerging market.

Fuji

For years, Kodak and Fuji have been battling for dominance in the global film market. Both control roughly a third of the total market. For years, Kodak has largely controlled the market in the US, holding over 80 percent of the market. In early 1996, however, Fuji began slashing its film prices by as much as 25 percent, and began to creep up on Kodak.[28] Equally troublesome to Kodak is the fact that Fuji's financial strength gives it much more flexibility for the future. In 1996, Fuji grossed $11 billion in sales, with profits of $757 million; moreover, Fuji enjoyed a net cash position of about $4.5 billion as well as access to cheap borrowing in Japan. It consistently spends about 7 percent of sales on R&D.[29] Like Kodak, Fuji has jumped into the digital camera business. With its lean cost structure, Fuji seems poised to be successful in the digital age. It has built a reputation for price, quality, and sharp marketing. With its huge cash reserve, technological edge, and marketing savvy, Fuji just might have what it takes to win in the new digital marketplace.

EASTMAN KODAK IN 1998:
RESOURCES AND CAPABILITIES

Critical to Kodak's ability to establish leadership in the new world of digital imaging was its ability to marshal its considerable base of resources and organizational capabilities, while building the additional capabilities needed to succeed in this technologically fast-moving field.

After almost a century of global leadership in the photographic industry, Kodak brings with it an enormous base of resources and expertise. At the market end, Kodak's brand and its worldwide distribution are probably its most important resources. Its ability to bring new products to consumers' attention and to support these products with one of the world's best known and most widely respected brand names is a huge advantage in a market where technological change creates uncertainty for consumers. At the same time, these resources are most valuable in relation to Kodak's existing distribution channels, which are primarily through retail photography stores, film processors, and professional photographers. Kodak's entire digital strategy is built around providing consumers with a pathway to digital imaging though Kodak's existing retail network, while introducing more advanced digital imaging systems to Kodak's professional market. If, however, digital imaging reaches the mass market through consumers' personal computers, there is the possibility that consumers download digital images directly from their camera to their PCs and printers without the need for traditional retailers and film processors.

In terms of technology, Kodak's leadership in photography has been based upon silver halide imaging. The transition from chemical to digital imaging only partly negates Kodak's traditional capabilities. C. K. Prahalad, the guru of competence-based strategy, who played a key role in shaping Kodak's early-1990s strategic vision of becoming a leader in digital imaging, sees Kodak's imaging capabilities as transcending specific imaging technologies. Fundamental to Kodak's ability to make the transition from chemical to digital imaging is its color management capability. And, even with digital images, for most uses users prefer a printed version. In the transfer of digital images to paper, Kodak possesses a powerful technology base, especially in thermal printing. In addition, digital imaging R&D stretching back to the early 1980s has given Kodak a strong knowledge base, even though most of this has not yielded success in the market. As *Business Week* observed when Fisher joined Kodak: "The basic know-how of combining electronic image capture and color management has been Kodak's for years. Kodak is a world-beater in electronic sensors, devices that see and capture an image, and has a raft of patents in color thermal printing. It also has the best understanding of color management software, which matches the colors you see on the screen with what's on the printed page." The key weakness, noted *Business Week*, was in bringing Kodak's technology to market. Most of Kodak's innovations in digital photography have been high-priced products for the professional market. In the consumer market, Kodak has been handicapped by marketers who have little understanding of the digital world.

In building the technical capabilities necessary to play a leading role in developing the market for digital imaging, Kodak recognized that it must draw upon the resources and capabilities of other companies. To this end, Kodak would need to establish collaborative relationships with companies that were leaders in microelectronics, consumer electronics, and computer software. Yet establishing fruitful collaboration with other companies also requires the managerial capabilities needed to foster and guide inter-firm alliances. Historically, Kodak had been an internally focused, go-it-alone corporation with limited experience of close collaboration with other companies. Yet, if Kodak was to be an architect of the new digital imaging industry and influence, even own, technical standards, it would need to build a network of collaborating companies – in much the same way that Motorola had done in wireless communication. Under Fisher's leadership, Kodak established alliances with Microsoft, Intel, Hewlett-Packard, Canon, and a range of smaller companies.

The role of networks of alliances and collaborative relationships was one factor that distinguished the new world of electronic imaging from Kodak's traditional photographic industry. Another was the sheer pace of change. Traditionally, Kodak had been a technological leader, and, because it had dominated the market for photographic products so effectively, it had been able to choose the pace at which it developed new technologies and the time when they would be embodied in new products. Moreover, the pattern of new product development had been a systematic one that began in the lab and worked through engineering and marketing into new products. The field of microelectronics was altogether a faster-moving field, where no company could expect or hope to dominate any substantial area of technology. The implications for the speed of new product development, for cross-functional integration, and for initiatives unbounded by organizational structure or formalized procedures were far-reaching. A key issue for Kodak was whether its history and location three thousand miles from California's Silicon Valley could permit it to develop the organizational capabilities needed to thrive in a hyper-competitive environment.

To build new technological, product development, and marketing capabilities, Kodak needed to change its culture, and to change its culture it needed new management skills and new management styles. The 1997 refocusing and cost-cutting initiatives were accompanied by major changes among the top management team. A key feature of these changes was bringing in managers whose thinking was not dominated by the Rochester culture. Although Dan Carp (appointed as COO in January 1997), Robert Keegan (new head of the Consumer division), and Patrick Siewart (new head of the Professional division) were all Kodak insiders, all had spent the major part of their careers outside of Rochester. Other top managers were brought from outside the company: Daniel Palumbo, new head of marketing, came from Procter & Gamble; Willy Shih, new head of the Digital Imaging division, had previously worked at Silicon Graphics, DEC, and IBM.

Looking Ahead

George Fisher recognized that the pursuit of leadership in digital imaging must be reconciled with increased profitability and better cash flows. This meant tighter cost control and smaller R&D and capital expenditure budgets. Inevitably, Kodak would need a more selective and parsimonious approach to developing digital imaging. In particular, it would be forced to rely increasingly upon collaboration with other companies. The challenge of maintaining leadership in digital imaging and playing a central role in setting industry standards for digital images was daunting given the diversity and rapid development of the core technologies and the extent of competition from other companies. Moreover, the finances available were limited by the factors pressuring Kodak's traditional photographic business, notably continued competition from Fuji and the Asian economic crisis.

At a press conference in New York in May 1998, Fisher outlined the key elements of his strategy for realizing Kodak's digital future while continuing to reduce Kodak's cost base:

As you know, we met today with members of the Institutional Investors Community. We had one key theme for that meeting, change. How much Kodak is changing – and will change – as we create a business model to reduce our cost structure and enable us to grow.

Our 1997 performance was unacceptable. So we're changing the way we do business. Here, are some examples:

- Our shift to a performance-based culture is moving ahead rapidly. In less than a year, roughly one-third of our senior management team has changed.
- We're taking large amounts of cost out of the company, faster than we ever have;
- We're changing the business model, which will enable us to operate at lower gross profit margins;
- We're strengthening Kodak's worldwide marketing capability;
- In digital, digitization and networking, we are expanding through partnerships; and,
- We're repositioning into new businesses, such as Kodak Polychrome Graphics.

These changes are going to get this company back on the path to profitable growth. Stated succinctly, this is our strategy:

Our business is pictures – enabling consumers and business customers around the world to take, make and use pictures for memories, for information, or for entertainment, whenever and wherever they desire.

We will grow by fulfilling our customers' needs better than anyone. In so doing, our objective is:

- To grow our global market share;
- To provide unparalleled levels of customer and employee satisfaction; and,
- To achieve at least a 10% average increase in earnings per share, over time.

Now let me give you a progress report on our business model and the cost-reduction changes. First, we are on track to instill a performance-based culture throughout Kodak. Since we met with you last May, we have installed new leadership in key areas. In addition, since last May, we've placed six new directors on Kodak's Board.

In our cost-reduction program, we are on track to take out at least $1 billion by year-end 1999. We will exit 1998 with overall costs reduced by $500 million. As promised, we are doing this:

By trimming SG&A; By refocusing our R&D investment; By driving down Cost of Goods Sold; and, By changing how we participate in digital.

In terms of SG&A, worldwide employment is down over 9,000 positions, or 9%, from total employment of just over 100,500 in the third quarter last year. We are on plan to achieve the overall reductions we told you about last fall.

In Research & Development, we are on track to remove $100-to-$150 million by the end of 1998. We're concentrating on technology areas that have the most meaningful prospects for us.

In Cost of Goods Sold, we are on track to double the cost-of-quality improvements we currently bring to the bottom line. Through the first quarter, we have achieved $60 million in COGS productivity improvements.

In marketing, we are putting in place programs that will make better use of the power of the Kodak brand. Among other actions, we are adding marketing talent – and revamping our worldwide Consumer marketing structure.

Now, turning to digital imaging: We are aggressively trimming our losses in digital imaging throughout Kodak. In the first quarter, our losses were $55 million, down from approximately $130 million in the fourth quarter, and $150 million in the third quarter of '97.

To improve performance, we are finding partners to share development expense, technical expertise, and risk and reward – partners like PictureVision, Heidelberg, and Sun Chemical. We announced another new partner yesterday, a very important one: Intel. And this partnership is – if you'll excuse the pun – "picture perfect."

Two premier global brands – Kodak and Intel – are joining together in a multi-year agreement to dramatically expand the picture business and jump-start our digital imaging strategy.

Building on each company's distinctive strengths, we will pioneer new ways to take, make and use pictures. Our collaboration will provide a new growth opportunity for film as the affordable, convenient, easy pathway to digital imaging. Together, we are committing about $150 million over three years to promote digital imaging products and services.

For consumers, this important agreement means that new ways to "take pictures further" through digitization and electronic imaging become convenient, affordable and accessible very soon. This happens no matter how "wired" or "unwired" those consumers may be.

For example, our agreement envisions that in 1999, with Intel's collaboration, our U.S. Qualex photofinishing labs will be able to convert consumers' roll film into Picture CDs at prices – and on turnaround schedules – comparable to today's conventional photoprocessing. We will have a fall market test before we do this.

But Picture CDs are only the beginning. We will also work with Intel to standard digital camera reference designs. Together, our two companies are best-positioned to set standards for critical digital imaging components and technology.

Expect to hear more from us next month about what the Kodak–Intel partnership will offer.

Let me also briefly update you now on where we are with PictureVision. We are in the process of consolidating the Kodak Picture Network with the PictureVision network, into a common service called "Kodak PhotoNet Online." This will take about another 60 days. The consolidation accelerates our growth in network services by at least 18 months, while containing our investment.

The consolidated network forms the foundation for an industry-leading, retailer-friendly photo network service, with unmatched reach and rapidly growing membership.

Kodak PhotoNet Online will be accessible in the U.S. at more than 9,000 retail points served by PictureVision . . . at 40,000 locations served by Qualex . . . and from home desktops. Longer-term, Kodak Picture Maker kiosks will also join the network. We have over 13,000 of these kiosks in place now, and expect to add about 5,000 more over the coming year. By offering consumers an easy way to re-use images that were first captured on film, Kodak PhotoNet Online is yet another way we are expanding the picture business.

I also want to comment on how Kodak's digital performance is improving, relative to the three "investment categories" we outlined last November. Those three categories are:

- Non-strategic, non-performers to quit or sell
- Strategic performers to strengthen and keep
- Strategic investments that continue to drive the digital opportunity

As we told you in November, we are exiting businesses that we no longer view as strategically important to our focus on pictures – and that are not generating value. For example, we are exiting the low-end photo scanner business, and we have ceased developing CD writers. We have also announced that we will cease the manufacture of 14-inch optical disks.

Sub-$1,000 consumer digital cameras are an example of a digital imaging opportunity in the second category: areas to strengthen and grow. We continue to be a leader in the sub-$1,000 consumer digital camera market.

The new Intel relationship is an example of the third category: strategic digital investments that create new opportunities. We believe digital imaging growth will increase as images captured on film are digitized – so they can be shared, stored, manipulated or printed on-demand.

Most importantly, a consensus was building within Kodak as to the overall direction of the company's development of digital technology and digital imaging products. "If we think our past was film and our future is digital, we're going to have problems. But if we think of our past being pictures and our future being pictures, we'll use whatever technologies are available," said Fisher. As Willy Shih learned when he arrived at Kodak, digitization does not necessarily mean digital cameras. The key is to predict which aspects of imaging are most appropriate to digitization, and to develop products and systems that bring new technologies to market when the consumer is ready to embrace them. For the next few years Kodak is focusing more on digitalization of image manipulation, storage, and transfer than on digital image capture. In the consumer market, silver halide imaging is still vastly superior to digital imaging in terms of resolution and cost; however, there is great customer value to be gained from using digital technology to manipulate, store, retrieve, and print. Once scanned, digital images can be sent to relatives over the Net or be manipulated in various ways. Kodak's Image Magic print kiosks allow you to have your face attached to the body of a cheerleader. Image Magic Theatre allows you to pose with the Land Rover on Mars or with Godzilla.

That said, digital cameras are already an important battleground where Kodak is keen to establish leadership against both camera companies (Fuji, Canon, Olympus) and electronics companies (Hewlett-Packard, Epson). Shih reports: "We have a 20% world market share. We are among the top in dollar share in the U.S., we are No. 1 in Europe, and we do well in Japan. We have to pick where we add value and commoditize where we can't." To help its worldwide digital camera sales, Kodak bought 51 percent of Japan's Chinon Industries last year and will use the company for assembling the newest digital models.[30]

All these products are mere stepping-stones along the road to Kodak's digital future. Commercial and market success in these products is critical to Kodak building a market presence and providing cash flows to support Kodak's continuing investment in digital imaging. However, even more important is Kodak's ability to establish leadership in the underlying technologies of digital image capture, and image manipulation and transfer, through the software needed for file editing, file compression, and color management.

NOTES

1. S. C. Wheelwright and K. B. Clark, *Revolutionizing Product Development: Quantum Leaps in Speed, Efficiency and Quality*, New York: The Free Press (1992), pp. 151–5.

2. Paul Ericson, "Struggling with success," *Rochester Business Journal*, July 2, 1990.

3. Michael Cosgrove, "Executive dustup begs question: Can giant Kodak ever change?" *Business First–Buffalo*, May 10, 1993.

4. Linda Grant, "Can Fisher focus Kodak?" *Fortune Magazine*, January 13, 1997.

5. Ronald E. Yates, "Fisher exposes Kodak to Motorola experience: CEO sharpens focus, looks to technology," *Chicago Tribune*, April 14, 1996.

6. "Six Sigma" is a TQM process that attempts to approach zero defects in production.

7. Grant, "Can Fisher focus Kodak?"

8. Linda Grant, "The bears back off Kodak," *Fortune Magazine*, June 24, 1996.

9. Address to the Academy of Management, Boston, August 1997.

10. "Kodak's New Focus," *Business Week*, January 30, 1995, pp. 62–8.

11. http://www.kodak.com/aboutKodak/kodakHistory/kodak.shtml

12. Wheelwright and Clark "Revolutionizing product development."

13. Eastman Kodak Company, "Kodak leaders outline road ahead to get Kodak 'back on track'", Kodak press release, November 11, 1997.

14. http://www.moneynet.com/Inc.Link/cp.mhtml?HUB=MONEYNET&SEC=EK

15. There are presently over 100 corporate supporters of the FlashPix standard.

16. John C. Dvorak, "Inside track," *PC Magazine*, March 23, 1998.

17. Lisa Griem, "Starting to click: Retailers expect hot holiday sales of digital cameras this year," *Rocky Mountain News*, November 17, 1997.

18. William Patalon III, "Intel invades digital camera arena," *Rochester Democrat and Chronicle*, November 2, 1997.

19. "Nine companies form digital photo group," *Computer Link*, October 7, 1997.

20. Acquired from "Digital Camera Marketplace," http://www.mindspring.com/~koehncke/marketpl.htm

21. "Digital photography: Casio adapts its strategy," *Les Echos*, March 16, 1998.

22. Ibid.

23. "Japan's photographic industry," *The Economist*, August 30, 1997.

24. "Sony leads the U.S. market in digital camera sales," *Business Wire*, February 10, 1998.

25. Jim Seymour, "PC hardware under the tree," *PC Magazine*, January 6, 1998.

26. Eric Nee, "What have you invented for me lately?" *Forbes*, July 28, 1997.

27. More than half of the company's orders in 1995 were for products introduced during the last two years. *HP: Hazard-based Safety Engineering*, 2.

28. Edward W. Desmond, "What's ailing Kodak?" *Fortune*, October 27, 1997.

29. Ibid.

30. "Why Kodak still isn't fixed," *Fortune*, May 11, 1998.

CHAPTER SIX

ORGANIZATIONAL RESTRUCTURING WITHIN THE ROYAL DUTCH/SHELL GROUP

Robert M. Grant prepared this case solely to provide material for class discussion. The author does not intend to illustrate either the effective or ineffective handling of a management situation. The author may have disguised certain names or other identifying information to protect confidentiality.

In 1998, the Royal Dutch/Shell Group of Companies (Shell) was emerging from one of the most ambitious and far-reaching organizational restructurings of its 91-year history. The restructuring had involved the shift from a predominantly geographically organized structure to a primarily business sector-organized structure, the elimination of over 1,000 corporate positions, the sale of much of Shell's London headquarters, and a redesign in systems of coordination and control.

The restructuring had been precipitated by a combination of factors, the implication of which was the realization that Shell would need to change the way it did business if it was to retain its position as the world's largest energy and chemicals company and offer an adequate return to shareholders in a deteriorating industry environment.

By 1997–98, it was clear that the changes were bearing fruit. Head office costs had been reduced and the benefits of improved coordination at the sectoral level were evident from the ongoing restructuring within Chemicals and the merging of European downstream activities into a joint venture with Texaco. However, with oil prices falling below $15 a barrel and competition for new investment opportunities increasing sharply, Shell's bottom line deteriorated substantially between 1996 and 1998.

At the same time, Shell's competitors were not standing still. BP, once government-owned and highly bureaucratized, had become one of the world's most dynamic, profitable, and widely admired oil majors, and its merger with Amoco would make it almost as big as Shell. Mobil, Chevron, Texaco, and Arco had emerged from phases of restructuring much leaner and more entrepreneurially driven. In terms of financial performance, Shell remained in the shadow of Exxon, which showed a remarkable capacity to defy falling oil prices and world economic turmoil to consistently generate a return on capital that was far superior to that of Shell.

The announcement of Shell's third-quarter earnings for 1998 renewed anxieties among Shell executives and external observers over the future of the Group. While there was consensus that the changes made in the 1995 restructuring were broadly in the right direction, there was a growing feeling that the reorganization had not gone far enough. Shell remained a highly complex organization where lines of responsibility and accountability were diffused, central direction remained weak, and a highly decentralized organization coexisted with a large corporate bureaucracy. Had enough been done to squeeze excess costs out of Shell and to turn its sprawling multinational empire into an enterprise capable of deploying its huge resources with speed and clear direction?

HISTORY OF THE ROYAL DUTCH/SHELL GROUP

The Royal Dutch/Shell Group is unique among the world's oil majors. It was formed from the 1907 merger of the assets and operations of the Netherlands-based Royal Dutch Petroleum Company and the British-based Shell Transport and Trading Company. It is the world's biggest and oldest joint venture. Both parent companies trace their origins to the Far East in the 1890s.

Marcus Samuel inherited a half share in his father's seashell trading business. His business visits to the Far East made him aware of the potential for supplying kerosene from the newly developing Russian oilfields around Baku to the large markets in China and the Far East for oil suitable for lighting and cooking. Seeing the opportunity for exporting kerosene from the Black Sea coast through the recently opened Suez canal to the Far East, Samuel invested in a new tanker, the *Murex*. In 1892, the *Murex* delivered 4,000 tons of Russian kerosene to Bangkok and Singapore. In 1897, Samuel formed the Shell Transport and Trading Company, with a pecten shell as its trademark, to take over his growing oil business.

At the same time, August Kessler was leading a Dutch company to develop an oilfield in Sumatra in the Dutch East Indies. In 1896 Henri Deterding joined Kessler and the two began building storage and transportation facilities and a distribution network in order to bring their oil to market.

The expansion of both companies was supported by the growing demand for oil resulting from the introduction of the automobile and oil-fuelled ships. In 1901 Shell began purchasing Texas crude, and soon both companies were engaged in fierce competition with John D. Rockefeller's Standard Oil. Faced with the might of Standard Oil, Samuel and Deterding (who had succeeded Kessler as chairman of Royal Dutch) began cooperating, and in 1907 the business interests of the two companies were combined into a single group, with Royal Dutch owning a 60 percent share and Shell a 40 percent share (a ratio that has remained constant to this day).

The group grew rapidly, expanding East Indies production and acquiring producing interests in Romania (1906), Russia (1910), Egypt (1911), the US (1912), Venezuela (1913), and Trinidad (1914). In 1929 Shell entered the chemicals business, and in 1933 Shell's interests in the US were consolidated into the Shell Union Oil Corporation. By 1938, Shell crude oil production stood at almost 580,000 barrels per day out of a world total of 5,720,000.

The post-war period began with rebuilding war-devastated refineries and tanker fleet, and continued with the development of new oilfields in Venezuela, Iraq, the Sahara, Canada, Colombia, Nigeria, Gabon, Brunei, and Oman. In 1959, a joint Shell/Exxon venture discovered one of the world's largest natural gas fields at Groningen in the Netherlands. This was followed by several gas finds in the southern North Sea; and then between 1971 and 1976 Shell made a series of major North Sea oil and gas finds.

During the 1970s, Shell, like the other majors, began diversifying outside of petroleum:

- In 1970 it acquired Billiton, an international metals mining company, for $123 million.
- In 1973 it formed a joint venture with Gulf to build nuclear reactors.
- In 1976–7 it acquired US and Canadian coal companies.
- In 1977 it acquired Witco Chemical's polybutylene division.

By the beginning of the 1980s, Shell had built global metals and coal businesses and established several smaller ventures including forestry in Chile and New Zealand, flower growing in the Netherlands, and biotechnology in Europe and the US.

The 1980s saw a reversal of Shell's diversification strategy with several divestments of "non-core businesses" and a concentration on oil and gas – especially upstream. One of Shell's major thrusts was to increase its presence within the US. After acquiring Belridge Oil of California, it made its biggest investment of the period when it acquired the minority interests in its US subsidiary Shell Oil for $5.4 billion.

SHELL'S ORGANIZATION STRUCTURE PRIOR TO 1995

Shell's uniqueness stems from its structure as a joint venture and from its internationality – it has been described as one of the world's three most international organizations, the other two being the Roman Catholic Church and the United Nations. However, its organizational structure is more complex than either of the other two organizations. The structure of the Group may be looked at in terms of the different companies which comprise Royal Dutch/Shell and their links of ownership and control, which Shell refers to as *governance responsibilities*. The Group's structure may also be viewed from a management perspective – how is Royal Dutch/Shell actually managed? The day-to-day management activities of the Group, which Shell refers to as *executive responsibilities*, are complex, and the structure through which the Group is actually managed does not correspond very closely to the formal structure.

The Formal Structure

From an ownership and legal perspective, the Royal Dutch/Shell Group of Companies comprises four types of company:

- *The parent companies.* Royal Dutch Petroleum Company N.V. of the Netherlands and the Shell Transport and Trading Company plc of the UK own the shares of the group holding companies (from which they receive dividends) in the proportions 60 percent and 40 percent. Each company has its shares separately listed on the stock exchanges of Europe and the US, and each has a separate Board of Directors.
- *The group holding companies.* Shell Petroleum N.V. of the Netherlands and The Shell Petroleum Company Ltd. of the UK hold shares in both the service companies and the operating companies of the Group. In addition, Shell Petroleum N.V. also owns the shares of Shell Petroleum Inc. of the US, which itself is the parent of Shell Oil Company.
- *The service companies.* During the early 1990s, there were nine service companies located either in London or The Hague. They were:
    - –Shell Internationale Petroleum Maatschappij B.V.
    - –Shell Internationale Chemie Maatschappij B.V.
    - –Shell International Petroleum Company Limited
    - –Shell International Chemical Company Limited
    - –Billiton International Metals B.V.
    - –Shell International Marine Limited
    - –Shell Internationale Research Maatschappij B.V.
    - –Shell International Gas Limited
    - –Shell Coal International Limited

    The service companies provide advice and services to the operating companies; however, they are not responsible for operations.
- *The operating companies* (or "opcos") comprise some 200 companies in over 100 countries (the 1993 annual report listed 244 companies in which Shell held 50 percent or more ownership). They varied in size from Shell Oil Company, one of the largest petroleum companies in the US in its own right, to small marketing companies such as Shell Bahamas and Shell Cambodia Company. Almost all of the operating companies operate within a single country. Some had activities within a single sector (exploration and production (E&P), refining, marketing, coal, or gas); others (such as Shell UK, Shell Canada, and Norske Shell) operated across multiple sectors. Figure 6.1 shows the formal structure of the Group.

Coordination and Control

Managerial control of the Group is vested in the Committee of Managing Directors (CMD), which forms the Group's top management team. During the early 1990s, the Committee comprised five Managing Directors. These were the three-member Man-

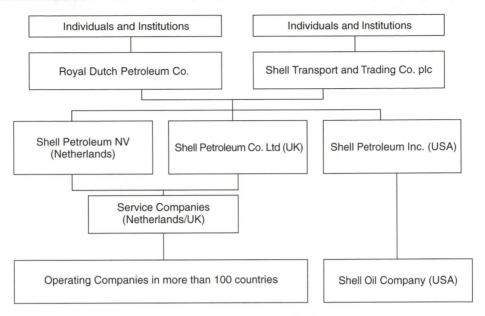

Figure 6.1 The formal structure of the Royal Dutch/Shell Group

agement Board of Royal Dutch Petroleum and the Chairman and Vice Chairman of Shell Transport and Trading. The chairmanship of CMD rotates between the President of Royal Dutch Petroleum and the Managing Director of Shell Transport and Trading. Thus, in 1993, Cor Herkstroter (President of Royal Dutch) took over from J. S. Jennings (Managing Director of Shell Transport and Trading) as Chairman of CMD, and Jennings became Vice Chairman of CMD. Because executive power is vested in a committee rather than a single chief executive, Shell has lacked the strong individual leadership that has characterized oil majors with authoritarian CEOs wielding centralized power.

The CMD provides the primary linkage between the formal (or *governance*) structure and the management (or *executive*) structure of the Group. The CMD links together the parent companies and the group holding companies since the members are Board Members of both.

The combination of diffused executive power at the top together with operating authority and financial responsibility dispersed through nearly 250 operating companies has meant that, compared with every other oil major, Shell was highly decentralized. However, the operational and economic realities of the oil industry meant that each operating company could not be autonomous – the companies were interdependent through the linkages between upstream and downstream, between refining and chemicals, and through common financial and technological needs. Within the Group, coordination was achieved through the service companies. During the early 1960s, Shell created, with the help of McKinsey & Company, a matrix structure within its service companies to manage its operating companies. This structure was viewed as a critical ingredient of Shell's ability to reconcile the independence

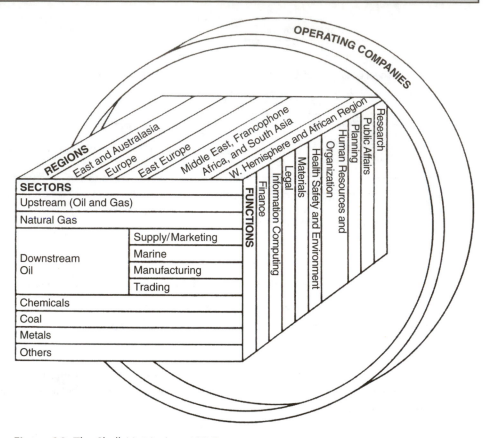

Figure 6.2 The Shell Matrix (pre-1996)

of its operating companies with effective coordination of business, regional, and functional commonalties. This matrix organization continued into the 1990s (see Figure 6.2).

The three dimensions of this matrix were represented by principal executives of the service companies, who were designated "coordinators." Thus, the senior management team at the beginning of 1995 included the following:

> *Committee of Managing Directors*
> ■ Chairman
> ■ Vice Chairman
> ■ + three other Managing Directors
>
> *Principal executives of the service companies*
> ■ Regional coordinators:
>   –Europe
>   –Western Hemisphere and Africa
>   –Middle East, Francophone Africa, and South Asia
>   –East and Australasia

- Sector coordinators:
  - –E&P Coordinator
  - –Chemicals Coordinator
  - –Coal/Natural Gas Coordinator
  - –Metals Coordinator
  - –President – Shell International Trading
  - –Marine Coordinator
  - –Supply and Marketing Coordinator
- Functional coordinators:
  - –Director of Finance
  - –Group Treasurer
  - –Group Planning Coordinator
  - –Manufacturing Coordinator
  - –Group HR and Organization Coordinator
  - –Legal Coordinator
  - –Group Public Affairs Coordinator
  - –Group Research Coordinator
  - –Director of the Hague Office
  - –Director of the London Office

Strategic Planning at Shell

Within this three-way matrix, it has traditionally been the geographical dimension that was the most important. At the root of this emphasis on coordination within geographical areas was the existence of the operating companies as the basic operational, financial, and strategic entities – almost all the operating companies were defined on a country basis. This was reinforced through the strategic planning process, which put its main emphasis on planning at the national and regional levels.

Shell's planning system was viewed as one of the most sophisticated and effective of any large multinational. It was much discussed and widely imitated. Its main features were the following:

- A strong emphasis upon long-term strategic thinking. Shell's planning horizon extended 20 years into the future – much further than the four- or five-year planning that most companies engage in. Unlike most other companies, the basis for these strategic plans were not *forecasts* but *scenarios* – alternative views of the future which allowed managers to consider strategic responses to the different ways in which the future might unfold.
- A breadth of vision, and emphasis on the generation and application of ideas rather than a narrow focus on financial performance. Shell's planning department was receptive to concepts and ideas drawn from economics, psychology, biochemistry, biology, mathematics, anthropology, and ecology. As a consequence, Shell pioneered many new management techniques, including multiple scenario analysis, business portfolio planning, cognitive

mapping, and the application of organizational learning concepts to planning processes.

■ More generally, Shell was in the vanguard of the transition from the role of the strategy function as *planning* towards one where the primary roles of strategy were encouraging *thinking about the future*, developing the capacity for *organizational learning*, promoting *organizational dialogue*, and facilitating organizational *adaptation* to a changing world.

Planning at Shell was primarily bottom-up. The CMD identified key issues, set strategic direction, and approved major projects, and the planning department formulated the scenarios. However, most strategic decisions and initiatives originated among the operating companies. The role of the planning staff and the regional and sector coordinators was to coordinate the operating company strategic plans.

FORCES FOR CHANGE

Between the early 1970s and the early 1990s, the world petroleum industry was transformed by a number of fundamental changes.[1] The growing power of the producer countries was seen not just in the sharp rise in crude oil prices during the first oil shock of 1974, but even more fundamentally in the nationalization of the oil reserves of the international majors. By the 1990s, the list of the world's top 20 oil and gas producers was dominated by state-owned companies such as Saudi Aramco, Petroleos de Venezuela, Kuwait Oil, the Iranian and Iraqi national oil companies, Pemex (Mexico), and Russia's Gasprom and Lukoil. In addition, the old-established majors faced competition from other sources. The "new majors," integrated oil companies such as Elf Aquitaine (France), Total (France), ENI (Italy), Nippon Oil (Japan), Neste (Finland), and Respol (Spain), were expanding rapidly, while in North America and the North Sea independent E&P companies such as Enterprise Oil, Triton, and Apache were becoming significant global players. Between 1970 and 1990, the share of world oil production of the "Seven Sisters" fell from 31 percent to 7 percent.[2]

The loss of control over their sources of crude oil was a devastating blow for the majors – their whole strategy of vertical integration had been based around the concept of controlling risk through owning the downstream facilities needed to provide secure outlets for their crude oil. As market transactions for crude oil and refinery outputs became increasingly important, so prices became much more volatile. Between 1981 and 1986, crude prices fell from $42 a barrel to $9 before briefly recovering to $38 in the wake of the Iraqi invasion of Kuwait, and then resuming their downward direction.

Between 1985 and 1993, almost all the world's oil majors underwent far-reaching restructuring. Restructuring involved radical simultaneous changes in strategy and organizational structure in a compressed time-frame. Key features of restructuring by the oil majors were:

■ Reorienting their goals around shareholder value maximization.
■ Greater selectivity in their strategies, involving the divestment of unprofitable businesses, refocusing around core petroleum and gas businesses, withdraw-

TABLE 6.1
Employment among the oil majors ('000)

	1996	1993	1990	1995
Shell	101	117	136	142
Elf Aquitaine	85	94	92	78
ENI	83	106	128	125
Exxon	79	91	101	147
Total	57	50	43	41
BP	53	73	118	132
Mobil	43	62	68	72
Amoco	42	46	53	48
Chevron	41	48	50	62
Texaco	29	33	40	57
Atlantic Richfield	23	25	28	31

Source: Fortune.

ing from countries where investments were not justified by the returns being earned, and outsourcing those activities that could be performed more efficiently by outside suppliers.

- Cutting back on staff, especially at the corporate level. (Table 6.1 shows changes in numbers of employees among the majors.)
- Reducing excess capacity through refinery closures and sales and scrapping of ocean-going tankers.
- Decentralization of decision-making from corporate to divisional levels and from divisional to business unit levels at the same time as giving divisions and business units full profit and loss responsibility.
- Shifting the basis of organizational structure from geographical organization around countries and regions to worldwide product divisions (many of the majors formed worldwide divisions for upstream activities, downstream activities, and chemicals).
- "Delayering" through eliminating administrative layers within hierarchical structures. For example, Amoco broke up its three major divisions (upstream, downstream, and chemicals) and had 17 business groups reporting direct to the corporate center. Mobil also broke up its divisional structure, and created 13 business groups. (The Appendix shows the organization structure of several of the majors.)

SHELL, 1990–1995

The only one of the major oil companies which did not undergo radical restructuring between 1985 and 1993 was Shell. The absence of restructuring at Shell appeared to reflect two factors:

- Shell's flexibility had meant that Shell had been able to adjust to a changing oil industry environment without the need for discontinuous change. For example, Shell had been a leader in rationalizing excess capacity in refining and shipping, in upgrading its refineries with catalytic crackers, in establishing arms-length relationships between its production units and its refineries, in moving into natural gas, and in taking advantage of opportunities for deepwater exploration.
- Because of Shell's management structure, in particular the absence of a CEO with autocratic powers, Shell was much less able to initiate the kind of top-down restructuring driven by powerful CEOs such as Larry Rawl at Exxon, Jim Kinnear at Texaco, Serge Tchuruk at Total, or Franco Bernabe at ENI.

Nevertheless, during the early 1990s, a combination of forces was pushing the CMD towards more radical top-down change. The most influential of these pressures was dissatisfaction over financial performance. The early 1990s were difficult years for the industry. The fall in oil prices to the mid-teens meant that returns from the traditional fount of profit – upstream – were meager. At the same time refining and chemicals suffered from widespread excess capacity and price wars. Yet investors and the financial community were putting increased pressure on companies for improved return to shareholders. The CMD was forced to shift its attention from long-term development to short-term financial results. Against a variety of benchmarks, Shell's profit performance looked less than adequate:

- Cost of capital was the most fundamental of these – during the early 1990s Shell was earning a return on equity that barely covered the cost of equity.
- Long-term stability was a further goal. Top management asked, "What rate of return is needed to provide the cash flow needed to pay dividends and replace assets and reserves?" The returns of 1990–4 were somewhat below this figure.
- Shell's rates of return, margins, and productivity ratios were below those of several leading competitors.

Table 6.2 shows performance data for Shell during 1992–7.

Evidence of the potential for performance improvement through restructuring was available from inside as well as from outside the Group. During the late 1980s and early 1990s quite radical restructuring measures among the operating companies in Canada, the US, the UK, South Africa, Germany, Malaysia, and France revealed convincing evidence of the potential for cost savings through changes in organizational structure, process redesign, and outsourcing.

The top managers of those operating companies that had been in the vanguard of cost cutting were increasingly resentful of the corporate structure. By 1994, Shell employed 6,800 people in its central organization (in London and The Hague) and in its corporate research and support functions. Even allowing for the differences in organizational structure between Shell and its competitors, this was bigger than the corporate and divisional administration of any other oil and gas major. As the opcos struggled to reduce their own costs and improve their bottom-line performance, so they became antagonistic towards what they saw as a bloated corporate center

TABLE 6.2
Royal Dutch/Shell Group: performance data, 1992–1997

	1997	1996	1995	1994	1993	1992
Gross sales ($ bill.)	171.7	172.0	150.7	129.1	125.8	128.4
Operating profit ($ bill.)	15.3	17.1	12.5	9.6	8.9	9.2
Net income ($ bill.)	7.8	8.9	6.9	6.2	4.5	5.4
ROCE (%)	11.4	13.2	10.6	10.4	7.9	9.0
ROE (%)	12.8	15.1	11.8	11.5	8.7	9.7
Capital expenditure ($ bill.)	13.4	12.1	11.8	10.5	9.5	10.4
Employees ('000)	105	104	106	107	117	127

The data are for continuing operations only. Hence, Shell's numbers of employees shown in Table 6.1 differ from those here because of acquisitions and disposals.

whose support and services were little valued by the opcos. Many viewed the elaborate matrix structure as failing to provide effective coordination of the opcos. For example, despite the important roles of the regional coordinators, in Europe

- the UK refineries were selling into Spain and Portugal;
- Shell's Marseilles refinery was supplying Belgium;
- natural geographical units such as Scandinavia were split between different opcos; and
- Europe-wide initiatives such as launching the Shell credit card had faced huge difficulties.

As Chairman Cor Herkstroter noted:

> Many Operating Companies are sending us clear signals that they feel constrained by the management processes of the Service Companies, that the support and guidance from them is ineffective or inefficient, and that the services are too costly. They do not see the eagerness for cost reductions in the Operating Companies sufficiently mirrored in the center.[3]

The essential issue, however, was to prepare Shell for an increasingly difficult business environment:

> While our current organization and practices have served us very well for many years, they were designed for a different era, for a different world. Over the years significant duplication and confusion of roles at various levels in the organization have developed. Many of you notice this on a day-to-day basis.
>
> We anticipate increasingly dynamic competition. We see the business conditions of today, with flat margins and low oil prices continuing into the future. In addition, there will be no let up on all players in the industry to strive for higher productivity, innovation quality and effectiveness.

Our vision of the future is one of increasing competitive surprise and discontinuity, of increasing change and differentiation in skills required to succeed; and of increasing demands by our people at the front line for accountability within a framework of clear business objectives, and with access to a global source of specialist expertise.[4]

The Change Process

Within Shell, proponents of organizational change, including the heads of several of the opcos, the finance function, and Group Planning, had had little success in persuading the Committee of Managing Directors of the need for large-scale change. In May 1993, Cor Herkstroter took over as Chairman of the CMD. A Dutch accountant, who had spent his entire career at Shell, Herkstroter was an unlikely pioneer of change. Fellow executives described him as a private, Old World personality without much charisma, and with a preference for written communication. Nevertheless, Herkstroter was widely respected for his intelligence and courage. "He's Shell's Gorbachev," said Philip Mirvis, a consultant working with Noel Tichy at Shell.[5]

Faced with growing evidence of suboptimal financial performance and an over-complex, inward-looking organizational structure, Herkstroter called a meeting of Shell's 50 top managers at Hartwell House, an English country manor, in May 1994. The meeting was a shock for the CMD. The request for frank discussions of the reasons for Shell's lagging return on capital provided a series of barbed attacks on top management and sharp criticism of the service company organization. The corporate center was castigated for taking months to approve operating company budgets and for the general laxness of financial controls. E&P coordinator Robert Sprague tossed a blank transparency onto the overhead projector and commented, "I don't know what to report, this issue is really a mess." The meeting had a powerful impact on the CMD: "We were bureaucratic, inward looking, complacent, self-satisfied, arrogant," observed then-Vice Chairman John Jennings. "We tolerated our own underperformance. We were technocratic and insufficiently entrepreneurial."[6] The outcome was the appointment of a high-level team to study Shell's internal organization and come up with options for redesign.

The team, set up in July 1994, was headed by Ernst van Mourik-Broekman, the head of HR, together with Basil South from Group Planning, Group Treasurer Stephen Hodge, an executive from Shell France, and the head of Shell's gas business in the Netherlands. The internal team was joined by three senior consultants from McKinsey & Company: two from the Amsterdam office and one from the London office.

The starting point for the internal team was a program of interviews with 40–50 managers at different levels within the company. This provided a basis both for assessing the existing structure and for generating ideas for change. The role of the McKinsey consultants was to provide perspective, to challenge the ideas of the Shell team, to introduce the experiences of other large multinationals (ABB for instance), to provide the back-up research needed to refine and test out ideas and concepts, and to organize the program of work and consultation.

By October 1994, the group had prepared a diagnosis of the existing Shell structure together with a suite of options for reorganization. During October and November, a series of workshops were conducted, mainly in London, to explore in greater detail the specific dimensions of change and to clarify and evaluate the available options. Each workshop team provided input on a specific area of change. The results of this exercise were written up towards the end of November, and a report was submitted to CMD which identified the areas for change and the options.

During December 1994, the team spent two "away days" with the CMD to identify the objects of change and how the different options related to these. The result was a blueprint which the team wrote up mid-December. After six or seven drafts, the report was approved by CMD during the weekend of Christmas. At the beginning of January, the report was circulated to the chief executives of the main opcos and the coordinators within the service companies with a request for reactions by the end of January. In the meantime, Chairman Herkstroter gave a speech, directed to all company employees, to prepare them for change by indicating the need for change and the likelihood of job losses, but without any specifics as to the organizational changes that were likely to occur.

The driving force behind the redesign was the desire to have a simpler structure in which the reporting relationships would be clearer and thus to allow the corporate center to exert more effective influence and control over the operating companies. A simpler structure would help eliminate some of the cost and inertia of the head office bureaucracies that had built up around Shell's elaborate committee system. There was also a need to improve coordination between the operating companies. This coordination, it was felt, should be based upon the business sectors rather than geographical regions. Globalization of the world economy and the breakdown of vertical integration within the oil majors had meant that most of the majors had reorganized around worldwide business divisions. As was noted above, most of the majors formed upstream, downstream, and chemicals divisions with worldwide responsibility. For Shell, achieving integration between the different businesses within a country or within a region was less important than achieving integration within a business across different countries and regions. For example, in exploration and production, critical issues related to the development and application of new technologies and sharing of best practices. In downstream, the critical issues related to the rationalization of capacity, the pursuit of operational efficiency, and the promotion of the Shell brand.

By the end of January, a broad endorsement had been received. In February a two-day meeting was held with the same group of Shell's 50 senior managers that had initiated the whole process some ten months earlier. The result was a high level of support and surprisingly little dissent. The final approval came from the two parent company Boards. On March 29, 1995, Cor Herkstroter, Chairman of the Committee of Managing Directors, gave a speech to Shell employees worldwide outlining the principal aspects of a radical reorganization of the Group, which were to be implemented at the beginning of 1996.

In the meantime, two totally unexpected events only increased the internal momentum for change. While Shell faulted itself on its ability to produce a return on capital to meet the levels of its most efficient competitors, in managing health, safety, and the environment it considered itself the leader of the pack. Then came the Brent Spar incident. A carefully evaluated plan to dispose of a giant North Sea oil platform in the depths of the Atlantic produced outcry from environmental groups, including Greenpeace. Consumer boycotts of Shell products resulted in massive sales losses, especially in Germany. Within a few months, Shell was forced into an embarrassing reversal of its decision.

A few months later the Nigerian military regime executed Ken Saro-Wiwa, a prominent Nigerian author who had protested Shell's poor environmental record in his country. Again, Shell was found to be flat-footed and inept at managing its public relations over the incident. The handling of the Brent Spar and Nigerian incidents convinced many that Shell's top management was both unresponsive and out of touch. "We had to take a good look at ourselves and say, 'Have we got it right?'" said Mark Moody-Stuart, then a Managing Director. "Previously if you went to your golf club or church and said, 'I work for Shell,' you'd get a warm glow. In some parts of the world that changed a bit."[7]

THE NEW SHELL STRUCTURE

The central feature of the reorganization plan of 1995 was the dismantling of the three-way matrix through which the operating companies had been coordinated since the 1960s. In its place, four business organizations were created to achieve closer integration within each business sector across all countries. It was intended that the new structure would allow more effective planning and control within each of the businesses, remove much of the top-heavy bureaucracy that had imposed a costly burden on the Group, and eliminate the power of the regional fiefdoms. The new structure would strengthen the executive authority of the Committee of Managing Directors by providing a clearer line of command to the business organizations and subsequently to the operating companies, and by splitting central staff functions into a Corporate Center and a Professional Services Organization. The former would support the executive role of the CMD; the latter would produce professional services to companies within the Group. Figure 6.3 shows the new structure.

At the same time, the underlying principles of Shell's organizational structure were reaffirmed:

- The decentralized structure based on the autonomy of the Shell operating companies vis-à-vis the Group was to be maintained.
- The new structure continued the distinction between *governance* and *executive responsibility* which was described above. Thus, the formal structure of parent companies, holding companies, operating companies, and service companies was continued without significant changes. The Boards of these companies discharged the governance functions of the Group including exercise of shareholder rights, the fulfillment of the legal obligations of the companies, and the appointment and supervision of the managers who fulfill executive responsibilities. It was the management structure where the major changes occurred, especially within the service companies.

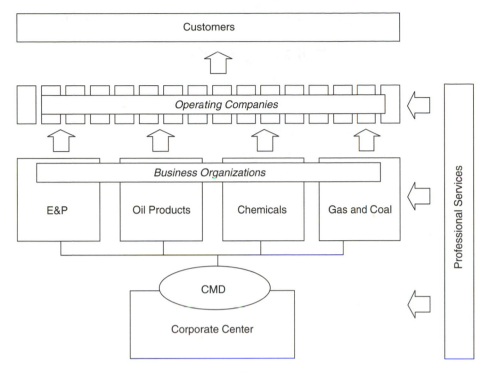

Figure 6.3 Shell's management structure, 1996

The Formal Structure

As noted, the formal corporate structure shown in Figure 6.1 was little changed. The principal changes in the formal structure were changes involving the identities and roles of the service companies to create a closer alignment with the new management structure. Thus, the new Corporate Center and Professional Services Organization were housed within Shell International Ltd. (in London) and Shell International B.V. (in The Hague). Other service companies housed the new Business Organizations. Figure 6.4 shows the relationship between the new management structure and Shell's formal legal structure.

The Management Structure

The new organizational structure can be described in terms of the four new organizational elements – the Business Organizations, the Corporate Center, Professional Services, and the Operating Units – together with the two organizational units that continued from the previous structure, the operating companies and the Committee of Managing Directors.

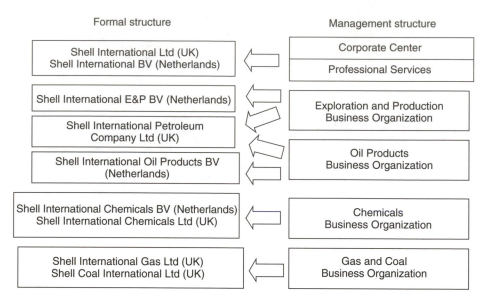

Figure 6.4 The service companies in 1996: links between the formal structure and the management structure

The Business Organizations

The central features of the new organization structure were the new Business Organizations. The CMD was supported by four Business Organizations: E&P ("upstream"), oil products ("downstream"), chemicals, and gas and coal. The Business Organizations were headed by Business Committees made up of a number of Business Directors appointed by the CMD. These Business Directors included:

- Business Directors with responsibility for particular business segments. For example, among the members of the E&P Business Committee in 1998 were J. Colligan, Regional E&P Business Director for Asia-Pacific and South America, H. Roels, Regional E&P Business Director for Middle East and Africa, and R. Sprague, Regional E&P Business Director for Europe.
- Certain of the operating companies were so important that their Chief Executives were also Business Directors. For example, in 1998, the E&P Business Committee included A. Parsley, Managing Director of Shell E&P International Venture B.V., while the Oil Products Business Committee included M. Warwick, President of Shell International Trading and Shipping Co. Ltd., and P. Turberville, President of Shell Europe Oil Products B.V.
- A Business Director for Research and Technical Services.
- A Business Director for Strategy and Business Services.

The Business Committees were accountable to CMD for

- the strategy of their business area;
- endorsing the capital expenditure and financial plans of the operating companies and business segments within their business area;
- appraising operating company and business segment performance; and
- the availability of technical, functional, and business services to the operating companies within their business sector.

Chairing each of the Business Committees was a member of the CMD. Thus, in early 1998, E&P reported to Managing Director P. B. Watts, Oil Products to Managing Director S. L. Miller, Chemicals to Vice Chairman M. Moody-Stuart, and Gas and Coal to Managing Director M. van den Bergh.

The Corporate Center
This supported the CMD in its role in

- setting the direction and strategy of the Group;
- growing and shaping the Group's portfolio of investments and resources;
- enhancing the performance of Group assets; and
- acting as custodian of the Group's reputation, policies, and processes.

In addition, the Corporate Center provided internal and external communication for the CMD. Apart from supporting the work of the CMD, the Corporate Center assisted the parent companies and the group holding companies in managing their financial, tax, and corporate affairs. The Corporate Center represented the other two dimensions of Shell's former matrix organization. For example, the Director for Planning, Environment and External Affairs chaired the meetings of Shell's Technology Council and Health, Safety and Environment Council. Also, the Corporate Advice Director undertook ad hoc country reviews.

The Corporate Center comprised six directorates:

- Planning, Environment and External Affairs
- Corporate Advice (supporting each of the Managing Directors in their regional roles as well as responsibility for IT, security, contracting and procurement)
- Group Treasurer
- Group Controller
- Human Resources
- Legal

In addition to these directorates, the Corporate Center also included the Head of Group Taxation, the Chief Information Officer, the Head of Intellectual Property, the Head of Contracting and Procurement, the Head of Group Security, the Head of Learning, and the Secretary to the CMD.

Professional Services
These new units provided functional support for the operating companies and service companies within the Group. They offered their services on an arms-length

basis and competed with external service providers for the business of the operating companies. They were also able to provide services to third-party customers outside the Group. The services provided included:

- Finance (e.g., treasury services, accounting, tax advice)
- HR (e.g., recruitment, training)
- Legal
- Intellectual property (intellectual property protection, licensing)
- Contracting and procurement
- Group Security (security advice)
- Shell Aircraft Ltd. (corporate jets)
- Office services (e.g., accommodation, personnel services)
- Health (medical services, environmental and occupational health advice)

Each Professional Services unit was headed by the relevant director from the Corporate Center. For example, HR was headed by the HR Director; legal and intellectual property services were headed by the Legal Director.

The operating companies

In the new organizational structure, the operating companies retained their role as the primary business entities within Shell. Each operating company was managed by a Board of Directors and a Chief Executive. The Chief Executive of an operating company was responsible to his/her Board and to his/her Business Director for the effective management of the operating company. The Chief Executive's responsibilities included the following:

- Setting the company's strategic aims against the backdrop of any guidelines established by the Business Committee
- Providing leadership to put the strategic aims into effect and instill an entrepreneurial company culture
- Setting internal financial and operating targets and overseeing their achievement
- Supervising the management of the business and setting priorities
- Effective reporting on the company's activities and results to the Group[8]

Operating Units

The superimposition of the Business Organizations on top of the operating companies created a problem for Shell because the operating companies were defined by country rather than by business sector and included activities which crossed business sectors. Hence, to achieve alignment between the new Business Organizations and the operational activities of the Group, Operating Units were created:

> In the context of the Group organizational structure, Operating Unit refers to the activities in one of the Group Businesses which are operated as a single economic entity. An Operating Unit can coincide with an Operating Company, be a part of an Operating Company or straddle part or all of several Operating Companies.[9]

Thus, where an operating company was in one business only, the operating company was the relevant Operating Unit. However, multi-business operating companies, such as Shell UK and Shell Australia, which included upstream, downstream, chemical, and gas businesses, were divided into separate Operating Units in order to align operating activities with the new Business Organizations. Each of these Operating Units was headed by a manager with executive responsibilities who reported to the relevant Business Director. Where several Operating Units operated in a country under different Chief Executives, the Managing Director with responsibilities for that particular region appointed one of them as a "country chairman" to fulfill country-level responsibilities (with regard to matters of taxation, conformity with national legislation, national government relations, and the like).

In addition, some Operating Units spanned several operating countries. In order to achieve more effective integration across countries and to save on administrative and operating costs, the trend was to form Operating Units which combined businesses in several countries. Thus, in Europe there was a desire to run chemicals and oil products as single business entities.

Changing Culture and Behavior

Changing the organizational structure was seen as insufficient to generate the kinds of performance improvements that Shell thought it needed to move to the head of the pack. The criticisms leveled at Shell for being bureaucratic, inward looking, slow, and unresponsive were not about organizational structure, they were about behavior and attitudes. In any organizational change, a new structure may provide the right context, but ultimately it is the effects on individual and group behavior that are key.

During 1996 and 1997, the Shell management development function moved into a higher gear. Organizational development and change consultants included Noel Tichy from Michigan Business School, Larry Selden from Columbia, McKinsey & Company, Boston Consulting Group, and Coopers & Lybrand. These were in addition to Shell's internal change management team known as LEAP (Leadership and Performance Operations). The result was a substantial increase in Shell's management development and organizational development activities. *Fortune* magazine reported:

> This army has been putting Shell managers through a slew of workshops. In early February, teams from the gasoline retailing business in Thailand, China, Scandinavia and France spent six hours in a bitter Dutch downpour building rope bridges, dragging one another through spider webs of rope, and helping one another climb over 20-foot walls.
>
> The Shell managers especially liked Larry Selden. He teaches people to track their time and figure out whether what they're doing contributes directly to growth of both returns and gross margins. Selden calls this "dot movement," a phrase he has trademarked and which means moving the dot on a graph of growth and returns to the north-east. "The model is very powerful" says Luc Minguet, Shell's retail manager in France. "It's the first time I've seen such a link between the conceptual and the practical. And I realized I was using my time very poorly."

In a particularly revealing exercise, the top 100 Shell executives in May took the Myers-Briggs personality test, a widely-used management tool that classifies people according to 16 psychological types. Interestingly, of its top 100 managers, 86% are "thinkers," people who make decisions based on logic and objective analysis. Of the six-man CMD, 60% are on the opposite scale. They are "feelers" who make decisions based on values and subjective evaluation. No wonder all those "thinkers" had such a hard time understanding the emotion behind Nigeria and Brent Spar. And no wonder the CMD gets frustrated with the inability of the lower ranks to grasp the need for change.[10]

PROGRESS 1996–1998

The most evident short-tem impact of the reorganization was a substantial reduction in Service Company staffs. Towards the end of 1995, Shell began shrinking its head offices in London and The Hague in anticipation of the introduction of the new organizational structure at the beginning of 1996. During 1996, the downsizing of central services and administrative functions within the Service Companies accelerated. During 1996, one of the two towers at the London Shell Centre was sold and was converted into residential apartments.

The quest for cost reductions did not stop at the Service Companies but extended to the operating companies as well. Between 1995 and 1997, unit costs were reduced by 17 percent in real terms, and between 1994 and 1997, savings in procurement costs amounted to $600 million each year. A priority for the Group was rationalization of capacity and reductions in operating costs in its downstream business. To facilitate this, Shell embarked upon three major joint ventures:

- The amalgamation of Shell Oil's downstream assets in the western US with those of Texaco
- The amalgamation of Shell's European downstream businesses with those of Texaco
- The merging of Shell's Australian downstream business with that of Mobil

Restructuring in Shell's other businesses included a swap of oil and gas properties with Occidental and the creation of a single global chemicals business. The chemicals business has demonstrated particularly clearly the benefits of global integration. In addition to cost savings of around 7 percent each year, investment decisions became better coordinated. "The Center's full control over chemicals, for instance, led Shell to put a new polymer plant closer to customers in Geismar, Louisiana, instead of near the existing plant in Britain. Two years ago that plant automatically would have been added to the UK fiefdom."[11]

In September 1998, Mark Moody-Stuart, who had succeeded Cor Herkstroter as Chairman of the CMD in June, announced further restructuring measures aimed at reducing Shell's cost base. Against a background of declining oil and gas prices and weakening margins in refining and chemicals, Moody-Stuart reaffirmed Shell's commitment to the target of 15 percent ROACE (return on average capital employed) by 2001, even though the ROACE for 1998 was expected to be well below the projected level of 12–12.5 percent. While restructuring so far had reduced costs significantly,

TABLE 6.3
**Royal Dutch/Shell Group: financial performance during
first nine months of 1998 ($ bill.)**

	1998	1997
Net sales	21.98	31.09
Net income	4.09	6.12
Net assets	62.67	63.25
Capital expenditure	11.06	9.33

Source: www.shell.com

Moody-Stuart asserted that Shell would be willing to take further radical measures if its programs did not deliver the performance gains that were needed. For example, in refining, Shell was closing its Shellhaven refinery and reducing capacity at Berre in France.

The streamlining of Shell's administrative structure with a view to bringing Shell's operating companies closer to their customers would also continue. To this end, he announced the closures of big national head offices in the UK, the Netherlands, Germany, and France.[12]

Despite the progress in reducing costs and improving responsiveness and global integration, any performance gains from the reorganization and subsequent restructurings were more than offset by the continued deterioration in the business environment of the oil and gas industry. Shell's third-quarter results announced on October 22, 1998 shocked investment analysts with declines in both revenue and net income of about 28 percent for the first nine months of 1998, as compared with the same period in 1997 (see Table 6.3).

TOWARDS A NEW MILLENNIUM

Among Shell-watchers both in the investment community and in the oil business there was little doubt that the 1996 reorganization had contributed substantially to the efficient and effective management of the Group. The stripping away of much of the administrative structure in the Group head offices in London and The Hague, the elimination of the regional coordinating staffs, and the closure of some of Shell's biggest national headquarters not only reduced cost, but seemed to be moving Shell towards a swifter, more direct style of management. The restructuring of chemicals and downstream businesses revealed both a tough-mindedness and a decisiveness that few had associated with the Shell-of-old.

The question in most people's minds was whether Shell had gone far enough. Despite the emphasis on simplicity, accountability, and clear lines of authority, compared with its leading competitors Shell's structure remained byzantine. While the new Business Organizations had done much to eliminate the multiple reporting relationships of the old matrix and provide a basis for greater global integration, there were several features of the new organization that concerned both insiders and outsiders. It was notable that the reorganization had applied to Shell operations outside of North America; Shell Oil of the US continued to lie outside of the new business committees in the same way that it had been outside of the old matrix. Although efforts had been made to improve coordination with Shell Oil (in particular the creation of the global chemicals business that was led by Henkes of Shell Chemicals Inc. of the US), the failure to incorporate Shell's biggest operating company in its reorganization suggested to many that Shell was still overcommitted to preserving the past.

Doubts were also expressed over the extent of Shell's new-found commitment to single-point accountability. Certainly, the dismantling of the old matrix had done much to reduce the diffusion of responsibilities and the multiplicity of reporting channels. Yet the creation of Business Committees to run the new Business Organizations pointed to a continuation of the Shell committee culture with its tradition of collective rather than individual accountability.

Shell's continuing commitment to its tradition of committee-based management and its wariness over the concentration of decision-making power in the hands of individual executives were indicated most clearly by the presence of the Committee of Managing Directors as the Group's top management team. Undoubtedly, the CMD provided a remarkable collection of experience and wisdom. But could such an executive body with its five-yearly rotation of the chairmanship between Dutch and British executives provide the impetus for continued change that would be needed in the new millennium? Increasingly it was being recognized by large, mature organizations that the critical role of top management was not so much to administer the existing organization as to provide the impetus for continued change to meet the requirements of the future. The evidence of business leaders such as Welch at GE, Ioccoca at Chrysler, Martinez at Sears Roebuck, Harvey-Jones at ICI, and Gerstner at IBM is that combating inertia within big, mature corporations requires a powerful CEO with commitment and determination. Shell's 1995–6 reorganization was the result of pressure for change building up over many years. Would the new structure be capable of providing continued adaptation to a rapidly changing business environment, or was the new structure one staging post on the road to further organizational transformation?

APPENDIX
THE ORGANIZATIONAL STRUCTURES OF OTHER OIL MAJORS

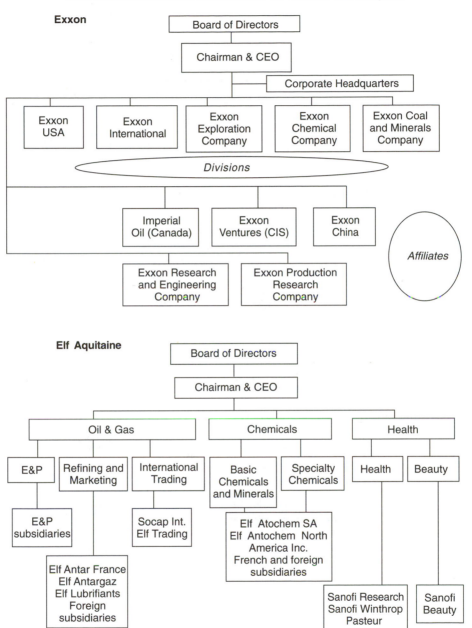

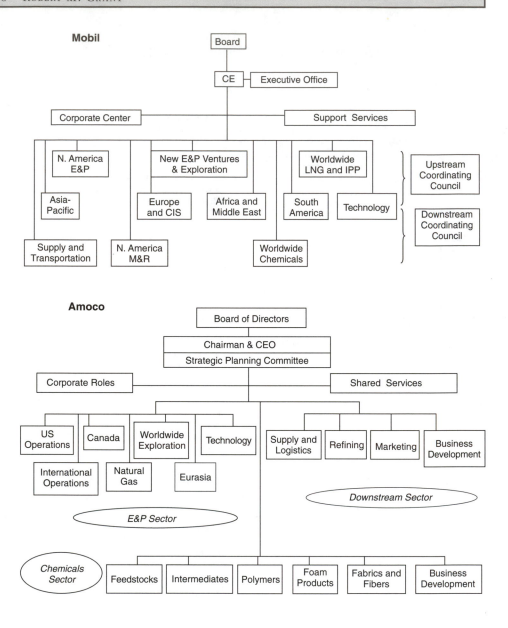

NOTES

1. This section draws from R. Cibin and R. M. Grant, "Restructuring among the world's largest oil majors," *British Journal of Management*. December 1996.

2. The "Seven Sisters" were the original international oil majors: Shell, Exxon, Mobil, BP, Chevron, Texaco, and Gulf. Gulf was acquired by Chevron in 1984.

3. C. A. J. Herkstroter, "Right for the times and right for Shell," Speech delivered in London, March 29, 1995.

4. Ibid.

5. "Why is the world's most profitable company turning itself inside out?" *Fortune*, August 4, 1997, pp. 121–5.

6. Ibid.

7. Ibid.

8. *Reference Guide to Group Organizational Structure*, Shell International Ltd., August 1996.

9. Ibid. p. 17.

10. "Why is the world's most profitable company turning itself inside out?"

11. Ibid.

12. "Shell shapes up for future," Speech by M. Moody-Stuart, San Francisco, September 18, 1998 (www.shell.com).

CHAPTER SEVEN

HARLEY-DAVIDSON, INC., JULY 1998

Robert M. Grant prepared this case, with the assistance of Luis Escudero, Nicole Flavin, Juan Trevino, Chris Gergen, and Bart Quillen, solely to provide material for class discussion. The author does not intend to illustrate either the effective or ineffective handling of a management situation. The author may have disguised certain names or other identifying information to protect confidentiality.

You've shown us how to be the best. You've been leaders in new technology. You've stuck by the basic American values of hard work and fair play . . . Most of all, you've worked smarter, you've worked better, and you've worked together . . . as you've shown again, America is someplace special. We're on the road to unprecedented prosperity . . . and we'll get there on a Harley.

President Ronald Reagan, speech at Harley-Davidson
plant, York, Pennsylvania, May 6, 1987

JULY 1998

Reporting on the company's second-quarter results, Harley-Davidson's president and CEO Jeffrey Bleustein expressed satisfaction at progress during the year:

> In addition to delivering another record quarter, we also achieved several significant milestones. We celebrated our 95th anniversary, introduced a new big twin engine, the Twin Cam 88, and announced plans to establish a motorcycle assembly operation in Brazil. These events created a lot of excitement and are part of our strategy for continuing to grow the worldwide demand for Harley-Davidson motorcycles.[1]

The results for the first half of 1998 were indeed spectacular. Despite the substantial investments that the company had made in growth and development – including expanding sales and distribution outside the US, the new assembly plant in Kansas City, the acquisition of Buell Motorcycle Company and Eaglemark Financial Services – gross margins had widened to 34.3 percent, and net income had increased by 12.6 percent over the year-ago period. Harley-Davidson (H-D) was well on track to meet its production target of 148,000 bikes for 1998.

For Jeff Bleustein, his first few months as CEO had focused upon consolidating the achievements of his predecessors Rich Teerlink and Vaughn Beals, as well as promoting new growth initiatives. Compared with the difficult years between the 1981 management buyout and the 1986 flotation when H-D was fighting for survival in a hostile world, the 1990s had been a period of uninterrupted success. Harley had displaced Honda as worldwide market-share leader in heavyweight motorcycles and despite an almost three-fold expansion of capacity, demand for Harleys continued to outstrip production. Steady growth in net income, from \$42 m in 1990 to \$174 m in 1997, was reflected in spectacular shareholder returns: \$100 invested in H-D stock at the 1986 initial public offering would have been worth \$4,067 by the end of 1997, an annual rate of return of 40 percent. Bleustein wanted to maintain the growth trajectory: in his first year as CEO, he authorized increased investment in production capacity, new product development, and overseas market development.

Yet despite this run of outstanding success, Bleustein was reminded of the advice of Intel founder Andy Grove. In his recent book, *Only the Paranoid Survive*, Grove emphasized the need to be constantly wary of threats from competitors and new market and technological trends. Bleustein realized that H-D could not afford to be complacent. The company continued to face rivalry from well-established global players such as Honda, BMW, Yamaha, and Kawasaki. At the other end of the scale, in addition to established specialist manufacturers such as Ducati and Moto Guzzi, there had been an influx of newcomers to the heavyweight motorcycle market such as Triumph, Polaris, and Excelsior-Henderson. If the world economy were to weaken, would there be sufficient demand for these expensive leisure toys to support H-D's continued prosperity and growth? Although Bleustein felt a general sense of unease about the future, identifying in precise terms the threats that H-D might face, and how H-D's strategy might be amended to take account of these threats was less evident to him.

THE HISTORY OF HARLEY-DAVIDSON

Harley-Davidson, Inc. was founded in 1903 by William Harley and brothers William Davidson, Arthur Davidson, and Walter Davidson. At this time, a motorcycle was no more than a bicycle with a small motor attached to it. Harley's 1903 model was made in the Davidson family shed and had a three-horsepower engine. Prior to World War I, Harley competed with about 150 other US motorcycle manufacturers. In 1909 Harley introduced its first two-cylinder, V-twin engine, featuring the deep, rumbling sound for which Harley motorcycles are known today.[2] Henry Ford's assembly-line concept (1913) and wartime orders pushed Harley out of the small-scale craft shed and into an era of mass production. In 1921 a Harley motorcycle won the first race in which machines reached speeds of over 100 miles per hour. This same year, H-D's new model featured a front brake and the distinctive Harley tear-drop gas tank. During its first three decades the industry consolidated: in 1910 there were close to 150 motorcycle producers, by 1929, Indian, Excelsior, and Harley accounted for the majority of US motorcycle sales. The Great Depression

TABLE 7.1
Annual production of motorcycles by Harley-Davidson

1901	1903	1913	1920	1933	1936	1948	1953
3	150	12,904	28,189	3,700	9,812	31,163	14,050

1966	1975	1981	1986	1987	1988	1989	1990
36,310	75,403	41,586	36,700	43,300	50,500	58,900	62,500

1991	1992	1993	1994	1995	1996	1997	
68,600	76,500	81,700	95,500	105,104	118,800	132,300	

Source: www.harley-davidson.com

killed Excelsior, and Indian closed in 1953, leaving Harley the sole American manufacturer of motorcycles. Table 7.1 shows H-D's production over the century.

The post-war era was one of opportunity and problems. Post-war affluence and the rise of youth culture created a growing demand for motorcycles. However, this was satisfied primarily by imports. By 1959, Harley was still market leader with sales of $16.6 million,[3] but British imports amounted to about 30,000 bikes a year with BSA, Triumph, and Norton taking 49 percent of the US market.[4] In 1959, Honda entered the US market. The result was the rebirth of motorcycling in the US.

From 1960 to 1965, motorcycle registrations increased from under 600,000 to almost 1,400,000. The new motorcycle owners were not traditional motorcycle owners, and certainly not "The Wild Ones" portrayed by Marlon Brando in the 1953 gang-movie.[5] The new riders were students, office workers, and leisure riders, both men and women, who found the new lightweight two-wheelers produced by Honda, Suzuki, and Yamaha to be convenient, economical, and fun. Honda's 1963 advertising campaign featured the slogan: "You Meet the Nicest People on a Honda." By 1966, Honda accounted for 63 percent of the motorcycles sold in the US.[6] Initially, H-D benefited from the overall expansion in the motorcycle market induced by Honda. However, Honda soon moved up-market. In 1969 Honda introduced the CB750, a technically advanced, four-cylinder machine that severely dented the sales of H-D and Triumph in the heavyweight market.

Also in 1969, H-D was acquired by AMF, which proceeded to expand production capacity with the building of the York, Pennsylvania assembly plant. Boosting capacity to 75,000 units annually had disastrous consequences for product quality. A company audit in the mid 1970s revealed that more than half the cycles coming off the line were missing parts.[7] By the end of the 1970s, Honda had replaced H-D as market leader in heavyweight motorcycles in the US.

The Buyout

In 1981 H-D's senior managers, led by Vaughn Beals, organized a leveraged buyout. Harley emerged as an independent, privately owned company, but heavily laden with debt. The buyout coincided with one of the severest recessions of the post-war US economy and, especially troublesome for a highly leveraged business, a soaring of interest rates under the Fed's tight monetary policies. Registrations of heavyweight motorcycles fell during 1981 and 1982, and Harley's own sales plummeted. By 1982 its sales of bikes were down by more than a third on 1979. During 1981 and 1982, Harley-Davidson lost a total of $60 million. Redundancies came thick and fast: 30 percent of the office staff were dismissed, with similar cutbacks among hourly workers. "I can remember when we used to have 2,700 people working here," recalled Ken Beaudry, vice-president of AIW Local 209 adjacent to Harley's Milwaukee engine and transmission plant. "Now we've got 535 members left."

Rebuilding Manufacturing

The company's first priority was to systematically rebuild production methods and working practices with a view to cutting costs and improving quality. The new Harley management team had visited several Japanese auto-manufacturing plants and carefully studied Toyota's just-in-time (JIT) system. After a visit to Honda's Marysville, Ohio plant in the following year, CEO Vaughn Beals commented: "We were being wiped out by the Japanese because they were better *managers*. It wasn't robotics, or culture, or morning calisthenics and company songs – it was professional managers who understood their business and paid attention to detail."[8] Tom Gelb, senior VP of operations, offered similar comments:

> I came away, as many others did, thinking "There's no magic." The plants weren't filled with robots, and the three I saw were surrounded by people watching them. There's no super-duper machinery that's different from ours. I did notice that the labor pace was greater than ours by 20 to 30 percent, but the real difference between US and Japanese management is in the staff – the manufacturing engineers, the accountants, the salaried workers.

The first few years after the buyout saw a revolution in Harley's production methods. Less than four months after the buyout, Harley management began a pilot JIT inventory and production-scheduling program called "MAN" (Materials As Needed) in its Milwaukee engine plant. The objective was to reduce inventories and costs and improve quality control. Within a year, all H-D's manufacturing operations were being converted to JIT: components and sub-assemblies were "pulled" through the production system in response to final demand. Production and component deliveries occurred when they were needed, where they were needed, and in the exact quantity needed.[9] Its adoption required a systematic rethinking and redesign of supply-chain management and manufacturing management. One result was much closer relationships with a smaller number of suppliers.

The new system of manufacturing and purchasing was accompanied by fundamental changes in job design and human resource management at plant level. During the early 1980s, the new management sought to redefine the responsibilities of manufacturing employees and transform their relationship with management. A key element was to give machine operators more responsibility, including responsibility for the preventive maintenance of their machines and participation in discussions about quality improvement. This in turn required investments in retraining.

The goal, stated Beals, was "to achieve cost and quality parity with foreign competition." However, the goal was to be achieved, not by automation, but by changes in working practices, organization, and attitudes. Rod Willis of *Management Review* summarized the changes in manufacturing management:

> Armed with the latest in Japanese manufacturing concepts – or as much as they could pry from their often tight-lipped competitors – Beals and his cadre of top managers returned to Milwaukee to reorganize Harley Davidson. The first big change was in plant management structure. The traditional American hierarchy of responsibilities was replaced with a system in which each employee from the line up has "ownership" in running an efficient operation. Each plant is assigned four to seven area managers each responsible for everything that takes place in his or her area. Staff jobs were cut throughout the company and divided among area managers and line workers. There are no corporate or plant heads of quality control. The area managers can't blame problems on staff failures, and line workers can't blame faulty equipment for productivity problems unless there are serious malfunctions. The chickens come home to roost.

By eliminating staff functions, the company obtained a shallower organizational chart and big cost savings. "Our biggest savings came from decreasing the number of salaried staff," said Beals. "That is where the greatest improvements in productivity have occurred . . . The presence of those service functions tends to emasculate the basic line with regard to authority, and that's what we are trying to avoid . . . All the line workers are responsible for inspecting and making basic adjustments to the machinery they use and managers should run their parts of the plant fully. It's a long-term transition to making each plant a profit center." Similarly, line workers, who were once given quotas and told to meet them, were given a voice in setting realistic quotas based on actual production capacity and needs. As a result, they felt a sense of ownership in meeting those goals. "In the past, line workers had to wait for a repairman to come and fix broken or malfunctioning machinery; now they can make most repairs themselves."

The revolution in manufacturing occurred without large-scale investment in new capital equipment. The high leverage and weak cash flows of the 1980s meant that the improvements in productivity and quality had to occur without the benefits of the latest computer-controlled machine tools and flexible manufacturing systems. The installation in 1987 of eight Japanese-built computer-controlled machining centers at a cost of over $1.5 million was a major investment for H-D. Even with these constraints, the improvements in all aspects of manufacturing performance were spectacular. The company reduced its inventory levels, lowered its setup and changeover times for machinery, and radically improved the quality of its products. Improved quality meant reduced costs in other areas: scrap, rework, supplier corrective action, downgraded end product, warranty costs, loss of future sales, recall costs, and return costs.

Product Development and Design

While management had decided to "play the game the way the Japanese play it" in terms of quality control and operations management, it decided to play a different game in terms of products and marketing. Harley abandoned all notions of becoming a broad-line competitor and concentrated its efforts into developing the big-bike niche. Although the heavyweight segment had traditionally been the preserve of Harley and the European manufacturers, by the 1980s it had become dominated by the Japanese. Moreover, the appreciation of the US dollar between 1980 and 1986 made it increasingly difficult for US manufacturers to remain price competitive. To give it time to develop its capabilities and market position in the heavyweight segment, the company sought (and won) a temporary five-year tariff on imported Japanese heavyweight motorcycles.

To build its position within the heavyweight segment, H-D's strategy was to exploit its traditional image while at the same time appealing to a more affluent, up-market customer base. In terms of product policy, this meant emphasizing the traditional Harley style, but improving the products to meet the needs of buyers who had neither the time nor the skill nor the inclination to maintain, rebuild, and upgrade their own bikes. Under the leadership of William G. ("Willy G") Davidson, grandson of one of the founders, H-D put greater emphasis on product styling, bringing back many of the design and stylistic features of former Harley models. Many managers today credit the company's survival during the early and mid-1980s to the innovations in paint, trim, chrome, and exhaust-pipe shaping that Willy G and his team introduced. Under Willy G's leadership, Harley introduced a number of new models, for the most part developed at minimal cost by combining modified components from its two most popular old models, the heavy Elektra Glide and the lighter Sportster. The new models took traditional Harley features and carefully adjusted the styling to appeal to the modern buyer. Says Willy G, "Every little piece on a Harley is exposed, and it has to look just right. A tube curve or the shape of a timing case can generate enthusiasm or be a total turnoff. It's almost like being in the fashion business."[10] The new bikes mimicked many of the cosmetic innovations with which Harley fans had traditionally customized their bikes after purchase.

Even with its traditional appeal, it was essential for Harley to upgrade its product to meet the standards of performance, comfort, reliability, and ease of maintenance expected by the market in the 1980s. The developments were incremental and involved no major innovations. In 1984, Harley introduced its improved "Evolution" range of V-twin engines. The Gates Poly chain belt drive offered greater quietness and reliability in rear wheel drive. Other improvements have included redesigned engine mounts to reduce vibration, a new carburetor offering a smoother power delivery, an improved starter, and redesigned gear case, which helped Harley meet the 1986 Federal noise limit for motorcycles.

Increasing differentiation and widening market appeal meant more frequent new model introductions. However, to exploit economies of scale, key components were standardized. Thus, H-D based its model range around three engine types and four different frames.

Given the high level of brand loyalty among Harley owners, increasing market share meant capturing new customers, and new riders in particular. To this end, the 883cc Sportster, Harley's entry-level bike priced (in 1985) at below $4,000, played a particularly important role.

Marketing

Communicating the appeal of Harley ownership to a new breed of potential customers also presented a challenge to the company. As with all other aspects of H-D's turnaround strategy, the key was to achieve maximum bang for very few bucks. In the area of marketing, H-D's approach was to obtain wide-ranging exposure of the company, its products, and its heritage, while largely eschewing traditional mass advertising.

The key was to build upon Harley's identification with American values of independence, ruggedness, and dependability, while undermining Harley's association with rebellious, law-flouting motorcycle gangs. The company publicized widely its efforts and success in implementing TQM with articles in technical magazines such as *American Machinist*, *Quality*, and *Industrial Engineering*. President Reagan's visit to H-D's York plant created a torrent of publicity. To counter the antisocial image associated with motorcycle gangs, the new management put a heavy emphasis on patriotism, charity, and community involvement. Publicity events such as the Harley-sponsored rides to raise money for the Muscular Dystrophy Association, and its organization of a Los Angeles to Washington D.C. "Ride for Liberty" to raise donations for the restoration of the Statue of Liberty, not only promoted a favorable image, but generated substantial publicity for Harley-Davidson motorcycles.

By the beginning of 1988 it was apparent that Harley's attempts to extend its appeal to a whole new group of more affluent customers were making steady progress. Market research data showed that the median age of Harley customers was a little over 34 – much higher than the average for motorcycle customers as a whole. Their median household income was almost $40,000 and over half were married.

With solid gains in quality and reliability, H-D sought to win back sales to public authorities, most of which had been lost to its Japanese rivals. In 1987 Harley made sales of some 4,000 bikes to police departments and had chalked up some notable successes, including a switch by the California Highway Patrol from Honda to Harley.

It was not only in the motorcycle market that Harley-Davidson was able to exploit the strength of the Harley brand image. The Harley-Davidson name was licensed to suppliers of tee-shirts, jackets, underwear, jewelry, and toys. Although licensing income accounted for less than 1 percent of Harley's revenue from motorcycles and related products, it was almost all profit. In 1982, Harley began vigorously enforcing protection of its trademarks. From its own dealerships to tattoo parlors (where the Harley-Davidson logo was the most popular single tattoo design), Harley prohibited unauthorized use of its trademarks, and drove out bootleg products. The starting point was the major motorcycle trade shows. Initially Harley found that bootleg merchandise was so prevalent that legitimate Harley-licensed products were hard to find. The result was a rise in licensing income to Harley, plus tighter controls against the Harley name being used in connection with poor quality or pornographic products.

Central to H-D's marketing efforts was building the relationship between the company and its customers. If the appeal of the Harley motorcycle was the image it conveyed and the lifestyle it represented, then the company had to ensure that the experience matched the image. To increase H-D's involvement in its customers' riding experience it formed the Harley Owners' Group in 1983. Through HOG, H-D became involved in organizing charity events, and employees, from the CEO down, were encouraged to take an active role in HOG activities.

Distribution

Improving H-D's much-neglected distribution network was essential to the company's market objectives. Far too many of Harley's 620 US dealerships were poorly managed shops, operated by enthusiasts, with erratic opening hours, a poor stock of bikes and spares, and indifferent customer service. H-D began rebuilding its dealership network. Harley's dealer development program improved support for dealers while imposing higher standards of pre- and after-sales service, and requiring better dealer facilities. The dealers were obliged to carry a full line of Harley replacement parts and accessories, and to perform service on Harley bikes. Harley-Davidson placed a strong emphasis on training dealers to help them meet the higher service requirements, and encouraging dealers to better meet the needs of the professional, middle-class clientele that H-D was now courting.

Despite the tariff protection awarded by the Reagan Administration and the popularity of the models, Harley flirted with bankruptcy between 1984 and 1986. By 1987, however, after a period of stronger sales and a successful round of $49 million in debt financing (where Citicorp took a $10 million write-down on its original investment), Harley's financial condition stabilized.[11] Between 1986 and 1990, Harley's share of the heavyweight market grew from about 30 percent to over 60 percent, with demand outstripping production. During this time, management improved the quality and reliability of its product and also began to look at growth opportunities in retail clothing and sales abroad. In 1989, Harley established a subsidiary in the UK.

THE HEAVYWEIGHT MOTORCYCLE MARKET

In the 1990s Harley has experienced eight years of uninterrupted growth in the heavyweight motorcycle market (650+ cc). This market is comprised of three segments:

- *Cruisers*: "big, noisy, low riding, unapologetically macho cycles"[12] with loud V-twin engines
- *Touring bikes*: large motorcycles with seats designed for long rides
- *Performance bikes*: built for superior handling and acceleration, they have lighter, stiffer frames, and require a more forward, crouched seated position

Harley dominates the cruiser and touring segments of this market, capturing over 50 percent of overall heavyweight motorcycle sales in the US in 1997 (see Table 7.2). Cruiser motorcycles are big, powerful machines with an upright riding position. Their design reflects the dominance of styling over either comfort or speed. For the urban males (and some females) in Los Angeles, New York, Paris, and Tokyo, the cruiser motorcycle is practical transportation in congested metropolises, but is primarily a statement of style. The cruiser segment has practically been created by Harley. Most of the bikes in this segment feature V-twin engines, many with cylinder capacities that exceed those of a small family car. Harley's major competitors include Japanese companies with models based upon traditional Harley design (Honda's Shadow range, Yamaha's Virago, the Suzuki Intruder, and Kawasaki's Vulcan).

Touring bikes include cruisers specially equipped for longer-distance riding (such as several Harley models) and bikes specially designed for comfort over long distance (including the Honda Goldwing and the bigger BMWs). These tourers feature luxuries such as audio systems, two-way intercoms, and heaters. In touring bikes, Harley is challenged by the greater smoothness and comfort of the multi-cylinder, shaft-drive BMWs and Goldwings.

Performance models are based upon racing bikes. These are high-technology, high-revving engines with a heavy emphasis on speed, acceleration, and race-track styling with minimal concessions to rider comfort. The segment is dominated by Japanese motorcycle companies, with a significant representation of European specialists such as Ducati and Triumph. H-D entered this segment in 1993 with its involvement in the formation of Buell Motorcycles, and with the acquisition of Buell in 1998 is now more heavily committed.

COMPETITION

Although H-D was well established as the market-share leader in the US heavyweight market, in the global motorcycle industry it was only a medium-sized player. In the smaller sizes of motorcycle, it was the Japanese that dominated the US and the world markets. Outside of the US, H-D lagged behind Honda, Yamaha, and

TABLE 7.2
Harley-Davidson's motorcycle registrations, 1993–1997

	1993	1994	1995	1996	1997
United States	132,800	150,400	163,100	178,500	205,400
Harley-Davidson	63,400	69,500	77,000	79,936	93,491
Market share (650+ cc)	47.7%	46.2%	47.2%	44.8%	45.5%
Europe	218,600	201,900	207,200	224,688	250,293
Harley-Davidson	13,200	14,400	15,400	15,300	15,300
Market share (650+ cc)	6.1%	7.1%	7.4%	6.8%	6.1%
Japan/Australia	35,700	39,100	39,400	37,417	58,880
Harley-Davidson	6,700	7,600	7,900	8,200	9,700
Market share (650+ cc)	18.7%	19.4%	20.1%	21.9%	16.5%

Source: www.harley-davidson.com

Kawasaki, even in the heavyweight segment. However, the conventional segmentation into lightweight, middleweight, and heavyweight does not clearly define H-D's market. H-D's strength lies not in the heavyweight motorcycle market, but in just one part of this: the *super-heavyweight* segment, comprising bikes with cylinder displacement of more than 850cc. In the 650–850cc range, the Japanese dominance is nearly as great as in the lightweight and middleweight markets.

As result of its single-segment focus, H-D produces a much smaller volume of bikes than its major competitors. The most striking comparison is between H-D and Honda: H-D's 150,000 bikes a year are dwarfed by Honda's 5 million. These volume differences have important implications for H-D's ability to access scale economies.

Compared to its competitors, H-D is also much less diversified. Honda, BMW, and Suzuki are important producers of automobiles. It seems likely that there are benefits from sharing technology, engineering capabilities, and marketing and distribution know-how between automobile and motorcycle divisions. In addition, sheer size confers greater bargaining power with suppliers.

H-D's smaller size and scale has important implications for its investments in technology. Because of the costs involved, H-D does not have a separate research function, and it lags far behind its competitors in the application of motor vehicle technology. To a great extent, it has succeeded in making a virtue out of necessity – its motorcycles not only look old-style, the technology is old-style, even the new Twin Cam 88 engine launched in 1998 in an era of multi-valve, liquid-cooled, overhead camshaft engines. The Twin Cam 88 is a 1450cc traditional V-twin with push rods and is air-cooled. By contrast, BMW's R1200C cruiser model launched in 1997 with a star role in the James Bond movie "Tomorrow Never Dies," features shaft drive; a multi-valve, fuel-injected engine; triple-disc, anti-lock brakes; and road-hugging cornering from its advanced suspension system and low center of gravity. In contrast to its Japanese rivals, who have focused upon applying the latest automotive

TABLE 7.3
Market shares in heavyweight motorcycles, 1997 (%)

	North America	Europe	Japan/Australia
Harley-Davidson	48.3	6.1	16.5
Honda	18.6	25.0	30.1
Kawasaki	10.6	10.7	20.2
Suzuki	10.5	17.2	8.7
Yamaha	5.8	17.2	13.9
BMW	2.4	12.6	4.0
Other	3.8	11.2	6.6

Source: Harley-Davidson Annual Report, 1997.

technology to their new models, H-D has concentrated upon incremental refinements to its engines, frames, and gearboxes, whose basic design has remained fundamentally the same for the past 70 years. Unlike technological leaders such as Honda and BMW, H-D has been forced to outsource most of its technological needs. In 1997 it established a joint venture with Porsche AG to source and assemble motorcycle components. H-D was particularly interested in accessing Porsche's expertise in engine emission compliance.

Appendix 2 gives profiles of several competitors of H-D in the heavyweight motorcycle market, Table 7.3 compares market shares, and Table 7.4 shows price comparisons.

HARLEY-DAVIDSON IN THE 1990S

Brand Loyalty

Harley-Davidson has emerged as one of the archetypes of American style. The famed spread eagle signifies not just the brand of one of the world's oldest motorcycle companies, but an entire lifestyle that it is associated with. Harley-Davidson has been described as "the ultimate biker status symbol . . . a quasi religion, an institution, a way of life."[13] As a result, the "golden, all-American brand name" has earned a considerable following. In a recent annual report, Harley's Chairman and CEO Richard Teerlink wrote, "Most people can't understand what would drive someone to profess his or her loyalty for our brand by tattooing our logo onto his or her body – or heart . . . this indescribable passion is a big part of what has driven and will continue to drive our growth."

Tattoos, strong brand loyalty, and Harley's icon status have created a distinct marketing advantage for the company. Harley ran no domestic advertisements in 1996, but was ranked number 26 in the listing of the "World's Top 100 Brands" for that

TABLE 7.4
Heavyweight motorcycles: price comparisons, 1998

Manufacturer and model	Engine	Price ($)
H-D XLH 800 Sportster	V-twin, air-cooled, 840cc	5,845
H-D XL 1200S Sportster	V-twin, air-cooled, 1203cc	8,395
H-D DynaWide Glide	V-twin, air-cooled, 1340cc	14,775
H-D Bad Boy	V-twin, air-cooled, 1340cc	14,925
H-D Heritage Softtail Classic	V-twin, air-cooled, 1340cc	15,157
H-D FLSTS	V-twin, air-cooled, 1340cc	16,995
Honda Shadow ACE 750	V-twin, OHC, 745cc	6,299
Honda Pacific Coast	V-twin, liquid-cooled, 800cc	8,699
Honda Shadow Aero	V-twin, liquid-cooled, 1099cc	9,695
Honda Shadow ACE Tourer	V-twin, liquid-cooled, 1099cc	10,999
Suzuki Maurauder	V-twin, liquid-cooled, OHC, 805cc	5,999
Suzuki Intruder	V-twin, air-cooled, 1462cc	9,899
Kawasaki Vulcan 800	V-twin, 8-valve, OHC	7,999
Kawasaki Vulcan Classic	V-twin, air-cooled, 1470cc	11,590
Yamaha 750 Virago	V-twin, OHC, 749cc	6,499
BMW F650	Liquid-cooled, double OHC, 652cc	7,490
BMW R1200 Cruiser	Horizontal-twin, 1170cc	12,990
Polaris Victory V92C	V-twin, 4-valve OHC, 1507cc	13,595

Source: www.motorcycle.com

year.[14] In 1997, it spent a mere $1 million on advertising out of a total marketing budget of $20 million. Meanwhile, Harley cycles have been featured in ads for countless other products, providing millions of dollars worth of free advertising. For example, during the 1997 Super Bowl 100 Harleys were part of the half-time show, at no cost to the company. The brand is so strong that Harley closed down its branding department in 1995 citing it as unnecessary.[15]

Creating the Harley Owners' Group (HOG) was a crucial factor in building the brand image and consolidating the relationship between the company and its customers. HOG's web site describes the kind of emotion and atmosphere that the company is trying to deliver to customers through its HOG organization: "the feeling of being out there on a Harley-Davidson motorcycle links us like no other experience can. It's made HOG like no other organization in the world . . . The atmosphere is more family reunion than organized meeting." By becoming a HOG member, riders get a company pin and patch, a membership card, and a HOG atlas as well as a host of membership benefits including the *Hog Tales Magazine*, a bimonthly newsletter. The organization has also come to include the Ladies of Harley, "giving the women riders among us the recognition they deserve."[16] (Women now make up 12 percent of US Harley buyers.) When it first started, in 1983, the organization had 28 members. HOG currently has 365,000 members in 940 chapters throughout the world.[17] Run by Harley employees, HOG sponsors motorcycle events almost every weekend from April to November across the country.[18] Harley managers participate along with their spouses. Marketing chief Kathleen Lawler-Demitros explains, "We try to run our business by the maxim 'The sale begins after the sale.' HOG is one way we differentiate ourselves from our Japanese competitors."[19]

The loyalty and fervor of Harley owners is most evident from the participation in the rallies whose sole purpose is to celebrate the company and the bikes. When Harley turned 90 in 1993, more than 100,000 bikers from around the world rode into Milwaukee swelling total party crowd size to approximately 600,000. The celebration of the 95th anniversary in June 1998 was even bigger.

The involvement of H-D managers and employees in HOG and Harley rallies also provides opportunities for market research and continuous customer feedback. "We listen to our customers," says Jeff Bleustein. "We're building the motorcycles they are asking for."[20] Managers listen to customers directly through their own involvement with HOG events and Harley rallies. Harley's chief designer, Willy G. Davidson, and his wife have been going every year for twenty years to "Bike Week," an annual rally organized in Daytona Beach, Florida by the company for its customers. Asked about the design process at H-D, Willy G replied, "There is no manual, it's just drive and creative juices. We got input over a long time, from places like the Boot Hill Saloon and Sturgis, South Dakota about what our riders thought about the product."[21]

To continue growing its customer base and tap into a growing group of affluent baby boomers, H-D's marketing focus and target customer group have shifted. During the 1980s, the average Harley customer was 32 years old with a household income of $30,000. Today, the average customer is 44 years old with a household income of $72,000. Harley maintains an image of rebelliousness and non-conformity, but Harley riders have few associations with their Hell's Angel predecessors. HOG is a major supporter of the Muscular Dystrophy Foundation, and HOG members are the fourth-largest contributing group to the Jerry Lewis Telethon.

The dealers have played a central role in Harley's repositioning, growth, and fostering of customer loyalty. Forced initially by the company, over 500 of the 600 dealers in the United States have rebuilt, renovated, or substantially upgraded their stores. Dealers' showrooms have moved locations and gone from being gritty motorcycle shops to airy boutiques that feature a wide variety of items ranging from motorcycles to Zippo brand lighters. Recognizing that the dealers are the point of contact for the brand, Harley has also launched a $600,000 "Genuine Deal" campaign. The campaign is designed to build the Harley brand image, dealership loyalty, and dealership traffic. It is also geared to taking advantage of the growing parts and accessory business. Most parts and accessory sales occur during the first year of Harley motorcycle ownership, adding on average $3,500 in incremental retail sales.[22] As part of the Genuine Deal campaign dealers receive a Genuine Dealer promotion kit. The kit includes a television spot, three black-and-white small space ads, a radio ad, and a store-hours sign. The shift to selling clothing and collectibles as well as motorcycles and parts has been a major transition for many dealers.

TABLE 7.5
Harley-Davidson shipments 1997–1998

	Jan.–June 1997	Jan.–June 1998
Motorcycle shipments		
United States	48,211	52,650
Export	18,614	19,585
Motorcycle product mix		
Touring	20.9%	24.4%
Custom	54.7%	53.5%
Sportster	24.4%	22.1%
Buell motorcycle shipments		
United States	1,118	1,287
Export	989	1,520

Source: Harley-Davidson quarterly results (www.harley-davidson.com).

Sales

The effectiveness of H-D's strategy, particularly the power of the Harley image, is evident in the fact that, despite a fourfold increase in production capacity, demand for Harley motorcycles continues to outstrip supply. Every motorcycle that H-D makes has already been sold long before it comes off the production line. For many models, would-be buyers must join a waiting-list. One result is that used bikes frequently sell at higher prices than new bikes; customers are willing to pay a premium to get a used Harley now rather than waiting a year or more before a dealer can ship the product. More generally, the rate of price depreciation of used Harleys is very low. Hence, the high price of the original purchase is mitigated by high resale values. At the same time, H-D has benefited not only from the appeal of its own products, but from the expansion of the market. While the overall motorcycle market in the US has seen little growth during the 1990s, the heavyweight segment has been an area of robust growth. Since 1993, registrations of heavyweight motorcycles in the US have grown at a rate of about 15 percent each year, with projected growth rates of 12–15 percent per year for the next decade. H-D's revenues and profits have also benefited from a shift in demand from the cheaper Sportster models to the more expensive models among the touring and custom ranges (see Table 7.5).

Extending the Brand

For both H-D and its dealers, the proportion of revenue and profit contributed by the sales of parts, accessories, and "general merchandise" (clothing and collectibles) has grown over time (see Table 7.6). During 1998, general merchandise were running

TABLE 7.6
Harley-Davidson's sales of parts, accessories, and general merchandise, 1986–1997 ($ million)

	1986	1990	1991	1992	1993	1994	1995	1996	1997
Parts and Accessories	35.7	80.2	94.3	103.6	127.8	162.0	192.1	210.2	241.9
General merchandise	9.4	29.8	36.0	52.1	71.2	94.3	100.2	90.7	95.1

Source: Harley-Davidson financial statements (www.harley-davidson.com).

close to 20 percent ahead of 1997, accounting for about 6 percent of total sales. Brand extensions include MotorClothes apparel and collectibles. Harley has also introduced a new line of denim products and the Spring MotorClothes line.

Only a small proportion of the clothing, collectibles, and other products bearing the Harley-Davidson trademark are sold through the H-D dealership network. Most of this business is a pure licensing operation where H-D's role is to sign the licensing agreements, collect the royalties, and ensure that the trademark is not devalued. The clothing bearing the Harley-Davidson logo has extended far beyond motorcycle apparel. For example, Nice Man Merchandising supplies children's clothing under the Harley brand. A giftware company is licensed to supply Harley holiday bulb ornaments, music boxes, and a Road King pewter motorcycle replica. In Europe, L'Oreal licensed the Harley name for a line of cologne. The first Harley-Davidson Cafe is in midtown Manhattan. The cafe is styled after a Hard-Rock Cafe and contains a gift shop serving up a gamut of Harley gift items including leather-clad Harley Barbie dolls. A second Harley Cafe recently opened in Las Vegas.

Eaglemark Financial Services

Eaglemark Financial Services was launched in 1993 with minority investment by H-D, and was later acquired. It was established to provide financial services to H-D dealers and customers, helping them to do business with H-D. It offers wholesale and retail financing, extended service contracts on Harley bikes, motorcycle insurance, and dealer insurance. More closely linked to its core motorcycle business has been H-D's expansion into financial services. Consumer finance is a critical service for any company selling big-ticket consumer durables. Prior to the formation of Eaglemark, H-D offered financing through Ford Motor Credit. In 1997, Eaglemark launched the Harley-Davidson Chrome VISA card.

In the first half of 1998, Eaglemark earned an operating income of $8.9 million, about 6 percent of H-D's total operating income, and up from $5.6 million a year previously.

TABLE 7.7
Harley-Davidson facilities, 1997

Location	Function	Total employment
Wisconsin		2,400
Milwaukee	Corporate Headquarters, parts/accessories sales, R&D	
Wauwatosa	XL Engine/Transmission production, Product Development Center	
Menomonee Falls	FL Engine/Transmission production	
Franklin	Parts/Accessories Distribution Center	
Tomahawk	Fiberglass parts production/painting	
Pennsylvania		2,600
York	Final assembly plant, parts and painting	
Missouri		350 by 1998
Kansas City	Manufacturing, painting	

Source: Harley-Davidson *Annual Report*, 1997.

Operations and Purchasing

Facilities
At the heart of H-D's business is its Milwaukee head office and nearby plants. The Milwaukee plants are responsible for engines and components. Under AMF's ownership the York, Pennsylvania assembly plant was opened. To alleviate the continuing pressure on capacity (since the 1986 IPO, H-D's motorcycle output has tripled), the Kansas City plant was opened in 1998. This plant will concentrate upon manufacturing Sportster models. Together with the Buell Motorcycle operation (see below), H-D's output will be close to 150,000 units in 1998. All plants are unionized. Table 7.7 gives information on H-D's facilities.

European headquarters, based in Windsor, England, manages H-D Motor Company's activities in European, African, and Middle Eastern markets. The European heavyweight market is the largest worldwide, 18 percent bigger than the US. In the Asia-Pacific region the major markets are Japan and Australia/New Zealand. In "Other Asia," H-D's sales are primarily in Malaysia, Singapore, Thailand, and Hong Kong. Japan has a wholly owned subsidiary that services its 35 dealers. Three independent distributors service 55 Australian dealers.

Purchasing and supplier management
A large proportion of the final price of a Harley motorcycle is accounted for by the cost of bought-in components. Because H-D is unable to purchase in the volumes of rivals such as Yamaha and Suzuki, and does not possess the additional clout that Honda and BMW enjoy because of their big automotive operations, purchasing is a

critical and problematic area for H-D. Purchasing managers are at senior levels within the H-D management structure. Says Garry Berryman, H-D's director of purchasing, "If purchasing is at a second or third tier level then it is too deep in the organization to have the early influence that it needs. In the 1990s, Harley made organizational changes to ensure that purchasing would be directly represented in the same group that wrestles with all the company's high-level strategic issues."[23]

In 1992, Harley extended its program of quality improvement to encompass its suppliers. It established a supplier advisory council (SAC) to expose supplier executives to the best practices of other suppliers in the Harley network.[24] Says Berryman, "Through the SAC, we're able to take some of the entrepreneurial aspects of our smaller, privately held suppliers and inject that enthusiasm, spirit, and energy into those that may be larger, publicly held companies." In this way, the SAC not only serves to improve purchasing efficiency, but also provides a forum to share information, ideas, and strategy. The SAC, says Berryman, is a way "to leverage the successes that occur in one area across the broader organization."[25] The SAC is made up of 16 suppliers, representing a cross-section of Harley's more than 400 OEM suppliers. Each SAC member contacts 9–12 other first-tier suppliers to get their input on various issues under review: costs, quality, scheduling, and strategy. The primary goal of the SAC is to spread best practices within Harley's supplier base and to improve the quality of Harley's own practices. Says Berryman, "The knowledge, leadership, and intelligence represented in our supplier council brings our capabilities well beyond what we could do with internal resources." Increased communication and coordination with suppliers is viewed as instrumental in improving Harley's new product development process. Says Leroy Zimdars, Harley's director of purchasing development, "We want suppliers to be deeply involved, at an early stage, in new product development. We'll use the SAC as a sounding board for how the supply base accepts the new structure, and we can react to it. The input is very candid, due to the close relationship between the SAC and the rest of the supply base."

Organizational Structure and Employee Empowerment

Following the management buyout of 1981, H-D's new management group systematically rethought management–employee relationships, employee responsibilities, and organizational structure. The result was a transformation in employee commitment and job satisfaction. "What other company has employees who tattoo the company name on their bodies? Or offers not just a job but a lifestyle?" observed an assembly-line worker at Harley's Milwaukee plant. Harley has a no-lay-off policy, 12 weeks of paid maternity leave, and unlimited sick days for salaried staffers.

The process of management innovation continued when Harley's new Northland Plant went on-line in Kansas City in January 1998. The plant's management structure and working methods reflected the company's desire to make further advances in employee commitment and self-management. "I'm not aware of anybody anywhere doing anything that emulates this," says plant chief Karl Eberle.[26] In contrast to the traditional layout of Harley's other plants, the Northland Plant does not have a management space that oversees floor production from a glassed-in office upstairs.

Instead, the plant manager and other administrators work in a "bullpen area" on the floor and in the center of the 330,000 square foot building.

In an effort to engage and motivate the entire plant workforce, management developed a novel operating structure different from anything else within the company. The structure comprises three types of teams:

- *Natural work groups* – every worker belongs to a work group, with 8–15 people per group
- *Process operating groups* – comprised of representatives from each work group, there are four process operating groups; each oversees one of the plant's four operating divisions: paint, assembly, fabrication, and engine production
- *Plant leadership group* – a 14-member committee, responsible for governing the facility; comprised of the plant manager, the presidents of both unions representing the plant workforce, four elected representatives from the process groups, an elected representative from maintenance, and six administrators

Harley is betting on this less hierarchical, team-based structure to improve employee motivation and accelerate the learning process at its new plant. Says plant chief Eberle, "We recognize there is a tremendous benefit – financially, psychologically, quality-wise, output-wise – to be gained by engaging the workforce."[27]

Harley Headquarters: from Hierarchy to Teams

The movement toward a flatter, more team-based organizational structure is also evident in recent changes occurring in Harley's overall corporate structure. "In our new organization," explains Clyde Fessler, VP for business development, "the Harley-Davidson Motor Company has been divided into three broad, functional areas called Circles. They are: the Create Demand Circle (CDC), the Produce Product Circle (PPC), and the Provide Support Circle (PSC). Each Circle is composed of the leaders representing the functions within it. The flexibility of the organization extends even to the decision of which functional areas are identified within a given circle. It is quite possible that Circle definitions may shift from time to time, depending on the demands of the business."[28] Like the team structure developed for the new Kansas City plant, each Circle operates as a team with the leadership role moving from person to person, depending on what issue is being addressed. Individual Circles meet once a month, and all three Circles meet together quarterly.

Overall coordination is provided by the Strategic Leadership Council (SLC), which is made up of individuals nominated by each of the three Circles. Explains Fessler:

> The role of the SLC is to resolve issues that have not been settled previously by consensus in Circle meetings. Leadership of the Council also rotates, shifting to the Circle representative who "owns" the topic being discussed ... The Circle format is especially valuable in that it facilitates systems thinking in our strategy implementation. If the marketing function plans to focus on a specific product, the Circles provide an opportunity to get feedback from manufacturing about timing and availability. If the manufac-

turing function needs to shut down its operations to upgrade equipment, the Circle structure allows all the affected functions to be involved in the decision. We have now been working with this organizational design for three and a half years. And we would probably all agree that the shift from hierarchy to Circles has not been easy – practicing consensus decision-making never is. However, defining the roles and responsibilities of each functional Circle and each Circle member has brought clarity, which in turn stimulates dialogue, trust, and eventually, non-threatening confrontation . . . Collaborative interdependent teams may not be able to move as quickly as the single decisive leader in a hierarchy, but they can be more innovative and resourceful and, ultimately, more effective in today's complex business climate.[29]

International Marketing

A key part of H-D's growth strategy is expanding its sales outside of the US and Canada. Europe is the focal point of H-D's overseas ambitions, simply because it is the largest heavyweight motorcycle market in the world. "A few years ago," says Harley CEO Bleustein, "our prime focus was the domestic market, and the rest was gravy. That view had to change. If our growth is to continue, Europe will have to play a significant part." Europe is also a huge challenge for H-D. Unlike in the US, H-D has never had a major position in Europe and it must fight to take market share from the market leaders: BMW, Honda, Kawasaki, and Yamaha. Harley launched its first large-scale European advertising campaign in the summer of 1998. The direct-response ads ran in style-conscious magazines such as *GQ* and *Esquire* in Europe with the intention of building up data on European potential customers and enhancing H-D's existing customer base.

   A critical issue for international marketing is the extent to which the products and the Harley image need to be adjusted to meet the needs of overseas markets. Harley's image is rooted in American culture, and thus seems central to their appeals to European and Asian customers. "The US and Harley are tied together," says Hugo Wilson of Britain's *Bike* magazine, "the guy who's into Harleys here is also the guy who owns cowboy boots. You get a Harley and you're buying into the US mystique."[30] At the same time, the composition of demand and the customer profile is different in overseas markets. The European motorcycle market differs significantly from the American market in that 70 percent of the heavy motorcycle market is for performance bikes (such as the popular Japanese high-power, lightweight, racing-style bikes), while the touring/cruiser bikes such as those Harley makes account for only 30 percent. European buyers tend to be knowledgeable and highly style conscious. Also, European roads and riding style are different from the US. As a result, Harley has modified its 1998 models to the needs and tastes of its European customers. The US Sportster, for example, has a straight handlebar instead of curled buckhorns and a new suspension system to improve cornering. The name has also changed to the "Custom 53." The Harley Softail has also received a new look, becoming the "Night Train." As in the US, Harley management regards the after-sale value of biker clubs and events as a critical differentiator for its product. The biggest Harley gathering ever planned was for June 20, 1998 in Austria, when some 10,000 European Harley owners were expected to gather in celebration of the company's 95th anniversary.

The European heavyweight market grew strongly during the mid- to late 1990s, especially in Italy, where a new customer base of Italian youth has driven sales. "Sales to those 25 and younger are about 3% among the world's motorcycle manufacturers," says Carlo Talamo, owner of 40 Numero Uno Harley Stores scattered around Italy. "In Italy [the youth market] is 37%."[31] However, despite growing sales, Harley has found it difficult to increase its market share significantly in Europe. The high price of Harleys and the rising value of the US dollar during the late 1990s have given Japanese and European manufacturers a competitive edge.

Buell Motorcycle Company

Harley regards Buell as an important extension of its market position and a potential market winner in Europe. Founded by ex-Harley engineer Erik Buell in the 1980s, Buell Motor Co. produces bikes that synthesize the comfort and style of a Harley cruiser with the high-performance attributes of a sports bike. Harley purchased a 49 percent stake in Buell in 1993, and more recently gained majority ownership. Buell bikes use Harley engines and other components, but mount them on a lighter, stiffer frame. The superior handling and acceleration of Buell models are appealing to the European market, where customers are younger and tend to put greater value on sporty performance and a cheaper price tag.

In the US, the Buell bikes are also targeted for a younger, more price-sensitive and performance-oriented market. In the US, the typical Buell customer is seven years younger and the price tag is about $10,000 compared to an average Harley price of $15,000.[32] To appeal to this younger segment, Harley has been using slogans such as "Pull Some Gs" and "Different in Every Sense" to advertise Buell bikes.[33] In addition, the company formed the Buell Riders Adventure Group (BRAG) modeled after HOG. Buell produced 4,462 units in 1997 and plans to increase that number to 5,500 by the end of 1998.[34]

LOOKING AHEAD

As he examined in detail the budget projections for the third quarter of 1998, Bleustein considered the remarkable achievements of H-D over the past decade and a half. From 40,000 bikes a year, H-D had grown to produce over 150,000 bikes in 1998, with capacity rising to 200,000 units per year. Yet even with expanded output and a big price premium over rival machines produced by Japanese competitors, H-D still faced a waiting-list for most of its models.

Did H-D really need to worry about competition? A Harley was a Harley. All the market research pointed to the improbability of Harley customers buying a look-alike Japanese machine, even if it was cheaper and embodied more advanced technology. And yet, the competitive situation was changing. In Europe, Harley was a relative newcomer – it was BMW, Triumph, Ducati, and Moto Guzzi which represented motorcycling tradition. In the US, H-D faced a new breed of competitor, US manufacturers such as Polaris and Excelsior which directly challenged H-D with retro-styled big bikes that also sought to recreate American motorcycle nostalgia. As H-D expanded its market share from a single segment – the US super-heavyweight market – it inevitably was drawn into competition with companies that possessed greater size, resources, and technological capabilities than H-D. Indeed, the Buell subsidiary represented a direct attack upon the performance bike market long dominated by the Japanese.

Apart from competition, there was also the question of whether the market for heavyweight motorcycles would continue to grow. The demand for Harley bikes had been remarkably resilient to downturns in the general economy. However, the world seemed to be moving into a new era of economic uncertainty. Warnings of global recession were hardly encouraging to any company that sold a leisure product costing up to $20,000 a unit. But the risks were not simply from a deteriorating economy. H-D, Bleustein reminded himself, was in the business, not of selling motor-cycles, but of selling a lifestyle. Would this lifestyle have the same appeal in the decade of the 2000s as in the 1990s?

APPENDIX 1
HARLEY-DAVIDSON, SUMMARY OF FINANCIAL STATEMENTS, 1994–1998

TABLE 7.A1
Harley-Davidson: summary of financial statements, 1994–1998 ($ million, except per-share data)

	1994	1995	1996	1997	1st half 97	1st half 98
Net sales	1,159	1,350	1,531	1,762	871.2	983.7
Gross profit	358	411	490	586	288.5	327.4
Operating Income						
Motorcycle and related products					135.5	154.3
Financial services	—	3.6	7.8	12.4	5.6	8.9
Selling, admin., engineering					(4.6)	(5.2)
Total income from operations	153.6	180.8	228.4	270.0	136.4	158.0
Interest income	1.7	0.1	3.3	7.9	3.7	1.4
Other income/(expense)	1.2	(4.9)	(4.1)	(1.6)	2.0	(1.8)
Income before taxes	156.4	176.0	227.6	276.3	142.1	157.7
Provision for income taxes	60.2	64.9	84.2	102.2	52.6	57.5
Net Income	104.3	112.5	166.0	174.1	89.5	100.1
Earnings per share (diluted)	$0.62	$0.73	$0.94	$1.13	$0.59	$0.66
Balance sheets	*1994*	*1995*	*1996*	*1997*	*June 1997*	*June 1998*
Assets						
Current assets						
Cash and cash equivalents	59.3	31.5	142.5	147.5	144.5	154.5
Finance receivables, net	—	169.6	183.8	249.3	237.7	346.1

TABLE 7.A1 *Continued*

Balance sheets	1994	1995	1996	1997	June 1997	June 1998
Accounts receivable, net	143.4	134.2	141.3	102.8	198.7	91.3
Inventories	173.4	84.4	101.4	117.5	101.4	131.5
Other	20.1	20.3	44.0	43.0	40.9	44.6
Total current assets	405.6	337.2	613.1	704.0	644.1	724.1
Property, plant, equipment	262.8	284.8	409.4	528.9	454.1	562.0
Total assets	739.2	1,000.7	1,230.0	1,598.9	1,453.4	1,746.1
Liabilities and stockholder's equity						
Current liabilities						
Current portion of finance debt	18.2	2.7	8.6	90.6	56.3	126.0
Accounts payable	64.0	102.6	100.7	106.1	117.4	294.5
Total current liabilities	216.3	233.2	251.1	361.7	324.4	420.4
Finance debt	0	164.3	258.1	280.0	250.0	280.0
Other long-term liabilities	89.7	108.6	70.3	62.1	70.0	63.3
Post-retirement benefits	n.a.	n.a.	65.8	68.4	67.2	70.2
Total stockholders' equity	433.2	494.6	662.7	826.7	741.7	912.1
Total liabilities & stockholders' equity	739.2	1,000.7	1,230.0	1,598.9	1,453.4	1,746.0

Cash flows	1994	1995	1996	1997	1st half 97	1st half 98
Operating activities – net cash flow	80.8	169.1	228.3	309.7	100.6	166.7
Capital expenditures	(94.7)	(113.0)	(178.8)	(186.2)	(76.3)	(69.1)
Investing activities	(96.6)	(187.8)	(213.8)	(406.5)	(138.7)	(177.4)
Financing activities	(2.6)	(10.5)	96.5	101.8	40.1	17.7

Source: Harley-Davidson financial statements (www.harley-davidson.com).

APPENDIX 2
HARLEY-DAVIDSON'S COMPETITORS

Excelsior Henderson Motorcycle Manufacturing Company (Excelsior)

In the early 1990s two brothers, Dave and Dan Hanlon, bought the trademarks to a pre-war motorcycle manufacturer, Excelsior and Henderson. Formed in 1876, Excelsior Supply Co. was one of the top three US motorcycle manufacturers at the turn of the century along with Indian Motorcycle and Harley-Davidson. Its motorcycle was the first to break the 100 mph barrier. However, the company was liquidated during the Depression (1931). Over 60 years later, the Hanlon brothers are trying to resuscitate its image by manufacturing, marketing, and selling cruisers and touring bikes under the Excelsior brand name. The Hanlons feel that the Excelsior brand "evokes an authentic American motorcycling heritage and lifestyle"[35] and will be able to create a mystique similar to that associated with the Harley name.

The Hanlons have developed a prototype of a retro-style cruiser with the latest technology and accessories, such as electronic fuel injection, a four-valve cylinder, and an overhead cam engine. The Super X, the inaugural model, is "reminiscent of the classic American heavyweight cruiser" and will be sold through independent dealers at a sticker price between $17,000 and $20,000 (a price comparable to the high-end Harley "Fat Boy"). The first bike will be produced during the first quarter of 1998 with 5,500 orders already awaiting delivery. It is estimated that the company will need to sell 5,000 bikes per year to achieve break-even. Excelsior is projecting sales of $5.4 million in 1998 and $284 million in 2002.

Excelsior is a development-stage company with no revenue recorded to date and a reported net loss in 1997 of $5.9 million and a $2.5 million loss in 1996. Construction of the company's new administrative and manufacturing facility in Belle Plain, MN, was financed through a 1997 $28 million IPO and a $1.7 million State of Minnesota equipment financing bond. The facility will manufacture 20,000 bikes per year by 2003 and will include a motorcycle heritage museum. Since neither of the two brothers is experienced in motorcycle manufacturing and sales, the Hanlons have formed a top management team, which includes VP of Manufacturing and Operations Allan Hurd (a former production engineer at Triumph who assisted in the rejuvenation of that brand), and VP for Sales and Marketing Dave Auringer, who created the Sea-Doo dealership network. Auringer has already singed up 36 independent dealers (some of whom are Harley-Davidson dealers) with promised margins of 25 percent.[36] Dealers are already carrying Excelsior merchandise and accessories such as leather jackets and T-shirts which generated $100,000 sales in 1997.

Polaris

A leading snowmobile, ATV (all-terrain vehicle), and personal watercraft maker since the 1950s, Polaris will launch a new cruiser, the Polaris Victory, in the spring of 1998. With a retro look and new technology, Victory will target the high-margin, high-growth cruiser market dominated by Harley. Victory will have the biggest available V-engine (1507cc), overhead cams, and electronic fuel injection. High-tech engineering has also "eliminated some of the noise and vibration associated with a Harley."[37] The Victory will be positioned to compete with technologically advanced Honda, Suzuki, Kawasaki, and Yamaha cruisers, even though its price of $13,000 places it above most Japanese models. Polaris says that the plan is to "compete with Japanese on price, quality, and technology." The company stresses its "made in the USA" appeal to attract customers away from these foreign competitors and is counting on its previous experience making personal watercraft and ATVs to beat the competition. According to CEO Wendel, "We met these guys in snowmobiles and ATVs and we beat their asses off."[38] Polaris does have past success with taking on Japanese competitors. In the early 1990s, Polaris entered the personal watercraft and the ATV markets, both dominated by Japanese competitors – Kawasaki and Honda

TABLE 7.A2

Comparative financial data for Harley-Davidson, Polaris, and Excelsior ($ million, except per-share data)

	Harley-Davidson		Polaris		Excelsior	
	1996	1997	1996	1997	1996	1997
Balance sheet data						
Assets						
Current assets						
Cash	142.50	147.50	5.8	1.2	9.40	24.20
Trade receivables	141.30	102.79	36.2	42.6	0.00	0.00
Finance subsidiary receivables	183.80	293.33	0.0	0.0	0.00	0.00
Inventories	101.39	117.48	122.9	139.4	0.00	0.00
Other	44.14	42.96	28.5	34.1	0.01	0.11
Finance receivables (net)	154.26	249.35	0.0	0.0	0.00	0.00
Property and equipment (net)	409.43	528.87	93.5	98.0	0.23	13.40
Intangible assets (net)	40.90	38.70	24.4	23.5	0.14	0.20
Other	82.26	77.96	40.4	45.8	0.23	10.20
Liabilities						
Current liabilities	251.10	361.69	161.4	191.0	0.41	3.30
Long-term debt	250.00	280.00	35.0	24.4	0.00	13.70
Other	136.17	130.54	0.0	0.0	0.00	0.00
Shareholders' equity	662.72	826.67	155.3	169.2	9.60	31.20
Income statement data						
Sales	1,531.20	1,762.60	1,191.9	1,048.3	0.00	0.00
COGS	1,041.10	1,176.40	928.1	785.8	0.00	0.00
Gross profit	490.10	586.20	263.8	262.5	0.00	0.00
SG&A	224.35	262.91	138.1	142.7	1.41	3.9
R&D	37.30	53.30	28.3	26.7	1.27	2.60
Operating income	265.75	323.29	97.4	93.1	(2.68)	(6.50)
Non-operating expenses:						
Interest expense (income)	(3.30)	(7.87)	4.3	2.8	0.00	0.00
Taxes	84.20	102.20	35.0	36.8	0.00	0.00
Other expenses (income)	(18.52)	1.57	(4.20)	(11.80)	(0.17)	(0.63)
Net income	203.37	227.39	62.3	65.3	(2.51)	(5.87)
Net income per share	$1.10	$1.15	$2.24	$2.45	$(0.43)	$(0.65)

Sources: www.harley-davidson.com; www.polarisindustries.com; http://sec.gov

respectively. Since then, Polaris has gained the number two market share in ATV sales (37 percent of Polaris' 1996 revenue), and challenged Kawasaki's dominance of the personal watercraft market by gaining significant market share and brand recognition.

With $1.2 billion in revenues (1996) and 45 percent profit margins, Polaris is a very efficient and aggressive company with high-tech manufacturing capabilities and a wide distribution network of 2,000 dealers. Over 600 dealers have been selected to offer the Victory, and the company is counting on cross-selling opportunities with its other vehicles (28 percent of Polaris customers already own a motorcycle).[39] Aside from its distribution network, the company is also leveraging its engineering and manufacturing capabilities. Engineering of the new cruiser was performed in-house, lowering development costs, and production and assembly will take place at two plants that have extra capacity. As a result, the Victory was developed on a $20 million budget, and Polaris will reach break-even at 4,000 motorcycles per year (3 percent of the current cruiser market).

Polaris anticipates becoming a significant player in the motorcycle market in a few years by developing a line of touring, cruiser, and performance bikes with projected sales of $500 million by 2003. The company will limit production to 3,000 Victory cruisers this year, but will move to expand capacity to 40,000–50,000 per year.[40] Polaris is known as an efficient, low-cost manufacturer. Despite a decline in sales in 1996, the company reported its ninth year of increased earnings primarily due to cost-cutting measures and new engine-sourcing arrangements.[41]

BMW

Even though BMW sold ten times more cars than motorcycles in 1996, the company is committed to supporting and developing its line of bikes. In 1996 motorcycles contributed DM 1 billion to the company's DM 60 billion revenues.[42] BMW Motorcycles will celebrate its 75th anniversary in 1998 and its bikes have led the way to technical innovation, pioneering such things as advanced suspension systems, anti-lock brakes, and fuel injection.[43] Because of these technological innovations, BMW motorcycles have lower operating costs than the competition. In a recent comparison of Kawasaki and BMW touring bikes, the California Police Department estimated an operating cost of 1.9 cents per mile for the Kawasaki model tested, compared to an operating cost of 1.7 cents per mile for the BMW model tested.[44] The company has always been associated with a high technical and quality standard, and its motorcycles are also known for reliability, safety, and comfort. BMW is repositioning its motorcycle brand to build on this reputation but at the same time disassociate motorcycles from its luxury cars.[45]

BMW offers a full line of performance and touring bikes, and recently it has introduced its first cruiser, the R1200C. The motorcycle was introduced in 1997 as part of the latest James Bond movie, "Tomorrow Never Dies," and became BMW's best-selling bike in its first model year.[46] R1200C includes the latest technological innovations and safety features; however, it departs from the retro look favored by other producers. In creating the bike, BMW assumed that in the future "high performance cruisers will replace retro-look customs with a sportier look and feel."[47] The R1200C would be the first in this category. At a price of $23,600, the cruiser will be priced $2,000 above a comparable Harley model. However, the BMW motorcycle can command a premium due to its unsurpassed features such as anti-lock disc brakes (the only motorcycle to have this technology), superior acceleration performance,

TABLE 7.A3
Comparative financial data for Honda and BMW ($ million)

	Honda		BMW	
	1996	1997	1996	1997
Balance sheet data				
Assets				
Current assets				
Cash	2,894	2,035	437	451
Trade receivables	3,077	2,525	299	443
Finance subsidiary receivables	9,187	11,261	—	—
Inventories	4,442	4,395	1,084	1,186
Other	5,293	5,458	2,689	2,900
Property and equipment (net)	8,353	8,387	2,419	2,662
Intangible assets (net)	—	—	55	41
Other	532	536	2,717	3,041
Liabilities				
Current Liabilities	14,577	14,516	4,393	4,816
Long Term Debt	5,918	6,153	36	35
Other	2,095	1,956	1,346	2,146
Shareholders' equity	11,190	11,971	3,927	3,727
Income statement data				
Sales	41,477	45,383	18,269	20,200
COGS	29,406	31,336	11,633	12,966
Gross profit	12,071	14,047	6,636	7,234
Other operating income	—	—	584	491
SG&A	7,148	8,119	6,833	7,219
R&D	2,007	2,211	n.a.	n.a.
Operating income	2,916	3,717	386	506
Non-operating expenses				
Interest	222	194	—	—
Taxes	1,282	1,760	212	351
Other expenses (income)	(351)	(212)	(138)	(105)
Net income	1,763	1,975	313	260

See Table 7.A2 for comparable figures for H–D.
Exchange rates used:
   Yen/Dollar 1996: 124.08yen/$
   Yen/Dollar 1997: 130.10yen/$
   DM/Dollar 1996 and 1997: 1.77DM/$

Sources: http://www.honda.com and http://www.bmw.com

and a liquid-cooled engine (which allows the bike to idle in traffic and hot weather).[48] Half of R1200C buyers are those who already own a Harley, and the other half are those who own a Japanese motorcycle. BMW will introduce a new cruiser model in 1998 and a new touring model in 1999.[49]

Honda

Honda Motor Co. has been manufacturing motorcycles since 1948 and entered the US market in 1959, first with cheaper, lightweight bikes, before quickly moving into the higher-priced segments such as performance and touring bikes. Today, it is the world's largest motorcycle manufacturer, with 5,198,000 bikes produced in 1997 (vs. 54,000 made by BMW and 132,000 made by Harley).[50] The company holds 27 percent of the total US motorcycle market, a close second to Harley-Davidson. (See Table 7.3 for US market share data.) Honda is a superior engineering company and its motorcycles have traditionally been "on the leading edge of technology."[51] Its performance bikes have dominated motorcycle racing for decades and are associated with the world's greatest racers. In the early 1970s the company also had great success with street and touring bikes with the introduction of the style-setting CB750K0 in 1969 and the Goldwing, the world's first long-distance touring bike, in 1975.[52] Honda's motorcycles are technically superior to most of the competition, and are offered at a lower price owing to the company's scale and efficient distribution advantages. In 1998, Honda plans to revise its line of ten motorcycles to celebrate its 50th anniversary in the motorcycle business.[53]

Smaller competitors

Ducati,[54] a "highly regarded but underfunded [Italian] company" attracts customers by leveraging its legendary reputation for high-performance stylish motorcycles. Traditionally, the company has concentrated on the performance segment of the market and sells about 4,000 of these motorcycles in the US each year. However, in 1998 Ducati is expanding into the touring bike market in an effort to double its sales.

Triumph,[55] a British manufacturer, began motorcycle production in 1902. By 1909 the company was producing 3,000 bikes per year and by the 1950s became one of the world's most renowned motorcycle brands (in part thanks to its appearance as Marlon Brando's bike in the classic movie "The Wild One"). However, by the 1970s the company faced financial problems and was forced to liquidate in 1983. Primarily due to the efforts of its current head John Bloor, the company revived in the early 1990s and began development and production of new models. In 1996 the company produced 50,000 bikes (touring, cruisers) and unveiled plans to introduce a new performance motorcycle. The company's most popular model (25 percent of production capacity) is a cruiser, Thunderbird. Thunderbird's styling is similar to that of the 1960s Triumph model with the same name and the bike is positioned to capture a part of the lucrative heavyweight cruiser market.

Big Dog Motorcycles,[56] produces high-end, customized cruisers for prices that often exceed those of comparable Harleys (between $18,000 and $26,000). The company produces 300 bikes per year and primarily sells to customers who do not want to "buy a Harley and put thousands of dollars in it to get it up to real world standards."

Other Japanese competitors

Several Japanese companies followed Honda's example and entered the US motorcycle market in the 1970s. Yamaha, Suzuki, and Kawasaki began with sales of small, lightweight motorcycles and moved into the "heavyweight" segments of cruisers and touring bikes. Most compete on technological innovation and low price driven by the economies of scale of these large companies. However, while these companies had great success in gaining share in the overall motorcycle market (see Table 7.3), they have captured only 25 percent of the cruiser market, where the Japanese product competes less effectively against the "Made in the USA" Harley mystique.

NOTES

1. "Harley-Davidson reports record second quarter sales and earnings," Harley-Davidson press release, July 13, 1998 (www.harley-davidson.com).
2. Ibid.
3. Ibid.
4. Boston Consulting Group, "Strategy alternatives for the British motorcycle industry," Her Majesty's Stationery Office, London, July 30, 1975; quoted in Richard T. Pascale, "Perspectives on strategy: the real story behind Honda's success," *California Management Review*, March 23 (Spring 1984): 47–72.
5. Pascale, "Perspectives on strategy."
6. Ibid.
7. Peter Reid, "How Harley beat back the Japanese," *Fortune*, September 25, 1989.
8. Ibid.
9. Ruth W. Epps, "Just-in-time inventory management: implementation of a successful program," *St. John's University Review of Business*, September 22, 1995.
10. Ibid.
11. Ibid.
12. Gary Strauss, "Born to be bikers," *USA Today*, November 5, 1997.
13. Marc Ballon, "Born to be wild," *Inc*, November 1997, p. 42.
14. Nicholas Korkham, *The World's Greatest Brands*, New York: Macmillan, 1996.
15. Ibid.
16. http://www.harley-davidson.com/experience/family/hog
17. Ibid.
18. Reid, "How Harley beat back the Japanese."
19. Ibid.
20. Lillie Guyer, "Escape roads," *Auto Week*, February 23, 1998.
21. Tom Tucker, "Davidson clan member recalls Harley's U-turn," *Daytona Beach News Journal*, March 16, 1996.
22. S. Eisenberg, "Harley-Davidson company report," Cibc Oppenheimer, October 14, 1997.
23. Ann Millen Porter, "One focus, one supply base," *Purchasing*, June 5, 1997.
24. Kevin R. Fitzgerald, "Harley's supplier council helps deliver full value," *Purchasing*, September 5, 1996.
25. Porter, "One focus, one supply base."
26. Stephen Roth, "Harley's goal: unify union and management," *Kansas City Business Journal*, May 16, 1997.
27. Ibid.
28. Clyde Fessler (H-D VP for Business Development), "Rotating leadership at Harley-Davidson: from hierarchy to interdependence," *Strategy & Leadership*, July 17, 1997.
29. Ibid.

30. Marco R. della Cava, "Motorcycle maker caters to the continent," *USA Today*, April 22, 1998.

31. Ibid.

32. "Harley battles to stay on top of US biker revival," *Financial Times*, April 22, 1998.

33. Chris Reidy, "Wheels are in motion for area Harley dealer," *Boston Globe*, April 24, 1998.

34. "Harley battles to stay on top of US biker revival."

35. "Excelsior Henderson selects J. D. Edwards to provide smooth ride to growth," *Business Wire*, March 24, 1998.

36. "Motorcycles," *The Orlando Sentinel*, November 13, 1997; and Ballon, "Born to be wild."

37. Macario Juarez, "City business to help debut American Harley rival," *Albuquerque Tribune*, December 18, 1997.

38. Paul Klebnikov, "Clear the roads, here comes Victory," *Forbes*, October 20, 1997.

39. Ronald Ahrens, "Harley faces competition from Polaris bike," *Star Tribune*, December 20, 1997.

40. Strauss, "Born to be bikers."

41. James Miller, "Spotlight on: Polaris Industries," *Anchorage Daily News*, March 15, 1998.

42. http://www.bmw.com

43. Richard Truett, "Motorcycling has long run in the BMW family," *The Orlando Sentinel*, March 5, 1998.

44. John O'Dell, "Giving chase: BMW wants to break Kawasaki's and Harley's hold on the police market," *Los Angeles Times*, September 21, 1997.

45. "BMW in control with Bond bike cruiser," *The San Diego Union Tribune*, March 14, 1998.

46. Truett, "Motorcycling has long run in the BMW family."

47. Adrian Blake, "Two motorcycle giants celebrate anniversaries," *The Toronto Star*, April 11, 1998.

48. O'Dell, "Giving chase"; and *The Evening Post* (Wellington), November 21, 1997.

49. Jean Halliday, "BMW bikes get 'bridge' print ad effort for spring," *Advertising Age*, March 30, 1998.

50. http://www.honda.com; http://www.bmw.com; and Table 7.1.

51. Blake, "Two motorcycle giants."

52. Ibid.

53. Ibid.

54. Valerie Morris, "Ducati's market challenge," *Business Unusual*, CNN, April 17, 1998.

55. http://www.georgian.net/rally/triumph

56. http://www.bigdogmotorcycles.com

CHAPTER EIGHT

STEINWAY & SONS

This case was prepared by Professors Suresh Kotha (the School of Business Administration, University of Washington) and Roger Dunbar (Stern School of Business, NYU) with assistance from Joseph H. Alhadeff (Stern, MBA, '95), Gerald Tennenbaum (Stern, MBA, '95), and Professor Xavier Martin (Stern) as the basis for class discussion rather than to illustrate either effective or ineffective handling of an administrative situation.

A Steinway is a Steinway. . . . There is no such thing as a "better" Steinway. Each and every Steinway is the best Steinway.

Theodore Steinway

Bruce Stevens sat in the chair where Henry Z. Steinway, the last of Steinway family dynasty, once sat. Across the table from him was Bob Dove, the firm's executive vice-president. They were discussing issues concerning the growing size of the Chinese market and Steinway & Sons' strategy to enter this market.

The 1990s was a period of change for the music industry. Foreign competition in the mid-price upright-piano market was intense. Further, in addition to well entrenched players from Japan, Yamaha and Kawai, two South Korean firms, Young Chang and Samick, were emerging as strong competitors. Moreover, Yamaha and Young Chang had already established a presence in China. Forecasts indicated that the future market for pianos will be concentrated in Asia.

This case discusses Steinway & Sons' history, the evolution of its value system, and the current market conditions facing the firm. It highlights the issues faced by Steinway & Sons as its top management formulate their strategy towards the growing Chinese piano market.

COMPANY BACKGROUND

The Steinway Family Years – 1853 to 1971

Steinway & Sons was founded in 1853 by Henry E. Steinway, Sr. and his sons, Henry, Jr., Charles, and William. In 1854 the firm entered and won its first competition. A year later, it won first prize at the American Institute Fair in New York. By 1860,

Steinway & Sons had built a manufacturing facility at 52nd Street and Fourth (now Park) Avenue, on the site now occupied by the Waldorf Astoria Hotel. Here, 350 men produced 30 square pianos and 5 grands per week. In 1864, the firm opened a showroom on 14th Street. In 1865 sales topped $1,000,000.

From the beginning, piano building at Steinway & Sons was a family affair. Each of the Steinway sons concentrated on gaining expertise in a different aspect of piano manufacturing: William was a "bellyman" who installed the piano soundboards, Henry, Jr. focused on piano "finishing," and Charles concentrated on "voicing" the piano. By 1854, the Steinways were employers and the family members had become managers. Henry E., Sr. was in charge overall, while Henry, Jr. focused on research and development, Charles on managing the plant, and William on marketing.

Music historians consider the competition at the 1867 Paris Exhibition as the turning point in the piano industry because it was there that the "American" system of cast-iron frames, heavier strings, solid construction, and more powerful tone took the competitive honors from the European pianos. The jury report gave the Steinway piano a slight edge over the other major US manufacturer, Chickering & Sons, due to its expression, delicate shading, and a variety of accentuations.

With this recognition, Steinway's domestic piano sales and exports grew rapidly, requiring greater production capacity. In 1870, under William's leadership the firm purchased 400 acres of remote farm land in Astoria, Queens with the idea of moving the factory from Manhattan. By 1873, the factory was operating, and Steinway-sponsored employee housing, transport, and other facilities were built. Two years later, the firm opened a showroom in London. Ten years later, to avoid US labor issues and build a global presence, the firm built a factory in Hamburg, Germany. Pianos manufactured there were marketed in Europe and exported to the rest of the world. Even today, these two factories remain the only manufacturing centers.

In the 1870s, low-cost piano producers were a significant competitive threat. Conflict emerged between William and Theodore concerning the best way to respond. (C. F. Theodore was the fourth son of the founder and had joined the firm following his brothers' deaths in 1865.) The choice was to continue to emphasize class and high quality as William favored, or to make inexpensive models as advocated by Theodore. William's view won out. Ever since, the firm has remained steadfast in its focus on the high-end segment of the market.

At the turn of the century, the public developed an interest in "player" pianos. Steinway & Sons, however, showed no interest in these add-on technologies. Sales of "player" pianos plummeted after radio broadcasting began in 1920. In contrast, Steinway's sales continued to climb. They were supported by extensive advertising and a generous sponsorship program which deployed 600 Steinways to support concert artists.

Successive generations of Steinways sought to follow the founder's advice: "We provide customers with the highest quality instrument and services, consistent with Steinway's reputation for excellence, by building the finest piano in the world and selling it at a reasonable profit." This approach was threatened when the US economy entered a depression in the 1930s and the firm's survival was at stake. To market pianos to people of more modest means with smaller homes, Steinway developed and introduced two new models, the 5 feet 1 inch (now popularly known as the "baby grand") and a 40 inch upright (vertical) piano. With the outbreak of World War II, sales dropped again.

When piano making resumed in 1946, the television set was at the center of the American home, not the piano. The task of rebuilding Steinway & Sons fell to Henry Z. Steinway, a fourth generation Steinway, who took over the responsibility for manufacturing. His brother John took over promotions and marketing. To help consolidate the firm financially, Henry Z. sold Steinway Hall on 57th street in Manhattan (the company's showroom), and leased back the lower two floors.

In the 1960s, new competition emerged from Asia. Yamaha and Kawai began exporting thousands of pianos to the United States. A Yamaha piano sold for about one half the price of the equivalent Steinway model. By the early 1970s, the Japanese threat raised doubts about the future of Steinway & Sons and the entire US piano industry. Henry Z. decided to sell:

> Among the active family members, none were getting younger. And no young Steinways were interested in the firm. In the mid-twenties, two stockholder managers could get in a room and do anything they wanted. With the depression, shares were diluted bringing many new owners. The New York factory was located in an area hostile to manufacturing. Other piano makers had moved South to where they appreciated manufacturers. If we chose to move, we needed lots of capital.

In 1972 the firm was sold and merged into the CBS Musical Instruments Division. Henry Z. observed:

> Japan represents both an opportunity and a menace. As the largest market in the world for new pianos, having surpassed the US, possibly Steinway could enter that market effectively with the aid of CBS. Conversely, free from restraints imposed by antitrust legislation in the US, one huge company [Yamaha] has the avowed purpose of overcoming Steinway. Why CBS and not General Motors or US Steel? CBS wanted us at a price we thought right. More importantly, we thought CBS could and would handle our product in the right way.

The CBS Years – 1972 to 1984

CBS increased capital spending from $100,000 annually to $1–2 million. Workers received the medical and retirement benefits of other CBS employees. These were a big improvement over what had been provided previously. To facilitate continuity, Henry Z. remained president. Nevertheless, many concerns soon arose. According to industry reports:

> Once CBS entered upon its own period of decline, Steinway was plagued by bureaucratic confusion, changing strategies and parades of efficiency experts. There were four Steinway presidents in [16 years]. "Quality control" slipped. . . . There were pianists who began to say that the Steinway was no longer a great instrument; the market for half-century old rebuilt Steinways boomed.[1]

Recalling the top management changes under CBS, Henry Z. Steinway observed:

> Each new [division] president wanted to do something different. It was like riding a different horse every six months – first it was quality, then it was volume, then it was automation. It was not a bad time. Generally, though, the firm was drifting from one program to another. Also, I got so many memos from the parent corporation [CBS Musical Instruments Division] that after a while, I simply ignored them. I also thought it was rather amusing that I reported to the head of the division in California who, in turn, reported to a guy at the [CBS] headquarters just a few blocks from our offices in Manhattan.

Further, CBS often showed little regard or understanding for Steinway's established traditions. An example concerned hiring practices. The Steinway tradition encouraged workers to bring their relatives to work for the firm. It was believed this was a good way of preserving established skills and it also encouraged loyalty and a reliable, motivated work force. Under CBS, however, such "nepotism" was strictly forbidden. Fed-up Henry Z. retired from the firm in 1980.

During the early 1980s, under the fourth CBS president, quality was revived and the firm introduced a new upright. This new 52 inch piano was aimed at institutions and music schools. Then CBS decided to divest all of its music businesses. The *Smithsonian Magazine* reported:

> That announcement alone nearly completed what earlier sloppiness and mismanagement could not. . . . In 1984, the year of the sale, Steinway was earning $8 million on $60 million in revenues. The sale, involving at least 18 interested parties, dragged out over a period of ten months. There were rumors that the factory would be sold for its real estate value. CBS claimed to be concerned over the future of the company, but finally it needed cash to fend off attempts to take it over. And so CBS sold Steinway & Sons in haste, along with three other musical instrument companies, for less than 50 million – a much smaller sum than was offered earlier by serious devotees of the instrument.[2]

This brought morale among Steinway workers to an all-time low.

The Birmingham Years – 1985 to 1995

CBS sold Steinway & Sons and the rest of its Musical Instruments Division to John and Robert Birmingham, two brothers from Boston who had made their fortune in Massachusetts through a family-owned heating-oil business. As the Steinway work force had just survived the uncertainty and confusion of the CBS years, they were not predisposed to trust strangers. Nevertheless, in December, 1985, the Birminghams took control.

Lloyd Meyers, the last CBS president, had tried to organize a leveraged buyout. Following the firm's acquisition he left, as did the chief financial officer. Bruce Stevens became president. Before the sales force had been managed by a two-day-a-week manager, now the Birminghams placed it under Frank Mazurco, a long time

Steinway district-sales manager. The number of US dealers was reduced from 152 to 92. A program was established to strengthen the ties between Steinway & Sons and its dealers. A formal 5-day program for technicians was established to provide hands-on training at both the New York and Germany plants. Additionally, the firm instituted a 3-year strategic planning process. To instill more "discipline" into manufacturing, top management replaced the factory manager with Daniel Koenig, a manufacturing engineer who had spent 21 years at GE.

Under Koenig, the firm introduced state-of-art machines for manufacturing some components such as hammers so tolerances could be brought within carefully established limits. Further, the whole "action-mechanism" department was reorganized and moved into a single location. New programs such as statistical process control were introduced. Engineers were hired and provided with state-of-art computer-aided design technology. Their goal was to document the design and manufacturing process using old Steinway drawings, many of which dated back to the turn of the century.

These changes were viewed as controversial by some employees, music critics, and other followers of the firm. They observed that changes introduced by top management seemed aimed primarily at increasing efficiency to the detriment of Steinway's historical traditions of craftsmanship and quality. Steinway management countered by arguing that employing a modern, scientific approach to manufacturing was not a break with, but rather a continuation of, Steinway traditions.

In 1991, Steinway & Sons introduced a new line – the Boston Pianos – designed to compete in the mid-range piano market, where prices are around $10,000. This line was designed by Steinway & Sons and manufactured at Kawai's factory in Japan. According to Bruce Stevens:

> Steinway dealers had suggested that a logical step up strategy to a Steinway piano was needed. The availability of many competent lower-priced pianos made making a Steinway sale to a novice pianist harder to justify. We decided that a new line of mid-priced pianos were necessary.

Steinway dealers now had a piano they could offer to compete against similarly-priced pianos made by Yamaha, Young Chang, Kawai, and Samick. Currently, the Boston line includes four grand-piano models ranging in length from 5 feet 4 inches to 7 feet 2 inches, as well as four vertical models ranging in height from 44 to 52 inches. The line does not include a full-size, concert grand. As they were originally intended strictly as an export from Japan, the Boston pianos sell for 25 percent more than Japanese domestic pianos.

According to John Birmingham, perhaps the most important ingredient that the new owners brought to Steinway was their attitude. Noted John:

> We did not purchase the company to move it and make a fortune in real estate, or to silk-screen Steinway t-shirts, or to go public and make a killing on the stock offering. It was our intention to operate the Steinway piano business in a vigorous and creative way. Our guiding principle has been to guard and nurture the quality and integrity of the Steinway piano.

During the Birminghams' tenure, worker morale was gradually re-established. Discussions between management and workers evolved so appropriate modernization of technical equipment occurred while respect for the unique aspects of the craft mode of production associated with a Steinway piano was maintained. In 1995, one the firm's harshest critics from the *New York Times* acknowledged the following:

> A recent tour of the Steinway's factory in Queens showed an apparently serious effort to improve the instrument. The final stages of manufacture receive more attention than they did a few years ago. Outside technicians have also reported improvements in Steinways, a heartening sign.[3]

Enter Selmer Company, 1995

In 1995, Steinway & Sons was purchased by the Selmer Company, Inc. for around $100 million. This firm based in Elkhart, Indiana has manufacturing facilities in La Grange, Illinois, Cleveland, Ohio, and Monroe, North Carolina. The Steinway & Sons management team installed by the Birminghams remains intact and in charge.

Commenting on the merger, Dana Messina, an investment banker and a controlling shareholder of Selmer's parent corporation, noted:

> The combination of Steinway and Selmer is an exciting opportunity for both of the companies and their employees. Our extensive investigation has made it clear that Steinway's New York factory today produces excellent instruments of a quality unequaled in many years, and the Steinways made in the company's Hamburg factory continue to dominate the European and Asian concert scene. . . . We intend to continue the mission of producing great instruments that has been pursued by Steinway.

The new owners made an IPO stock offering to raise $60 million in August 1996.

THE STEINWAY LEGACY

There are two fundamentals in understanding the origins of the Steinway legacy: technical innovation and marketing. Around 1800, the piano's identity was still in its formative stages, but by the 1850s, the piano's basic structure was defined. This permitted the Steinways to model and improve the form of the piano and, ultimately, the entire industry.

Building Technical Capabilities

In 1850, producers were working to make piano performance more reliable and louder. This was because new piano works by romantic composers were appearing and they demanded a broader range of tones. In addition, larger concert halls were being built. These developments served to establish a need for pianos with a louder tone. The general objective of Steinway & Sons' efforts was to develop pianos that were reliable and offered a more powerful tone.

Experimentation at Steinway & Sons was done primarily by two of the founder's sons, Henry, Jr. and Theodore. These Steinway brothers experimented and developed theories about improvements to both the design and the manufacture of pianos. In 1911, Alfred Dolge chronicled the history of the piano industry. He described Theodore's approach as follows:

> Step by step he [Theodore] invaded the fields of modern science, investigating and testing different kinds of wood in order to ascertain why one kind or another was best adapted for piano construction, then taking up the study of metallurgy, to find a proper alloy for casting iron plates which would stand the tremendous strain of 75,000 pounds of the new concert-grand piano that was already born in his mind, calling chemistry to his aid to establish the scientific basis for felts, glue, varnish oils, – in short, nothing in the realm of science having any bearing on piano construction was overlooked.[4]

Over a 50-year period starting in 1857, the firm obtained 58 patents for various innovations to piano design. At international exhibitions in Europe, the Steinways proudly showed off their new methods and basked in the resulting acclaim. One consequence was that their methods were copied widely, especially in Europe. By the 1870s, the "Steinway System" was well recognized and by the end of the century it became the *de facto* industry standard.

During the mid-nineteenth century, many new industrial technologies emerged to cause a revolution in piano manufacturing. Steinway & Sons was at the forefront of these developments, implementing innovative and unique approaches to piano manufacturing. At their large facility opened in 1860, they standardized various parts of the piano to facilitate volume manufacturing, refitting, and servicing. Yet though the firm used increased mechanization to produce standardized components, it retained a "craft" approach for other components and for assembling pianos. The combination of the mechanized technologies and individual craft skills quickly became a hallmark of the Steinway approach to piano manufacture.

Building Reputation

From its beginnings, Steinway & Sons faced intense competition from rivals such as Chickering and Mason & Hamlin in the US, and Erard and Broadwood in Europe. Facing this competition, the firm sought to present its product to highlight not only the unique construction of the Steinway piano but also its "superior" sound.

To do this, the firm entered its pianos in contests that compared manufacturers' products. In 1854, for example, the firm exhibited a square piano at the Metropolitan Fair held in Washington, D.C., and received a prize medal. A year later, Steinway & Sons entered the American Institute Fair in New York and the judges awarded it first prize from among 19 competitors.

[Steinway & Sons'] great triumph came at the great fair of the American Institute in New York in 1855, where their overstrung square piano with full iron frame created a sensation in the piano world. As a result their business expanded so rapidly that in 1859 the erection of that mammoth factory on Fifty-third Street and Fourth Avenue, New York, became a necessity.[5]

To gain international recognition, Steinway & Sons, along with 130 other manufacturers, entered the International Exhibition held at the Crystal Palace in London in 1862. Steinway & Sons was recognized as the best American manufacturer and was awarded a first prize. The main prize went to Broadwood. In 1867, the firm entered the Paris Exposition along with 178 other firms. Both Steinway and Chickering were awarded gold medals at this exposition.

Winning by not competing

At the major manufacturers' competition held in Vienna in 1873, around two thirds of the pianos exhibited were built according to the Steinway system. Steinway & Sons did not compete, having reached an agreement with Chickering not to participate so as to avoid continuation of the shrill accusations that had arisen between the two rivals after the Paris Exposition.[6] With the competition over, however, the judges issued a statement regretting that Steinway & Sons, the celebrated inaugurators of the new piano-making system, had chosen not to exhibit. From the standpoint of enhancing their reputation for making a superior piano, Steinway & Sons "won" in Vienna by not competing.

Industry rivalries also prevented Steinway & Sons from participating at the 1893 World's Fair held in Chicago and 15 eastern firms joined this boycott. As expected, W. W. Kimball, a Chicago piano manufacturer, won the highest award. At this time, Steinway & Sons was promoting a US tour of the Polish virtuoso Ignance Jan Paderewsky. Paderewsky was invited to play at the exhibition's inauguration, but only if he would play on a piano entered in the competition. Paderewsky countered that he could only play on a piano he was used to playing. The organizers relented and Paderewsky played his Steinway. Again, Steinway & Sons enhanced their reputation by not competing.

A Steinway is a Steinway

Steinway & Sons always sought to establish a reputation for itself as the firm that built the "best" piano for musicians, especially concert artists. It also sought to establish itself as being a contributor to, supporter for, and leader of the cultural arts. As Dolge noted:

They never relaxed in letting the public know that they manufactured a fine piano. William Steinway, with far-seeing judgment, was not satisfied only to use printer's ink with telling effect, but he also began to educate the public to appreciate good music. Steinway Hall was erected, the Theodore Thomas orchestra generously supported and the greatest piano virtuosos from Rubinstein to Joseffy engaged for concerts, not only in New York but in all large cities of the United States and Canada.[7]

Steinway Hall, designed and built by William Steinway in 1866, was the largest concert hall in New York City. Notes Dolge:

The opening of this hall was the inauguration of a new era in the musical life of America. Anton Rubinstein, Annette Essipoff, Teresa Carreno, Fannie Bloomfield-Zeisler, Rafael Joseffy, Eugene D'Albert, Leopold Damrosch and Anto Seidl made their bows to select audiences from the platform of Steinway Hall. William Steinway knew that the American people needed musical education. He provided it.[8]

Steinway Hall served as New York City's leading concert hall until 1890, when it was replaced by the newly built Carnegie Hall.

Concert artist endorsements were another method used by Steinway & Sons to convince the public that their pianos were superior. Initially, the effort at Steinway & Sons was largely opportunistic and informal. But the benefits of more large-scale efforts were recognized as a result of the 215-concert US tour in 1872 by the virtuoso Anton Rubinstein, who was sponsored by Steinway & Sons. Rubinstein and his Steinway dazzled audiences. In 1891, the Steinway-sponsored concert tour of the Polish virtuoso Ignance Jan Paderewsky was also a great success. Paderewsky cleared an unprecedented $200,000 from his tour but the promotional value to Steinway & Sons was immeasurable.

Concerts, the artist, and the sponsor all received ecstatic press coverage. In 1912, Charles Steinway, the president of Steinway & Sons, observed: "It was without doubt the most effective of all advertising methods we employed, since it not only made the piano and its maker widely known, but assisted in laying the foundation for a broad national culture."

Though Steinway & Sons has never offered to reduce the price of its pianos, it has sought endorsements from New York's social elite.[9] To this and other groups, the firm presents itself as offering a high quality product worthy of a high price. Still today, the price of Steinway pianos is the highest in the industry. Often this price is nearly double that of Yamaha, the firm's most competitive rival in the United States.

Steinway & Sons has consistently emphasized its commitment to the cultural enrichment of the nation and the world. The firm's promotions argue, for example, that the act of buying a piano was not the same as the act of buying a Steinway. Buying a Steinway is depicted as a high achievement, an indication of an appreciation for high cultural taste. The firm also built an international presence. Dolge noted:

> Having established the fame of his piano in America beyond dispute, William [Steinway] looked for other worlds to conquer, and opened a branch house in the city of London about the year 1875. Steinway Hall in London was formally opened in 1876. In 1880 Hamburg factories were started, to supply the ever-growing European Trade.[10]

The Hamburg facility was established primarily to challenge the domination of European piano markets by companies such as Bechstein, Bluthner, and Ibach. At the time, the firm was the only piano maker that served all well-known concert artists in every major city in America and in Europe. According to Fostle, an author and keyboard expert, "A Steinway piano soon became recognized as an admired cultural icon in any refined home, a necessary element on any prominent concert stage, and part of the necessary baggage of any prominent pianist."[11]

Building a Marketing Approach

Like its competitors, Steinway & Sons originally sought out and paid for endorsements from prominent concert artists. Over time, however, Steinway and other firms ceased paying for endorsements. Concert artists, however, still chose to endorse the Steinway piano over others. Today, more than 90 percent of all classical music concerts featuring a piano soloist are performed on a Steinway concert grand piano.[12] This endorsement from a group of experts has remained stable for many decades. Music schools and conservatories such as Juilliard, Oberlin, and Indiana University have always showed a great fondness for Steinways.

Steinway & Sons sought to be associated with high culture, style, status, and class. In 1855, the firm started advertising daily in the *New York Times*. Gradually, Steinway & Sons moved to much more extensive advertising campaigns.

> To the astonishment and chagrin of the older and more conservative houses in the piano trade, William [Steinway] started an aggressive and heretofore unheard-of advertising campaign. As a competent judge he knew that his factories turned out the best pianos that could possibly be made, and he was bent not only on letting the world know it, but on making the world believe it, as he did. This was revolutionary, even shocking, but William persisted until he carried his point.[13]

Steinway as an investment

In 1900, Steinway & Sons hired N. W. Ayer & Son, the oldest full-service advertising agency in the country, to promote Steinway pianos. Ayer & Son emphasized that many potential Steinway buyers were not only interested in music but were greatly interested in class and status. Their interest in owning a Steinway would increase as the class and status associated with the Steinway name could be emphasized.

Systematically, the firm broadened the message in its promotions. Firm advertising emphasized, for example, that one did not "buy" but "invested" in a Steinway, that there was no such thing as a better Steinway but just the best Steinway, that being the owner of a Steinway was more important than being able to play it, and that a Steinway piano was always made just a little bit better than was necessary. Steinway advertising was targeted to emphasize, as appropriate, family values, the contributions to art and music of Steinway & Sons, Steinway's technical excellence, or some combination of these. Forging a link with the art community, the firm commissioned paintings showing famous artists and composers, past and present, linked to the Steinway piano. The "timeless" excellence of a Steinway was emphasized.

> The commission and use of modern art in Steinway ads of the 1920s was an extension of the advertising style that the New York firm [N. W. Ayer & Son] had employed for decades. . . . [W]ith Steinway the association was natural. However much another product's image was improved by its proximity to art, it remained a mere product. The Steinway itself became art.[14]

In the 1920s, the program to make sure all outstanding concert artists used a Steinway grew to include over 600 supported artists. With a consistent and overwhelming advertising message and its US competition in retreat, the firm convinced the public that a Steinway was the only "artistic" piano.[15]

According to *Forbes* magazine, a Steinway piano outperforms Mercedes-Benz automobiles, power boats, wine, and gold as luxury items for investment. A Steinway created between 1929 and 1958 is now worth 5.9 times its original cost; for those dating from 1959 to 1978 the factor of appreciation currently stands at 2.8 times. Piano rebuilders are known to scour the world in search of old Steinways because, regardless of its age or neglect, a Steinway grand can often be restored to its original magnificence.

The 1970s and 1980s saw new competition emerge from Asian competitors. Of particular interest was Yamaha's announced intention to "overtake" the status associated with a Steinway. Yamaha's president claimed this would be done by promoting Yamaha's sound quality and tone along with the status and class associated with the Yamaha name. Despite Yamaha's avowed threat to overtake the status of Steinway & Sons, the firm's reputation as producer of the best sounding piano has remained pretty much intact. Back in 1911, Dolge noted:

> Just as a most masterful copy of a Raphael or Correggio will ever be only a copy and far from the original, so it has proved impossible to produce a piano equal to the Steinway piano, even though the Steinways were copied to the minutest detail. No art product can be duplicated by copying.

MANUFACTURING STEINWAYS

Manufacturing a Steinway piano is a labor intensive and time consuming process. A Steinway concert grand piano is one of the world's most complex pieces of hand-built machinery. It consists of over 12,000 parts and requires about a year to complete. Approximately 300 craftspeople have a hand in its development.

The 44,000 square feet New York factory supplies dealers in North and Latin America, while the Hamburg plant manufactures pianos for sale through dealers and distribution in Europe, Africa, and Asia. The New York manufacturing facility manufactured about 67 percent of Steinway pianos sold in 1995. This facility consists of many linked buildings that house the factory and Steinway's offices. In 1985, 260 direct workers and 61 non-direct workers were involved in manufacturing pianos. The production workers are represented by Local 102 of the United Furniture Workers, a small two-company local that has bargained with Steinway management for decades. In 1986, wages averaged approximately $9.00 per hour ($12 including fringes). About 25 percent of the skilled artisans are paid via piece rates, while other workers are paid on a straight-time basis. Throughout the factory there are workers who represent families that have been with the firm for generations. Currently, the work force has a multinational cast of first-generation immigrants. Over 17 languages are spoken in the factory.

The factory is part lumber mill, part fine-cabinet works, part manual-crafts assembly line, and part studio for industrial craftsmen and women working an art acquired through many years of apprenticeship. Although the buildings have undergone significant changes over the years, the piano-making operations have hardly changed for over a century.

The lumber mill

The mill, the factory's lumber yard, carries approximately 1.5 million board-feet of select woods (costing approximately over $2 million) such as hard rock maple and sitka spruce, among others. Twice a year, the firm's wood technologist, Warren Albrecht, goes to Canada and the American Northwest to identify wood of sufficient quality and grain to be used by Steinway. These woods are first air-dried in the open for about 18 months and then kiln-dried using computer controlled equipment that was recently installed. Reduction of the wood's moisture content through drying is essential for the instrument's acoustics. Through years of trial and error, the firm has managed to establish ideal moisture content and drying times for each of the instrument's various wooden components. It is here, via the world's finest woods, that the origins of what eventually becomes a Steinway piano lie.

Rim-bending operations

This operation focuses on the piano's rim (the curved sideboard giving grand pianos their shape and support) and the sound board (the board found inside the piano case that is specially tapered to reflect the sound made when strings are struck). A concert grand's rim requires a 22-feet-long, three-and-a-half-inches wide board of hard rock maple wood. Because boards of this length rarely occur in nature, thin slats of maple laminates (18-layers thick) are glued together to form the piece. When bent, this wooden piece forms the piano's familiar outer and the hidden inner rim that extends below the sound board and frame. Steinway's processes for bending the inner and outer board date back over a century and remain unique in the industry. According to Steinway's long-time executives, it is this process that provides the instrument with greater strength and durability.

The rim-bending room consists of 8 piano-shaped forms of steel whose perimeters are fitted with screws and clamps. With the glue holding the 18 layers of laminates (for concert grands) still wet, the piece is manually pressed against the form and secured by iron pinions.[16] The bent rim is then heated by high frequency radio waves. Although technically the rim is ready in minutes, rather than in hours, for the next process, it remains in the iron form for 24 hours. Once removed, the piece is stacked in a humidity-controlled environment for 10 weeks. This curing period ensures that the rim retains its bent form. Following the waiting period, it is planed, sanded, and cross braced, following which a key-bed and a pin-block are inserted. Slowly the rim is transformed into a unitary piano case.

The sound board assembly

In another part of the factory, highly skilled wood workers create the piano's sound board. The sound board consists of 20 spruce boards, selected from the same lot of wood, meticulously cleared of any imperfections. These boards are matched for grain and color and glued along their lengths. Once glued, the board is thinned (in certain places) and tapered towards the ends. By the application of support ribs to its underside, the board is also slightly crowned. Then a bridge, the clef-shaped support for the strings, is affixed.

The action mechanism
The "guts" of the piano consists of the keys and action. Together the keys and action constitute the mechanism by which depressing the key causes the corresponding hammer to strike the string and return to its original resting place.[17] Once assembled, the actions are mated with the piano's keys and the entire "key-action assembly" mechanism is regulated to ensure proper movement. After being regulated the key-action assembly is moved to another part of the factory where the keys are weighted to ensure that they provide the appropriate touch and recoil. Proper touch and recoil results in the even-feel of a piano, an important trait of the legendary "Steinway experience." The mechanism is then fitted to a piano case. The foundation which supports the key-action assembly is the spruce key-bed.

The final assembly
The joining of the piano case and an iron plate to support the strings is carried out in the factory's "belly" room. The "bellying" process involves attaching the iron plate and the sound board to the inner rim of the piano case. This process takes up to eight hours over the course of two days. During this process, the sound board is securely affixed to the piano case using a special hot glue that ensures a good seal between the board and the piano case. The board installation process is critical for the proper resonance of the strings and multiple measurements are taken to ensure a proper fit.

Once the hot glue sets, the clamps holding the board in place are removed and the cast-iron plate is lowered into the case. Accurate installation of the plate ensures the proper bearing of the bridge, which then helps maintain the right pressure on the piano's strings; too little or too much pressure results in an instrument sounding weak or muffled. With the sound board and iron plate installation complete, the piano is ready for stringing. The stringing process involves the hammering of pins into a pin-block underneath the iron plate and inserting of about 243 strings. After the instrument is strung it passes through a "banger" which mechanically "pounds" every key about 8,000 times, all within a 45-minute time period. This "aging" process ensures that the sound notes emanating from the instrument are stable. The instrument is then regulated to ensure its moving parts – the key-action mechanism – interact properly.

The Steinway piano comes in flat and glossy finishes; the flat finish is the trademark of the Queens factory and the glossy finish is the mark of the Hamburg factory. Each piano receives five coats of lacquer prior to the insertion of the sound board and iron plate, but is not truly finished until the time of shipment. Once assembled, pianos are polished and rubbed in a manually intensive process.

The tone regulating department
Many of the sound-related operations are carried out in the tone regulation department by Steinway's most skilled technicians. Highly skilled "artisans" (as the firm

prefers to call them) optimize the final tone of the piano and do all the fine-tuning. For the concert grands, this process can take as long as a week per piano.

Tuning involves adjusting the piano strings to get the proper tonal quality and voicing entails final adjustments to the shape of the hammer, the feel of the felt, the movement and position of actions. With the personality or voice of the piano exposed, final adjustments are completed to optimize the instrument's sound qualities. The time taken to complete this process varies from 8 to 24 hours. The need to accommodate for the variations in the production process during the tuning and voicing processes contributes to the distinctive sound that each Steinway piano produces. Also, given the nature of the craft production process, each step is contingent upon the previous steps being accomplished properly and there is little room for error. Each piano sounds and feels a bit different. The firm allows prospective buyers to play several pianos and pick the one they think sounds best.

By the time a piano is assembled, strung, tuned, and voiced, it has gone through 25 to 30 quality checkpoints. The workers responsible for sound board placement, stringing, and tone adjustment and other "big jobs" often sign their work. According to one Steinway's tuner, "It's an aspiration of everybody to be immortal, and so, like an artist who signs his painting, I sign the piano. I put into the piano the best of myself."[18] In the 1980s, the late John Steinway observed:

> A Steinway is a Steinway only because we don't cut any corners. We make quality, nothing but the top quality we can make. My great-grandfather started that when he started the firm, 135 years ago. I often say we are probably thick-headed and stubborn; we stick to our principles. But it works.[19]

Arthur Loesser has chronicled the history of the piano and describes the sound of the Steinway concert grand piano most eloquently:

> The end result of the Steinway effort was a tone-producing tool of matchless strength and sensitiveness. . . . It was a marvelous kind of sound for the music that people loved then: thick, thundering piles of chord, booming batteries of octaves, and sizzling double jets of arpeggios. But the single Steinway tone, struck gently and held, also worked its ineffable spell, taking an endless, yearning time to die.[20]

In 1986, the total direct-labor costs for a grand piano averaged between $1,350 and $2,050, and for vertical pianos, averaged between $600 and $800. The material costs for a grand piano averaged between $1,900 and $3,600, and for vertical pianos, they averaged between $1,200 and $2,200. The firm produced about 2,500 pianos in 1988 in New York.

Historically, grand pianos have accounted for the bulk of Steinway's production. Steinway offers eight models of the grand pianos that range in length from 5 feet 1 inch for a baby grand to 9 feet for the largest concert-style piano. The smaller grands are sold to both individual and institutional customers, while the concert grands are sold primarily to institutions. Grand pianos are at the premium end of the piano market in terms of quality and price, with the Steinway grands dominating the high end of the market with retail prices ranging from $27,600 to $101,200 in the United States. Steinway produces vertical pianos to satisfy the needs of institutions and other customers who are constrained by space limitations but unwilling to compromise on quality. Steinway's four models of vertical pianos range in height from 45 inches to 52 inches.

THE MARKET AND COMPETITION

According to a 1990 survey conducted by the Gallup Organization for the American Music Conference, slightly more than four in ten (43 percent) US households contained at least one amateur instrumental musician. The survey reported that about 42 million "music-making" households existed in the United States. However, the proportion of households with one or more amateur musicians dropped from 46 percent in 1985 to 43 percent in 1990. About 44 percent of piano players were male and 56 percent were female.

Generally, players were under the age of 35 (the median age was 28). Among the musical instruments, piano and the guitar topped the list with about 40 percent of players playing the piano and 17 percent the guitar. Also, amateur musicians came from households that had a higher median income level ($45,860) than the total population ($37,640) and were headed by an adult with more than a high school education.[21]

Domestic Competition

In the 1960s, US piano manufacturers were first confronted with Japanese piano imports. The Japanese firms offered high quality pianos at a much lower price than US manufacturers. By 1968, two Japanese firms, Yamaha and Kawai, were selling 10,000 units annually. Together, they captured 5 percent of US upright sales and 28 percent of US grand piano sales.

The 1980s saw further significant change in the US piano market. Yamaha introduced the first all-digital synthesizer which could effectively produce a range of high quality sounds. Yamaha's introduction of the synthesizer effectively undercut the low-end acoustic piano market. In fact, sales of acoustic pianos declined from a high of 233,000 at the beginning of the 1980s to 50,000 units annually in 1994. As sales of upright pianos continue to decline, grand piano sales have increased (see Exhibits 8.1 and 8.2).

Though Japan and Korea held 11 percent of the US market in 1980, they held 38 percent of it by 1985. In the meantime, several US firms closed. Currently, only two US firms, Steinway & Sons and Baldwin, continue to make pianos. Several foreign firms, on the other hand, now have US manufacturing facilities. Kawai operates a plant in North Carolina, and Samick has a manufacturing facility in California. Currently, the high-volume producers are located in Japan, Korea, China, and the Soviet Union.

US piano market in 1995
In 1995, the musical instrument industry in the US generated retail sales of approximately $5.5 billion. The acoustic piano segment, which represents approximately

EXHIBIT 8.1:
Historical sales of pianos in the United States

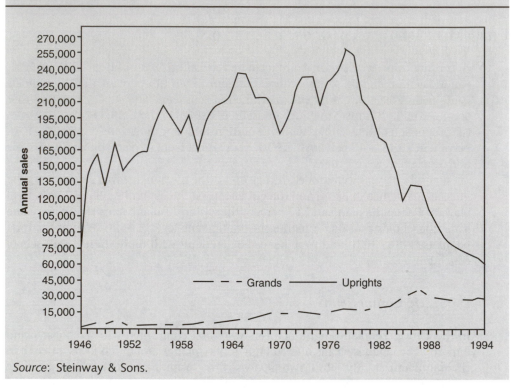

Source: Steinway & Sons.

11 percent of the total musical instrument industry, had retail sales of $598 million in 1995, up 7 percent from 1994.[22] This included an 11 percent increase for grand pianos over feet in length. During the period from 1991 to 1995, total dollar sales of grand pianos increased at an average annual rate of over 7 percent from $287.8 million to $371.8 million. Vertical pianos' dollar sales, in contrast, increased at an average rate of only 1.5 percent during the same period.

Steinway's domestic market share of the grand piano market was approximately 7 percent in 1995. Approximately 90 percent of Steinway unit sales were sold on a wholesale basis, with the remaining 10 percent being sold directly by Steinway at one of its five company-owned retail locations. Steinway & Sons operates five retail stores in New York, New Jersey, London, Hamburg, and Berlin. The West 57th Street store in New York City, known as Steinway Hall, is one of the largest and most famous piano stores in the world. Steinway pianos are sold by dealers in 45 states across the United States. The firm's major markets are in and around major metropolitan areas. The two largest regions in terms of sales are California and New York, which together accounted for approximately 20 percent of domestic wholesale revenues in 1995 (see Exhibit 8.3). The institutional segment of the US piano market, which includes music schools, conservatories, and universities, represented less than 10 percent of Steinway's domestic sales.[23] Steinway's largest dealer accounted for approximately 8 percent of sales in 1995, while the top 15 accounts represented 28 percent of sales.

In 1994, the firm sold 2,698 grand pianos worldwide (see Exhibit 8.4 for a history of Steinway grand piano sales). During this year, the firm reported a net income of $3.1 million on sales of $101 million (see Exhibit 8.5). Approximately 50 percent of Steinway's total sales were in the US, 37 percent were in Europe, and the remaining 13 percent were in Asia. Steinway's market share in Japan and Korea combined is less than 1 percent. Germany, Switzerland, France, the United Kingdom, and Italy accounted for the greatest percentage of sales outside the Americas. Steinway's largest European markets were Germany and Switzerland.

Steinway pianos are primarily purchased by affluent individuals with incomes in excess of $100,000 per year. The typical customer is over 45 years old and has a serious interest in music. Steinway's core customer base consists of professional artists and amateur pianists, as well as institutions such as concert halls, conservatories, colleges, universities, music schools, and other institutions. Customers purchase Steinway pianos either through one of the company's five retail stores or through independently owned dealerships. Over 90 percent of the firm's piano sales in the US are to individuals. In other countries, sales to individuals are a smaller percentage of the total sales.

Baldwin

This firm was founded by Dwight H. Baldwin, a music teacher, in 1862 as a retail piano business in Cincinnati. In 1865, Mr. Baldwin hired Lucien Wulsin as a bookkeeper. In 1870, he made him a partner in the enterprise. Until his death in 1912, Wulsin shaped Baldwin's development. Branch stores were opened in Indianapolis, Louisville, and other Ohio towns. In 1887, when M. Steinert & Company from Boston and a holder of a Steinway franchise opened a retail store in Cincinnati, Steinway & Sons canceled Baldwin's Cincinnati franchise. Wulsin responded by planning Baldwin's first manufacturing facilities and production started in Chicago in 1889. To sell Baldwin pianos, Wulsin introduced a dealer consignment program whereby the dealer only paid for the piano after it had been sold. The company also experimented with installment sales contracts. This combination of consignment selling and installment contracts led to the firm's rapid growth at the turn of the century. Baldwin's successful approach was copied by most other piano manufacturers.

Rapid growth of the firm in the 1950s and the inadequacies of the company's manufacturing facilities in Cincinnati convinced the company to move south. Eventually, five plants were opened, three in Arkansas, one each in Mississippi and Juarez, Mexico. Baldwin's offering included a line of high quality grand pianos and a line of relatively inexpensive verticals assembled in the firm's highly automated Arkansas plants.

During the 1970s, the firm transformed itself into a conglomerate, Baldwin-United Corp, and acquired banks, savings and loans, and insurance companies by running up a sizable debt which led it to file for bankruptcy protection in 1983. A

EXHIBIT 8.2:
Sales of US pianos by product type, 1992, 1987, and 1982

Product type	1992			1987			1982		
	Firms with shipments of $100,000 or more	Units[a]	Value[a] ($mil.)	Firms with shipments of $100,000 or more	Units[a]	Value[a] ($mil.)	Firms with shipments of $100,000 or more	Units	Value ($mil.)
Verticals, uprights, consoles, 37" or less in height	1	—	—	3	40,900	38.5	6	32,600	21.1
Verticals, uprights, consoles, more than 37" in height	7	53,700[b]	84.1[b]	5	52,100	75.1	14	141,400	141.5
Grand pianos	3	5,500	53.5	3	7,700	58.2	8	7,100	32.2

[a] No. of units shipped and value of shipments reported are for all producers in the industry, not just for those with shipments valued at greater than $100,000.
[b] Represents combined figures for all vertical and uprights. Figures for 37" or less are not available separately.

Source: US Bureau of Census, 1987.

EXHIBIT 8.3:
Steinway's top ten US markets, 1994

City	Sales ($000)
New York City	6,007
Los Angles	2,643
Baltimore/Washington D.C./Virginia	2,250
Dallas	1,642
Phoenix	1,438
Boston	1,144
San Francisco	1,078
Salt Lake City	848
Minneapolis/St. Paul	793
Detroit	605

Source: Steinway & Sons.

EXHIBIT 8.4:
Historical Steinway unit sales, 1965–1994

Year	US grands	Foreign grands	Total grands	Year	US grands	Foreign grands	Total grands
1994	1,720	978	2,698	1979	1,815	1,357	3,172
1993	1,631	887	2,518	1978	1,819	1,334	3,153
1992	1,344	917	2,261	1977	1,590	1,372	2,962
1991	1,550	1,438	2,988	1976	1,908	1,241	3,149
1990	2,117	1,459	3,576	1975	1,875	1,160	3,035
1989	2,096	1,385	3,481	1974	2,001	937	2,938
1988	2,144	1,283	3,427	1973	1,919	1,131	3,050
1987	2,144	1,237	3,381	1972	1,809	1,212	3,021
1986	1,763	1,369	3,132	1971	1,540	1,173	2,713
1985	1,337	1,291	2,628	1970	1,470	1,142	2,612
1984	1,876	1,340	3,216	1969	1,806	1,163	2,969
1983	2,036	1,263	3,299	1968	1,932	1,250	3,182
1982	1,677	1,141	2,818	1967	1,603	1,043	2,646
1981	2,041	1,394	3,435	1966	1,770	1,056	2,826
1980	1,897	1,349	3,246	1965	1,659	1,259	2,918

Source: Steinway & Sons.

EXHIBIT 8.5:
Steinway & Sons: income statement and balance sheet ($000)

	1990	1991	1992	1993	1994
Income statement data					
Net sales	92,037	98,816	89,240	89,714	101,896
Gross profit	33,673	35,586	30,759	26,139	31,636
Operating income	10,096	9,124	4,556	1,919	8,795
Income (loss) from continuing operations	3,077	2,753	(2,930)	(3,009)	2,847
Net income (loss)[a]	3,618	2,825	(10,335)	(3,009)	3,115
Ratio of earnings to fixed charges[f]	2	2	1	—[g]	2
Other data					
EBITDA[b]	13,500	13,535	9,591	6,067	13,068
Nonrecurring charges[c]	1,861	2,319	2,532	2,047	1,658
Interest expenses, net	3,448	3,186	3,307	4,390	3,842
Depreciation and amortization[d]	1,669	2,099	2,675	2,695	2,664
Capital expenditures[e]	2,451	1,889	1,936	1,237	1,145
Steinway grand pianos sold (in units)	3,558	3,282	2,648	2,245	2,569
Margins					
Gross profit, %	37	36	44	29	31
EBITDA, %	15	14	11	7	13
Balance sheet data					
Current assets	68,306	70,120	73,300	56,259	58,760
Total assets	85,701	87,832	91,784	72,677	76,019
Current liabilities	30,327	32,078	45,602	31,896	32,969
Long-term debt	31,921	29,395	28,715	26,394	25,379
Redeemable equity	3,614	4,227	1,471	1,000	270
Stockholders' equity	9,066	10,606	3,690	767	4,935

[a] Net loss for the fiscal year ended June 30, 1992 includes loss from discontinued operations of $7,405 as a result of Steinway's September 14, 1992 disposition of its Gemeinhardt Company, Inc. subsidiary.

[b] EBITDA represents earnings before tax expense (benefit), adjusted to exclude certain nonrecurring charges and charges related to previous ownership, which are not expected to recur. While EBITDA should not be construed as a substitute for operating income or a better indicator of liquidity than cash flow from operating activities, which are determined in accordance with generally accepted accounting principles, it is included herein to provide additional information with respect to the ability of the Company to meet its future debt service, capital expenditure and working capital requirements. EBITDA is not necessarily a measure of the Company's ability to fund its cash needs. See the Consolidated Statement of Cash Flows of Selmer and Steinway and the related notes thereto included in this Prospectus. EBITDA is included herein because management believes that certain investors find it to be a useful tool for measuring the ability to service debt.

[c] Nonrecurring charges represent certain costs and expenses primarily consisting of certain executive compensation and benefits and office related expenses of Steinway which, as a result of the Merger, are not expected to recur.

[d] Depreciation and amortization for the fiscal year ended June 30, 1994 excludes approximately $563 of amortization of deferred financing costs written off pursuant to a debt refinancing effected in April 1994 (see note 6 to Steinway's financial statements).

[e] Capital expenditures of Steinway exclude expenditures for additions to the Concert and Artist Piano Bank.

[f] For purposes of this computation, fixed charges consist of interest expense and amortization of deferred financing costs and the estimated portion of rental expense attributable to interest. Earnings consist of income (loss) before taxes plus fixed charges.

[g] Earnings were inadequate to cover fixed charges by $3,065 for the year ended June 30, 1993.

EXHIBIT 8.6:
Baldwin Piano & Organ Company (US$000)

	1995	1994	1993
Sales	122,634	122,347	120,658
Net income	3,960	345	4,561
Total assets	101,429	97,460	89,928
Stockholders' equity	54,114	50,154	49,892

Baldwin Piano & Organ Company is the largest (US) domestic manufacturer of keyboard musical instruments and manufactures or distributes all major product classes of pianos and electronic organs. The company also manufactures grandfather clocks, wooden cabinets and printed circuit boards utilized in a wide variety of products outside of the music industry. Musical products and other accounted for 72% of 1995 revenues; electronic contracting, 23.2% and financing services, 4.7%.

Source: Compact Disclosure Database, 1996.

year later, R. S. Harrison and Harold Smith led a $55 million leveraged buyout of the company's piano and organ operations and reestablished the firm as a dedicated keyboard manufacturer.

Baldwin has over 800 dealers in the United States. Its dealership base and broad product line help attract students and other low-end users who generally stay with a Baldwin piano as they upgrade. In 1987, the firm sold 175,000 pianos, a figure well below the 282,000 units it sold a decade earlier. In this year, it had excess capacity in its Arkansas facility and obtained a contract from Yamaha to manufacture the Everett piano line. Actions for Baldwin pianos are assembled at the Juarez plant. In 1995, the firm reported a net income of $3.9 million on sales of $122 million (see Exhibit 8.6).

Japanese Competitors

In the early part of the century, due to a lack of quality components, impoverished circumstances, and a work force that was uninformed about the subtleties of instrument design and construction, there was little piano manufacturing in Japan. Starting after the Second World War, however, two Japanese companies, Yamaha and Kawai, quickly became important piano manufacturers. Figures for the 1980s indicated that these two firms together made more pianos than any other nation. In 1954, only 1 percent of Japanese homes owned a piano; currently, more than 20 percent do. In contrast to Steinway & Sons, the Japanese approach to piano manufacture emphasizes automation and assembly-line operations.

Yamaha Corporation

Founded in 1887 as Nippon Gakki, Yamaha's main plants are near Hamamatsu. From the time of its founding, the firm has built pianos.[24] It first exported pianos to the US in 1960. By the 1970s, Yamaha had developed a strong reputation for making high quality pianos. In the US, it took significant market share away from US producers. The company uses innovative engineering, and automated manufacturing. The firm markets its pianos world wide.

In 1987, its centenary year, Yamaha was the world's leading musical instrument maker. It commanded 30 percent of the world piano market, 40 percent of the organ market, and 30 percent of the wind instrument market. Currently, the firm markets a line of grands, uprights, consoles, and studio pianos manufactured in either Georgia in the US, or Hamamatsu in Japan. These pianos are the company's pride; concert grands are a measure of its aspirations. Yamaha currently commands around 55 percent of the Japanese piano market.

In 1983, Genichi's son, Hiroshi Kawakami took over the leadership of Yamaha. Under his leadership Yamaha established several close working relationships with other firms in the late 1980s and 1990s. In 1984, Yamaha contracted with Kemble & Co. of England to make pianos for it (Yamaha). In 1986, it contracted with Baldwin in the US to make the Everett piano line. In 1988, it established Tienjin Yamaha Electronic Musical Instruments to produce musical instruments in China. Further, it obtained an option to buy 25 percent of Schimmel Pianofortefabrik in Germany. More recently, Yamaha holds a 60 percent ownership of a $10 million joint venture with Jiangzhu Piano, China's largest piano manufacturer, located in Guangzhou, China. In 1996, the joint venture started producing pianos at a monthly rate of 1300 units. In 1995, the firm reported a net income of $61.6 million on sales of over $5.5 billion (see Exhibit 8.7).

Kawai Musical Instruments

In 1889, while he was an employee of Yamaha, Koichi Kawai, the founder of Kawai Musical Instruments, began his piano research. He developed the first rudimentary assembly line to make pianos. He was the first in Japan to design and build a piano action. Prior to his effort, all Japanese manufacturers had imported their actions from the US or Germany. Mr. Kawai began the production of upright pianos a year after building his first piano action. It was the cost advantage of his domestically produced action that gave him a foothold in the fledgling Japanese market. Soon he began building grand pianos.

In 1955, Koichi's son, Shigeru Kawai, took over as president. He has overseen its growth and the introduction of modern technology. In 1956, the firm had one plant, 546 employees, and production capacity was 1,776 units. By 1996, Kawai had 9 factories and employed over 7,000 people who produced over 100,000 pianos. The firm's main manufacturing center, Ryuyo Grand Piano Facility, was opened in 1980. This facility is known for the efficient methods that have been developed by the firm to build grand pianos. Kawai emphasizes the engineering, research and development, quality control, technological innovation, and skill that go into its pianos. Shigeru's son, Hirotaki Kawai, is expected to take over leadership of the firm.

EXHIBIT 8.7:
Yamaha Corporation (US$000)

	1995	1994	1993
Sales	5,576,860	4,348,744	4,210,910
Net income	61,665	−38,854	15,913
Total assets	5,327,507	4,518,696	4,151,752
Stockholders' equity	1,702,343	1,424,758	1,353,630

Yamaha Corporation's major products are musical instruments including pianos, electronic organs, digital musical instruments, wind instruments and percussion instruments and audio equipment. Audio and musical instruments accounted for 61% of fiscal 1995 revenues; electronic equipment and metal products, 18%; household utensils, 12% and other including sports goods and housing equipment, 9%. The company has 58 consolidated subsidiaries, 26 in Japan and 32 overseas. Overseas sales accounted for 30.5% of fiscal 1995 revenues.

Source: World Scope Database, 1996.

In its advertising, Kawai emphasizes the number of institutions and music venues – e.g., prominent universities, symphony orchestras, opera companies, music centers, theater companies, churches, music studios, and hotels around the world – that have purchased the Kawai piano. In 1995, however, the firm reported a loss of $2 million on sales of $877 million. This loss was attributed to the lingering economic recession facing firms in Japan (see Exhibit 8.8).

Korean Competitors

In 1964, the Korean government decided to promote musical instrument manufacture. To support this effort, it passed a prohibitive tariff on imported luxury goods like pianos. Three firms immediately benefited from this protection. They were Samick, which had already established its piano manufacturing facility, Young Chang, which formed a joint venture with Yamaha, and Sojin, a division of Daewoo. Industry assessments state that, "despite a harsh environment and a lack of Western musical tradition, Young Chang and Samick made the transformation from primitive manufacturers to global powerhouses in record time. Over the past century, no other manufacturers have come so far so fast."[25] Recently, Hyundai became an additional Korean piano manufacturer. In the 1990s, with growing labor and raw material shortages, Samick and Young Chang have shifted their production to locations with either lower costs or better access to raw materials or markets.

EXHIBIT 8.8:
Kawai Musical Instruments (US$000)

	1995	1994	1993
Sales	877,742	881,114	899,657
Net income	(2,733)	(2,200)	1,180
Total assets	—	—	530,666
Stockholders' equity	—	—	235,114

This firm is the second largest musical instruments company in Japan. It is also an OEM supplier of pianos to the Boston Piano Co., wholly-owned subsidiary of Steinway Musical Properties. Pianos accounted for 25% of fiscal 1995 revenues; electronic equipment and metal products, 8%; other including musical instruments, 9%; metallic parts for electronic instruments, 13%; other products, 10%; Music Schools, other 35%. Overseas sales accounted for 11% of fiscal 1995 revenues.

Source: Japan Company Handbook.

Samick

Established in 1958 by Hyo Ick Lee, Samick has grown into one of the world's largest producer of pianos, with its main plant in Inchon. The firm produced 18,000 grand pianos in 1995. Samick pianos feature cabinets designed by Kenneth Benson and incorporate a high-tension imperial-German scale. In making its pianos, Samick makes extensive use of computer-controlled equipment to shape parts and perform finishing operations.

In 1989, Samick Music Corporation, a wholly owned subsidiary of Samick, opened a 85,000-square-feet facility in California to assemble vertical pianos. In 1991, monthly production at the facility had reached 325 units. While case parts were American, actions, backs, and hardware were all imported by Samick.

Recently, Samick opened parts producing facilities in Indonesia and China. Parts from these plants are then shipped to the firm's main plant at Inchon for assembly. These new facilities have allowed Samick to hold costs down and minimize price increases. Samick offers the best warranty in the industry – ten years on the piano, plus a life time warranty on the iron plate, the sound board, and the pin block. In 1995, the firm reported a net income of $13 million on sales of $291 million (see Exhibit 8.9). At the end of 1996, Samick filed for a bankruptcy protection due to financial difficulties partly resulting from its piano operations.

Young Chang

Young Chang was founded by three brothers. Jai-Sup Kim, who had studied engineering, Jai-Young Kim, who had studied finance at New York University, and Jai-Chang Kim, who had studied music. In 1956, they began to produce pianos in a

EXHIBIT 8.9:
Samick Corporation (US$000)

	1995	1994	1993
Sales	291,512	243,287	254,125
Net income	13,350	225	14,062
Total assets	477,887	474,387	414,575
Stockholders' equity	31,037	26,737	25,000

Pianos accounted for 54.5% of fiscal 1995 revenues; guitars, 28.5%; amplifiers, 16.8%; and other, 0.2%.

Source: World Scope Database, 1996.

small storefront in Seoul, South Korea. They also secured distribution rights to Yamaha pianos in South Korea. In 1962, they became the first musical instrument manufacturer in South Korea and built their first assembly plant in Seoul in 1964.

In 1967, they entered into a partnership with Yamaha Corporation, receiving technical assistance to acquire the production skills necessary to create instruments capable of competing with those made in Japan, the US, or Europe. In 1971, they began exporting. In 1975, Yamaha and Young Chang parted ways. And in 1976, they opened their second factory in Inchon, which they further expanded in the late 1980s. In 1979, Young Chang America was established.

Young Chang's economies-of-scale in combination with its advanced manufacturing processes have resulted in one of the best price/value offerings in the market today. Also, with an annual production capacity of 200,000 pianos, Young Chang is the largest piano manufacturer in the world. The firm produces around 110,000 piano units annually including 13,000 grand pianos. It holds over 50 percent of the expanding, domestic Korean market (around 150,000 units per year) and currently has over 4,000 employees. It offers a complete line of vertical and grand pianos as well as guitars. The firm sees piano manufacturing as a totally integrated activity and so it has facilities for making all the significant parts of a piano.

In 1990, Young Chang acquired Kurzweil (a music keyboard manufacturer) for $20 million. In 1993, Young Chang acquired its own timber mill in Tacoma, Washington for $32 million. In 1995, it opened a $40 million production facility in Tienjin, China with an annual production capacity of 60,000 units. As J. S. Kim observes:

> In the short term, our balance sheet would look stronger if we were to stay out of China. But it is obvious that the future for the piano industry is in China and companies not willing to make the investment are in great jeopardy.

The firm anticipates that the Chinese market will eventually be the world's largest. In 1995, the firm reported a net income of $9.6 million on sales of $262 million (see Exhibit 8.10).

EXHIBIT 8.10:
Young Chang (US$000)

	1995	1994	1993
Sales	262,158	258,489	225,716
Net income	9,650	8,209	3,368
Total assets	302,437	292,172	233,889
Stockholders' equity	131,818	135,698	126,536

Young Chang, the largest piano producer in South Korea, produces digital pianos, guitars, electronic organs and other musical instruments, along with acoustic pianos. The company has six subsidiaries, two each in the United States and China and one each in Canada and Germany. In 1994, export sales accounted for 37% of total revenues. Acoustic and digital pianos accounted for 80% of fiscal 1995 revenues; synthesizers, 5.5%; guitars, 2%; and other, 12.5%.

Source: World Scope Database, 1996.

European Competitors

Although German piano manufacturers make high quality, high priced pianos, they have been severely tested by the low-priced Asian competitors. As a consequence of this competition, the number of piano makers has fallen from a few hundred to 10. All surviving firms faced financial difficulties in the 1990s. In 1995, total annual production in Germany was over 20,000 units, with 20 percent being grand pianos. Bechstein Gruppe, Inc., the manufacturer of Bechstein and Zimmerman pianos, had annual sales of around DM30 million. Recently, however, this group filed for bankruptcy protection.

Other firms included Blüthner of Leipzig, which produced about 400 pianos annually with 50 percent marked for export, and Schimmel in Braunschweig, which held around 11 percent of the German market. Schimmel had a close relationship with Yamaha, which marketed Schimmel pianos in Japan. Steinway & Sons of Hamburg produced around 1,000 grands and 200 uprights annually and exported around 300 grands to Japan.

While English firms were world renowned during Steinway's formative years, today there is little piano manufacturing in England. The manufacturing that does occur involves subcontracting from non-British makers. The most prominent is Kemble & Co., a firm which employs 100 people and makes pianos for Yamaha (Japan) and Schiedmeyer (Germany).

In Austria, Bösendorfer continues to make a limited number of high-end concert grands and upright pianos for its parent, Kimball International. Kimball, until recently, was a US domestic piano maker with a single plant in Indiana. This facility, however, closed in 1995. Significant numbers of pianos are made in the former Soviet Union. Until recently, few of these pianos have appeared in the US. Some imports are starting to appear. Perhaps the best known brand in the US is the Belarus piano from Borisov.

CURRENT ISSUES FACING MANAGEMENT

US domestic grand piano unit sales increased 42 percent from 1992 to 1995. This increased growth was largely attributable to the economic recovery in the US as well as increased marketing efforts by major producers of pianos.

Growing Importance of China

Industry forecasts indicated that the future market for pianos will be concentrated in Japan, Korea, and China. Bruce Stevens acknowledged that:

> Although the Steinway Piano has an excellent reputation in Asia and is the piano of choice in virtually every Japanese concert venue, Steinway has not historically focused significant selling or marketing efforts in these markets.

In light of this, Steinway & Sons recently positioned a full-time employee in Japan to head its Asian effort. According to Bob Dove, the firm's executive vice-president, these efforts were beginning to show some results:

> The Boston Piano currently has around 5 percent of the Japanese market in terms of units, and a higher percentage, about 8 percent, in terms of value (since the Boston line is more expensive than your average piano). We are optimistic about future sales of both Boston and Steinway pianos in Japan. We believe the Boston piano is significantly better than that offered by competitors at similar prices.

Due to the recent ownership changes and the growing importance of the Asian markets, top management was interested in finding ways to further penetrate the Asian market. Notes Dove:

> The merger of Steinway & Sons with the Selmer Company and its woodwind and band instruments has introduced a number of new strategic possibilities. The future demand for the band instruments made by Selmer is predictable from demographic data, peaking as larger cohorts of children enter high school. So this gives the new company a pre-dictable source of demand for its products. So far as growth is concerned, pianos are important and there is no doubt that growth in demand for pianos will occur mainly in Asia and so this is the current focus of company attention. . . . There are also other instruments that have high quality standards and which have high sales and growth rates, e.g. guitars. These may be areas which offer new opportunities for the enlarged firm. Finally, the Steinway brand name, itself, is unsurpassed in terms of its positive reputation. In the future, this too could be used in a number of different ways.

Additionally, Steinway's key managers were intrigued about the possibility of Steinway & Sons entering the Chinese market. China, in particular, was being considered because estimates indicated that the Chinese domestic production of pianos had risen from 43,000 units in 1987 to more than 100,000 units in 1994. The Chinese government policy of "one child per family" had encouraged parents to spend more on their children, and this, many observes believed, may keep the continuing level of unsatisfied demand for pianos relatively high. Moreover, children in school were being taught to appreciate music and this was likely to impact demand positively. In 1994, there were four main piano producing centers in China including Beijing (30,000 units), Shanghai, Guangzhou (50,000 units), and Yingkuo in Liaoning province. By 1996, Tienjin in North China had also become a center of acoustic piano production as Young Chang had established a plant there.

Dove, however, was skeptical:

> All expect that China will be the world's largest market for pianos. However, since the price of pianos is currently set very low [the average price of a piano in China was around $1,100] the reported levels of untapped demand there are probably a bit illusory. Further, there are already large piano-making facilities in China such as Young Chang's and Yamaha's factories. It is not clear there is need for additional production capacity.

Although the demand at current prices far outstrips supply, it was uncertain how increase in prices might affect demand. Bob Dove believed that Steinway's current approach was appropriate:

> Given the emphasis on culture in China, the country's rapidly growing income levels, the small families and the interest parents have in their children, one can expect the usual developments to occur so far as piano penetration is concerned. But this takes time and people don't start off their interest in music by buying a Steinway. Rather, they work up to a Steinway. We already have an active Steinway dealership in Hong Kong and this firm has opened a branch in Shanghai. Currently, [therefore], we should be just watching to see how things develop.

Moreover, he was optimistic about other Asian markets:

> Other Southeast Asian countries like Japan, South Korea, Hong Kong, Taiwan and Singapore have already achieved higher general wealth levels and have meaningful piano penetration into homes. These countries, therefore, should be more immediate targets for both the Steinway and Boston line of pianos.

Among the many proposals being considered was whether Steinway & Sons should build a plant in Asia, perhaps in China. This new facility was to help service the demand for pianos in Asian markets. Observed Dove:

> Ideally, because quality is such an important issue and the desire to "do the job right" is so strong, it would be better for all Steinways to be built in one place. Perhaps standardized and mass-produced components could be supplied from different sources and could reduce costs, but for assembly and to do the other processes involving specialist skills, it would be better to have the Steinway piano built in a single place.

Irrespective of the approach the firm decided to pursue with respect to China and other Asian markets, Dove commented that:

> In considering what to do, Steinway & Sons had to remember two things. First, the company has built up a tremendous brand name and enjoys an unsurpassed reputation for quality. So first, anything we do must be consistent with the idea that we are the "keepers of the flame." Second, as Henry Z. Steinway said, "capital loves growth." To generate growth, we have to add value.

NOTES

1. E. Rothstein, "To make a piano it takes more than tools," *Smithsonian*, November, 1988.
2. Rothstein, 1988.
3. E. Rothstein, "Made in the USA, once gloriously, now precariously," *The New York Times*, May 28, 1995.
4. A. Dolge, *Pianos and Their Makers*, Covina, CA: Covina Publishing Company, 1911, p. 303.
5. Dolge, p. 302.
6. Both Chickering and Steinway attempted to depict the results of the Paris Exposition as confirming they, and not their rival, were the leading US piano manufacturer. This competition escalated into a notorious series of claims and counter-claims as each firm claimed additional endorsements and awards in an effort to convince the public they had "really won" in Paris.
7. Dolge, p. 174.
8. Dolge, p. 309.
9. As judges, newspaper proprietors, music publishers, teachers, reverends, music critics, or others prominent in New York social or cultural circles indicated they'd like to buy a Steinway, the firm offered them generous credit terms to encourage the purchase. By having a Steinway in influential New York homes, Steinway & Sons calculated its status by association tended to grow.
10. Dolge, p. 309.
11. D. W. Fostle, *The Steinway Saga*, New York: Scribner, 1995.
12. Currently, the Concert Artists' Department maintains a bank of 330 Steinway concert-grand pianos spread out in about 160 cities. Once an artist achieves sufficient stature to be considered eligible by the Steinway & Sons to receive concert service, he or she is offered the opportunity to use Steinway pianos for all performances, the only expense being the cost of hauling the piano to the recital hall.
13. Dolge, p. 309.
14. C. H. Roell, *The Piano in America, 1890–1940*, Chapel Hill: The University of North Carolina Press, 1989, p. 180.
15. The firm's ads necessarily were, and are, devoted to maintaining an appeal to a minority audience of high culture that has not been swept into mass society. Hence the promotion of Steinway as art. According to the world-famous classical pianist Jose Feghali: "Steinways are a work of art; if they weren't, we wouldn't be playing them. . . . You can walk into a room with 10 pianos and it's like playing 10 different instruments."
16. To prevent damage and facilitate conductivity, a brass strap, the length of the piece, is placed on the exterior side. The wet glue, along with the wood's slightly elevated moisture content, permits the laminates that form the wooden piece to slide against each other just enough to permit bending.
17. The piano key covers are made from a mock ivory polymer, in deference to the ban on ivory imports. The action consists of 17 different wooden parts

including machined wooden parts, Brazilian deer hide, felt covered maple hammers, metal pins, and Teflon impregnated wool bushings. The components of the action are milled on the third floor and then assembled on the second floor. The design of the actions, much like the rest of the piano, only works if all of the milled parts fit together perfectly. Employees were trained in determining the exact fit and to spot problems through visual and physical inspection of the action components.

18. "Steinway's Key . . . One at a time," *Associated Press International*, 1985.

19. Ibid.

20. Quoted in R. V. Ratcliffe, *Steinway & Sons*, San Francisco: Chronicle Books, 1985, p. 102.

21. American Music Conference, *Music USA, 1991*, pp. 21–23.

22. The US acoustic piano market consisted of two important segments – grands and verticals (uprights). Grand pianos are larger and give a louder, more resonant sound. The grands were more expensive and the market for such pianos was generally smaller than that for verticals, and fewer firms were involved in their manufacture.

23. Steinway provides restoration services and sells piano parts from its New York, London, Berlin, and Hamburg locations. It also provides tuning and regulating services. Restoration, repair, tuning, and regulating services are important because they lead to potential new customers. In 1995, restoration services and piano parts accounted for approximately 7 percent of revenue, with gross margins of approximately 29 percent.

24. In 1950, Genichi Kawakami took over the leadership of the firm from his father. In 1953, Genichi toured the US and Western Europe and was struck by the emphasis being placed on recreational products and the waning interest in musical instruments. He returned home determined to stimulate an interest in musical instruments in Japan and opened a chain of franchised music schools which have since graduated 4 million students. There are currently 10,000 franchised schools and many have a showroom for Yamaha instruments on the ground floor.

25. *The Music Trades*, January, 1991.

CHAPTER NINE

AMAZON.COM

Assistant Professor Suresh Kotha and Emer Dooley, both from the University of Washington, School of Business Administration, prepared this case as the basis for class discussion rather than to illustrate either effective or ineffective handling of an administrative situation.

Amazon is the beginning of a completely new way to buy books. . . . It could increase book sales quite dramatically by making it easier for people to find the books they want.

Alberto Vitale, Chairman, Random House Inc.

It is projected that as many as 52 million people worldwide will be using the Internet by the year 2000. The typical Internet user in 1996 was young, affluent, and well educated. The potential size and affluence of this target market has led many observers to coin the phrase the "Internet Gold Rush." Not unlike the California gold rush of 1849 where prospectors lost everything, pickings in the Internet gold rush so far have been extremely limited. Most commercial web sites – they number in the thousands – generate no revenue and cost upward of $500,000 a year to maintain and operate. Losses by major corporations are so widespread that Don Logan, CEO of Time Warner, declared publicly that the (Time Warner) web site, "Pathfinder," gave a "new definition to the term black hole." Although historically every gold rush has been a net loss, there have always been the successful few who buck the trend and garner extraordinary rewards. This case explores the efforts of one such entrepreneur, Jeffrey Bezos, and his on-line bookstore – Amazon.com – on the World Wide Web.

Amazon.com provides a singular case in which the frequently hyped World Wide Web is actually changing how consumers buy products and services. Not content to just transplant the traditional book retailing format to the World Wide Web, Jeff Bezos, the founder behind Amazon.com, is attempting to transform it through technology that taps the interactive nature of the Internet. At Amazon.com like-minded bibliophiles can meet, discuss books, swap raves and pans, and, most importantly, spend money. Over the past two years, Bezos has quietly built a fast-growing business. His web site on the World Wide Web (http://www.amazon.com) has become an underground sensation for thousands of book-lovers around the world who spend hours perusing its vast electronic library, reading other customers' amusing on-line reviews, and ordering books. This case describes how Bezos has managed to build a rapidly growing business on the Internet and the challenges he currently faces as other firms attempt to imitate his model of competition.

COMPANY BACKGROUND

In 1994, Jeffrey Bezos, a computer science and electrical engineering graduate from Princeton University, was the youngest senior vice-president in the history of D. E. Shaw, a Wall Street-based investment bank. During the summer of that year, one statistic about the Internet caught his imagination – Internet usage was growing at 2,300 percent a year. His reaction: "Anything that's growing that fast is going to be ubiquitous very quickly. It was my wake-up call."

He left his job, drew up a list of 20 possible products that could be sold on the Internet and quickly narrowed the prospects to music and books. Both had a potential advantage for on-line sale: far too many titles for a single store to stock. He chose books.

> There are so many of them! There are 1.5 million English-language books in print, 3 million books in all languages worldwide. This volume defined the opportunity. Consumers keep demonstrating that they value authoritative selection. The biggest phenomenon in retailing is the big-format store – the "category killer" – whether it's selling books, toys, or music. But the largest physical bookstore in the world has only 175,000 titles. . . . With some 4,200 US publishers and the two biggest booksellers, Barnes & Noble and Borders Group Inc., accounting for less than 12 percent of total sales, there aren't any 800-pound gorillas in book selling.[1]

In contrast, the music industry had only six major record companies. Because these companies controlled the distribution of records and CDs, they had the potential to lock out a new business threatening the traditional record-store format.

To start his new venture, Bezos left New York City to move west, either to Boulder, Seattle, or Portland. As he drove west, he refined and fine-tuned his thoughts and his business plan. In doing so, he concluded that Seattle was his final destination. Recalls Bezos:

> It sounds counterintuitive, but physical location is very important for the success of a virtual business. We could have started Amazon.com anywhere. We chose Seattle because it met a rigorous set of criteria. It had to be a place with lots of technical talent. It had to be near a place with large numbers of books. It had to be a nice place to live – great people won't work in places they don't want to live. Finally, it had to be in a small state. In the mail-order business, you have to charge sales tax to customers who live in any state where you have a business presence. It made no sense for us to be in California or New York. . . . Obviously Seattle has a great programming culture. And it's close to Roseburg, Oregon, which has one of the biggest book warehouses in the world.[2]

Renting a house in Bellevue, a Seattle suburb, Bezos started work out of his garage. Ironically, he held meetings with prospective employees and suppliers at a nearby Barnes & Noble superstore. He also raised several million dollars from private investors. Operating from a 400-square-foot office in Bellevue, he launched his venture, Amazon.com, on the Internet in July 1995.

At first Bezos was concerned that sales would be so slow he wouldn't be able to meet the 10-book minimum that distributors require. Improvising, he combed through a big distributor's catalog and found a book entry he suspected wasn't actually available – an obscure publication about lichen (a thallophytic plant). His plan was simple: if the firm needed three books, it would pad the order with seven copies of the lichen book.

As it happened this plan wasn't necessary, as word about the new venture spread quickly across the Internet and sales picked up rapidly. Six weeks after opening, Jeff moved his new firm to a 2,000-square-foot warehouse. Six months later, he moved once again to a 17,000-square-foot building in an industrial neighborhood in Seattle. Estimates for the first year of operations indicate that Amazon.com revenues were about $5 million. These revenues are comparable to a large Barnes & Noble superstore.

THE BOOK PUBLISHING INDUSTRY

The United States is the world's largest market for books, with retail sales accounting for about $25.5 billion in 1995. Book publishing is one of the oldest and has traditionally been one of the most fragmented industries in the United States, with over 2,500 publishers.[3] Exhibit 9.1 shows the structure of the US publishing industry.

Publishers

Books are sold on consignment basis, and publishers assume all the risk. They accept returns on unsold books guaranteeing their distributors a 100 percent refund. They provide money and contracts to prospective authors and decide how many copies of the book to print. Typically a "first-run" print for a book can vary from 5,000 to 50,000 copies. However, best-selling authors' first-run prints are generally set at around 300,000 copies.

In practice, trade and paperback publishers print far more copies than will be sold. About 25 percent of all books distributed to wholesalers are returned and at times these percentages run as high as 40 percent for mass-market paperbacks. According to industry experts, 20–30 percent for hard-cover books returns is considered acceptable, 30–50 percent is considered high, and anything above 50 percent is considered disastrous. Publishers drastically reduce the price after a certain period in a process known as "remaindering" (offering books to discount stores, jobbers, and other vendors). Apart from the material cost of returns and the lost revenue they represent, the industry spends millions of dollars each year transporting books back and forth. Profit margins in publishing are driven by book volume, which in turn hinges on the size of each print run. Book publishers generally depend on 10 percent of titles for profit, with 90 percent barely breaking even.[4]

EXHIBIT 9.1:
Book publishing market structure

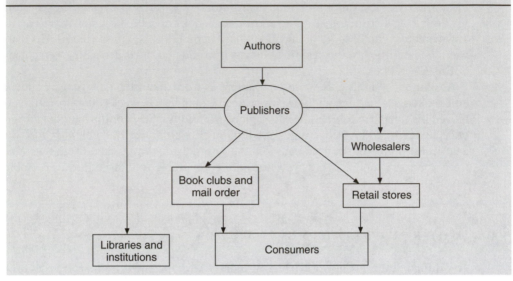

The "big three" – Warner Books, Simon & Schuster, and Pearson – accounted for 21 percent of sales in 1995. The 20 largest book publishing companies in the US commanded over 60 percent of all retail sales. Warner Books, a subsidiary of Time Warner, the United States entertainment giant, was the largest publisher, with sales of $3.7 billion in 1995. Simon & Schuster, a division of Viacom Corporation, ranked second with sales reaching $2.17 billion. These two leaders are followed by Pearson, a group that owns the *Financial Times*, which recorded sales revenues of $1.75 billion. Exhibit 9.2 illustrates the margins on a typical hard-cover book.

Wholesalers

Books are distributed by wholesalers. Wholesalers take orders from independent booksellers and chains and consolidate them into lot-orders for publishers. Publishers supply wholesalers, who in turn supply the thousands of retail bookstores located throughout the country. According to industry estimates, in 1996 wholesalers accounted for almost 30 percent of publishers' sales. Unlike publishing and retailing, wholesalers are highly concentrated with firms such as Ingram Book Co. commanding the major share (50 percent in 1995) of the market. Competition revolves around the speed of delivery and the number of titles stocked. Ingram, for instance, receives more than 70 percent of its orders electronically and offers one-day delivery to about 82 percent of its US customers. In 1994 the average net profit for

EXHIBIT 9.2:
Profit margins for a "typical" book

Book list price	$19.95	
Revenue to publisher (i.e. price paid by wholesaler or bookstore)	10.37	48% discount off suggested retail price
Manufacturing cost	2.00	Printing, binding, jacket design, composition, typesetting, paper, ink
Publisher overhead	3.00	Marketing, fulfillment
Returns and allowances	3.00	
Author's royalties	2.00	
Total publishing costs	10.00	
Publisher's operating profit	0.37	Returns amount for 3.7%

wholesalers was less than 1.5 percent. This figure was down from the traditional margins of about 2 percent a few years earlier.[5]

Technological advances have made warehouse operations more efficient and this in turn has made it possible for wholesalers to provide attractive discounts to retailers. Also the types of books wholesalers are supplying to retailers are changing. Increasingly, bookstores are relying on wholesalers for fast-selling titles and less-popular backlist books.[6] However, with the emergence of superstores, the large retailers such as Barnes & Noble and Borders Books & Music, are no longer using wholesalers for initial orders of major titles. In 1994, for example, Borders Books & Music bought more than 95 percent of its titles directly from publishers.

Retail Bookstores

Retail bookstores, independents and general retailers accounted for between 35–40 percent of industry revenues (Exhibit 9.3). Also 1995 marked the first year in which bookstore chains sold more books than independents.[7] From 1975 to 1995, the number of bookstores in the United States increased from 11,990 to 17,340, and these bookstores, accounted for about 21 percent of the total retail book sales. The superstores, the new Goliaths of retailing, such as Barnes & Noble and Borders Books & Music, accounted for about 15 percent of all retail sales. Estimates suggest that from 1992 through 1995, superstore bookstore sales grew at a compounded rate of 71 percent while nonsuperstore sales grew at a rate of 4 percent. According to Rick Vanzura of Borders Books & Music: "When one of our superstores opens up near one of our mall stores, the mall store tends to lose 10 to 15 percent of its sales. But the superstore is doing a lot more business – say, seven times – what the mall store was doing."

EXHIBIT 9.3:
Book sales in 1994 by various distribution channels

Channel	% of total sales
Bookstore chains, independents and general retailers	35–40
Mail order and book clubs	21
Sales to college book stores	17
Schools	15
Libraries and other institutions	10

Experts cautioned that in smaller markets a shake-out was inevitable.[8] Mr. Vlahos, a spokesman for the American Booksellers Association, noted:

> In the three years from 1993 to 1995, 150 to 200 independent-owned bookstores went out of business – 50 to 60 in 1996 alone. . . . By contrast in the same period, approximately 450 retail superstore outlets opened, led by Barnes & Noble and the Borders Group, with 348 openings.[9]

Independent booksellers believed the growth of superstores may be reaching saturation point. However, notes Leonard Riggio, the chairman of Barnes & Noble: "We are so far from reaching the saturation point [because] we are in the midst of one of the biggest rollouts in the history of retail." But even as Barnes & Noble and Borders entered city after city, as many as 142 US metropolitan markets still did not have a book superstore. According to Amy Ryan, a Prudential Securities analyst, the current rate of expansion could continue at least through the year 2000. In her opinion, this is because the United States could support about 1,500 such large stores.[10]

Institutions and Libraries

There are more than 29,000 private, public and academic libraries in the United States.[11] Because of its stability and size, this market is crucial to publishers. Since libraries order only what they want, this lowered the overhead costs associated with inventory and return processing, making this market a relatively profitable one for publishers. Moreover, as hard-cover trade books have become relatively expensive, many readers are borrowing them from libraries, rather than purchasing them outright. Industry experts observed that about 95 percent of general titles published in any year sold less than 20,000 copies; of that amount, about 55 percent is purchased by libraries. Libraries also frequently repurchase titles to replace worn-out and stolen books. By doing so, they kept the backlist sales healthy.

EXHIBIT 9.4:
The various product categories

Trade books. This segment includes general interest hardcover and paperback books sold to adults and juveniles. Trade books accounted for almost 30% of publishers' revenues in 1994. According to an industry group, books sold to adults increased by more than 30% between 1991 and 1995. Juvenile book sales, which showed a double-digit growth rate in the late 1980s and early 1990s, leading to many publishers, however, were much slower, at 1.1% in 1994. This slow growth was attributed to a decline in the number of popular titles and increased spending by children on toys and games.

In 1995, Random House Inc., Bantam Doubleday Dell, Simon & Schuster, HarperCollins, and Penguin were some of the leading firms that competed in this product category.

Professional books. Over 165 million professional books were sold in 1995, accounting for $3.9 billion. Since 1991 professional book sales have grown at a compound annual rate of 3.0% (in units). Legal publishing was the largest segment of the professional-books category, with the scientific and technical category coming in second place. The long-term outlook for this category was good because employment in the medical, legal, scientific, and business professions was expected to grow strongly.

In 1995, Thomson Corp. was the largest professional books publisher, with sales of $1.99 billion. Professional book revenues comprised 31% of Thomson's total revenues. Reed Elsevier ranked second with 1994 sales of $1.63 billion, and was followed by Wolters Kluwer and Times Mirror with $1.07 billion and $775 million in sales respectively.

Mass market books. These are books produced by publishers who get a significant proportion of sales through magazine wholesalers and outlets such as newsstands and drugstores. This category includes bestsellers that have shelf-lives about three to six weeks. Although the cost of acquiring the paperback rights to a best-selling hardcover title can cost millions of dollars, the per-unit fixed costs for printing are small because print runs are as large as 500,000. However, when return rates, which typically exceed 40%, are factored in, profit margins are typically less than 12%.

The largest publishers are Random House Inc. Bantam Doubleday Dell, Simon & Schuster, and HarperCollins.

Mail Order and Book Clubs

The year 1995 witnessed a significant drop in the mail-order book business. This drop in sales was attributed to the growth of large discount-sale retailers. Publishers' book club sales on the other hand rose steadily, gaining 9 percent in 1994 and in early 1995. The strong growth in this segment was attributed to the increasing popularity of specialized book clubs which focused on favorite baby-boomer interests such as gardening and computers.

The industry sells a variety of books which include: trade, professional, mass market, El Hi (elementary high school) and college text-books and others. Each of these categories varied in terms of sales, competition, profitability, and volatility (see Exhibits 9.4 and 9.5).

EXHIBIT 9.4: *Continued*

El-Hi text books. El-Hi or elementary-high school books accounted for 30% of all books sold in 1994. El-Hi is driven by state adoption and enrollment levels and books are sold to school systems on a contract basis. The development of materials for schools is a capital intensive process that typically takes up to five years to develop for most new programs. Per-pupil expenditures as well as the number of students are expected to grow through the year 2000. This implied moderately strong annual growth (about 3 to 4%) for El-Hi textbooks through the remainder of the decade.

The big publishers are owned by media conglomerates such as News Corp., Times Mirror, and Paramount. The largest El-Hi publisher in 1995 was McGraw Hill, followed by Paramount (the parent company of Prentice Hall and Silver Burdett), Harcourt Brace, and Houghton Mifflin.

College textbooks. College publishing is the most profitable category. The cost of producing a college text is lower than in the El-Hi market, because the texts are typically prepared by university faculty members and used individually. However, the unit sales tend to be small and used textbook sales generally accounted for 20%–40% of total sales. The US Department of Education was forecasting a decline in college enrollments for 1996, and slow growth thereafter. College textbook sales, which grew by 4.4% in 1995 to 155 million books, were expected to decline in the future.

In 1995, Prentice Hall (owned by Paramount) was the largest college publisher, followed by HB College (owned by Harcourt General), International Thomson, McGraw-Hill, and Irwin (a division of Times Mirror).

A survey commissioned by American Booksellers Association found that some 106 million adults purchased about 456.9 million books in any given quarter. The survey which looked at book-buying habits of consumers during the calendar year 1994 revealed that six in 10 American adults (60 percent) say they purchased at least one book in the last three months. Annually that corresponds to 1.8 billion books sold, an average of 17 books per book-buying consumer a year. The average amount paid for the three most recent books purchased by consumers in the last 30 days was about $15.

Emergence of "Virtual" Bookstores

The two hardest challenges for bookselling – physically distributing the right numbers of books to bookstores and getting the word about serious books out to potential readers – are getting a more than trivial assist from the new on-line technologies.

The rapid growth of the Internet businesses was spreading to book publishing. According to Larry Daniels, director of information technologies for the National Association of College Stores:

EXHIBIT 9.5:
Sales and profit margins by product category

Product category	1993 ($m)	1994 ($m)	Profit margins in 1993 (%)
Trade books			
Hardcover books for adults	1,069.0	1,187.0	0.6
Paperback books for adults	586.4	674.5	13.7
Books for juveniles	431.6	439.9	7.7
Bibles, hymnals, and prayer books	45.6	54.7	12.4
Mass market paperbacks	998.7	1,202.8	3.1
Business, medical, scientific, & technical	813.5	891.6	8.0
El-Hi textbooks and materials	1,977.8	1,836.8	14.9
College textbooks and materials	1,586.7	1,611.3	15.8

Source: Standard and Poor Industry Surveys, July 20, 1995.

> Booksellers' concern revolves around the potential for publishers to deal directly with consumers and the media on the Internet. . . . The phenomenon could mean the elimination of middlemen such as bookstores.[12]

Moreover, Daniels notes that there is also the potential for publishers to be "disintermediated," because computer-literate writers can now publish and distribute their own works on-line.

However, the leading publishing houses are skeptical of electronic book-publishing capabilities and remain uncertain about the Internet's future in the sale of physical books. Despite such skepticism, selling on-line was a fast-growing phenomenon. A plethora of bookstores were selling books on the Internet. Companies such as Amazon.com, Bookserver, Book Stacks Unlimited, Cbooks Express, Pandora's, and the Internet Bookstore are growing at the self-reported rates of 20 to 35 percent a month. Of the $518 million expected to be sold on-line in 1996 on the Internet, books sales are a small segment relegated to the "other" category. Total book sales on-line accounted for less that 1 percent of overall book sales. However, since the amount of money Americans spend on books is projected to reach $31 billion by 2000, selling on-line is expected to grow further.

COMPETING ON THE WORLD WIDE WEB

A virtual bookstore

Unlike traditional bookstores, there are no bookshelves to browse at Amazon.com. All contact with the company is done either through their World Wide Web page [at http://www.amazon.com] or by e-mail. At the firm's web site, customers can search for a specific book, topic or author, or they can browse their way through a book catalog featuring 40 subjects. Visitors can also read book reviews from other customers, the *New York Times*, *Atlantic Monthly*, and Amazon.com's staff. Customers can browse, fill up a virtual shopping basket, and then complete the sale by entering their credit card information or by placing their order on-line and then phoning in their credit card information.[13] Customer orders are processed immediately. Books in stock (mostly bestsellers) are packaged and mailed the same day. When their order has been shipped customers are notified by e-mail. Orders for nonbestsellers are placed with the appropriate book publisher by Amazon.com immediately.

Shunning the elaborate graphics that clutter so many web sites on the Internet, Amazon.com instead loads up its customers with information. For many featured books, it offers capsule descriptions, snippets of reviews and "self-administered" interviews posted by authors. More importantly, the firm has found a way to use the technology to offer services that a traditional store or catalog can't match. Notes Bezos:

> An Amazon customer can romp through a database of 1.1 million titles (five times the largest superstore's inventory), searching by subject or name. When you select a book, Amazon is programmed to flash other related titles you may also want to buy. If you tell Amazon about favorite authors and topics, it will send you by electronic mail a constant stream of recommendations. You want to know when a book comes out in paperback? Amazon will e-mail that too.[14]

Additionally, the firm offers space for readers to post their own reviews and then steps out of the way and lets its customers sell to each other. For example, recently a book called *Sponging: A Guide to Living Off Those You Love* drew a chorus of on-line raves from customers, one of whom remarked: "This gem is crazy! Flat Out. Hysterical. You'll have a good laugh, but wait! Let me let you in on a lil' secret – it's useful!" This book swiftly made it onto Amazon.com's own bestseller list. Notes Bezos:

> We are trying to make the shopping experience just as fun as going to the bookstore, but there's some things we can't do. I'm not interested in retrofitting the physical bookstore experience in the virtual world. Every few weeks, someone around here asks, 'When are we going to do electronic book signings?' We still haven't done them. The experience of book signings works best in the real world.[15]

But he is fast to add:

> There are so many things we can do on-line that can't be done in the real world. We want customers who enter Amazon.com to indicate whether they want to be "visible" or "invisible." If they choose "visible," then when they're in the science fiction section, other people will know they're there. People can ask for recommendations – "read any good books lately?" – or recommend books to others. I'm an outgoing person, but I'd never go into a bookstore and ask a complete stranger to recommend a book. The semi-anonymity of the on-line environment makes people less inhibited.[16]

When asked why people come to their site, Bezos responds:

Bill Gates laid it out in a magazine interview. He said, "I buy all my books at Amazon.com because I'm busy and it's convenient. They have a big selection, and they've been reliable." Those are three of our four core value propositions: convenience, selection, service. The only one he left out is price: we are the broadest discounters in the world in any product category. . . . These value propositions are interrelated, and they all relate to the Web.[17]

At Amazon.com all books are discounted. Bestsellers are sold at a 30 percent discount and the other books at a 10 percent discount. Notes Bezos:

We discount because we have a lower cost structure than physical stores do. We turn our inventory 150 times a year. That's like selling bread in a supermarket. Physical bookstores turn their inventory only 3 or 4 times a year.[18]

The firm's small warehouse is used only to stock bestsellers and consolidate and repack customer orders. Moreover, only after the firm receives a paid customer order does it request the appropriate publisher to ship the book to Amazon.com. The firm then ships the book to the customer. The firm owns no expensive retail real estate and its operations are largely automated.

Industry observers note that although Amazon.com discounts most books, it levies a $3 service charge per order, plus 95 cents per book. And it can take Amazon a week to deliver a book that isn't a bestseller, and even longer for the most esoteric titles. Also, some people don't like providing their credit card number over the Internet.

Virtual Customer Service

According to the firm about 44 percent of the book orders come from repeat customers.[19] To keep customers interested in Amazon.com, the firm offers two forms of e-mail-based service to its registered customers. "Eyes" is a personal notification service in which customers can register their interests in a particular author or about their favorite topic. Once registered, they are notified each time a new book by their favorite author or about their favorite topic is published. "Editor's service" provides editorial comments about featured books via e-mail. Three full-time editors read book reviews, pour over customer orders, and survey current events to select the featured books. These and other free-lance editors employed by the firm provide registered users with e-mail updates on the latest and greatest books they've been reading. These services are automated and are available free of charge.

According to Bezos, such services are vital for success on the Internet:

Customer service is a critical success factor in any retail business. But it's absolutely make-or-break on-line. If you make customers unhappy in the physical world, they might each tell 6 friends. If you make customers unhappy on the Internet, they can each tell 6,000 friends with one message to a newsgroup. If you make them really happy, they can tell 6,000 people about that. You want every customer to become an evangelist for you.[20]

Additionally, the firm's employees compile a weekly list of the 20 most obscure titles on order, and Bezos awards a prize for the most amusing. Recent entries include: *Training Goldfish Using Dolphin Training Techniques*, *How To Start Your Own Country*, and *Life Without Friends*. Amazon.com drums up all these orders through a mix of state-of-the-art software and old-fashioned salesmanship.

Associates Program

According to Mark Breier, vice-president of marketing at Amazon.com, the firm is currently growing at the rate of 20–30 percent a month. Part of the reason for this rapid growth is the firm's Associates Program. The program was designed to increase traffic to Amazon.com by creating a referral service from other web sites to Amazon.com's 1.1 million book catalog. An associates web site, such as Starchefs – which features cookbook authors – recommends books and makes a link from its web page to Amazon's catalog page for the books. The associated web site then earns referral fees for sales generated by these links. Partners receive weekly referral fee statements and a check for the referral fees earned in that quarter. More than 7,000 sites have already signed up under this program and earn a commission of 8 percent of the value of books bought by the referred customer. Notes Bezos, "[The] Web technology has made it possible to set up micro-franchises, and with zero overhead."[21]

Operating Philosophy

Unlike traditional bookstores, there are no salespeople at Amazon.com. Moreover, the firm is open for business 24 hours a day and has a global presence. Customers from 125 countries have purchased books from the firm. This list includes Bosnia, where more than 25 US soldiers have placed orders. The firm is devoid of expensive furnishings, and money is spent sparingly. Notes Bezos:

> We made the first four desks we have here ourselves – all our desks are made out of doors and four-by-fours. . . . My monitor stand is a bunch of old phone books. We spend money on the things that matter to our customers and we don't spend money on anything else.[22]

According to Mark Breier, although the firm advertises in print, it spends a substantial amount on web advertising. According to Jupiter Communications, the firm spent over $340,000 for the first half of 1996 and ranked 34th in web ad spending. Because Amazon.com is an Internet-only retailer, web advertising gives it a unique opportunity to track the success of an ad by the number of click-throughs to the store's web site and the number of Internet surfers who actually purchase something. Industry analysts estimate that between 2 percent and 3 percent of people who see an ad on the Web will actually click-through to see more. Advertising is done mainly in the large-circulation news papers such as *The Wall Street Journal*, *New York Times*, and *San Jose Mercury News*, and on the Internet search-

EXHIBIT 9.6:
Company's organizational structure and top management

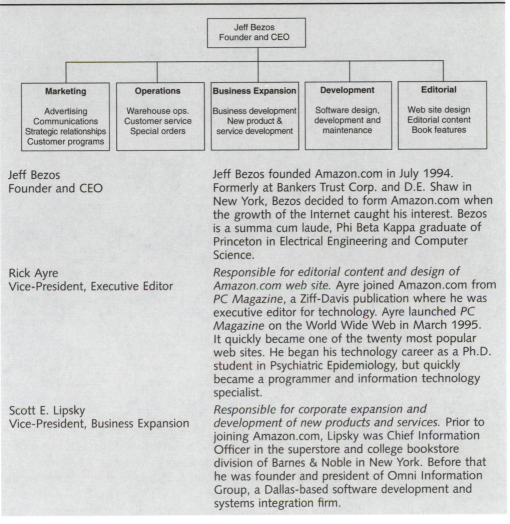

	Jeff Bezos Founder and CEO			
Marketing	**Operations**	**Business Expansion**	**Development**	**Editorial**
Advertising Communications Strategic relationships Customer programs	Warehouse ops. Customer service Special orders	Business development New product & service development	Software design, development and maintenance	Web site design Editorial content Book features

Jeff Bezos
Founder and CEO

Jeff Bezos founded Amazon.com in July 1994. Formerly at Bankers Trust Corp. and D.E. Shaw in New York, Bezos decided to form Amazon.com when the growth of the Internet caught his interest. Bezos is a summa cum laude, Phi Beta Kappa graduate of Princeton in Electrical Engineering and Computer Science.

Rick Ayre
Vice-President, Executive Editor

Responsible for editorial content and design of Amazon.com web site. Ayre joined Amazon.com from *PC Magazine*, a Ziff-Davis publication where he was executive editor for technology. Ayre launched *PC Magazine* on the World Wide Web in March 1995. It quickly became one of the twenty most popular web sites. He began his technology career as a Ph.D. student in Psychiatric Epidemiology, but quickly became a programmer and information technology specialist.

Scott E. Lipsky
Vice-President, Business Expansion

Responsible for corporate expansion and development of new products and services. Prior to joining Amazon.com, Lipsky was Chief Information Officer in the superstore and college bookstore division of Barnes & Noble in New York. Before that he was founder and president of Omni Information Group, a Dallas-based software development and systems integration firm.

engine sites such as Yahoo! and Lycos, the Microsoft Network, and Microsoft's Slate magazine. Amazon.com keeps its banner ads simple, with just a few words and a web address.[23] Recently, the firm has started advertising on CNN.

The decision to locate Amazon.com in Seattle appears to be paying off. The firm has been able to attract some Microsoft veterans. For instance, Jodi de Leon, the firm's advertising manager, is a Microsoft veteran. See Exhibit 9.6 for an illustration of how the firm is organized and a brief description the firm's management.

EXHIBIT 9.6: *Continued*

Mark Breier Vice-President, Marketing	*Responsible for corporate marketing and sales.* From 1994 to 1996 Breier was vice-president of marketing at Cinnabon World Famous Cinnamon Rolls, where he established the marketing department and contributed to annual sales growth of more than 30 percent. Prior to joining Cinnabon, Breier managed core brands and led new product introductions at Dreyer's Grand Ice Cream (1988 to 1994), Kraft, Inc. (1986 to 1988) and Parker Brothers (1985 to 1986). From 1981 to 1984 Breier was president and co-founder of Amazing Events Unlimited, which specialized in entertainment and promotional events. He holds a B.A. in Economics from Stanford University and an M.B.A. from Stanford University's Graduate School of Business.
Shel Kaphan Vice-President, Development	*Responsible for development including the design and maintenance of Amazon.com's web site.* Kaphan joined Amazon.com in October 1994. Prior to joining Amazon.com, he held senior engineering positions at Kaleida Labs, Frox and Lucid and has worked for 20 years designing hardware and software systems and services. Kaphan holds a B.A. in mathematics, cum laude, from the University of California, Santa Cruz.

Amazon had 110 employees in October 1996. Of these, 14 employees manage customer support and seven employees attend to marketing. In addition, a few employees manage "content" on the firm's web site, including such tasks as web page updating and formatting book reviews for display. The vast majority of the remaining employees work on developing software tools for operating on the Internet. According to Julia King, an executive assistant in marketing, "This is a very driven place. Hours are typically 8 to 8 and many people work weekends. Jeff spends every waking hour on this business." Bezos, for example, lives just a few minutes away, but keeps a sleeping bag in his office for all-nighters.

When asked to differentiate this firm from potential rivals, Bezos notes:

People who just scratch the surface of Amazon.com say – "oh, you sell books on the Web" – don't understand how hard it is to actually be an electronic merchant. We're not just putting up a Web site. We do 90 percent of our customer service by e-mail rather than by telephone. Fourteen of our 110 employees do nothing but answer e-mail from customers. There are very few off-the-shelf tools that help do what we're doing. We've had to develop lots of our own technologies. There are no companies selling software to manage e-mail centers. So we had to develop our own tools. In a way this is good news. There are lots of barriers to entry.[24]

In discussing the technical side of the business, Bezos explains:

[W]e have the best programmers, the best servers in the world. We use 64-bit Digital Alpha servers with 500 megabytes of RAM. It's worked very well for us. All of the stuff that actually matters to our customers, we buy the very best.[25]

Explosive Growth

Since July 1995 Amazon has doubled in size every 2.4 months.[26] By August 1996, sales were growing at 34 percent a month. Although estimates vary, the company's gross revenues are expected to be around $17 to $19 million for 1996. When the company was founded in 1995, the plan was to be profitable in five years. As of October 1996 the firm claims to have exceeded expectations and has made its business plan more aggressive. According to Bezos:

> We're not focused on trying to make the company profitable. If we're profitable any time in the short term, it'll just be an accident.[27]

Irrespective of the firm's profitability, interest in the new venture remains strong. The firm recently attracted $8 million from Kleiner, Perkins, Caufield & Byers, a venture-capital firm based in Silicon Valley that has funded firms such as Sun Microsystems and Netscape.

Bezos is focused on expanding Amazon.com: "In the year 2000, our goal is to be one of the world's leading bookstores. Since the world's leading bookstores are billion-dollar companies, people impute that [this figure is our target]."[28] But he quickly dismisses fears that his firm could ever spell the end of traditional bookstores.

> Amazon.com is not going to put bookstores out of business. Barnes & Noble is opening a new superstore every four days. Borders is opening a new superstore every nine days. . . . I still buy half of my books at bookstores. Sometimes I want the book right now, not tomorrow. Sometimes I just like to get out of the office and go to a nice environment. What you're going to see – and it's happening already – is that physical bookstores will become ever-nicer places to be. They are going to have more sofas, better lattes, nicer people working there. Good bookstores are the community centers of the late 20th century. That's the basis on which they're going to compete. There is plenty of room for everyone.[29]

Adds Bezos:

> We believe we're expanding the market for books. With this new way of selling books on the Web we can expose people to far more books than before. People buy books from us that they won't find in bookstores. And we're growing rapidly in this stagnant market.

CHALLENGES FACING AMAZON.COM

Bezos acknowledges that many strategic challenges remain. In particular, two challenges demand his immediate attention. His first concern is to find innovative ways

---

EXHIBIT 9.7:
Amazon.com's Customer Bill of Rights

Amazon's Bill of Rights, which claims that as a customer there is:

1. *No obligation.* Eyes & Editors Personal Notification Services are provided free of charge, and you are under no obligation to buy anything.
2. *Unsubscribing.* You can unsubscribe or change your subscriptions at any time.
3. *Privacy.* We do not sell or rent information about our customers. If you would like to make sure we never sell or rent information about you to third parties, just send a blank e-mail message to never@amazon.com

---

to fruitfully use the massive database his firm has been accumulating about his customers without alienating them. The second, more threatening development is the emerging copycat ventures offering books on the Internet.

The "Massive" Database

During 1995–6, Amazon.com has been building a detailed purchasing history and profile of its customers. Notes Alberto Vitale, chairman of Random House Inc.: "Amazon is creating a database that doesn't exist anywhere else. Book publishers have never had much market data about readers, and some are already salivating for a peek into Amazon's files."[30] Yet customers who buy books from Amazon are assured of privacy by the Amazon Bill of Rights (see Exhibit 9.7).

Bezos is concerned that his customers might be outraged if he turns over this information to other marketers. To him the Web is the ultimate word-of-mouth medium. Still he is considering whether a plan to let publishers offer hand-picked Amazon customers books at discounted prices before their publication date should be implemented.

The Emerging Competition

More than half of the Internet's computers reside in the United States, with the rest spread out among connected networks in 100 other countries. Estimates of the number of Internet users (and more importantly the number of potential users) vary widely (see Exhibit 9.8). The number of businesses joining the Internet has risen dramatically over the past year, and growth hasn't been limited to large corporations (see Exhibit 9.9 for some leading sites on the Internet). From July 1994 to July 1995, the number of hosts on the Internet rose from 3.2 million to 6.6 million. By the end of the decade, 120 million machines are expected to be linked to the Internet.[31]

Every day approximately 150 new businesses come onto the Net, and their total number is estimated to be about 40,000. Most of these companies use the Web as a public relations tool to promote their products and services.[32] More than 35 million

EXHIBIT 9.8:
Varying estimates of Internet users in 1996

Source	Date	Definition	Users (millions)
Intelliquest	Jul. 1996	U.S. internet users	35.0
Louis Harris	May 1996	U.S. internet users	29.0
International Data Corp.	May 1996	WWW surfers	23.5
Computer Intelligence	May 1996	Year-end 1995 (U.S. internet users)	15.0
Hoffman/Novak	Apr. 1996	U.S. internet users	16.4
Wall Street Journal	Mar. 1996	North American home/office users	17.6
Morgan Stanley	Feb. 1996	1995 Net/Web users	9.0
Matrix	Feb. 1996	1995 Worldwide Internet users	26.4
Find/SVP	Jan. 1996	U.S. users who use any Internet service except email	9.5

Source: CyberAtlas, August, 1996.

EXHIBIT 9.9:
Leading sites on World Wide Web

In a June 1996 survey of 1,100 Web-based businesses, 31 percent claimed to be profitable, and 28 percent more said that they would be profitable in the next 12 to 24 months. Here are a few of the most prominent Web success stories:

- Auto-byTel – Founder Peter Ellis claims his car buying service will turn a profit on $6.5 million in revenues this year.
- CDnow – Started in the basement of their parents' home, Jason and Matthew Olim expect to reach $6 million in sales in 1996, triple last year's revenue, while maintaining an 18 percent operating margin.
- Netscape – Netscape already sells $1.5 million worth of its products over the Net each month.
- ONSALE – This auction house, founded by Jerry Kaplan (of Go fame), is on a $45 million annual run rate.

Source: ActivMedia, May, 1996, and Business Week, 1996.

Americans now use the Internet – 9 million of whom joined in 1996 alone. From a commercial perspective, the demographics of Internet and World Wide Web users makes them part of an extremely attractive market segment. The average age of computer users is 39, while the average age of a typical Internet user is 32. About one in 10 Internet users (more than 3 million) is under 18 and uses the Internet

EXHIBIT 9.10:
Internet forecast by market and product segments ($ millions)

Forecast by market segment[a]				1995	2000
Network services (ISPs)				300	5,000
Hardware (routers, modems, computer hardware)				500	2,500
Software (server, applications)				300	4,000
Enabling services (electronic commerce, directory services, web tracking)				20	1,000
Expertise (system integrators, business consultants)				50	700
Content and activity (online entertainment, information, shopping)				500	10,000
Total market				1,670	23,200

Forecast by product segment[b]	1996	1997	1998	1999	2000
Computer products	140	323	701	1,228	2,105
Travel	126	276	572	961	1,579
Entertainment	85	194	420	733	1,250
Apparel	46	89	163	234	322
Gifts/flowers	45	103	222	386	658
Food/drink	39	78	149	227	336
Other	37	75	144	221	329
Total	518	1,138	2,371	3,990	6,579

[a] *Source*: Hambrecht & Quist, December, 1995.
[b] *Source*: Forrester Research Inc., May, 1996.

from home or school. About 64 percent of the Internet users have at least a college degree with a median household income of $60,000.[33]

The global Internet market is expected to soar to $23 billion by 2000 (Exhibit 9.10). Estimates for 1996 indicate that the World Wide Web has attracted more than 100,000 retailers, with some spending more than $1 million each on eye-popping sites. Yet worldwide retail sales on the Web amounted to just $324 million in 1995, which averages out to slightly more than $3,000 in sales per retailer.[34] In 1996 about 2.7 million people used the Internet for shopping or to obtain commercial services such as banking or travel information.

Recent forecasts suggest that while Internet merchants will sell about $518 million in goods in 1996, on-line retailing revenues are likely to grow to about a $6.6-billion business by the end of this century.[35] Notes Bezos:

> We're by far the largest bookseller out there in terms of the number of titles we offer for sale and the services we provide. We are, for all intents and purposes, competing against a vacuum right now. That's not going to last.[36]

EXHIBIT 9.11:
Partial list of virtual bookstores on the Web in October 1996

- *Bookserver.* This firm was founded by brothers David and Michael Mason from the family garage in Tennessee. Since its founding the firm has moved to a mall in Lavergne, Tennessee.
- *CBooks Express.* This Internet startup specializes in technical books and computer-related materials.
- *Pandora's Books Ltd.* This firm features out-of-print science fiction and fantasy books to read when Star Trek reruns can't be found.
- *The Internet Book Shop.* This firm claims that it is the biggest on-line bookstore in the world with over 912,000 titles. The firm lets you track your order on-line.
- *Macmillan Information Superlibrary.* This web site is an attempt to pull together Macmillan's various print, reference and electronic publishing efforts. Its bookstore however carries only 6,000 titles.
- *The Cosmic Web.* This is a non-profit book center dedicated to circulating "words of inspiration and evolutionary answers that awaken souls to the infinitude of our experience as planetary beings."
- *Dial-A-Book.* This venture focuses on selling books in a downloadable format.
- *Moe's Books.* This firm specializes in used books. The firm searches 1,500 affiliated stores to bring you the used books you're looking for. Customers get to specify the condition they would like the book to arrive in.

Bezos' concerns about potential competition are not far fetched. During mid-1996 the Internet witnessed a plethora of virtual bookstores sprouting on the Internet. Exhibit 9.11 provides a partial list of virtual bookstores on the Internet. Not surprisingly, many of these new virtual bookstores are modeled after Amazon.com. For example, Bookserver was founded with a mere $20,000 by brothers David (26) and Michael (23) Mason and originally operated from their family garage. This firm claims to offer more than a million book titles. Additionally, the firm specialized in finding books for customers. Books were offered in English, German, Dutch, and Spanish at discounts similar to Amazon.com and at half the shipping fees charged by Amazon.com. According to David, the store's sales have increased steadily by about 20 percent a month since founding. This growth has enabled the firm to shift operations from the family garage to a strip mall in Lavergne, Tennessee. Bezos was also concerned about the prospect of new competition from some of high-tech's and retailing's mightiest players: a new joint venture between Wal-Mart Stores Inc. and Microsoft Corp., Amazon.com's neighbor in nearby Redmond, Washington.

Elliot Bay Books, a Seattle-based independent bookstore, had set up a web site to establish an Internet presence. Further, a report in the *Seattle Times* indicated that both Barnes & Noble and Borders, the giants in the industry, expect to offer on-line services this year (1997).[37]

In response Bezos is considering novel ways to attract new customers and, at the same time, maintain his existing customer base. One of the options under consideration is to customize offerings for each and every customer. Describes Bezos:

We want to "redecorate the store" for every customer. We can let people describe their preferences, analyze their past buying patterns, and create a home page specifically for them. If you're a big mystery reader, we can show you the three hottest new mystery novels and highlight one from an author you've bought before. These interactive features are going to be incredibly powerful. And you can't reproduce them in the physical world.[38]

Yet he is concerned and is searching for ways by which Amazon.com could stay ahead of this emerging competition. Although sales were increasing, he sees this as a continuing challenge:

Our customers are loyal right up to the point somebody offers them a better service. That's the dimension on which we compete. The goal of Amazon.com has to be to make sure that we are the preeminent brand name associated with on-line bookselling in the year 2000. I think we have a huge opportunity to build an interactive retailing company beyond books.[39]

Paul Hilts, technology editor of *Publishers Weekly*, remains guarded:

It remains to be seen whether online bookselling will completely transform the industry. Their [Amazon.com] timing was exquisite, and they promoted the heck out of it. Everyone will have their eyes on them to see how it goes.[40]

NOTES

1. "Who's writing the book on web business?" *Fast Company*, October–November, 1996, pp. 132–133.
2. *Fast Company*, October–November, 1996.
3. U.S. Bureau of the Census, 1992.
4. "World book market 'faces further consolidation.'" *Financial Times*, October 2, 1996, p. 16.
5. *Publishers Weekly*, January 1, 1996.
6. Although the best-selling books get the bulk of the attention and marketing dollars, "backlist" books are considered the "bread and butter" of the industry. A backlist is the publishing company's catalog of books that have already appeared in print. Estimates indicated that as much as 25 to 30 percent of a publisher's revenues come from this source. Backlisted books have predictable sales with occasional bumps, such as when a subject matter loses favor with the consumers or when an author dies. Since these books require no editing and little promotion, they are generally profitable. Moreover, print runs are more easy to predict, resulting in fewer returns to publishers.
7. *Philadelphia Business Journal*, September 27, 1996.
8. *Publishers Weekly*, March 11, 1996. Superstores, originally confined to big metropolitan areas, were increasingly entering markets with populations of 150,000 or less. Industry estimates indicated that superstores had to make around $200 a square foot to turn a profit. A typical Barnes & Noble super-

store needed, for example, $3 to $4 million in sales revenues to break even. Some industry observers questioned whether such cities can support one or more of these mammoth stores and whether superstores in these locations could sell enough books to turn a profit.

9. "A nonchain bookstore bucks the tide," *The New York Times*, September 8, 1996.

10. Compounding the competition from superstores, many independent booksellers claimed to be unfairly treated by publishers. They claimed that publishers offered bookstore chains better prices and greater promotional support than independents. In response, the American Booksellers Association (ABA) brought an antitrust suit against six publishers, five of which have been settled favorably out of court. The only remaining ABA suit was against Random House Inc.

11. *Standard and Poors Industry Surveys*, July 20, 1995.

12. *The Christian Science Monitor*, September 18, 1996.

13. When the company first started, only 50 percent of the people were prepared to enter their credit card number on Amazon's web page. The other half phoned it in. However, within a year this ratio had changed to 80 : 20.

14. *The Wall Street Journal*, Thursday, May 16, 1996.

15. *Fast Company*, October–November, 1996.

16. *Fast Company*, October–November, 1996.

17. *Fast Company*, October–November, 1996.

18. *Fast Company*, October–November, 1996.

19. "Booked up on the Net," *Seattle Times*, January 5, 1997.

20. *Fast Company*, October–November, 1996.

21. "Amazon.com forges new sales channel," *Web Week*, August 19, 1996.

22. *Upside*, October 1996.

23. Web advertising is gaining increasing legitimacy. Revenue for advertising on the World Wide Web rose 83 percent to $46.4 million in the second quarter of 1996. The figure is expected to reach $312 million by the end of 1996. This amount is still quite small in comparison to the $30 billion spent on television advertising each year.

24. *Fast Company*, October–November 1996.

25. *Upside*, October 1996.

26. *Financial Times*, October 7, 1996.

27. *Upside*, October 1996.

28. *Upside*, October 1996.

29. *Fast Company*, October–November 1996.

30. "Reading the market: How a Wall Street whiz found a niche selling books on the Internet," *Wall Street Journal*, May 16, 1996.

31. Estimates provided by the Internet Society, 1996.

32. Statistics from *Internet World*, November, 1995 and TDM Software and Consulting.

33. Nielsen Media Research, 1995.

34. Based on data from International Data Corp. 1996.

35. Forrester Research Inc., May 1996.

36. *Upside*, October 1996.

37. *Seattle Times*, January 5, 1997.

38. *Fast Company*, October–November 1996.

39. *Seattle Times*, January 5, 1997.

40. *Seattle Times*, January 5, 1997.

CHAPTER TEN

STARBUCKS CORPORATION (A)

This case was prepared by Melissa Schilling and Assistant Professor Suresh Kotha, both from the University of Washington, School of Business Administration, as the basis for class discussion rather than to illustrate either effective or ineffective handling of an administrative situation.

Starbucks Corporation is a Seattle, Washington-based coffee company. It roasts and sells whole bean coffees and coffee drinks through a national chain of retail outlets/restaurants. Originally only a seller of packaged, premium, roasted coffees, the bulk of the company's revenues now comes from its coffee bars, where people can purchase beverages and pastries in addition to coffee by the pound. Starbucks is credited with changing the way Americans view coffee, and its success has attracted the attention of investors nationwide.

Starbucks has consistently been one of the fastest growing companies in the United States with over 1,000 retail outlets in 1996. Over a five-year period starting in 1991, net revenues increased at a compounded annual growth rate of 61 percent. In fiscal 1996, net revenues increased 50 percent to $696 million from $465 million for the same period the previous year (see Exhibit 10.1). Net earnings rose 61 percent to $42 million from the previous year's $26 million. Sales for Starbucks have been continuing to grow steadily, and the company is still a darling of investors, with a PE ratio of 58.

To continue to grow at a rapid pace, the firm's senior executives have been considering international expansion. Specifically, they are interested in Japan and other Asian countries, where Starbucks had little or no presence. Japan, the world's third largest coffee consumer after the United States and Germany, represented both a challenge and a huge opportunity to the firm. To explore what changes in Starbucks' strategy were required, and the questions that might arise during expansion, this case looks at the firm's entry strategy into Japan and the nature of the issues facing the firm during early 1997.

THE COMPANY BACKGROUND

In 1971, three Seattle entrepreneurs – Jerry Baldwin, Zev Siegl, and Gordon Bowker – started selling whole bean coffee in Seattle's Pike Place Market. They named their store Starbucks, after the first mate in *Moby-Dick*. By 1982, the business had grown to five stores, a small roasting facility, and a wholesale business selling coffee to local restaurants. At the same time, Howard Schultz had been working as VP of US operations for Hammarplast, a Swedish housewares company in New York, marketing coffee makers to a number of retailers, including Starbucks. Through selling to Starbucks, Schultz was introduced to the three founders, who then recruited him to bring marketing savvy to the company. Schultz, 29 and recently married, was eager to leave New York. He joined Starbucks as manager of retail sales and marketing.

A year later, Schultz visited Verona, Italy for the first time on a buying trip. As he strolled through the piazzas of Milan one evening, he was inspired by a vision. He noticed that coffee was an integral part of the romantic culture in Italy; Italians start their day at an espresso bar, and later in the day return with their friends. (For a history of the coffeehouse, see Exhibit 10.2.) There are 200,000 coffee bars in Italy, and about 1,500 in Milan alone. Schultz believed that given the chance, Americans would pay good money for a premium cup of coffee and a stylish, romantic place to enjoy it. Enthusiastic about his idea, Schultz returned to tell Starbucks' owners of his plan for a national chain of cafes styled on the Italian coffee bar. The owners, however, were less enthusiastic and did not want to be in the restaurant business. Undaunted, Schultz wrote a business plan, videotaped dozens of Italian coffee bars and began looking for investors. By April 1985 he had opened his first coffee bar, Il Giornale (named after the Italian newspaper), where he served Starbucks coffee. Following Il Giornale's immediate success, Schultz opened a second coffee bar in Seattle, and then a third in Vancouver. In 1987, the owners of Starbucks agreed to sell to Schultz for $4 million. The Il Giornale coffee bars took on the name of Starbucks.

Convinced that Starbucks would one day be in every neighborhood in America, Schultz focused on expansion. In 1987 he entered Chicago, four years later he opened in Los Angeles and in 1993 he entered the District of Columbia. Additionally, he hired executives away from corporations such as PepsiCo. At first, the company's losses almost doubled, to $1.2 million from fiscal 1989 to 1990 as overhead and operating expenses ballooned with the expansion. Starbucks lost money for three years running, and the stress was hard on Schultz, but he stuck to his conviction not to "sacrifice long-term integrity and values for short-term profit."[1] In 1991 sales shot up 84 percent, and the company turned profitable. In 1992 Schultz took the firm public at $17 a share.

Always believing that market share and name recognition are critical to the company's success, Schultz continued to expand the business rather aggressively. Notes Schultz, "There is no secret sauce here. Anyone can do it." To stop potential copycats, he opened 100 new stores in 1993, and another 145 in 1994. Additionally, he acquired the Coffee Connection, a 25-store Boston chain, in 1994.

Everywhere Starbucks has opened, customers have flocked to pay upwards of $1.85 for a cup of coffee (latte). Currently (1997), the firm operates stores in most

EXHIBIT 10.1:
Selected financial data (in thousands, except earnings per share)

As of and for the fiscal year ended:	Sept. 29, 1996 (52 Wks)	Oct. 1, 1995 (52 Wks)	Oct. 2, 1994 (52 Wks)	Oct. 3, 1993 (53 Wks)	Sept. 27, 1992 (52 Wks)
Results of operations data:					
Net revenues					
Retail	$600,067	$402,655	$248,495	$153,610	$89,669
Specialty sales (institutional customers)	78,655	48,143	26,543	15,952	10,143
Direct response (mail order)	17,759	14,415	9,885	6,979	3,385
Total net revenues	696,481	465,213	284,923	176,541	103,197
Operating income	56,993	40,116	23,298	12,618	7,113
Provision for merger costs[a]	—	—	3,867	—	—
Gain on sale of investment in Noah's[b]	9,218	—	—	—	—
Net earnings	$ 42,128	$ 26,102	$ 10,206	$ 8,282	$ 4,454
Net earnings per common and common equivalent share – fully-diluted[c]	$ 0.54	$ 0.36	$ 0.17	$ 0.14	$ 0.09
Balance sheet data:					
Working capital	$238,450	$134,304	$ 44,162	$ 42,092	$40,142
Total assets	726,613	468,178	231,421	201,712	91,547
Long-term debt (including current portion)	167,980	81,773	80,500	82,100	1,359
Redeemable preferred stock	—	—	—	4,944	—
Shareholders' equity	451,660	312,231	109,898	88,686	76,923

[a] Provision for merger costs reflects expenses related to the merger with The Coffee Connection, Inc. in fiscal 1994.

[b] Gain on sale of investment in Noah's of $9,218 ($5,669 after tax) results from the sale of Noah's New York Bagel, Inc. stock in fiscal 1996.

[c] Earnings per share is based on the weighted average shares outstanding during the period plus, when their effect is dilutive, common stock equivalents consisting of certain shares subject to stock options. Fully-diluted earnings per share assumes conversion of the company's convertible subordinated debentures using the "if converted" method, when such securities are dilutive, with net income adjusted for the after-tax interest expense and amortization applicable to these debentures.

Source: From the consolidated financial statements of the company.

EXHIBIT 10.2:
The history of the coffeehouse

Coffee made its way up the Arabian peninsula from Yemen 500 years ago. At that time, coffeehouses were regularly denounced as "gathering places for men, women and boys of questionable morals, hubs of secular thought, centers of sedition and focal points for such dubious activities as the reading aloud of one's own poetry."

In Turkey and Egypt, coffeehouses were meeting places for "plotters and other fomenters of insurrection." In Arabian countries, it was considered improper for a Muslim gentleman to sit at a coffeehouse – it was deemed a waste of time and somewhat indecent to gather and discuss secular literature, though these activities later became the rage in European coffeehouses.

In seventeenth-century London, coffeehouses were suggested as an alternative to the growing use of alcohol. Coffeehouses were a very popular place for the masses to gather since in a coffeehouse, a poor person could keep his seat and not be "bumped" if a wealthier person entered. Coffee houses became known as "penny institutions" where novel ideas were circulated.

Around the turn of the century, espresso was invented in Italy. The name refers to the method of forcing high-pressure water through the coffee grounds, rather than the standard percolation techniques. Espresso and cappuccino rapidly became the preferred beverage of the coffeehouse, and today most Italians and many other Europeans spurn the canned coffee that has been so popular in America.

Sources: *Chicago Tribune*, Feb. 28, 1993, and the *Los Angeles Times*, Dec. 6, 1992.

of the major metropolitan areas in the US and Canada, including Seattle, New York, Chicago, Boston, Los Angeles, San Francisco, San Diego, Austin, Dallas, Houston, San Antonio, Las Vegas, Philadelphia, Pittsburgh, Cincinnati, Minneapolis, Portland, Atlanta, Baltimore, Washington, D. C., Denver, Toronto, and Vancouver, B. C. Its mail-order business serves customers throughout the United States. Enthusiastic financial analysts predict that Starbucks could top $1 billion by the end of the decade (see Appendix).

In 1996, Starbucks employed approximately 16,600 individuals, including approximately 15,000 in retail stores and regional offices, and the remainder in the firm's administrative, sales, real estate, direct response, roasting, and warehousing operations. Only five of the firm's stores (located in Vancouver, British Columbia) out of a total of 929 company-operated stores in North America were unionized. Starbucks has never experienced a strike or work stoppage. Management was confident that its relationship with its employees was excellent.

Currently the firm is organized as a matrix between functional and product divisions. The firm's functional divisions include: Marketing; Supply Chain Operations (Manufacturing, Distribution, Purchasing); Human Resources; Accounting; International; Planning and Finance; Administration (facilities, mail); Communications and Public Affairs; and Merchandising (the group that focuses on product exten-

EXHIBIT 10.3:
Top management at Starbucks

Howard Schultz is the founder of the company and has been chairman of the Board and chief executive officer since its inception in 1985. From 1985 to June 1994, Mr. Schultz was also the Company's president. From September 1982 to December 1985, Mr. Schultz was the director of retail operations and marketing for Starbucks Coffee Company, a predecessor to the Company; and from January 1986 to July 1987, he was the chairman of the Board, chief executive officer, and president of Il Giornale Coffee Company, a predecessor to the Company.

Orin Smith joined the company in 1990 and has served as president and chief operating officer of the Company since June 1994. Prior to June 1994, Mr. Smith served as the Company's vice president and chief financial officer and later, as its executive vice president and chief financial officer.

Howard Behar joined the Company in 1989 and has served as president of Starbucks International since June 1994. From February 1993 to June 1994, Mr. Behar served as the Company's executive vice president, sales and operations. From February 1991 to February 1993, Mr. Behar served as senior vice president, retail operations of the Company and from August 1989 to January 1991, he served as the Company's vice president, retail stores.

Scott Bedbury joined Starbucks in June 1995 as senior vice president, marketing. From November 1987 to October 1994, Mr. Bedbury held the position of worldwide director of advertising for Nike, Inc. Prior to joining Nike, Inc., Mr. Bedbury was vice president for Cole and Weber Advertising in Seattle, Washington, which is an affiliate of Ogilvy and Mather.

Michael Casey joined Starbucks in 1995 as senior vice president and chief financial officer. Prior to joining Starbucks, Mr. Casey served as executive vice president and chief financial officer of Family Restaurants, Inc. from its inception in 1986. During his tenure there, he also served as a director from 1986 to 1993, and as president of its El Torito Restaurants, Inc. division from 1988 to 1993.

Vincent Eades joined Starbucks in April 1995 as senior vice president, specialty sales and marketing. From February 1993 to April 1995, Mr. Eades served as a regional sales manager for Hallmark Cards, Inc. From August 1989 to February 1993, Mr. Eades was general manager of the Christmas Celebrations business unit at Hallmark Cards, Inc.

sions for food and beverages). The firm's product-based divisions include: Retail North America (this division accounts for the bulk of the company's business and is split into regional offices spread throughout the United States); Specialty Sales and Wholesale Group (handles large accounts such as restaurants); Direct Response (a division that focuses on mail order/Internet-related orders); International; and Licensed Concepts Unit. Because of the overlap in these divisions (e.g., Marketing and Retail North America), many employees report to two division heads. Notes Troy Alstead, the company's Director of International Planning and Finance, "We have avoided a hierarchical organization structure, and therefore we have no formal organization chart." Exhibit 10.3 provides a partial list of Starbucks' top management.

EXHIBIT 10.3: *Continued*

Sharon E. Elliott joined Starbucks in 1994 as senior vice president, human resources. From September 1993 to June 1994, Ms. Elliott served as the corporate director, staffing and development of Allied Signal Corporation. From July 1987 to August 1993, she held several human resources management positions with Bristol-Myers Squibb, including serving as the director of human resources – corporate staff.

E. R. (Ted) Garcia joined Starbucks in April 1995 as senior vice president, supply chain operations. From May 1993 to April 1995, Mr. Garcia was an executive for Gemini Consulting. From January 1990 until May 1993, he was the vice president of operations strategy for Grand Metropolitan PLC, Food Sector.

Wanda J. Herndon joined Starbucks in July 1995 as vice president, communications and public affairs and was promoted to senior vice president, communications and public affairs in November 1996. From February 1990 to June 1995, Ms. Herndon held several communications management positions at DuPont. Prior to that time, Ms. Herndon held several public affairs and marketing communications positions for Dow Chemical Company.

David M. Olsen joined Starbucks in 1986 and has served as the Company's senior vice president, coffee since September 1991. From November 1987 to September 1991, Mr. Olsen served as its vice president, coffee, and from February 1986 to November 1987, he served as the Company's director of training.

Deidra Wager joined Starbucks in 1992 and has served as the Company's senior vice president, retail operations since August 1993. From September 1992 to August 1993, Ms. Wager served as the company's vice president, operation services. From March 1992 to September 1992, she was the company's California regional manager. From September 1988 to March 1992, Ms. Wager held several operations positions with Taco Bell, Inc., including having served as its director of operations systems development.

Source: Starbucks Corporation, 1997.

MARKET AND COMPETITION

Americans have a reputation for buying the cheapest coffee beans available. Most American coffee buyers have to fight growers to keep them from just showing them the culls. Much of the canned coffee on American supermarket shelves is made from the robusta bean – considered to be the lowest quality coffee bean, and the highest in caffeine content. Japanese, German, and Italian buyers, in contrast, are known for buying the best beans, primarily Arabica. There are many different types and grades of Arabica and robusta beans, though for years Americans have treated them as a generic commodity.[2]

The US Coffee Industry

US coffee consumption peaked in 1962. At that time Americans were drinking an average of 3.1 cups per day. However, from the 1960s to the 1980s coffee con-

EXHIBIT 10.4a:
US consumption of coffee and other beverages (cups per person per day)

	1985	1986	1987	1988	1989	1990	1991	1992	1993	1994	1995
Total coffee	1.83	1.74	1.76	1.67	1.75	1.73	1.75	n.a.	1.87	n.a.	1.67
By sex:											
Male	1.91	1.80	1.89	1.86	1.85	1.86	1.92	n.a.	2.11	n.a.	1.81
Female	1.76	1.68	1.64	1.50	1.66	1.60	1.59	n.a.	1.64	n.a.	1.54
By age:											
10–19 years	0.12	0.09	0.11	0.14	0.11	0.16	0.12	n.a.	0.15	n.a.	0.16
20–29 years	1.24	1.06	0.99	0.94	0.99	0.96	0.83	n.a.	0.89	n.a.	0.69
30–59 years	2.65	2.43	2.56	2.35	2.46	2.34	2.40	n.a.	2.62	n.a.	2.35
60 plus	2.20	2.40	2.18	2.17	2.30	2.32	2.44	n.a.	2.38	n.a.	2.11

n.a. = not available.

Source: National Coffee Association of U.S.A., 1995 Report.

EXHIBIT 10.4b:
US specialty coffee consumption (% of the population drinking)

	1993	1995	Male[a]	Female[a]
Espresso	0.6	0.9	0.9	0.9
Cappuccino	1.1	1.2	0.7	1.6
Latte	0.5	0.4	0.3	0.5

[a] Based on 1995 figures.

Source: National Coffee Association of U.S.A., 1995 Report.

sumption declined, bottoming out at an average consumption of 1.8 cups per day, or $6.5 billion annually. Over the past decade, coffee demand has been stagnant, with growth only occurring in some of the specialty coffees (see Exhibits 10.4a, 10.4b and 10.4c). Whereas three-fourths of all Americans were regular coffee drinkers in the 1960s, today only half of the US population consumes coffee.[3]

There has been a marked consumer trend towards more healthful fare, causing overall coffee consumption to decline. Although the coffee industry had expected decaffeinated coffee brands to increase, decaffeinated sales in the grocery stores have been steadily dropping, making decaffeinated coffee one of the fastest-declining categories in the supermarket.[4] Industry observers note that many consumers are disappointed with the flavor of decaffeinated coffees and have opted to give up coffee entirely. Demand for better tasting coffees has also hurt the instant coffee market,

EXHIBIT 10.4c:
US consumption in gallons (per person per year)

	1990	1991	1992	1993	1994E	1995P
Soft Drinks	47.6	47.8	48.0	49.0	50.6	51.0
Coffee[a]	26.2	26.6	26.5	25.4	23.4	21.2
Beer	24.0	23.3	23.0	22.9	22.6	22.5
Milk	19.4	19.4	19.1	18.9	18.9	18.8
Tea[a]	7.0	6.7	6.8	6.9	7.1	7.4
Bottled Water	8.0	8.0	8.2	8.8	9.2	9.6
Juices	7.1	7.6	7.1	7.0	7.0	7.0
Powdered drinks	5.7	5.9	5.8	5.5	5.4	5.3
Wine	2.0	1.9	2.0	1.7	1.7	1.6
Distilled spirits	1.5	1.4	1.3	1.3	1.3	1.3
Total	148.5	148.6	147.8	147.4	147.2	145.7

[a] Coffee and tea data are based on a three-year moving average to counterbalance inventory swings, thereby portraying consumption more realistically.

P = Projected, E = Estimates.

Source: John C. Maxwell Jr., *Beverage Industry, Annual Manual 1995/1997*.

with sales of instant coffee declining too. While the instant coffee technology impressed consumers following its introduction in 1939, younger coffee consumers appear to be spurning instants.

The Growth of the Gourmet Segment

The more faithful coffee drinkers have turned to the gourmet decaffeinated coffees, specialty flavors, and whole bean coffees. According to the Specialty Coffee Association of America (SCAA), the gourmet coffee segment grew by more than 30 percent each year for the past three years. The SCAA predicted that by 1999 specialty coffee will capture about 30 percent of the market (up from 17 percent in 1988) for combined retail sales of $5 billion. Also by 1999, the number of espresso bars and cafes is expected to grow to more than 10,000, up from 4,500 in 1994, and 1,000 in 1989.

Sales of specialty coffee have climbed steadily. For instance, in 1969 the retail sales volume of specialty coffee totaled just under $45 million. However, sales grew to more than $2.0 billion in 1994. During 1994, the specialty coffee segment represented about 19 percent of all coffee sold. This figure was up from 10 percent in 1983. However, by 1996 about 30 percent of all coffee drinkers consumed specialty coffees. This amounted to a customer base of approximately 35 million people in the United States. Today, specialty coffees such as espressos and lattes have become so popular that they are being offered in drive-through cafes and coffee stands through-out many parts of the United States.[5]

Some analysts attribute the explosive growth in specialty coffees to the poor economy. They note that as people scale back in other areas, they still need their "minor" indulgences. Although many people cannot afford a luxury car, they can still afford a luxury coffee.[6] Despite this growth, some analysts anticipate trouble on the horizon for the specialty coffee business. As evidence, they cite several indicators. For instance:

- In many markets some of the smaller coffee houses have closed due to excessive competition.
- In Los Angeles, the city council (in response to complaints about rowdy late-night patrons) was considering an ordinance that would require coffeehouses open past midnight to obtain a license. This move, suggest analysts, is a sign that the coffee business is maturing.
- The cost of coffee beans is expected to rise in the near future, tightening margins for coffee merchants. Coffee farmers are switching to more profitable fruit and vegetable crops, reducing the world's supply of coffee beans.

Competition for the Gourmet Segment

Starbucks faces two main competitive arenas – retail beverages and coffee beans. Starbucks' whole bean coffees compete directly against specialty coffees sold retail through supermarkets, specialty retailers, and a growing number of specialty coffee stores. According to senior executives at Starbucks, supermarkets pose the greatest competitive challenge in the whole bean coffee market, in part because supermarkets offer customers the convenience of not having to make a separate trip to "a Starbucks' store." A number of nationwide coffee manufacturers, such as Kraft General Foods, Procter & Gamble, and Nestlé, are distributing premium coffee products in super-markets, and these products serve as substitutes for Starbucks' coffees. Additionally, regional specialty coffee companies also sell whole bean coffees in supermarkets.

Starbucks' coffee beverages compete directly against all restaurant and beverage outlets that serve coffee and a growing number of espresso stands, carts, and stores. Both the company's whole bean coffees and its coffee beverages compete indirectly against all other coffees on the market. Starbucks management believe that their customers choose among retailers primarily on the basis of quality and convenience, and, to a lesser extent, on price.

Starbucks competes for whole bean coffee sales with franchise operators and independent specialty coffee stores in both the United States and Canada. There are a number of competing specialty coffee retailers. One specialty coffee retailer that has grown to considerable size is Second Cup, a Canadian franchiser with stores primarily in Canada. In 1996 there were 235 Second Cup stores in Canada. Second Cup also owns Gloria Jean's Coffee Bean and Brother's Gourmet, both franchisers of specialty coffee stores that are primarily located in malls in the United States. Gloria Jean's, founded in 1979, operated 249 retail stores with about $125 million in annual sales in 1996. Brother's Gourmet is a Florida-based coffee chain with almost 250 franchisee-owned locations in the Chicago area.

Seattle's Best Coffee (SBC) competes fiercely with Starbucks on Starbucks' own turf, Seattle. This firm is following Starbucks' lead in national expansion. However, unlike Starbucks, SBC sells franchise rights to its stores in order to expand rapidly with limited capital. SBC takes advantage of Starbucks' market presence by waiting for Starbucks to invest in consumer education. Then, once customers are familiar with the concept of gourmet coffees, SBC enters that market. In following this approach, the firm has had an easier time finding franchisees. SBC intends to operate 500 stores by 1999.

Starbucks also competes with established suppliers in its specialty sales and direct response (mail order) businesses, many of whom have greater financial and marketing resources than Starbucks has. Lately, competition for suitable sites to locate stores has also become intense. Starbucks competes against restaurants, specialty coffee stores, other stores offering coffee stands within them (e.g., bookstores, clothing retailers, kitchenware retailers) and even espresso carts for attractive locations. In many metropolitan areas a single square block may have four or five different coffee beverage stores. This level of competition prompted Brother's Gourmet Coffee to abandon its 1995 expansion plans after it determined that the market was almost saturated and that Starbucks was already in all of its markets. Finally, the firm also competes for qualified personnel to operate its retail stores.

THE STARBUCKS LEGACY

In establishing Starbucks' unique approach to competition, Schultz had four companies in mind as role models: Nordstrom, Home Depot, Microsoft, and Ben & Jerry's. Nordstrom, a national chain of upscale department stores based in Seattle, provided a role model for service and is part of the reason that each employee must receive at least 24 hours of training. Home Depot, the home improvement chain, was Schultz's guideline for managing high growth. Microsoft gave Schultz the inspiration for employee ownership, resulting in Starbucks' innovative Bean Stock Plan. And Ben & Jerry's was his role model for philanthropy; Starbucks sponsors community festivals, donates money to CARE for health and literacy programs in coffee-growing countries, and donates to charity any packages of coffee beans that have been open a week.

Schultz's goal is to: "Establish Starbucks as the premier purveyor of the finest coffee in the world while maintaining our uncompromising principles as we grow." He has since articulated six guiding principles to measure the appropriateness of the firm's decisions (see Exhibit 10.5).

Securing the Finest Raw Materials

Starbucks coffee quality begins with bean procurement. Although many Americans were raised on a commodity-like coffee composed of Arabica beans mixed with less-expensive filler beans, Starbucks coffee is strictly Arabica, and the company ensures

EXHIBIT 10.5:
Starbucks' Mission Statement and guiding principles

Mission Statement

Establish Starbucks as the premier purveyor of the finest coffee in the world while maintaining our uncompromising principles as we grow.

Guiding principles

- Provide a great work environment and treat each other with respect and dignity.
- Embrace diversity as an essential component in the way we do business.
- Apply the highest standards of excellence to the purchasing, roasting and fresh delivery of our coffee.
- Develop enthusiastically satisfied customers all of the time.
- Contribute positively to our communities and our environment.
- Recognize that profitability is essential to our future success.

that only the highest quality beans are used. Dave Olsen, the company's senior vice president and chief coffee procurer, scours mountain trails in Indonesia, Kenya, Guatemala and elsewhere in search of Starbucks' premium bean. His standards are demanding and he conducts exacting experiments in order to get the proper balance of flavor, body and acidity. He tests the coffees by "cupping" them – a process similar to wine tasting that involves inhaling the steam ("the strike" and "breaking the crust"), tasting the coffee, and spitting it out ("aspirating" and "expectorating").[7]

From the company's inception, it has worked on developing relationships with the countries from which it buys coffee beans. Traditionally, most of the premium coffee beans were bought by Europeans and Japanese. Olsen has sometimes had to convince coffee growers that it is worth growing premium coffees – especially since American coffee buyers are notorious purchasers of the "dregs" of the coffee beans. In 1992 Starbucks set a new precedent by outbidding European buyers for the exclusive Narino Supremo bean crop.[8] Starbucks collaborated with a mill in the tiny town of Pasto, located on the side of the Volcano Galero. There they set up a special operation to single out the particular Narino Supremo bean, and Starbucks guaranteed to purchase the entire yield. This enabled Starbucks to be the exclusive purveyor of Narino Supremo, purportedly one of the best coffees in the world.[9]

Vertical Integration

Roasting of the coffee bean is close to an art form at Starbucks. The company currently operates three roasting and distribution facilities: two in the Seattle area, and one in East Manchester Township, York County, Pennsylvania. In the Seattle area, the company leases approximately 92,000 square feet in one building located in Seattle, Washington, and owns an additional roasting plant and distribution facility of approximately 305,000 square feet located in Kent, Washington.

Roasters are promoted from within the company and trained for over a year, and it is considered quite an honor to be chosen. The coffee is roasted in a powerful gas-fired drum roaster for 12 to 15 minutes while roasters use their sight, smell, hearing and computers to judge when beans are perfectly done. The color of the beans is even tested in an Agtron blood-cell analyzer, with the whole batch being discarded if the sample is not deemed perfect.

The Starbucks Experience

According to Schultz, "We're not just selling a cup of coffee, we are providing an experience." As Americans reduce their alcohol consumption, Schultz hopes to make coffee bars their new destination. In order to create American coffee enthusiasts with the dedication of their Italian counterparts, Starbucks provides a seductive atmosphere in which to imbibe. Its stores are distinctive and sleek, yet comfortable. Though the sizes of the stores and their formats vary from small to full-size restaurants, most are modeled after the Italian coffee bars where regulars sit and drink espresso with their friends.

Starbucks stores tend to be located in high-traffic locations such as malls, busy street corners, and even grocery stores. They are well lighted and feature plenty of light cherry wood. Further, sophisticated artwork hangs on the walls. The people who prepare the coffee are referred to as "baristas," Italian for bartender. And jazz or opera music plays softly in the background. The stores range from 200 to 4,000 square feet, with new units tending to range from 1,500 to 1,700 square feet. In 1995, the average cost of opening a new unit (including equipment, inventory and leasehold improvements) was about $377,000. The firm employs a staff of over 100 people whose job is to plan, design and build the unique interiors and displays. The Starbucks interiors have inspired a slew of imitators.

Location choices so far have been easy; Starbucks opens its cafes in those cities where its direct mail business is strong. By tracking addresses of mail-order customers to find the highest concentration in a city, Starbucks can ensure that its new stores have a ready audience. Although this would normally imply cannibalizing its mail order sales, mail order revenues have continued to increase.

The packaging of the firm's products is also distinctive. In addition to prepared Italian beverages such as lattes, mochas and cappuccinos, the retail outlets/restaurants offer coffee by-the-pound, specialty mugs, and home espresso-making machines. *Biscotti* are available in glass jars on the counter. Many of the firm's stores offer light lunch fare including sandwiches and salads, and an assortment of pastries, bottled waters and juices. Notes George Reynolds, a former senior vice president for marketing:

> [Starbucks'] goal is to make a powerful aesthetic statement about the quality and integrity of their products, reaffirming through their visual identity the commitment they feel to providing the very best product and service for customers.

The company has also developed unique strategies for its products in new markets; for instance, for its passport promotion, customers receive a frequent buyer bonus stamp in their "passport" every time they purchase a half-pound of coffee. Each time a customer buys a different coffee, Starbucks also validates their "World Coffee Tour." Once a customer has collected ten stamps, they receive a free half-pound of coffee. The passport also contains explanations of each type of coffee bean and its country of origin.

Despite the attention to store environment and coffee quality, Starbucks' effort at bringing a premium coffee and Italian-style beverage experience to the American market could have been lost on consumers had the company not invested in consumer education. Starbucks employees spend a good portion of their time instructing customers on Starbucks' global selection of coffee and the different processes by which the beverages are produced. Employees are also encouraged to help customers make decisions about beans, grind, and coffee/espresso machines and to instruct customers on home brewing. Starbucks' consumer education is credited with defining the American espresso market, paving the way for other coffee competitors.[10]

Building a Unique Culture

While Starbucks enforces almost fanatical standards about coffee quality and service, the policy at Starbucks towards employees is laid-back and supportive. They are encouraged to think of themselves as partners in the business. Schultz believes that happy employees are the key to competitiveness and growth:

> We can't achieve our strategic objectives without a work force of people who are immersed in the same commitment as management. Our only sustainable advantage is the quality of our work force. We're building a national retail company by creating pride in – and stake in – the outcome of our labor.[11]

Schultz is also known for his sensitivity to the well-being of employees. Recently when an employee had come to tell Schultz that he had AIDS, he reassured him that he could work as long as he wanted to, and that when he left, the firm would continue his health insurance. After the employee left the room, Schultz reportedly sat down and wept. He attributes such concern for employees to memories of his father:

> My father struggled a great deal and never made more than $20,000 a year, and his work was never valued, emotionally or physically, by his employer. . . . This was an injustice. . . . I want our employees to know we value them.

A recent article on the firm in *Fortune* points out:

> Starbucks has instituted all sorts of mechanisms for its Gen X-ers to communicate with headquarters: E-mail, suggestion cards, regular forums. And it acts quickly on issues that are supposedly important to young kids today, like using recycling bins and improving living conditions in coffee-growing countries. To determine the extent to which Starbucks has truly identified and addressed the inner needs of twenty somethings would require several years and a doctorate. But anecdotally, the company appears to be right on the money.[12]

On a practical level, Starbucks promotes an empowered employee culture through employee training, employee benefits programs, and an employee stock ownership plan.

Employee training

Each employee must have at least 24 hours of training. Notes *Fortune*:

> Not unlike the cultural blitz of personal computing, Starbucks has created one of the great marketing stories of recent history, and it's just getting started. The company manages to imprint its obsession with customer service on 20,000 milk-steaming, shot-pulling employees. It turns tattooed kids into managers of $800,000-a-year cafes. It successfully replicates a perfectly creamy caffe latte in stores from Seattle to St. Paul. There is some science involved, and one of its primary labs happens to be Starbucks' employee training program.[13]

Classes cover everything from coffee history to a seven-hour workshop called "Brewing the Perfect Cup at Home." This workshop is one of five classes that all employees (called partners) must complete during their first six weeks with the company. This workshop focuses on the need to educate the customer in proper coffeemaking techniques.

Store managers (who have gone through facilitation workshops and are certified by the company as trainers) teach the classes. The classes teach the employees to make decisions that will enhance customer satisfaction without requiring manager authorization. For example, if a customer comes into the store complaining about how their beans were ground, the employee is authorized to replace them on the spot. While most restaurants use on-the-job training, Starbucks holds bar classes where employees practice taking orders and preparing beverages in a company training room. This allows employees to hone their skills in a low-stress environment, and also protects Starbucks' quality image by allowing only experienced baristas to serve customers.[14] Reports *Fortune*:

> It's silly, soft-headed stuff, though basically, of course, it's true. Maybe some of it sinks in. Starbucks is a smashing success, thanks in large part to the people who come out of these therapy-like training programs. Annual barista turnover at the company is 60% compared with 140% for hourly workers in the fast-food business. 'I don't have a negative thing to say,' says Kim Sigelman, who manages the store in Emeryville, California, of her four years with the company. She seems to mean it.[15]

Employee benefits

Starbucks offers its benefits package to both part-time and full-time employees with dependent coverage available. Dependent coverage is also extended to same-sex partners. The package includes medical, dental, vision and short-term disability insurance, as well as paid vacation, paid holidays, mental health/chemical dependency benefits, an employee assistance program, a 401k savings plan and a stock option plan. They also offer career counseling and product discounts.[16]

Schultz believes that without these benefits, people do not feel financially or spiritually tied to their jobs. He argues that stock options and the complete benefits package increase employee loyalty and encourage attentive service to the customer.[17] Notes Bradley Honeycutt, the company's vice president, HR services and international: "[Our] part-timers are on the front line with our customers. If we treat them right, we feel they will treat [the customers] well."[18] Sharon Elliot, HR senior vice president offers another explanation, "Most importantly, this is the right thing to do. It's a basic operating philosophy of our organization."

Despite the increased coverage, Starbucks' health care costs are well within the national average, running around $150 per employee per month. This may be due, in part, to the fact that its employees are relatively young, resulting in lower claims. Half of the management at Starbucks is under 50, and retail employees tend to be much younger. Starbucks is betting on the increases in premiums being largely offset by lower training costs due to the lower attrition rate. Comments *Fortune*:

> It has become boilerplate public relations for corporations to boast about how much they value their people. But Starbucks really does treat its partners astonishingly well. The pay – between $6 and $8 an hour – is better than that of most entry-level food service jobs. The company offers health insurance to all employees, even part-timers. . . . Walk into just about any Starbucks, and you'll see that these are fairly soft hands: Some 80% of the partners are white, 85% have some college education beyond high school, and the average age is 26.

The Bean Stock Plan
Employee turnover is also discouraged by Starbucks' stock option plan known as the Bean Stock Plan. Implemented in August of 1991, the plan made Starbucks the only private company to offer stock options unilaterally to all employees. After one year, employees may join a 401(k) plan. There is a vesting period of five years; it starts one year after the option is granted, then vests the employee at 20 percent every year. In addition, every employee receives a new stock option award each year, and a new vesting period begins. This plan required getting an exemption from the Security Exchange Commission, since any company with more than 500 shareholders has to report its financial performance publicly – a costly process that reveals valuable information to competitors.

The option plan did not go uncontested by the venture capitalists and shareholders on the board. Craig Foley, a director and managing partner of Chancellor Capital Management Inc. (the largest shareholder before the public offering), noted that, "Increasing the shareholders substantially dilutes our interest. We take that very seriously." In the end he and others were won over by a study conducted by the company that revealed the positive relationship between employee ownership and productivity rates, and a scenario analysis of how many employees would be vested. Foley conceded that: "The grants are tied to overachieving. If you just come to work and do your job, that isn't as attractive as if you beat the numbers."[19]

Since the Bean Stock Plan was put into place, enthusiastic employees have been suggesting ways to save money and increase productivity. The strong company culture has also served as a levy against pilferage; Starbucks' inventory shrinkage is less than half of 1 percent.

In 1995 Starbucks demonstrated that its concern for employee welfare extended beyond the US borders. After a human-rights group leafleted the stores complaining that Guatemalan coffee pickers received less than $3 a day, Starbucks became the first agricultural commodity importer to implement a code for minimum working conditions and pay for foreign subcontractors.[20] The company's guidelines call for overseas suppliers to pay wages and benefits that "address the basic needs of workers and their families" and to allow child labor only when it does not interrupt required education.[21] This move has set a precedent for other importers of agricultural commodities.

Leveraging the Brand

Multiple channels of distribution

While Starbucks has resisted offering its coffee in grocery stores, it has found a variety of other distribution channels for its products. Besides its stand-alone stores, Starbucks has set up cafes and carts in hospitals, banks, office buildings, supermarkets and shopping centers. In 1992 Starbucks signed a deal with Nordstrom to serve Starbucks coffee exclusively in all of its stores. Nordstrom also named Starbucks as the exclusive coffee supplier for its restaurants, employee lunchrooms and catering operations. As of 1992, Nordstrom was operating 62 restaurants and 48 espresso bars. A year later, Barnes & Noble initiated an agreement with Starbucks to implement a "cafe-in-a-bookshop" plan.

Other distribution agreements have included office coffee suppliers, hotels, and airlines. Office coffee is a large segment of the coffee market. Associated Services (an office coffee supplier) provides Starbucks coffee exclusively to the 5,000 northern California businesses it services. Sheraton Hotel has also signed an agreement to serve Starbucks coffee. In 1995 Starbucks signed a deal with United Airlines to provide Starbucks coffee to United's nearly 75 million passengers a year.[22]

While Starbucks is the largest and best-known of the coffeehouse chains and its presence is very apparent in metropolitan areas, the firm's estimates indicate that only 1 percent of the US population has tried its products. Through these distribution agreements and the new product partnerships it is establishing, Starbucks hopes to capture more of the US market.

Brand extensions

In 1995, Starbucks launched a line of packaged and prepared teas in response to growing demand for tea houses and packaged tea. Tea is a highly profitable beverage for restaurants to sell, costing only 2 cents to 4 cents a cup to produce.[23]

Starbucks coffee is not sold in grocery stores, but its name is making its way onto grocery shelves via a carefully-planned series of joint ventures.[24] An agreement with PepsiCo Inc. brought a bottled version of Starbucks' Frappuccino (a cold, sweetened coffee drink) to store shelves in August of 1996. A similar product released a year before, called Mazagran, was a failure and was pulled from the shelves; however, both Starbucks and PepsiCo had higher hopes for Frappuccino.[25] Starbucks also has an agreement with Washington-based Redhook Ale Brewery to make a product called Double Black Stout, a coffee-flavored stout. In another 50–50 partnership,

Dreyer's Grand Ice Cream Inc. distributes seven quart-products and two bar-products of Starbucks coffee ice cream.

Other partnerships by the company are designed to form new product associations with coffee. For instance, Starbucks has collaborated with Capitol Records Inc. to produce two Starbucks jazz CDs, available only in Starbucks stores. Starbucks is also opening tandem units with Bruegger's Bagel Bakeries and had bought a minority stake in Noah's New York Bagels in 1995. This minority stake has since been sold.

INTERNATIONAL EXPANSION

From the beginning, Schultz has professed a strict growth policy. Although many other coffeehouses or espresso bars are franchised, Starbucks owns all of its stores outright with the exception of license agreements in airports.[26] Despite over 300 calls a day from willing investors, Schultz feels it is important to the company's integrity to own its stores. Further, rather than trying to capture all the potential markets as soon as possible, Starbucks goes into a market and tries to completely dominate it before setting its sights on further expansion. As Alstead points out, "Starbucks hopes to achieve the same density in all of its markets that they have achieved in Seattle, Vancouver and Chicago."

In 1996, the firm opened 307 stores (including four replacement stores), converted 19 Coffee Connection stores to Starbucks, and closed one store. In 1997, Starbucks intends to open at least 325 new stores and enter at least three major new markets in North America including Phoenix, Arizona, and Miami, Florida. Moreover, Schultz plans to have 2,000 stores by the year 2000.

Some analysts believe that the US coffee bar market may be reaching saturation. They point to the fact that there have been some consolidations, as bigger players snap up some of the smaller coffee bar competitors.[27] Further, they note that Starbucks' store base is also maturing, leading to a slowdown in the growth of unit volume and firm profitability. Higher coffee costs have also cut into margins, intensifying the competition in what has now become a crowded market. Recognizing this, Starbucks has turned its attention to foreign markets for continued growth. Notes Schultz, "We are looking at the Asia-Pacific region as the focus of our international business."

Expansion into Asian Markets

In 1996 the firm invested $1.5 million and established a subsidiary called Starbucks Coffee International Inc. The focus of this subsidiary will be on penetrating the Asia-Pacific region. According to Kathie Lindemann, the director of international operations at Starbucks:

> We are not overlooking Europe and South America as areas for future expansion. But, we feel that expanding into these regions is more risky than Asia. The Asia-Pacific region we feel has much more potential for us. It is full of emerging markets. Also con-

sumers' disposable income is increasing as their countries' economies grow. Most important of all, people in these countries are open to Western lifestyles.

This international subsidiary consists of 12 managers located primarily in Seattle, Washington. Together these managers are responsible for: the developing of new businesses internationally, financing and planning of international stores, managing international operations and logistics, merchandising in international markets and, finally, for the training and developing of Starbucks' international managers. Since its establishment, this subsidiary has been responsible for opening Starbucks coffeehouses in Hawaii, Japan, and Singapore.[28]

Lindemann, commenting on Starbucks' approach to Asian markets, notes:

> At Starbucks we don't like the concept of franchising. Therefore, we decided to work with partners in Japan and other Asian countries. Our approach to international expansion is to focus on the partnership first, country second. Partnership is everything in Asia. We rely on the local connection to get everything up and working. The key is finding the right local partners to negotiate local regulations and other issues.

When asked to list the criteria by which Starbucks chose partners in Asia, Lindemann highlights six points:

> We look for partners who share our values, culture, and goals about community development. We are trying to align ourselves with people, or companies, with plenty of experience. We are primarily interested in partners who can guide us through the process of starting up in a foreign location. We look for firms with: (1) similar philosophy to ours in terms of shared values, corporate citizenship, and commitment to be in the business for the long haul, (2) multi-unit restaurant experience, (3) financial resources to expand the Starbucks concept rapidly to prevent imitators, (4) strong real-estate experience with knowledge about how to pick prime real estate locations, (5) knowledge of the retail market, and (6) the availability of the people to commit to our project.

Entry into Japan

In October 1995, Starbucks entered into a joint venture with Tokyo-based Sazaby Inc. This firm was expected to help Starbucks open 12 new stores in Japan by the end of 1997. This joint venture, amounting to 250 million yen ($2.33 million) in capitalization, is equally owned by Starbucks Coffee International and Sazaby. The Tokyo-based Sazaby, often recognized as a leader in bringing unique goods to the people of Japan, operates upscale retail and restaurant chains throughout Japan. Commenting on this joint venture, the president of Starbucks International, Howard Behar, notes:

> This powerful strategic alliance, which combines two major lifestyle companies, will provide the Japanese consumer a new and unique specialty coffee experience. . . . We look at this venture as though we're starting all over again, and in many ways, we are.

With Sazaby's assistance the firm opened two stores in Tokyo in September of 1996. The first outlet was in Tokyo's posh Ginza shopping district. The Ginza store

EXHIBIT 10.6:
Japan consumer preferences[a]

	1980	1985	1990	1994
Instant coffee	57.6%	59.2%	50.6%	45.4%
Regular coffee	33.3%	29.4%	33.1%	37.4%
Canned coffee	9.1%	11.4%	13.1%	17.3%
Total (cups per week)	7.4	9.02	9.52	10.36
Place of consumption[b]				
Home	55.8%	58.3%	56.6%	54.7%
Coffee shop	24.6%	11.6%	8.9%	8.0%
Work/school	15.4%	21.8%	23.9%	26.4%
Other	4.2%	8.3%	10.6%	10.9%

[a] Based on a survey from October 20 through November 7, 1994 by the All Japan Coffee Association. The survey reported that men aged between 25–39 years consumed the most coffee at 16 cups per week and girls between 12–17 years consumed the least at 3 cups.
[b] *Source: Tea & Coffee Trade Journal*, August, 1995.

was planned so that Japanese customers can have the same "Starbucks experience" offered in US stores. The firm's second store was located in Ochanomizu, a student area cluttered with colleges, bookstores and fast-food restaurants. Starbucks hopes that students and office workers in the neighborhood will come in to grab a cup of coffee and a light snack. At both stores customers can eat in the store or take out their purchases.

The food-and-drink menus in the firm's Japanese coffeehouses are similar to those in the United States. The firm offers 15 types of beverages, snacks such as cookies and sandwiches, coffee beans, and novelty goods such as coffee mugs and T-shirts. The firm's single-shot short latte costs 280 yen in Tokyo (about $2.50, a price that is roughly 50 cents more than in the United States). According to an industry report, a cup of coffee in Tokyo cost about 399 yen, on average, in August 1996.

Although the Japanese are not used to Italian-style coffee beverages, Starbucks executives believe that Japanese consumers are ready to embrace the Starbucks concept.[29] A report in the *Wall Street Journal* suggests that breaking into the Japanese market may not be easy (see Exhibit 10.6 and Exhibit 10.7):

> The Japanese haven't developed a taste for espresso drinks like caffe latte and caffe mocha; they drink a lot of instant coffee or ready-to-drink coffee in cans, as well as American-style hot coffee. Moreover, the Japanese coffee market may be saturated with many coffee shops and vending machines serving hot coffees. Coca-Cola alone has more than 800,000 vending machines that sell canned coffee.[30]

Similarly, a report in the *Nikkei Weekly* points out:

EXHIBIT 10.7:
Canned coffee sales in Japan (US$ millions)

	Market share (%)	1991	1992	1993	1994	1995
Coca Cola	40	2,718	2,396	2,635	2,899	3,189
UCC	12	653	718	790	869	965
Pokka	11	599	658	724	797	877
Daido	10	544	599	658	724	797
Nestlé	7	381	419	461	507	558
Others	20	1,089	1,198	1,317	1,449	1,594
Total	100	5,445	6,990	6,589	7,248	7,972

Canned coffee accounts for approximately 40% of total beverage sales in Japan, including soft drinks.

Source: *Advertising Age*, 1996.

Though Japan is the world's third largest coffee consumer, its coffee shops constitute a declining industry, with high operating costs knocking many small operators out of business. In 1992, there were 115,143 coffee shops in Japan, according to the latest government survey available. That figure is nearly 30% less than the peak in 1982.[31]

Japan's coffee culture revolves around the *kissaten*, a relatively formal sit-down coffeehouse. According to the All Japan Coffee Association, while US and German consumers consumed 18.1 and 10 million bags of coffee in 1994, respectively, the Japanese consumed 6.1 million coffee bags (one bag of coffee contains 60 kilograms of coffee beans).

Despite the absolute size of the Japanese coffee market, knowledgeable analysts note that Starbucks is likely to face stiff competition and retaliation from well-established players in Japan. Two of Japan's well-established coffee chains are the Doutor Coffee Company and the Pronto Corp.

Started in 1980, Doutor Coffee Company is Japan's leading coffee-bar chain. In 1996, it had over 466 shops in and around Tokyo. At times, the consumers refer to this firm as the McDonald's of coffeehouses since it provides a limited menu, and emphasizes self-service. In Doutor's shops seating is limited and counters are provided where customers can stand while they consume their beverages. The focus is on speed of service and quick turnover of customers. The average customer stay in a Doutor coffee shop is about 10 minutes, about one-third the stay in a typical *kissaten*. Close to 90 percent of the Doutor's coffeehouses are operated by franchisees, while the remaining 10 percent of the shops are operated directly by Doutor. A standard cup of coffee at Doutor costs 180 yen. The firm serves other refreshments, such as juice, sandwiches and pastries. It is reported that nearly 10 million customers per month visit Doutor coffeehouses. The firm has five shops in Ginza, the location where Starbucks opened its first store.[32]

Pronto Corp. is Japan's second largest coffee-bar chain. The firm opened its first shop in Tokyo in 1987. In 1996, it operated over 95 outlets, most of them in Tokyo. The firm's coffeehouses serve coffee and light snacks during the day, and at night they switch to neighborhood bar–type operations, serving alcoholic drinks and light meals. At Pronto, a standard cup of coffee costs 160 yen. Reacting to Starbucks' entry into Japan, Seiji Honna, president of Pronto Corp., notes:

> For the past few years, we've had this nightmare scenario that espresso drinks are going to swallow up Japan's coffee market. . . . And we won't know how to make a good cup of espresso. . . . [And now Starbucks' entry], if they really mean business, I think they'll probably put some of us out of business.[33]

But he goes on to comment:

> I don't think that the opening of the first Starbucks store in Japan would immediately be a threat to our business. . . . But Starbucks could become a strong competitor if it is able to gain consumer recognition in the next three years or so. In order to do so, Starbucks will need to have about 30 to 50 stores in the Tokyo area.[34]

Yuji Tsunoda, president of Starbucks Coffee Japan Ltd., indicates the company intends to have 100 directly-owned coffee bars in major Japanese cities in the next five years.

According to Kazuo Sunago, an analyst from Japan's leading advertising firm Dentsu Inc., Japanese coffee bars lack the creativity to stop a firm like Starbucks from making inroads in the Japanese coffee market.

> As traditional mom-and pop coffee shops die off, big chains are looking for more attractive formats. . . . But they are like a dry lake bed – void of new ideas. That's why the whole industry is stirred up about Starbucks.[35]

Comments Alstead: "The issue facing Starbucks is how, as we expand geographically and through expanding channels, will we be able maintain the Starbucks' culture?"

Appendix
Starbucks Corporation – A Brief History

1971   Starbucks Coffee opens its first store in the Pike Place Market – Seattle, Washington's legendary, open-air farmer's market.

1982   Howard Schultz joins Starbucks as director of retail operations and marketing. Starbucks begins providing coffee to fine restaurants and espresso bars in Seattle.

1983   Schultz travels to Italy, where he's impressed with the popularity of espresso bars. Milan, a city of the size of Philadelphia, hosts 1,500 of these bars.

1984   Schultz convinces the original founders of Starbucks to test the coffee bar concept in a new Starbucks store on the corner of 4th and Spring in downtown Seattle. Overwhelmingly successful, this experiment is the genesis for a company that Schultz will found in 1985.

1985   Schultz founds Il Giornale, offering brewed coffee and espresso beverages made from Starbucks coffee beans.

1987   In August, with the backing of local investors, Il Giornale acquires the Seattle assets of Starbucks and changes its name to Starbucks Corporation. The company has fewer than 100 employees and opens its first stores in Chicago and Vancouver, B.C. **Starbucks store total = 17**

1988   Starbucks introduces mail order catalog, offering mail-order service in all 50 states. **Starbucks store total = 33**

1989   Opens first Portland, Oregon store in Pioneer Courthouse Square. **Starbucks store total = 55**

1990   Starbucks expands corporate headquarters in Seattle and builds a new roasting plant. **Starbucks stores total = 84**

1991   Starbucks opens first stores in Los Angeles, California. Announces Starbucks' commitment to establish a long-term relationship with CARE, the international relief and development organization, and introduces CARE coffee sampler.

        Becomes the first US privately-owned company in history to offer a stock option program, Bean Stock, that includes part-time employees. **Starbucks store total = 116**

1992   Starbucks opens first stores in San Francisco, San Diego, Orange County and Denver. Specialty Sales and Marketing Division awarded Nordstrom's national coffee account. Completes initial public offering, with Common Stock being traded on the NASDAQ National Market System. **Starbucks store total = 165**

1993   Opens premier East Coast market: Washington, D.C. Specialty Sales and Marketing Division begins relationship with Barnes & Noble, Inc. as national account. Opens second roasting plant located in Kent, Washington. **Starbucks store total = 275**

1994   Opens first stores in Minneapolis, Boston, New York, Atlanta, Dallas and Houston. Specialty Sales and Marketing Division awarded ITT/Sheraton Hotel's national coffee account.

        The Coffee Connection, Inc. becomes wholly-owned subsidiary of Starbucks Corporation in June.

        Starbucks announces partnership with Pepsi-Cola to develop ready-to-drink coffee-based beverages.

        Completes offering of additional 6,025,000 shares of Common Stock at $28.50 per share.

        Schultz receives Business Enterprise Trust Award recognizing the company's innovative benefits plan. **Starbucks store total = 425**

1995   Starbucks opens first stores in Pittsburgh, Las Vegas, San Antonio, Philadelphia, Cincinnati, Baltimore and Austin. Specialty Sales and Marketing Division begins relationship with United Airlines.

        Starbucks and Redhook Ale Brewery introduce Double Black™ Stout, a new dark roasted malt beer with the aromatic and flavorful addition of coffee.

        Acquires minority interest in Noah's New York Bagels, Inc.

        Starbucks stores begin serving Frappuccino® blended beverages, a line of low fat, creamy, iced coffee beverages.

        Starbucks opens state-of-the art roasting facility in York, Pennsylvania, serving East Coast markets.

Announces alliance with Chapters Inc. to operate coffee bars inside Chapter's super-stores in Canada.

Announces partnership with Star Markets to open Starbucks retail locations within Star Market stores.

Develops framework for a code of conduct as part of a long-term strategy to improve conditions in coffee origin countries.

Starbucks Coffee International signs agreement with Sazaby Inc., a Japanese retailer and restaurateur, to form a joint venture partnership that will develop Starbucks retail stores in Japan. The joint venture is called Starbucks Coffee Japan, Ltd.

Forms long-term joint venture with Dreyer's Grand Ice Cream, Inc. to develop revolutionary line of coffee ice creams. **Starbucks store total = 676**

1996   Opens first stores in Rhode Island, Idaho, North Carolina, Arizona, Utah and Toronto, Ontario. Specialty Sales and Marketing Division awarded Westin Hotel's national coffee account.

Starbucks Coffee Japan, Ltd. opens first location outside North America in the Ginza district, Tokyo, Japan. Announces plans to develop 10 to 12 additional stores in the Tokyo metropolitan area over the next 18 months.

Starbucks Coffee International signs agreement forming Coffee Partners Hawaii, which will develop Starbucks retail locations in Hawaii.

First Starbucks store in Honolulu opens at Kalala Mall.

Starbucks Coffee International signs licensing agreement with Bonstar Pte. Ltd. to open stores in Singapore.

First licensed Singapore location opens at Liat Towers.

Direct Response Division reaches over seven million America Online (AOL) customers through Caffe Starbucks, a market place channel store that offers select Starbucks catalog products.

Announces that all Coffee Connection locations in the Boston area will become Starbucks stores during fiscal 1996.

Announces development agreement with three leading digital media companies – Digital Brands, Inc., Watts-Silverstein & Associates and Cyberstruction, Inc. – to develop a wide-ranging online strategy.

Unveils prototype store at Comdex Convention and Trade Show, Las Vegas, with Intel Corp., showcasing some of the technologies Starbucks will be testing over the next year in several stores.

Forms licensing arrangement with Aramark Corp. to put licensed Starbucks operations at various locations operated by Aramark.

Starbucks and Dreyer's Grand Ice Cream Inc. introduce six flavors of Starbucks™ Ice Cream and Starbucks Ice Cream bars, available in grocery stores across the United States. Starbucks Ice Cream quickly becomes the number one brand of coffee ice cream in the US.

North American Coffee Partnership (between Starbucks and Pepsi-Cola Company) announces a bottled version of Starbucks popular Frappuccino™ blended beverage will be sold in supermarkets, convenience stores and other retail points of distribution on the West Coast.

Starbucks commemorates the first anniversary of the Blue Note Blend coffee and CD with Blue Note 2, an encore collection of jazz from the Blue Note® Records label. The

Blue Note Blend coffee also returns for a limited engagement in the company's coffee lineup.

Celebrates the company's 25th anniversary with marketing program featuring the art, music and culture of 1971, the year Starbucks was born. **Current Starbucks store total = 1,015**

NOTES

1. *Success*, April, 1993.
2. The *Chicago Tribune*, July 1, 1993.
3. According to the *Berkeley Wellness Letter*, a newsletter from the University of California, 53 percent of all coffee in the United States is consumed at breakfast. Further, 11 percent of the US population drink decaf coffee, and 10 percent drink instant coffee. Of the people who drink instant coffee most are over the age of 55.
4. The *Wall Street Journal*, February 25, 1993. According to the National Coffee Association brewed coffee accounted for 85 percent of all coffee consumed in the US during 1995. This was followed by Espresso-based drinks (14 percent) and Express coffee (1 percent).
5. Espresso, despite its potent flavor, is lower in caffeine than the canned coffees offered in supermarkets. It is made with Arabica beans that are lower in caffeine content, and the brewing method yields less caffeine per cup.
6. The *Wall Street Journal*, February 25, 1993.
7. The *Sacramento Bee*, April 28, 1993.
8. This Colombian coffee bean crop is very small and grows only in the high regions of the Cordillera mountain range. For years, the Narino beans were guarded zealously by Western Europeans who prized their colorful and complex flavor. They were usually used for upgrading blends. Starbucks was determined to make them available for the first time as a pure varietal. This required breaking Western Europe's monopoly over the beans by convincing the Colombian growers that it intended to use "the best beans for a higher purpose."
9. The *Canada Newswire*, March 1, 1993.
10. Though *Consumer Reports* rated Starbucks coffee as burnt and bitter, Starbucks customers felt otherwise, and most of Starbucks' early growth can be attributed to enthusiastic word-of-mouth advertising. The typical Starbucks customer is highly proficient in the science of coffee beans and brewing techniques. The coffee bars even have their own dialect; executives from downtown Seattle businesses line up in force to order "tall-skinny-double mochas" and "2% short no-foam lattes."
11. *Inc.*, January, 1993.
12. *Fortune*, December 9, 1996.
13. *Fortune*, December 9, 1996.
14. *Training*, June 1995.
15. *Fortune*, December 9, 1996.
16. The decision to offer benefits even to part-time employees (who represent roughly two-thirds of Starbucks' 10,000 employees) has gained a great deal of attention in the press. According to a Hewitt Associates L.L.C. survey of more than 500 employers, only 25 percent of employers offer medical coverage to employees working less than 20 hours a week. It was difficult to get insurers to sign Starbucks up since they did not understand why Starbucks would want to cover part-timers.
17. *Inc.*, January, 1993.
18. *Business Insurance*, March 27, 1995, p. 6.
19. *Inc.*, January, 1993.

20. The *Wall Street Journal*, April 4, 1995.
21. The *Wall Street Journal*, October 23, 1995.
22. In the past, one interesting outlet for Starbucks coffee was Starbucks' deal with Smith Brothers, one of the Northwest's oldest dairies. Smith Brothers used to sell Starbucks coffee on its home delivery routes. The idea for the alliance actually came from the dairy, a supplier for Starbucks. Management at Smith Brothers began to wonder if Starbucks' rapid growth might prompt them to look for other dairies to supply their milk. A report in the Seattle *Times* (November 6, 1992) noted that Earl Keller, Sales Manager for Smith Brothers, got the idea that "Maybe if we were a good customer of theirs, it would be more difficult for them to leave us." In 1992, Smith delivered 1,000 pounds of coffee beans a week. The coffee was sold at the same price as in Starbucks' retail stores, and the only complaint has been that Smith does not carry all 30 varieties. The company no longer sells coffee through Smith Brothers.
23. The *Nations Restaurant News*, July 10, 1995.
24. According to Troy Alstead, "We are evaluating whether to offer our coffee in grocery stores, and we have done some private labelling of Starbucks coffee for Costco." The Specialty Coffee Association of America predicts that by 1999 supermarkets will account for 63 percent of all coffee sold in America. This will be followed by gourmet stores (14%), mass market (11%), mail order (8%) and other (8%).
25. Coke and Nestlé have signed a similar agreement to produce single-serving cold coffee drinks in specialty flavors such as French Vanilla, Mocha and Cafe Au Lait to compete with the Starbucks product.
26. Airports often grant exclusive concessions contracts to a single provider, e.g. Host Marriott. Since Starbucks wanted to tap these markets, they negotiated licensing arrangements with Marriott to run Starbucks stands in the airports that Marriott has under contract.
27. The *Washington Post*, August 1, 1995.
28. The Hawaii entry is based on a joint venture with the MacNaugton Group, a real estate development firm that has been responsible for the successful introduction of several well-known mainland firms such as Sports Authority, Office Max and Eagle Hardware stores into the Hawaiian Islands. Using this joint venture, the firm plans to develop approximately 30 stores throughout the Hawaiian Islands over the next three to four years. Starbucks' entry into Singapore is based on a licensing agreement with Bonvests Holdings Limited, a firm that is involved in property and hotel development, investment, related management services, waste management and building maintenance services, food and beverage retailing and marketing of branded luxury products in Singapore. Under this agreement (completed in December 1996), ten Starbucks coffee stores are expected to be opened within the first 12 to 15 months.
29. The *Puget Sound Business Journal*, June 21–27, 1996.
30. The *Wall Street Journal*, September 4, 1996.
31. The *Nikkei Weekly*, September 23, 1996.
32. According to a report in the *Nihon Keizai Shimbum* (June 18, 1988), Doutor is good at segmenting the coffee market. For instance, the firm has a coffee shop for just about every taste and service level. The low-end shops are located near train stations and busy areas where people are in a hurry. In residential locations, the firm operates Cafe Colorado where people can sit and chat for a while. The price of coffee in Cafe Colorado is double that of the firm's inexpensive coffee houses. The firm also caters to more upscale cus-

tomers via Cafe Doutor, where the ambience is more elegant and the coffee price is much higher.

33. According to a report in the *Wall Street Journal*, Honna spent time last year gathering intelligence on Starbucks' method in the United States. He report-

edly visited, incognito, more than 20 Starbucks coffee shops along the West Coast.

34. Reuters World Service, August 1, 1996.

35. The *Wall Street Journal*, September 4, 1996.

THUNDERBIRD
THE AMERICAN GRADUATE SCHOOL
OF INTERNATIONAL MANAGEMENT

CHAPTER ELEVEN

HONEYWELL INC. AND GLOBAL RESEARCH & DEVELOPMENT

In mid-1997, Steve Wilson, a Honeywell Technology Center (HTC) manager, thought back to the previous week's visit from a Chinese delegation interested in Honeywell Inc. (Honeywell) technology and products. These visits were becoming increasingly frequent. Wilson and other HTC managers were certain that there were many international opportunities for Honeywell, not just in China but throughout Asia and Eastern Europe. The dilemma was that HTC, Honeywell's research and development (R&D) organization, was centralized in Minneapolis, a long way from the potential new markets.

Recently, a Honeywell manager based in Asia had raised the following issues:

There are several reasons for spreading R&D capability around the world. One, time to market in today's world is probably the most significant competitive advantage a company can have. One way to get quicker time to market is to do R&D in multiple locations around the world so you have a 24-hour R&D process. Second, there are talented people around the world and by not taking advantage of those skills and talents that may exist in China or India or other places, a company is putting itself at a competitive disadvantage. Third, in many countries, including China, personal contacts and connections are invaluable in the business world and there is a great loyalty among alumni of certain institutions. American companies that have established relationships with these institutions may get access to alumni in important government positions down the road. Fourth, it's much easier to understand the unique product requirements of a country or region of the world if you spend time there. It's very hard to sit in Minneapolis and figure out the cooling control requirement for a Chinese air conditioning system if you have never been in an apartment building in China that has poured concrete walls that you can't run thermostat wire through.

There was a growing consensus that HTC had to become more international to support Honeywell's growth opportunities. However, before anything could be done, many issues had to be addressed. How should Honeywell attempt to build effective global R&D capabilities? HTC had developed a unique entrepreneurial, interaction-based culture. Could this culture be replicated outside the United States? How quickly should HTC move? Who would manage new R&D organizations? How would these organizations be funded? Should international R&D sites be centers of excellence for specific technologies, or should they be application centers using technology developed in Minneapolis, or should they be a combination of both?

HONEYWELL BACKGROUND

Honeywell had a long history of engineering and scientific achievement. In 1885, Albert Butz invented the damper flapper, a device that opened furnace vents automatically. Butz formed the Butz Thermo-Electric Regulator Co. in Minneapolis to market the product. In 1927, the firm, now known as the Minneapolis Heat Regulator Company, merged with its main competitor, Honeywell Heating Specialties of Wabash, Indiana. The new public company, named the Minneapolis-Honeywell Regulator Co. and headquartered in Minneapolis, became the leading U.S. firm in home heating controls.

Throughout the 1930s, Minneapolis-Honeywell expanded and diversified. In 1930, the first international subsidiary was opened in Toronto and in 1934, the first European subsidiary was established in the Netherlands. Between 1900 and 1937, the company evolved from manufacturing one thermostat to producing more than 3,000 control devices and its engineers received more than 1,000 patents. During World War II, Minneapolis-Honeywell became involved in mass-production of military instruments and equipment. This work lead to the development and production of an aircraft autopilot, positioning Minneapolis-Honeywell in the aeronautical engineering business. After the war, the firm reorganized its various defense-related businesses into the Military Products Group and by the late 1950s, military business represented one third of the company's sales. By the 1960s, the firm, now called Honeywell Inc., had become an important supplier for the U.S. space program.

In 1955, Honeywell formed a division called Datamatic to build computers. This division would eventually have a 10% market share. Honeywell's controls business also grew rapidly in the post-war period. In 1950, the firm acquired the Micro Switch Corporation, a manufacturer of switches, sensors, and manual controls used in myriad products such as cars, airplanes, appliances, air conditioning systems, and factory equipment. In 1953, Honeywell introduced its famous round thermostat, the Honeywell Round. Much of Honeywell's growth between 1960 and 1980 was the result of international growth and, in particular, demand from developing nations for home, building, and industrial controls.

The 1980s and early 1990s was a period of restructuring for Honeywell. Total employment dropped from 94,000 in 1985 to 50,000 in 1995. Cutbacks in U.S. defense spending had a dramatic effect on Honeywell's Space and Aviation Division. During a three-year period from 1991 to 1994, space and aviation revenue declined by $700 million to $1.4 billion. Space and aviation employment declined by half to about 11,000 and 3 million square feet of plant space was closed. In 1990, the defense business, which a few years earlier had accounted for almost half of total revenues, was spun off into a new organization. In 1986, Sperry Aerospace, a Phoenix-based firm manufacturing flight instrumentation, advanced avionics, and other electronics systems was acquired for $1.03 billion. The acquisition solidified Honeywell's position as the leader in aircraft navigation systems and flight controls. Also in 1986, after its market share dropped to 2%, the computer business was spun off into a joint venture of Compagnie des Machines Bull of France and NEC Corp. of Japan. In 1991, Honeywell exited the computer business.

Honeywell Sectors in 1997

Honeywell was organized around three industry sectors: home and building control, industrial control, and space and aviation control. Exhibit 11.1 shows summary financial information for Honeywell, Exhibit 11.2 shows a list of products, customers, and competitors, and Exhibit 11.3 shows segmented financial information by division and geographic region.

The home and building control division manufactured controls for heating such as thermostats, ventilation, humidification and air-conditioning equipment, home automation systems, lighting controls, building management systems and services, and home consumer products such as air cleaners and humidifiers.

The industrial control sector produced systems for the automation and control of process operations in industries such as oil refining, oil and gas drilling, pulp and paper manufacturing, food processing, chemical manufacturing, and power generation. For example, Honeywell controls were used in 24 of the world's 25 largest oil refineries. The industrial control sector also produced switches, sensors, and solenoid valves for use in vehicles, consumer products, data communication, and industrial applications.

The space and aviation sector was a leading supplier of avionics systems for the commercial, military, and space markets. Honeywell systems could be found on virtually every commercial aircraft produced in the Western world and were aboard every manned space flight launched in the United States. Products included automatic flight control systems, electronic cockpit displays, flight management systems, navigation, surveillance, and warning systems, and severe weather avoidance systems. In 1995, the Boeing 777 was launched, marking the successful launch of a new suite of Honeywell integrated avionics controls.

Of the three product sectors, home and building control was the most international because its products had potential applications in every country. The end customer was the homeowner and housing needs differed in every country. Most of the home and building control products sold in Europe were engineered and manufactured in European factories. For example, German homes were usually heated with hot water whereas in the U.S. forced air was the norm. As a result, various valves and boiler parts were developed in Germany for the German heating market. In other cases, the European products were close adaptations of products sold in the United States. There were also products, such as thermostats sold in the Netherlands, that were imported directly from the United States.

With its worldwide standards, space and aviation was the best defined international sector. Aviation products did not have to be localized, which meant that aviation could be operated as a centralized global business. Industrial control products, although not standard worldwide, tended to be less localized than home and building products because customers wanted similar controls worldwide in their plants.

International Opportunities

Honeywell's international organization is shown in Exhibit 11.4. European operations were headquartered in Brussels and the Asia-Pacific region was based in Hong Kong. Non-U.S. sales were $2.8 billion, equal to 39% of 1996 total sales. By the year 2000, non-U.S. sales were expected to increase to 45%. Much of this growth was projected for China and Eastern and Central Europe. With their high levels of air and water pollution and poor record of energy efficiency, these areas were large potential markets for Honeywell home and building and industrial controls. As one HTC researcher indicated, "the mess in Eastern Europe is a huge market for us."

In particular, the area of district heating was a large potential market for Honeywell. In Eastern Europe and China, most people had never used a thermostat in their homes. Apartments generally had no heating controls and their temperatures were determined by outputs of a central district heating facility. During the winter it was not unusual to see open windows in apartment buildings as residents tried to cool their apartments. Hot water for domestic radiators was provided by a central boiler in each region. On a designated day of the year, an official turned the heating on for the whole city; on another, it was turned off. Often, there were no valves on the radiators. The plumbing was often arranged so that if one occupier turned down the heating, the entire building would be affected. With district heating, Honeywell's goal was to provide a complete system from the boiler to the individual apartment unit. Honeywell could provide monitoring and control systems to improve productivity, save energy, reduce air pollution and provide better temperature control. To do this would require Honeywell home and building control and industrial control units to work closely together as a team. As an early entrant, Honeywell, which opened a Moscow office in 1974, was a major supplier of district heating controls in Eastern Europe.

Although Honeywell's Asian business accounted for only about 8% of sales, CEO Michael Bonsignore indicated that "Asia represents the greatest growth opportunity for Honeywell in the next 20 years."[1] Bonsignore added that he would like Asian businesses to reach $1 billion in sales by 2000 and to grow at a 20% compound rate or better. Honeywell's Asia-Pacific business had operations in 17 Asian countries

EXHIBIT 11.1:

Honeywell Inc. financial information (dollars and shares in millions except per share amount)

	1996	1995	1994	1993	1992
Sales					
Home and Building Control	$3,327.1	$3,034.7	$2,664.5	$2,424.3	$2,393.6
Industrial Control	2,199.6	2,035.9	1,835.3	1,691.5	1,743.9
Space and Aviation Control	1,640.0	1,527.4	1,432.0	1,674.9	1,933.1
Other	144.9	133.3	125.2	172.3	152.0
Total sales	$7,311.6	$6,731.3	$6,057.0	$5,963.0	$6,222.6
Operating profit					
Home and Building Control	$345.8	$308.6	$236.5	$232.7	$193.4
Industrial Control	254.9	233.8	206.6	189.7	156.9
Space and Aviation Control	163.3	127.6	80.9	148.1	175.8
Other	6.2	2.8		(1.8)	(9.5)
Total operating profit	770.2	672.8	524.0	568.7	516.6
Operating profit as a percentage of sales	10.5%	10.0%	8.7%	9.5%	8.3%
Interest expense	(81.4)	(83.3)	(75.5)	(68.0)	(89.9)
Litigation settlements				32.6	287.9
Equity income	13.3	13.6	10.5	17.8	15.8
General corporate expense	(91.9)	(97.6)	(89.3)	(72.6)	(95.7)
Income before income taxes	$610.2	$505.5	$369.7	$478.5	$634.7

Assets					
Home and Building Control	$2,144.3	$1,727.2	$1,529.8	$1,327.3	$1,302.4
Industrial Control	1,376.1	1,307.2	1,273.3	1,059.8	1,057.5
Space and Aviation Control	1,037.3	971.1	1,174.9	1,219.6	1,403.6
Corporate and Other	935.6	1,054.7	907.9	991.4	1,106.6
Total assets	$5,493.3	$5,060.2	$4,885.9	$4,598.1	$4,870.1
Additional information					
Average number of common shares outstanding	126.6	127.1	129.4	134.2	138.5
Return on average shareholders' equity	19.7%	17.1%	15.6%	18.4%	13.8%
Shareholders' equity per common share	$17.44	$16.09	$14.57	$13.48	$13.10
Price/earnings ratio	20.7	18.6	14.7	14.3	11.5
Percent of debt to total capitalization	31%	28%	32%	28%	28%
Research and development					
Honeywell-funded	$353.3	$323.2	$319.0	$337.4	$312.6
Customer-funded	$341.4	$336.6	$340.5	$404.8	$390.5
Capital expenditures	$296.5	$238.1	$262.4	$232.1	$244.1
Depreciation and amortization	$287.5	$292.9	$287.4	$284.9	$292.7
Employees at year end	53,000	50,100	50,800	52,300	55,400

Source: Honeywell 1996 Annual Report.

EXHIBIT 11.2:
Honeywell products, customers, and competitors

Sector	Representative customers	Competitors
HOME AND BUILDING CONTROL **Home and Building Products:** *Consumer Products:* Heaters; fans; humidifiers; vaporizers; electronic air cleaners; water filtration products; thermostats and home security systems. *Control Products:* Perfect Climate Comfort Center® System; SYSNet™ Facilities Integration System; thermostats; TotalHome® home automation system; HVAC equipment controls; integrated furnace and boiler controls; demand-side energy management systems; energy-efficient lighting equipment; utility services; water controls; direct-coupled actuators; zoning systems; media controls; heat recovery and energy recovery ventilators. **Building Solutions:** Installed systems; HVAC solutions (EXCEL 5000®); fire solutions (Excel Life Safety); security solutions (Excel Security Manager; open systems technology; performance contracting; compressed air management; isolation room controls; remove HVAC monitoring (ServiceNet®); and maintenance services.	Architects and developers; building managers and owners; consulting engineers; contractors; distributors and wholesalers; hardware and home center stores; heating, ventilation and air conditioning equipment manufacturers; home builders; physicians; consumers; airports; hospitals; hotels; manufacturing facilities; office and government buildings; restaurants; retail stores; education facilities; utilities; and security directors.	Johnson Controls; Siebe; Landis & Staefa; Emerson; White-Rodgers, Holmes; Alerton; Siemens; ADT and regional companies such as Andover.
INDUSTRIAL CONTROL **Industrial Automation and Control Products and Solutions:** Advanced control software and industrial automation systems for control and monitoring of continuous, batch and hybrid operations; process control instrumentation; industrial control valves; recorders; controllers; flame safeguard equipment; supervisory cell controllers; product management software; equipment controls; programmable controllers; communications systems for industrial control equipment and systems; and professional services, including consulting, networking, engineering and installation. **Sensing and Control Products and Solutions:** Solid-state sensors for position, pressure, airflow temperature and current; vision-based sensors; precision electromechanical switches; PC-based device level control.	Chemical plants; computer and business equipment manufacturers; data acquisition companies; food processing plants; medical equipment manufacturers; oil and gas producers; pharmaceutical companies; pulp and paper mills; refining and petrochemical firms; textile manufacturers; heat treat processors; utilities; package and material handling operations; appliance manufacturers; automotive companies; and aviation companies.	Asea Brown Boveri; Elsag-Bailey; Fisher-Rosemount; Siebe (Foxboro); Siemens; Yokogawa; Allen-Bradley; Banner; Cherry; Omron; Sprague; Telemecanique; Turck.
SPACE AND AVIATION CONTROL **Major Products:** Integrated cockpit avionics, including automatic flight controls, electronic display systems, flight management systems; Global Positioning System (GPS) based avionics; communications systems; Traffic Alert and Collision Avoidance Systems (TCAS); automatic test systems; helmet-mounted display and sighting systems; space instruments and sensors; and data management and processing systems.	Airframe manufacturers; international, national and regional airlines; corporate operators; NASA; prime U.S. defense contractors; and the U.S. Department of Defense.	Allied Signal; Litton; Kaiser; Rockwell International; Sextant.

EXHIBIT 11.3:
Segmented financial information

Home and Building Control

1996 sales mix

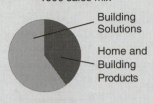

- Building Solutions
- Home and Building Products

- North America
- Europe
- Asia-Pacific
- Latin America

Financial results (dollars in millions)

	1996	1995	1994
Sales	$3,327.1	$3,034.7	$2,664.5
Operating Profits	$345.8	$308.6	$265.2*
Margin	10.4%	10.2%	10.0%

* Excluding special charges.

Industrial Control

1996 sales mix

- Sensing and Control
- Industrial Automation and Control

- North America
- Europe
- Asia-Pacific
- Latin America

Financial results (dollars in millions)

	1996	1995	1994
Sales	$2,199.6	$2,035.9	$1,835.3
Operating Profits	$254.9	$233.8	$221.0*
Margin	11.6%	11.5%	12.0%

* Excluding special charges.

Space and Aviation Control

1996 sales mix

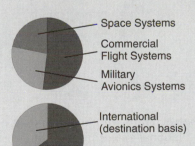

- Space Systems
- Commercial Flight Systems
- Military Avionics Systems

- International (destination basis)
- North America

Financial results (dollars in millions)

	1996	1995	1994
Sales	$1,640.0	$1,527.4	$1,432.0
Operating Profits	$163.3	$127.6	$100.5*
Margin	10.0%	8.4%	7.0%

* Excluding special charges.

Sources: Honeywell Inc., 1996 Annual Report.

EXHIBIT 11.4:
Honeywell International

President, Honeywell Asia-Pacific	President, Honeywell Europe	Vice President and GM, Latin America	President, Honeywell Canada
HQ, Hong Kong	HQ, Brussels	HQ, Sunrise, Florida	HQ, North York, Ontario

Affiliates: Australia, China, Hong Kong, Malaysia, New Zealand, Pakistan, Singapore, Taiwan, Thailand

Manufacturing: Sydney, Auckland, Taipei, Shenzhen, Tianjin

Joint Venture Manufacturing: Pune (India), Fujisawa, Hadano, Kamata, Isehara, Shanan, (Japan), Bupyong (South Korea)

Affiliates: Austria, Belgium, Bulgaria, Czech Republic, Denmark, Egypt, Finland, France, Germany, Hungary, Italy, Kuwait, The Netherlands, Norway, Oman, Poland, Portugal, Romania, Commonwealth of Independent States (Russia), Saudi Arabia, Slovak Republic, South Africa, Spain, Sweden, Switzerland, Turkey, Ukraine, United Arab Emirates, United Kingdom

Centers of Excellence and Manufacturing: Brussels, Belgium; Varkaus, Finland; Amiens and Grenoble, France; Amsberg, Maintal, Mosbach, Neuwied and Schönaich, Germany; Den Bosch and Emmen, The Netherlands; Porto, Portugal; Newhouse, Scotland; Geneva and Zurich, Switzerland

Affiliates: Argentina, Brazil, Chile, Mexico, Panama, Puerto Rico, Venezuela, Colombia, Ecuador

Centers of Excellence and Manufacturing: Caracas, Venezuela; Chihuahua, Ciudad Juarez, Districto Federal and Tijuana, Mexico; São Paulo, Brazil

Manufacturing: Ontario, Quebec

and Hong Kong. Its joint ventures included partnerships with South Korean conglomerate Lucky-Gold Star Group and China National Petrochemical, the world's third-largest petroleum refiner. About half of Honeywell's Asian sales were in China. Honeywell generated about $250 million in revenue in China and expected sales of at least $500 million by the end of the decade. In 1997, Honeywell began working with Beijing District Heating Co. to improve heating services for 20% of the capital's buildings, with the potential for expansion. As well, China needed more than 1,000 new aircraft over the next 15 years, which created opportunities for Honeywell avionics products.

Competition

Honeywell's home and building and industrial control competitors ranged from diversified global giants like Siemens and Asea Brown Boveri to small, specialized firms such as Andover Controls, a $70 million manufacturer of programmable, network-based building automation systems (see Exhibit11.2). In the space and aviation control sector, the set of competitors was much smaller and primarily U.S.-based.

Competitors in the home and building and industrial control sectors were, like Honeywell, intent on international growth. For example, Johnson Controls, Honeywell's largest U.S.-based competitor in home and building controls, had recently announced an R&D partnership with a Hong Kong university. In 1997, U.K.-based Siebe announced plans to establish a wholly-owned subsidiary in India, which would include engineering centers for industrial process control equipment. White-Rodgers, a division of Emerson Electric with a worldwide base of 23 sales, distribution and manufacturing sites, had made a commitment to expand its international presence. Even tiny Andover, based in Andover, Massachusetts, operated three technical centers outside the United States in the United Kingdom, Germany, and Hong Kong.

In addition to increasing internationalization, the controls industry had seen a wave of mergers, acquisitions, and alliances. In 1996, Electrowatt Group, a Swiss-based holding company, announced the formation of Landis & Staefa, Inc., a world-wide combination of Landis & Gyr and Staefa Control System. Landis & Staefa competed with Honeywell in home and building controls. Later in 1996, it was announced that Siemens AG was acquiring a 44.9% share in Electrowatt Group. Siemens, a Honeywell competitor in various product markets, was one of the world's largest organizations. Siemens had sales of more than $60 billion, 250 manufacturing sites in 42 countries, and subsidiaries and affiliates in more than 190 countries. In the United States alone, Siemens had more than 46,000 employees in over 400 office locations, 40 research and development facilities, and 80 manufacturing and assembly plants. In 1991 Siebe acquired U.S.-based Foxboro for $656 million. The Siebe group employed over 42,500 people and consisted of more than 150 companies located in 40 countries. In 1992, Emerson Electric bought Fisher Controls for $1.4 billion, forming the Fisher-Rosemount family of companies.

RESEARCH AND DEVELOPMENT

R&D was a focal point throughout Honeywell with technology seen as the key to marketplace differentiation. About 30% of Honeywell's current sales were from products introduced in the past five years. Honeywell was involved in two main R&D activities: R&D that supported Honeywell's worldwide product divisions and contract research funded by outside government agencies and firms. Including R&D

EXHIBIT 11.5:
Honeywell organization, 1997

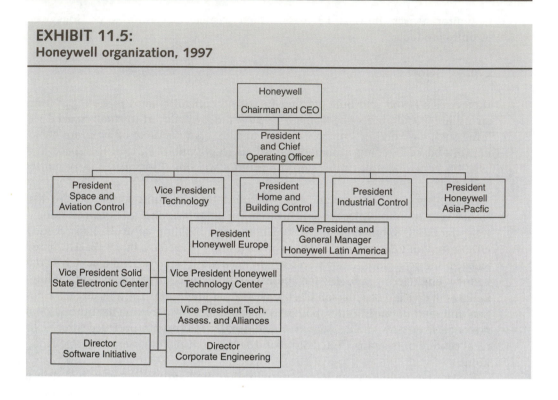

done both in the product divisions and by HTC, Honeywell funded $353 million of R&D in 1996 and contract work generated revenue of $341 million. Until the cutbacks in U.S. military spending in the early 1990s, most of the contract research was for military purposes. Although a significant amount of contract research still involved the Dept. of Defense, other funding agencies included NASA, Department of Commerce, and the Electric Power Research Institute. Increasingly, non-defense firms were forming alliances to jointly develop new technologies through contract research. Cooperative research with OEM customers also occurred. All of the outside contract funding was from U.S. sources, although several project applications were targeted outside the United States, such as a Dept. of Commerce power plant upgrade project in Ukraine.

HONEYWELL TECHNOLOGY CENTER

The Honeywell Technology Center (HTC) was Honeywell's primary research organization and supported the worldwide product divisions. As a corporate service organization, HTC's mission was to support the product divisions and develop technologies that had the potential to benefit multiple product divisions. This mission was expressed as:

EXHIBIT 11.6:
HTC organization, 1997

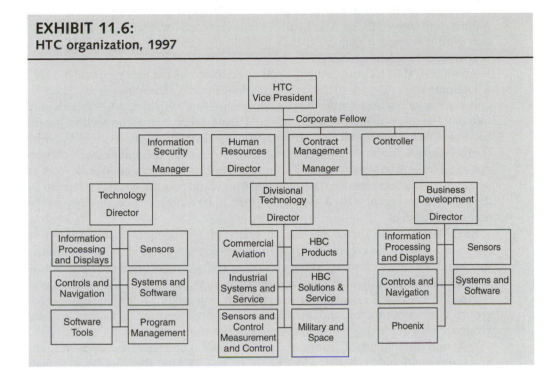

In partnership with Honeywell's businesses, we provide world-class technologies, processes, and product concepts that fuel Honeywell's global growth and profitability.

HTC, based in Minneapolis, employed about 575 people, including 300 engineer/scientists. Of these 300, 100 had Ph.D.s, and 180 had Bachelor or Master's degrees. With the exception of about 40 employees in Phoenix and 5 in Prague, all HTC employees were in two locations in the Minneapolis area. In 1996, HTC's spending was $90 million, which came from several sources: 50% from outside contracts, 40% allocated to HTC by Honeywell corporate management, and 10% funded directly by divisions for near-term projects.

HTC Organization

Exhibit 11.5 shows the Honeywell corporate organization and Exhibit 11.6 shows the HTC organization. Prior to 1993, Honeywell operated two corporate R&D organizations: the Sensors and Systems Development Center (SSDC) for home, building, and industrial R&D and the Systems and Research Center for space and aviation R&D. The Systems and Research Center was primarily involved in military research and was oriented to outside contracts. Because there was comparatively less outside contract work in the non-defense related controls area, SSDC R&D was focused on commercial applications and product division problems. In 1993 the two R&D groups were merged for both cost and synergy reasons. There was also a realization that with government military spending declining, Honeywell-funded R&D had to become more application-oriented.

About 350 HTC technical employees worked in one of the four technology areas whose managers reported to the HTC technology director. These four areas, controls and navigation, sensors, information processing and displays, and systems and software, were in turn broken down into 19 sub-areas headed by section heads. For example, controls and navigation R&D was divided into home and building control systems, industrial control systems, space and aviation guidance and control systems, and navigation systems. The role of the technology section head was to facilitate interaction between the product divisions and corporate R&D performed by the HTC. As one section head indicated, "I try to be a broker of technology to the product divisions."

R&D development cycles and the maturity of technologies influenced HTC's organization. Because commercial control technologies were more mature than the space and aviation technology, research in this area was more oriented towards how to apply the technology in existing and new products. As a result, the controls and navigation group was organized around markets and product lines. The other three groups were organized around technologies, and engineers and scientists in these groups tended to identify with technologies rather than products.

HTC had two additional groups of managers called Business Development managers and Divisional Technology Managers (DTMs). The five Business Development managers were responsible for generating outside contracts. Six DTMs provided an interface between the divisions and HTC, working closely with the technology section heads and the product divisions. The DTMs had two main responsibilities: 1) to understand the divisional business strategy; translate that strategy into short- and long-term technology needs; and disseminate that information in HTC as the basis for influencing investments in R&D and 2) to establish mechanisms for the transfer of mature technology from HTC to divisions. According to a DTM, the DTM's role was "to be a funnel for information transfer and dissemination."

Although HTC had a structure and clear lines of authority, HTC management believed that to operate effectively, the structure had to exist as a loose framework in order to support interaction among the engineers, scientists, and product divisions. According to an HTC manager:

> We are very good at quite a number of areas. I can bring together researchers in sensors, control theory, information processing, real time software and those are the guts of Honeywell products. We need to work from a systems perspective, which means we have to have interaction and networking.

HTC management saw their key role as ensuring that the interaction occurred.

> The researchers are the people that really make things happen here. As managers, our job is to make sure they have lights, food, and water to get things done.

THE RESEARCH PROCESS

Very little product development or product testing was done at HTC. HTC supported divisional product development by providing new technologies that could be incorporated into products and by developing concepts for new products. The actual development of new products was a divisional responsibility and each of Honeywell's product divisions had active engineering organizations. It was a divisional responsibility to turn new technology into something that was producible and salable. As such, most of the R&D done at the division level was product development and engineering work using existing technologies. Occasionally, if HTC was convinced a product should be developed immediately to create a market window and no division had the resources to react quickly, HTC might initiate product development. HTC might also approach a customer directly as the basis for generating divisional interest in a technology. As well, technology that would benefit only one division was normally viewed as R&D that should be funded at the division level rather than at corporate.

Within HTC, scientists and engineers competed for funding via various funding programs. The Home Run Program supported projects with low technical risk, an established market need, a large funding requirement, and an expectation of a rapid capital return. The Initiatives Program focused on innovative, technology-based funding with high risks and longer term payoffs. Technology Base Funding supported longer range division needs. Joint Projects provided for matching funds from divisions tied directly to divisional products needs.

There were many and varied linkages between HTC and the product divisions. In some cases, HTC engineers were assigned to divisions to support product development. The assignments could range from several weeks to a year. Nevertheless, it was acknowledged that it was difficult to get people to accept short-term assignments because of family and personal constraints.

Technology Transfer

Within the divisions, the perception of HTC had shifted in recent years as HTC increasingly stressed the importance of relevance and pushed this message deep within the organization. Relevance meant that HTC's goal should be to help the divisions serve their customers, as a manager remarked: "Our job in HTC is to transfer technology but we don't really transfer technology, we transfer solutions." As well, Honeywell was committing greater funds to technology transfer. Ten years ago, technology transfer was more ad hoc with fewer specific funding mechanisms available. This commitment to technology transfer was evident in the following comment from an HTC manager:

> We know that whatever we do is worthless until a division makes money from it. If they don't want the technology, we can't force them to take it.

The underlying philosophy of technology transfer was consistent throughout HTC. First, technology transfer required funding, which occurred through different mechanisms. Second, technology transfer was rarely a function of "how incredible the technology is." The technology had to be mature and its transfer had to be economically feasible in terms of cost effectiveness and ROI. Some successful technology transfers involved technology that had been developed five to ten years earlier. Third, there had to be an emotional commitment to the technology within a product division. The challenge for all technology transfers was to convince the product divisions that the technology was relevant and could provide customer solutions. The highest probability of technology transfer occurred when HTC and a division identified a specific divisional need that HTC could meet. An HTC manager described the difficulty in transferring technology:

> Half the battle is how badly the product division managers and engineers want the technology. If they don't want it, they aren't going to get it. Tech transfer is about interaction and begins with trust between two people. . . . Some of the best engineers in Honeywell divisions think they don't need HTC because they can do it themselves and because they think HTC gets to do all the fun stuff. There is some implication that I [as a division engineer] am not capable of getting my part of the job done so the hired guns from HTC are being brought in to get it done for me. And, I have to pay for it.

The key to establishing a successful match between HTC and the division was the network and personal contact-based system that allowed individual researchers to determine the technological needs of Honeywell. Researchers were expected to generate funding for their projects, which could be either internal or external funding. This forced researchers to be in close contact with the divisions, the customers, other researchers, funding agencies, and so on. By getting an outside research sponsor, researchers could control the support for their research. The same held true for Joint Projects funded by divisions and HTC. For example, researchers might go to a divisional engineer and convince him(her) of the relevance of a project; the engineer might interact with the HTC DTM; and the DTM would work between the division and HTC to ensure that the project was funded. An HTC manager offered this view:

> The real success stories come out of these contact scenarios where a researcher sells an idea either internally or externally. If they sell it externally, it is with the end goal of eventually selling it internally. We don't do research for the good of science. We do research that will lead to customer solutions.

For software, technology transfer often involved transferring individuals to teach the software and adapt it to applications. For home and building controls and its more mature technology, technology transfer often meant the transfer of hardware solutions. For space and avionics applications, the cost of the technology might be less important than the contribution of the technology to safety or reliability. For home and building controls, the cost of the technology was always an issue since there was a belief that customers were very reluctant to spend more money for basic controls such as thermostats, even if the technology was significantly better.

Technology Transfer Example

Technology transfer occurred in many different forms depending on the technology, the product division involved, project funding, and so on. The following discussion illustrates one example of a successful technology transfer. The project began with an idea from a university student intern working at HTC. The project was initially funded under the Initiatives Program, the internal HTC funding mechanism for advanced, long-range thinking. The project involved fuzzy control theory that was not initially directed at a product. As the project progressed, the Home and Building Control Systems Group saw some potential applications for the technology in the boiler control area. Some additional internal funding of around $50,000 was provided to do some modeling and simulation of the concept. Although discussions with the product divisions had not yet occurred, there was a belief that the technology could be useful to one of the European divisions.

The next step was to show some examples of the technology to product divisions. The initiation of the HTC–division interaction could occur in various forms, such as a monthly HTC report on internally developed HTC programs, a DTM presentation to the divisions, or a specific request from a division for a particular technology. The HTC objective in interacting with the divisions was to develop divisional interest for the project. In this example, a division in the Netherlands was interested. This division sold valves and other components for boilers used in homes for heating and hot water. Based on a proposal prepared by HTC engineers, the division agreed to participate in a Joint Project, which meant that the division and HTC would share project funding equally. By getting the division involved, product and market specifications could be developed. At this point, the personnel involved in the project included the Home and Building Control Systems Group section head, HTC engineers, a division development engineer, and a DTM. At the division level, the engineer would work with sales and marketing people to justify the funding.

The next phase was called build-and-test and could have been done at HTC or in the division. This decision was negotiated based on various constraints: scheduling, funding, personnel, and R&D skills. In this example, the build-and-test phase was carried out in the division. Initial results were promising and it was hoped that the product could be marketed to boiler OEMs by the end of 1997. If so, the entire phase from idea to market would be about five years. From the time that the division became aware of the technology and saw it as a potential product application was about two years.

HTC's RELATIONSHIP WITH HONEYWELL EUROPE

Technology transfer to the Honeywell Europe divisions had always been problematic. While the European divisions expected HTC to develop new technology, European managers often complained about the irrelevance of the technology for their markets, the cost of HTC, and their lack of contact with HTC. Although 25%

of Honeywell sales were in Europe, a much smaller percentage of R&D was carried out either in Europe or in Minneapolis for European solutions. Until about 1990, there was very little Honeywell R&D being done for Europe even though Europe was supporting central R&D financially, creating some bitterness in the European operation. Central R&D was primarily focused on the U.S. market. New product development in Europe was originating in the European divisional engineering groups.

An HTC manager recounted his experience in making a presentation to a group of Honeywell managers in Brussels. After making the presentation and outlining current technology initiatives in HTC, the Europeans indicated that they were unaware that HTC was working on such leading technologies. The manager continued:

> When I first went to Europe a few years ago it was clear to me how angry they were at the U.S. notion that HTC was going to provide good stuff. They also believed that most of the Honeywell resources were being harbored in the United States. There was not a feeling that they were equal members in getting the same resources for development as the U.S. divisions. That said, in the past few years there have been some very good technology transfer projects and they were done in the same way as in the United States – personal interaction, people spending time in the divisions, some short term relocations to Europe. Increasingly, there is acceptance that the paradigm of R&D jointly sponsored by HTC and the divisions is the best approach.

Over the past few years, relationships with Europe had begun shifting and HTC was becoming more responsive in addressing the needs of European businesses. The current Honeywell COO was an Italian who was previously head of Honeywell Europe and the CEO had also been the head of Europe. The head of Divisional Technology responsible for the DTMs was also spending a great deal of time in Europe. As well, there was now an HTC organization based in Europe, HTC Prague.

HTC Prague

In the early 1990s SSDC (the R&D organization that preceded HTC) managers were considering how to strengthen European R&D. With the collapse of the Iron Curtain and expectations of new Honeywell markets developing in Eastern Europe, the viability of an R&D organization somewhere in Eastern Europe was being debated. There was a belief that very strong technical skills could be found in countries like Poland and Russia. In 1992 an HTC scientist and former university professor in Czechoslovakia was attending a conference in Tampa. He met a Czechoslovakian from a research institute in Prague. With the Czech economy in transition and research funding drying up, the Czech scientist was interested in new opportunities. The HTC scientist returned to Minneapolis with reasonable assurance that a partnership with the Czech scientist could work. HTC Prague began with five former Czech university professors hired on a contract basis to do research in two areas: computational fluid dynamics, a technology area important for evaluating control product designs, and advanced boiler control technology. Honeywell's Eastern

Europe office was moved from Vienna to Prague and by 1997, the Honeywell sales organization in Prague had grown to more than 60 employees. Prague was viewed as an excellent entry point for what could be a huge business in controls for district heating.

In 1995 the Prague professors became Honeywell employees. The professors were very entrepreneurial and had established a reputation for getting things done. Compared to their counterparts in the universities, they were pleased to have access to funding and equipment to continue their research. In 1997, one of the Prague researchers came to Minneapolis for nine months to work on a district heating project. All of the HTC senior management team had been to Prague.

Several objectives were established for HTC Prague: 1) to develop specific technologies for Europe; 2) to assist in HTC technology transfers to Europe; 3) to provide access to activities and opportunities in Eastern Europe; and 4) to help alleviate Honeywell Europe concerns about the lack of support from HTC. Projects in HTC Prague were to be coordinated through HTC to ensure that Prague became an integral part of HTC and not a separate entity.

In 1997, HTC management conceded that it was too early to make an evaluation of HTC Prague's viability and future within Honeywell. For one thing, HTC Prague consisted of only five researchers, which limited the potential impact. As a manager indicated, "With only five people, it is not clear what Prague really is or can be." There were concerns that HTC Prague might become an application center rather than a true R&D center. One manager suggested that the Europeans were too accustomed to looking to the United States for new technology and therefore HTC Prague would have trouble building legitimacy. Moreover, other European divisions had questioned the decision to start an R&D organization in Prague rather than in say, Germany or Belgium. Other European managers offered a different perspective, suggesting that European divisions were already taking ownership of the technology being developed in Prague and viewed Prague as "their" technology center.

Several HTC managers were emphatic that Prague had to be expanded if it was to remain relevant. But, if Prague were to be expanded, when should it happen and could additional high quality technical talent be found for Prague? The model for HTC in the United States was to rely heavily on outside contracts. Would Prague be able to develop outside funding? Should Prague be given the tools and skills necessary to bid on outside contracts? If Prague were to be expanded, who would pay for the expansion: Honeywell Europe or HTC? Other managers suggested that perhaps Prague should remain at 5–6 people and additional R&D centers should be established close to other Honeywell operations, perhaps in Germany, Scotland or the Netherlands.

REASONS FOR CENTRALIZED R&D

Within Honeywell, reasons for and against centralized R&D were being actively debated. Reasons supporting centralized R&D included the following:

1.   The complexity of Honeywell products and systems is such that a large team of R&D people is needed in one location to ensure interaction occurs between scientists. For example, the control system for a refinery incorporated hundreds of other products. It is easy to share information when almost all HTC employees are in the same building and see each other regularly. Decentralization would reduce interaction and personal contacts.

> Technology transfer is based on personal contacts. This is one of the biggest challenges we have in trying to operate on a global basis. We have a system in HTC that works quite well and we are comfortable with it. What does it mean to deal with things around the world when we need to maintain our contact-based system?

> The strength of HTC is the world-class people we can bring to bear on a problem. How do we connect these people with the far-flung empire of Honeywell in order to bring together the expertise, know-how, and ability to make money?

> The biggest logistical issue is communications. You can't invent science with only one scientist. You need multiple disciplines and interaction. The various distributed R&D organizations must communicate with each other the same way they would if they were all in Minneapolis and could meet in the hallways or the cafeteria. That is extremely difficult to do. We are looking at new information technology but you also have to have interchanges of people. Without communication, remote R&D will only work for a little while because people will get out of touch. Once people go native they lose the advantage of outside views and new ideas coupled with the connection with the marketplace.

2.   One of the main functions of Honeywell's central R&D is to move ideas around the world. Decentralizing R&D would jeopardize this central dissemination function.

3.   When the product is a system comprising various parts, a team can be built using people from different areas. Scattering people geographically would make this difficult.

> A product like abnormal situation management for oil refineries requires sensors, controls, human interface, and so on. We have all the people in one place to put these technologies together. No division of the company has all these parts.

4.   If R&D scientists are too far from the central labs they risk becoming obsolete, migrating from R&D to the product divisions, or losing contact with central R&D. They may even think they are competing with central R&D.

> We have a group in Plymouth, which is only 15 miles from the Minneapolis location. When I talk to those guys, they feel like they are cut off from all kinds of things. To a degree, they are correct. We have a group in Phoenix that sometimes feel like they are in yonder land.

5.   If R&D is tied too closely with a division, there is the risk that the division will not have the long term orientation necessary for R&D, which could lead to complacency. Or, after assuming ownership of the R&D, the division may decide that a particular technology is no longer necessary and R&D efforts could decline. A central R&D organization can ensure stability in research efforts and implement controls to keep people motivated.

6.   Engineers and scientists interested in R&D prefer to work in a central R&D organization.

7.   What the non-U.S. and non-European divisions need now is localization of existing products, not new technology.

8.   The HTC culture would be difficult to transfer.

> How do you transfer the HTC culture outside the United States? HTC has developed a unique culture based on openness and interaction across different levels and technologies. The kinds of people we hire and attract are very entrepreneurial down to the youngest engineers. How do you duplicate this culture in a place like Prague? It is tough enough to do it in Phoenix.

9.   Before R&D could be localized, Honeywell had to develop more incentives to transfer technology.

> Although a few years ago I was committed to the idea of global technology management, I am not so sure now. The problem is that within Honeywell there are still expectations that solutions will come from the United States. Until that changes and funding is in place to support technology transfer outside the United States, creating new R&D organizations makes no sense. Right now, we do not have the financial incentives in place to transfer technology to Europe.

REASONS FOR DECENTRALIZED R&D

1.   Central R&D is too far removed from the customer, particularly customers outside the United States. It is impossible to develop customer solutions if you do not understand customer problems. The current remote sites in Phoenix and Prague benefit from being close to the divisions. Different parts of the world should logically be the focus for problems unique to their area. For example, tropical Asia has unique air conditioning requirements because of the heat and humidity.

> You need people immersed in all aspects of the culture to communicate with customers and other parts of Honeywell. There is a whole lot of networking that has to happen and it has to involve people from the HTC culture who know what is going on. People of this culture have to see with their own eyes what is going on outside the United States. We are not going to sell U.S. thermostats in Beijing. What they need and want is different, the amount of money the Chinese have to spend is different.

> You have to live with the culture to understand the opportunities. You cannot simply transfer technologies and product designs that are used in the United States. There have to be different solutions because the business models in different countries are different. Right now, the paradigm says that products come from the United States. There is a strong mix of prejudice and ignorance about international markets. For example, in the United States, air conditioning is the focus for home and building controls. In Europe, central air conditioning is much less common. We have a huge opportunity in district heating in Eastern Europe. In the United States, Honeywell has limited knowledge about district heating because it is hardly used here.

2. If the technology does not require interaction with other technologies, like the development of a particular sensor or flat panel displays, it may be better to have it located where the local support structure is strongest. The support could come from the product division or in a geographic area known for a particular technology.

3. Application developments may require close interaction with a customer in the customer's facility.

4. Putting R&D people in geographic business units would increase the relevance of R&D and increase the information flow from business units to R&D.

5. Future sales will be growing faster outside the United States and, therefore, people from all parts of Honeywell must be in the growing areas of the business.

6. Traveling to Europe, China and other locations outside the United States is expensive and time consuming. It would be better to have people on the ground in these locations.

7. Remote R&D facilities would facilitate technology transfers outside the United States.

8. Remote locations in countries like China provide a foothold that gives Honeywell credibility and makes it look like a committed Chinese business. It could also help in hiring local engineers and scientists.

9. Remote locations show the product divisions that Honeywell is serious about a particular region.

Along with the basic question of centralized versus decentralized R&D, there were additional issues associated with R&D:

- Would remote locations have to focus on unique technologies? How would those technologies be identified? Are there technologies that are unique to specific locations?

- Outside funding was critical to HTC. As part of a U.S. corporation, could a remote location gain access to outside funding? With greater R&D presence, could HTC gain access to funding from agencies such as the World Bank and the Asian Development Bank?

- What kind of controls must be in place to ensure that a remote location remained part of *central* R&D rather than becoming an offshoot of a product division?

- In Europe and Asia, with its diversity of countries and markets, where should HTC have a stronger presence?

- With an increasing shift to software as the key to product differentiation, how would this influence future Honeywell R&D?

- Within Honeywell, the allocation of HTC costs was based on divisional revenues. Was this allocation system appropriate given that some regions within the firm were growing faster than others?

- How would remote R&D locations be staffed. Would it make sense to move HTC people out of Minneapolis to new locations? If not, were skilled scientists available in other parts of the world? As an HTC manager commented:

The key thing about our culture is networking and sharing and bringing together different technologies. The only way you can create that culture in a remote R&D center is to take some of the HTC people and put them in China or Russia for a while. This would infect the new hires with "the way we do business." Then we will bring them back. We have had good luck getting people to go to different places.

FUTURE OPPORTUNITIES

In view of Honeywell's international growth opportunities, the issue of international R&D was becoming a high priority issue in HTC. For example, China's economy was growing so rapidly that some sort of HTC presence seemed inevitable. One line of thinking was that HTC should have employees based in China with a broad learning and exploration agenda. Another view was that until there was a clear understanding of the opportunities in China, it would not make sense to commit to expensive expatriate employees. A further issue was that in China, and Asia in general, there were no engineering staffs to adapt technologies for the local market. For the most part, products manufactured and sold in Asia were products transferred from American or European Honeywell divisions. Without an engineering staff in Asia, technology could not be transferred.

Further issues are evident in the following comments from HTC managers:

By the year 2000, sales outside the United States could be 60% of our business. At HTC we have to start experimenting in other parts of the world. Our mission is to help the divisions understand what they can do with our technology. If you ask them what they want, you will get the most ordinary ideas. If we work with their customers and understand that environment, we can link customers with our technology and come up with something completely different. If we are not out there looking at the world we will never grow the company. And, I can't hire someone in China to do this for me; someone from here has to go over there and get the HTC culture going.

Technology is technology; it is physical principles and science – there is nothing unique about the technology needed in Europe or Asia. However, the application needs seem to vary from region to region. Perhaps we should set up application groups around the world. The technology engine will remain in Minneapolis and Phoenix. These groups will be the selectors and appliers of those technologies given their knowledge of the region. If we go this way, we won't need the best researchers in Prague and other regions. We will need people who can apply technology and gain access to technology sources outside the United States. We have really not tapped into these non-U.S. sources.

The notion of distributed R&D is very important to me. I am convinced that HTC is going to become more distributed, not less. How we can create one large, global R&D organization and not 12 small ones is a big issue. Strategically, putting together other R&D centers in Beijing or Eastern Europe is going to become a way of life at HTC.

It is difficult enough making HTC work. Trying to replicate it somewhere else in the world is even more difficult. That is one of the reasons that Prague has remained small – we are not sure what to do with it. My view of what Prague should be will probably be radically different from other people's. In the United States, 20 years of evolution has allowed HTC to develop some unique capabilities. Can we wait for Prague or some other remote R&D center to naturally evolve over 20 years? What is the best way for a non-U.S. R&D organization to have an impact?

NOTE

1. DeSilver, D., "Honeywell Plans Asian Forays," *Minneapolis-St. Paul City Business*, June 21, 1996, p. 11.

CHAPTER TWELVE

DuPont Teflon®: China Brand Strategy

INTRODUCTION

Simon Lin, Marketing Manager for DuPont Greater China Teflon® Finishes, stood in the aisle of the Shanghai department store and watched the young well dressed couple as they inspected the various brands of non-stick cookware on display for sale. After several minutes of comparing the different brands, the wife pointed to the DuPont Teflon® logo on the packaging of one brand, and said something to her husband. He nodded approval, they picked up the boxed set of cookware and headed for the cashier. It was January 1996 and Lin was researching the Chinese cookware market for DuPont. For six years, DuPont had been involved in the Chinese cookware market, licensing its non-stick technology to local manufacturers for use on pots and pans. In spite of its efforts to develop the Chinese domestic cookware market and its Teflon® brand, sales had never reached expectations. Lin's project was to make a recommendation as to whether DuPont should continue with its current strategy, pull out of the market, or try some new approach. As he watched the young couple leave the store, he wondered what the company should do.

BACKGROUND ON DUPONT

In 1995, E. I. du Pont de Nemours and Company Inc. (DuPont) was a global industrial company with 193 years of continuous business. As a major producer of oil, natural gas and petroleum products and a leader in high-performance materials, specialty chemicals, pharmaceuticals, and agricultural products, it achieved 1995 revenues of US$42.2 billion and net income of US$3.3 billion. Although based in the United States, approximately 48% of the company's 1995 sales were outside the country. Exports from the United States were approximately US$4.0 billion, making it one of the largest US exporters. Of its almost 105,000 employees, approximately 35% worked outside the United States. According to *Fortune* in 1995, DuPont was the 13th largest US industrial and service corporation and the world's 58th largest industrial and service corporation. See Exhibit 12.1 for corporate financial highlights.

DuPont operated in approximately 70 countries worldwide, with about 175 manufacturing and processing sites that included 135 chemicals and specialties plants, five petroleum refineries, and 25 natural gas processing plants. It had more than 40 research and development labs and customer service labs in the United States and more than 35 labs in 11 other countries. See Exhibit 12.2 for a listing of countries with major DuPont operations.

Major product areas for DuPont included chemicals, fibers, films, finishes, petroleum, plastics, healthcare products, biotechnology, and composite products. The Chemicals segment included a wide range of commodity and specialty products used in the paper, plastics, chemical processing, refrigeration, textile and environmental management industries. The Fibers segment included a diversified mix of specialty fibers produced to serve end uses ranging from protective apparel, active sportswear and packaging to high-strength composites in aerospace. High volume fibers were produced for apparel and home fabrics, carpeting and industrial applications in consumer and industrial markets. The Polymers segment products included engineering polymers, elastomers, fluoropolymers, ethylene polymers, finishes and packaging films for industries such as packaging, construction, chemical processing, electrical, paper, textiles, and transportation. Its Life Sciences business segment consisted of Agricultural Products, with a focus on crop protection chemicals and biotechnology, and Pharmaceuticals. The Diversified Businesses segment included electronic materials and polymer businesses.

DuPont had an unparalleled portfolio of 2,000 trademarks and brands. Some of the company's best known brands were: Teflon® resins, SilverStone® non-stick finish, Lycra® brand spandex fiber, Stainmaster® stain-resistant carpet, Antron® carpet fiber, Dacron® polyester fiber, Kevlar® brand fiber, Corian® solid surface material, Mylar® polyester films, Tyvek® spunbonded olefin fabric, and Coolmax® and Cordura® textile fibers.

TEFLON® OVERVIEW

A DuPont chemist, Dr. Roy J. Plunkett, developed Teflon® in 1938 in DuPont's New Jersey laboratory. Plunkett was working with gases related to Freon® refrigerants, another DuPont product. He had frozen and compressed a sample of tetrafluoroethylene, which subsequently spontaneously polymerized into a white waxy solid to form polytetrafluoroethylene (PTFE). The invention of PTFE has been described

EXHIBIT 12.1:

E.I. du Pont de Nemours and Company 1995 corporate financial highlights ($ millions, except per share)

	Three months ended December 31		Year ended December 31	
	1995	1994	1995	1994
Sales	$10,385	$10,137	$42,163	$39,333
Other income	294	258	1,099	913
Total	10,679	10,395	43,262	40,246
Cost of goods sold and other expenses	7,930	7,656	31,162	29,238
Selling, general and administrative expenses	750	795	2,995	2,876
Depreciation, depletion and amortization	785	806	2,722	2,976
Exploration expenses, including dry hole costs and impairment of unproved properties	110	153	331	357
Interest and debt expense	197	124	758	559
Restructuring (B)	—	(88)	(96)	(142)
Total	9,772	9,446	37,872	35,864
Earnings before income taxes	907	949	5,390	4,382
Provision for income taxes	280	303 (C)	2,097	$31,655 (C)(D)
Net income	627	646	3,293	2,727
Earnings per share of common stock (E)	$1.13	$0.95	$5.61	$4.00
Dividends per share of common stock.	$0.52	$0.47	$2.03	$1.82

(A) Certain reclassifications of 1994 data have been made to conform to 1995 classifications.
(B) Reflects adjustments to 1993 estimated charges for asset write-downs, employee separation costs, facility shutdowns, and other restructuring costs.
(C) Includes a benefit of $30 from adjustment of prior-year tax provisions.
(D) Includes a benefit of $127 principally related to a favorable change in tax status resulting from a transfer of properties among certain North Sea affiliates.
(E) Earnings per share are calculated on the basis of the following average number of common shares outstanding:

	Three months ended December 31	Year ended December 31
1995	555,367,995	585,107,476
1994	680,929,485	679,999,916

EXHIBIT 12.1: *Continued*

Consolidated industry segment information

	Three months ended December 31		Year ended December 31	
	1995	1994	1995	1994
Sales				
Chemicals	$1,006	$970	$4,181	$3,760
Fibers	1,801	1,723	7,215	6,767
Polymers	1,716	1,639	7,037	6,318
Petroleum	4,468	4,470	17,660	16,815
Diversified Businesses	1,394	1,335	6,070	5,673
Total	$10,385	$10,137	$42,163	$39,333
After-tax operating income (A) (B) (C)				
Chemicals	$151	$125	$659 (D)	$386
Fibers	188	216	826 (D)	701
Polymers	175 (E)	194	841 (E)	717
Petroleum	89 (F)	118	655 (F)	680
Diversified Businesses	175	98	849 (G)	623 (G)
Total	778	751	3,830	3,107
Interest and other corporate expenses net of tax	(151)	(105)	(537)	(380)
Net income	$627	$646	$3,293	$2,727

(A) 1995 includes, from the third quarter, a charge of $24 for printing and publishing operations, principally for employee separation costs in Europe, a litigation provision of $13 related to a previously sold business, and adjustments in estimates associated with the third quarter 1993 restructuring charge, which result in the following net (charges)/benefits:

    Chemicals $ 3
    Fibers   4
    Polymers   3
    Diversified Businesses   (12)
                       $ (2)

(B) 1994 includes the following fourth-quarter (charges)/benefits:

    Chemicals $ 22 (1)
    Fibers   25 (1)
    Polymers   (5) (1)
    Diversified Businesses   (40) (1) (2)
                       $ 2

EXHIBIT 12.1: *Continued*

(1) Reflects adjustments in estimates associated with the third quarter 1993 restructuring charge.
(2) Includes charges of $63 for the "Benlate" DF 50 fungicide recall and $27 for the write-down of assets and discontinuation of certain products, and a benefit of $30 from adjustment of prior-year tax provisions.

(C) 1994 includes the following third-quarter (charges)/benefits:

Chemicals	$ (27) (1)
Polymers	16 (2)
Petroleum	(26) (2)
Diversified Businesses	34 (2)
	$ (3)

(1) Associated with discontinuation of certain products and asset sales and write-downs.
(2) Reflects adjustments in estimates associated with the third quarter 1993 restructuring charge. In addition, the Petroleum segment also includes additional charges for employee separation costs, a loss of $95 from write-down of certain North Sea oil properties held for sale and a benefit of $127 principally related to a favorable change in tax status resulting from a transfer of properties among certain North Sea affiliates.

(D) The Chemicals and Fibers segments reflect an additional benefit of $7 and $27, respectively, principally an adjustment of estimates associated with the third quarter 1993 restructuring charge.
(E) Includes a charge of $38 for costs to settle certain plumbing systems litigation.
(F) Includes a charge of $45 for write-down of certain North American and European assets.
(G) Also includes charges of $63 and $47 associated with "Benlate" DF 50 fungicide recall from the quarters ended June 30, 1995 and 1994, respectively.

E.I. du Pont Nemours and Company and consolidated subsidiaries consolidated industry segment information excluding impact of nonrecurring items

	After-tax operating income			
	Three months ended December 31		Year ended December 31	
	1995	1994	1995	1994
Chemicals	$151	$103	$649	$391
Fibers	188	191	795	676
Polymers	213	199	876	706
Petroleum	134	118	700	706
Diversified Businesses	175	138	924	676
Total	$861	$749	$3,944	$3,155
Less: interest and other corporate expenses net of tax	(151)	(105)	(537)	(380)
Total	$710	$644	$3,407	$2,775

EXHIBIT 12.2:
Countries with major DuPont operations

North America

Canada	Mexico	Puerto Rico
United States		

South America

Argentina	Brazil	Chile
Columbia	Trinidad & Tobago	Venezuela

Europe, Africa and the Middle East

Austria	Belgium	Czech Republic
Denmark	Dubai	Finland
France	Germany	Greece
Hungary	Ireland	Italy
Luxembourg	The Netherlands	Nigeria
Norway	Poland	Portugal
Russia	South Africa	Spain
Sweden	Switzerland	Turkey
United Kingdom		

Asia-Pacific

Australia	China	Hong Kong
India	Indonesia	Japan
Malaysia	New Zealand	Philippines
Republic of Korea	Singapore	Taiwan
Thailand	Vietnam	

as "an example of serendipity, a flash of genius, a lucky accident . . . even a mixture of all three." The discovery of PTFE was so important because it is inert to virtually all chemicals and is considered the most slippery material in existence. These unique properties have made it one of the most valuable and versatile technologies ever invented. The various applications of PTFE have contributed to significant advancements in areas such as aerospace, communications, electronics, industrial processes and architecture.

Registered as a trademark in 1945, Teflon® had become a familiar brand name worldwide. It was recognized for its use as a coating on cookware and as a soil and stain repellant for fabrics and textile products. It was DuPont's intention that the Teflon® brand and its various end-use applications be associated with reliable, high-quality products and processes that made life easier. DuPont was vigilant in protecting the brand to ensure that it was of maximum marketing value to DuPont and its business partners. As part of the brand strategy, the company developed a distinctive logotype for Teflon®. The logotype was designed to reflect the integrity and identity of the brand, and to be appropriate across a wide range of markets and applications. It was intended for use on products, packaging, labels, advertising and all other types of promotional material that might carry the brand name. Like the Teflon® trademark, the logotype was owned exclusively by DuPont and may only be used under license from DuPont.

Teflon® for Cookware

When people hear the brand name Teflon®, they usually think "non-stick." This association is the result of years of consistent brand support and a determination to maintain a strong global reputation. Teflon's® ability to shrug off whatever comes into contact with it led to the application of protective non-stick coatings to pots and pans. This made cookware featuring Teflon® easy to use and easy to clean. Since cleaning up after cooking can be a difficult and messy job, having pots and pans that come clean with just a wipe would be a welcome addition to the kitchen of any family. Since their introduction in the 1960s, over a billion pots and pans with DuPont non-stick surfaces have sold worldwide. Non-stick coatings can be bonded to aluminum, stainless steel, enameled steel, cast iron, glass, ceramics or plastics to form a smooth inner surface which releases food easily and wipes clean after use.

To meet a variety of cookware applications, DuPont developed various brands that differ in the formulation and thickness of the coating system. When combined with the thickness of the metal, the result was different quality and thickness levels. Teflon® was designed for regular use and offered excellent quality and value for money. Teflon® must be at least 25 microns thick with a two-layer system (primer and topcoat) that offers resistant, reliable, durable non-stick qualities. SilverStone® coatings are more durable for intensive use. SilverStone® has three layers with a combined minimum thickness of 35 microns, making it even more durable and resistant. SilverStone Supra® is a specially formulated super-durable coating for superior quality cookware. It was designed to meet the needs and demands of the most discerning user. It has three layers with a combined minimum thickness of 35 microns and includes an advanced primer and an extremely tough mid-coat.

Although DuPont developed non-stick technology and non-stick coatings in 1938, it was not until the 1960s that Tefal, a French cookware company, first introduced non-stick cookware, using DuPont technology. The first markets were North America and Europe. As non-stick cookware was accepted, it became popular in Japan and other parts of Asia. However, by the 1990s, these markets (i.e., North America, Europe and Japan) were considered "mature." Tefal went on to become one of the largest manufacturers of non-stick cookware in the world. Today, its operations are global and fully integrated.

Traditionally, DuPont had acted as a raw material supplier to cookware manufacturers by providing Teflon® brand non-stick coatings. In this approach, DuPont supplied non-stick technology to licensees who used Teflon® brand coatings on their cookware. Then, the Teflon® brand label was prominently displayed on the packaging of the licensee's cookware. The Teflon® label implied to the consumer that the cookware was quality made and dependable because it featured DuPont technology. In effect, DuPont partnered with licensee manufacturers in promoting their non-stick cookware brands through differentiation and by creating a "pull through" marketing strategy in which the Teflon® label attracted the retail buyer. This was due to Teflon's® high brand awareness among retail customers. For example, brand awareness levels in the US were at 98% for the Teflon® brand and at 95% for DuPont's premium non-stick brand, SilverStone®.

THE CHINESE COOKWARE MARKET

China's population in 1995 was 1.2 billion people. Its major population centers (with populations) were Shanghai (7.5 million), Beijing (5.8 million), and Tianjin (4.6 million). The average annual income was 5,500 RMB (approximately US$685), up from 2,140 RMB in 1990. Economic reforms instituted by the central government were having a favorable effect on industrial growth, family income, savings rates, and consumer spending. As their economic situation improved, Chinese citizens became interested in consumer goods.

Non-stick cookware featuring the Teflon® brand was first introduced to the Chinese retail market in 1989. Although the Chinese market had great potential, the non-stick cookware market experienced little growth over the ensuing years. By 1995, non-stick cookware represented less than 2% of the industry's "top-of-range" cookware[1] sales. However, products featuring the DuPont brand held about 80% of this small market segment. So, while the company's market share was strong, it was the non-stick cookware market in general that performed poorly.

Since sales of Teflon® coating (through license) were dependent on the sales of non-stick cookware, DuPont wanted to see the market grow. In investigating the market, Lin's research team discovered several important demand-side characteristics of the domestic cookware market that hindered the growth of non-stick cookware, some related to consumers and some to licensee manufacturers. First, Chinese consumers had traditionally used a different type of cookware than Western consumers, preferring round-bottomed steel woks to flat-bottomed fry pans and sauce pans. Although top-of-range cookware was the primary food preparation utensil, Chinese consumers also used pressure cookers and rice cookers. The preference for steel cookware was augmented by their use of metal cooking utensils, such as spoons and spatulas, instead of plastic or wood utensils. While Teflon® was stick resistant, repeated use of metal utensils on the coating could cause scratches that were detrimental to its performance.

A second factor was that Chinese cooking processes differed from Western cooking methods, which generally used lower temperatures and longer cooking times. In contrast, Chinese cooking methods favored relatively higher temperatures for shorter periods of time and with frequent stirring. The high heat and frequent stirring, which can cause abrasions, put increased stress on the non-stick properties of the finish. This difference was compounded by other, related factors. Chinese kitchens were generally much smaller than Western kitchens, which limited the number of cooking pans a family owned. Also, cooking gas was available only in urban areas, which accounted for only 20% of the country's population.

A third limiting factor was price. Non-stick cookware was significantly more expensive than steel cookware. For example, an iron or stainless steel wok may cost only 20 or 30 RMB and last for 8 to 10 years. By comparison, a 26 cm diameter pan with Teflon® non-stick coating may cost 80–150 RMB. With the average worker's monthly income being only about 500 RMB, non-stick cookware represented a major household purchase.

A fourth complicating factor was the consumer's perception of cookware. Traditional Chinese consumers believed that cooking in iron woks was good for a person's health, while using non-stick cookware was not good for one's health. This was a misconception because Teflon® was safe for cooking. In fact, Teflon® complies with the United States Food and Drug Administration (USFDA) regulations for use by consumers as a food-contact finish, which meant it caused no harmful effects when used. On a positive note, Chinese consumers perceived non-stick cookware as easy to clean, easy to use, and good for cooking fish and eggs.

There were also supply-side issues to be addressed. Industry analysts had identified several other barriers to further developing the market that were common to Chinese non-stick cookware manufacturers. First, the Chinese central government routinely designated a priority list of particular state-owned industries (known as "pillar industries") that were important to the further economic development of the country. These state-owned enterprises (SOEs) received special consideration from government agencies in becoming stronger domestic and international competitors. As non-stick cookware manufacturers were not on this list and, therefore, received no government support, developing the market and new products put a heavy financial burden on the individual companies and their partners.

Business financing and payment customs were another significant problem. Regardless of the credit terms offered to retailers, cookware manufacturers were heavily penalized by triangular debt, characterized by some industry analysts as "notorious." Payment terms from retailers routinely exceeded 90 days and long past due receivables were common. In addition, key raw materials, such as aluminum and non-stick coatings, were sold only on a letter-of-credit or cash basis. Combined with relatively high interest rates in 1995 and negative cash flow, cookware licensee manufacturers tended to self-impose low volume limits on how much non-stick cookware they would sell in the local market. By comparison, if the manufacturers sold only exports, all they needed to be concerned about was producing cookware, filling an overseas shipping container, and then sending it to their distribution customers. This was easier than selling to the domestic Chinese market, which had the use and cost issues noted above and potential account collection problems associated with local distributors.

When these severe financial burdens were coupled with the government's tight credit policy, some licensee manufacturers were cash-strapped and, by Western accounting standards, close to bankruptcy. Therefore, these numerous forces combined such that Chinese licensee manufacturers had neither the resources nor desire to develop the domestic non-stick market. From 1989 to 1995, DuPont used a "pull through" strategy that it had used in other countries. DuPont had licensing agreements with cookware companies that manufactured their own cookware featuring Teflon® non-stick coatings and used the Teflon® label on their packaging as a sign of high quality. Under this partnership arrangement, DuPont worked with Chinese licensees to develop the non-stick cookware market and build Teflon® brand awareness. Both parties benefited. DuPont helped to strengthen the Chinese brand by adding the Teflon® label to the packaging, and DuPont benefited through the revenue received from additional sales of cookware using its non-stick coating. By 1995, DuPont was working with six Chinese licensee manufacturers.

DuPont's Dilemma

After years of investing in and developing brand awareness in the Chinese domestic market, the market had shown some growth but not as much as was expected. According to estimates by industry analysts, three million units of non-stick cookware had been sold in China in 1995, less than 2% of the domestic cookware market. By comparison, for the same year, 15 million units of non-stick cookware were sold in Japan, and 50 million units were sold in the US, or 80% of the US market. In 1995, DuPont had spent US$1 million marketing non-stick cookware in China and two million units featuring Teflon® coatings had been sold. Over the years, the cost of market development for Teflon® products had exceeded the revenue that DuPont received from the sales of the products. While DuPont had seen this as investing for the future, it determined that it had to make a decision about its future participation in the Chinese domestic market: continue with the licensee partnerships as it had, find an alternative strategy for the domestic market, or pull out of the market.

Lin considered the options. Continuing with the current licensing strategy would not require any changes in operations or significant changes in financial commitment. DuPont could continue providing market development support to its licensee manufacturers. However, not only was this effort not realizing the full potential of the Chinese market, but the arrangement was not profitable for DuPont. The development cost exceeded the revenue that DuPont earned from non-stick cookware in the Chinese market. As a publicly traded company, DuPont had to account to its shareholders for its profits. If DuPont withdrew its market development support from the local cookware manufacturers, it could redirect its efforts to developing other products or markets. However, to do so would most likely be the end of any significant resources directed at developing the non-stick cookware market in China.

A second option was for DuPont to work more closely with the local manufacturers in developing the Chinese market. DuPont could help the manufacturers develop marketing programs for Teflon® non-stick cookware products. This could include advertising programs, point-of-sale displays and product demonstrations. Since DuPont hoped that the non-stick market would eventually turn profitable for them, being more involved with the licensee manufacturers could help this happen sooner. This would require them to be patient and see the Chinese non-stick cookware market as a long-term investment.

A third option that had been suggested was for DuPont to produce its own brand of non-stick cookware. Lin knew from the market research that the Teflon® brand was well recognized and respected by Chinese consumers and this awareness influenced their purchase decision. The young couple Lin had seen in the store confirmed that. DuPont had strong marketing skills so it would be relatively easy to develop and promote their own brand of cookware. Since the Teflon® brand was a determining factor in the purchase of non-stick cookware for Chinese consumers, having a DuPont brand was a logical extension. A new brand could allow them to extend the brand to other types of non-stick kitchen appliances, such as rice cookers.

However, this strategy required skills that the company did not currently possess. While DuPont was a manufacturing company, it had no experience in manufacturing cookware. It would either have to learn the process through internalization or rely on another company for the manufacturing. If it did this, how would it manage the relationship? Should it form a joint venture with one of it current licensee manufacturers or should it subcontract the manufacturing? If it decided to use a joint venture arrangement, DuPont would want a majority (>50%) ownership position for control purposes. In addition, there would probably be increased costs due to DuPont's high concern for product quality. If it went with a current licensee manufacturer, would the manufacturer see this as a threat to its own brand?

DuPont also would need to get the product to the consumer. This would require a distribution system. But DuPont currently did not have a system established for distribution, wholesalers, and marketing support. They would need to either create their own distribution channels or try to get into the established, although problematic, Chinese distribution channels. The distribution system in China varied from province to province. There was no national system in place. The system used by their licensee manufacturers involved many middlemen, was inefficient and used some business practices with which DuPont was not comfortable. Developing their own brand could require establishing a whole business system to accommodate the new products.

If they established their own brand, DuPont would need to begin by resolving these critical issues. Each approach had benefits and drawbacks. It was past noon and Lin decided to further consider the options over *wu tsao* before continuing his research.

NOTE

1. "Top-of-range" cookware refers to cookware that is used on top of an oven or cooking surface, as opposed to in an oven. This generally includes items such as pots, pans, and woks.

CHAPTER THIRTEEN

RICHARD BRANSON AND THE VIRGIN GROUP OF COMPANIES IN 1998

Robert M. Grant, with the assistance of Kimberly Bennett, David Glass, Kris Hammargren, Bach Lien Ho, Rene Houle, Jay Jacobs, Kristin Kraska, Shalini Lal, Mike Novy, Lisa Paganini, Mike Quintana, and Andrea Stueve, prepared this case solely to provide material for class discussion. The author does not intend to illustrate either the effective or ineffective handling of a management situation. The author may have disguised certain names or other identifying information to protect confidentiality.

As August drew to a close, it was clear that 1998 was turning out to be a challenging year for Richard Branson and his sprawling business empire. Although Branson continued to plan and launch new business ventures – current projects included Virgin Active, a chain of health clubs, and a wireless telephone service for the UK – several Virgin companies were experiencing difficult times:

- Virgin Rail Group was the subject of widespread complaints over lack of punctuality and poor customer service. Looking ahead, it faced massive investments in new rolling stock and the elimination of government subsidies.
- Virgin Express, Branson's Brussels-based European airline, had not yet reached break-even by the first half of 1998.
- Virgin Atlantic, the crown jewel of Branson's many business ventures, seemed to be making little headway in its campaign to stop the giant transatlantic alliance between American Airways and British Airways.
- The US launch of Virgin Cola was regarded as pure bravado by most observers. Virgin Cola was making heavy losses in the UK, where it had attracted much publicity but only 0.8 percent of the market. Its chances of establishing itself in the intensely competitive US market alongside giants such as Coke and Pepsi were viewed as forlorn – even with the eye-catching "Pammy" bottle modeled on the body of curvaceous "Baywatch" actress Pamela Anderson. Nor was the publicity generated by Virgin Cola wholly favorable. Elizabeth Toledo of the National Organization for Women commented: "I think the idea of using Virgin as a corporate logo was offensive to begin with and the Pammy soda

really just plays on schoolboys' fantasies. It seems juvenile but not unexpected from the Virgin companies."[1]

- The Virgin Retail Group, comprising the chain of Virgin Megastores, continued to lose money and was seen as in need of rationalization.

While intense media interest constantly enveloped Branson and the Virgin group, of late this interest had extended beyond Branson's new business ventures, his appearances with politicians and show-biz celebrities, and his hot-air ballooning, to explore the state of his business empire. A report in the *Economist* magazine in February 1998 pieced together the assets and profits of the various Virgin operating companies, most of which are owned by holding companies registered in the British Virgin Islands. The picture painted by the *Economist* was far from reassuring.

Virgin Travel is the only one of Mr. Branson's businesses to make a large profit – and most of this comes from his main airline. There are no publicly available accounts for the new Virgin Rail, which the company says is now profitable, or for Virgin's retail business outside Britain. The rest of Mr. Branson's firms, in both groups, lost money in total. Those firms that he controls (excluding Virgin Retail outside Britain) lost 28 million pounds on a turnover of some 84 million pounds. The firms that are jointly-owned are mostly recent start ups and mostly loss-making. Together they lost 37.5 million pounds; Mr. Branson's share of these losses was 15.4 million pounds.[2]

Moreover, the risks posed by the investment demands of Virgin Rail and the host of different Virgin start-ups, together with the risks of downturn in the highly cyclical airline business, point to substantial future risks. As the *Economist* noted, "In a recession, an empire founded on such principles may become over-extended. Cash flow could suddenly become inadequate to finance the expansion that is already underway. At that point the only way to raise money would be to borrow more, or to sell stakes in businesses – at a time when valuations might well be falling."

Picking up on a flurry of critical media reports on Branson and the Virgin group, the London *Independent* newspaper asked, "Is Branson's honeymoon finally over?"

Has the halo finally begun to slip? This weekend the man who was once ranked second only to Mother Teresa as a role model for the young is looking distinctly less saintly. The man is, of course, Richard Branson, boss of the Virgin empire, and this has not been one of his better weeks.

It began with a demolition job by the BBC Panorama program on the performance of his West Coast train franchise. It ended with a double-barreled assault from *The Spectator* and *The Economist*, both of which chose to make Mr. Branson the subject of less-than-flattering cover stories.

The Spectator's was a piece of ill-tempered polemic charting how Mr. Branson has risen to the top on a tide of litigation, news management and self-promotion. *The Economist* contained a more sober but telling assessment of the financial vulnerability of the Virgin companies and the way in which their true ownership is disguised by a web of offshore trusts.

Little of the information presented was that groundbreaking: Virgin has encountered such flak before and sailed through unscathed to stamp the brand on everything from air travel, bridal wear and a radio station to cola, vodka, personal pensions and cinemas.

But the combination of the twin attacks was enough to wipe the smile off that famously bearded face for once. Speaking yesterday from his chalet in the Swiss ski resort of Zermatt, Mr. Branson was not amused by the bad publicity, but accepted it might be partly his own fault. "We have been away for the week so we haven't been able to fire-fight properly," he reflected. "It could all be just a coincidence of course, but one of the things that came out of the court case was just how much money PR companies are being paid to keep an eye on Virgin. We have a lot of competitors and a lot of enemies out there."[3]

Further evidence of financial weaknesses in the Virgin group was supplied by the *Financial Times*. Analysis of Virgin's 13 biggest operating companies in the UK over a three-year period ending December 1997 pointed to negative cash flow and economic value added (EVA) during the past two years and a deteriorating interest cover. The *Financial Times* suggested that Branson might have to resort to raising long-term capital through stock market flotation of equity in some of his larger companies – an avenue that Branson was reluctant to go down because of the various irksome restrictions attached to running a publicly quoted company.

Publicly, Branson was dismissive of the analysis of both the *Economist* and the *Financial Times*. Each Virgin company, he argued, was financed on a stand-alone basis, hence attempts to consolidate the income and assets of the companies were irrelevant and misleading. Moreover, Branson has little regard for accounting profits, preferring cash flow and capital value as the critical performance indicators. Thus, most of the Virgin companies are growing businesses that are increasing in their real value and long-term cash-generating potential, even if accounting profits are negative. "The approach to running a group of private companies is fundamentally different to that of running public companies. Short-term taxable profits with good dividends are a prerequisite of public life. Avoiding short-term taxable profits and seeking long-term capital growth is the best approach to growing private companies."[4]

Even if Branson could shrug off attacks upon the profitability and financial security of his business empire, he realized that his Virgin group of companies was facing critical strategic and organizational issues, which could not be ignored for much longer. By 1998, the Virgin group had expanded from music and airlines into rail transport, vacations, vodka, cola drinks, cinemas, radio broadcasting, clothing, bridal shops, hotels, insurance, mutual funds, Internet services, and health clubs.

The extent of this expansion raised questions not just over financial resources but also over the two key resources common to the Virgin companies: the Virgin brand name and Branson himself. With regard to the brand, what was the range of businesses over which the brand could be applied without damaging its appeal or integrity? With regard to Branson, what should his role be in the management of his business empire? To what extent should he attempt to involve himself personally in guiding the various Virgin companies? Did the group need to establish a more systematic approach to management if synergies were to be exploited, value creation to be optimized, and risks managed?

Lying behind these questions was the issue of what Branson wanted to do with his own life. Up until now, Richard Branson and the Virgin companies had been inextricably entwined. Looking ahead, Branson could see the need to establish a management structure that could operate more independently of him. This would give greater freedom to him to pursue his many sporting and social interests, while making the company less vulnerable to his absences or to his possible injury or death in one of his high-profile, high-risk sporting exploits.

THE DEVELOPMENT OF VIRGIN

Richard Branson's business career began while he was a student at Stowe, a private boarding school. His start-up magazine, *Student*, was first published on January 26, 1968. The early success of the magazine encouraged Branson to leave school when 17 years old, before taking his final exams. Agreeing to the boy's request to leave, the headmaster offered the prophetic statement, "Richard, you will end up in prison or as a millionaire." Both predictions were to be fulfilled.[5]

This early publishing venture displayed features that would characterize many of Branson's subsequent entrepreneurial initiatives. Robert Dick provides an insightful discussion of these:

> Branson's brainchild *Student* magazine was a product of the 1960s, the decade when the post-war "baby-boomers" came of age. Across Western Europe and North America young people enjoyed educational, employment and lifestyle opportunities unknown to their parents, all made possible by rapid economic growth. The decade become known for its promotion of youth culture in which authority was challenged, fashions changed rapidly, and rock stars became global gurus of a new age.
>
> It was in such a climate that Richard Branson, tired of the boring inadequacies of the traditional school magazine and recognizing a "gaping hole in the market," founded his publication. Aimed at people aged 16 to 25, *Student* was to be the "voice of youth" and would "put the world to rights." Its eclectic style reflected its founder's ability to commission articles by celebrities and to identify subjects not touched by many well-established magazines. Norman Mailer, Vanessa Redgrave, and Jean-Paul Sartre contributed pieces which appeared among articles on sex, rock music, interviews with terrorists, and proposals for educational reform.
>
> The success of the magazine (Branson optimistically claimed a circulation of 100,000) promoted favorable notice in the national press. Branson was described in complimentary terms as "The editor, publisher and sole advertising manger . . . a teenage professional whose enthusiasm gets things done to an extent that would shame his elders." Certainly his energy and enthusiasm were needed to keep the organization going. The offices were transient, first in a friend's basement flat, later in a disused church. The staff – a closely organized cooperative of friends, acquaintances and hangers-on – distributed magazines, took copy and, frequently, avoided creditors. As Branson said at the time: "The staff all work for nothing. I supply them with somewhere to sleep and some food. It's not so much they are working for you as working with you."[6]

VIRGIN RECORDS

Branson's next venture was mail order records. Beginning with a single advertisement in the last issue of *Student* magazine, Branson found that he was able to establish a thriving business with almost no up-front investment and no working capital, and could easily undercut the established retail chains. The name "Virgin" was suggested by one of his associates who saw the name as proclaiming their commercial innocence, while possessing some novelty and modest shock-value. Virgin Records brought together Branson and his childhood friend Nik Powell, who took a 40 percent share in the company and complemented Branson's erratic flamboyance with careful operational and financial management. The start of a national postal strike in 1971 encouraged Branson to open his first retail store – on London's busy Oxford Street.

Expansion into record publishing was the idea of Simon Draper – one of Virgin's record buyers. Draper introduced Branson to Mike Oldfield, who was soon installed at Branson's Oxfordshire home with a fully equipped recording studio. "Tubular Bells", launched in 1973, was an instant hit, eventually selling over 5 million copies worldwide. The result was the Virgin record label, which went on to sign up bands whose music or lifestyles were unacceptable to the major record companies. Among the most successful (certainly the most outrageous) were the Sex Pistols, who were contracted to Virgin until the band's breakup following the arrest (for murder) and subsequent death of Sid Vicious.

The recession of 1979–82 was a struggle for Virgin. There was disaffection among many of Virgin Records employees, several business ventures were unsuccessful – including *Event* entertainment magazine – and Nik Powell left Virgin, selling his shareholding back to Branson in return for a million pounds and Virgin's cinema and video recording interests. Despite these setbacks, the 1980s saw rapid growth for Virgin Records with the signing of Phil Collins, Human League, Simple Minds, and Boy George's Culture Club. By 1983, the Virgin group was earning pre-tax profits of £2.0 million on total revenues of just under £50 million.

VIRGIN ATLANTIC AIRWAYS

Virgin Atlantic began with a phone call from Randolph Fields, a Californian lawyer who proposed founding a transatlantic, cut-price airline. To the horror of Branson's executives at Virgin Records, Branson was enthralled with the idea. On June 24, 1984, Branson appeared in a World War I flying outfit to celebrate the inaugural flight of Virgin Atlantic in a second-hand 747 bought from Aerolinas Argentina. With the launch of Virgin Atlantic Branson had embarked upon a perilous path strewn with the wreckage of earlier entrepreneurs of aviation, including Laker, Braniff, and People's Express. Unlike Branson's other businesses, not only was the airline business highly capital intensive, it also required a completely new set of business skills from Branson, in particular the need to negotiate with governments, regulatory bodies, banks, and aircraft manufacturers.

PRIVATE TO PUBLIC TO PRIVATE

By 1985, a transatlantic airfares price war and the investment needs of Virgin Atlantic had created a cash squeeze for Virgin. Branson became convinced of the need to expand the equity base of the group. He assigned Don Cruikshank, a Scottish accountant with an MBA from Manchester and Branson's group managing director, the task of organizing an initial public offering for Virgin's music, retail, and vision businesses, which were combined into the Virgin Group plc, a public corporation with 35 percent of its equity listed on the London, and later the NASDAQ, stock market.

Branson was not happy as chairman of a public corporation. He felt that investment analysts misunderstood his business and that the market undervalued his company. A clear conflict existed between the financial community's expectations of the chairman of a public corporation and Branson's personal style. With the October 1987 stock market crash, Branson took the opportunity to raise £200 million to buy out external shareholders.

As a private company, Virgin continued to expand, using both internal cash flows (in 1989, Virgin Atlantic Airways posted pre-tax profits of £10 million) and external financing. The retailing group moved aggressively into new markets around the world. The Virgin Megastore concept provided the basis for new stores in Japan, the United States, Australia, the Netherlands, and Spain. This growth was facilitated by the formation of a joint venture with Blockbuster Corporation, the US video-store giant. New ventures launched during the early 1990s included Virgin Lightships, an airship advertiser; Vintage Airtours, an operator of restored DC-3 aircraft between Orlando and Key West; Virgin Games producing video games; West One Television, a TV production company; and Virgin Euromagnetics, a personal computer company. Meanwhile, Virgin Atlantic Airways continued to expand. It gained the right to operate out of London's Heathrow Airport, won a court battle with British Airways requiring BA to transfer some of its Japanese air routes to Virgin, and pursued its plan to fly to 20 cities worldwide. Its transatlantic market share grew and the airline won many awards for its customer service.

VIRGIN IN THE 1990s

The cash demands of the airline business continued to pressure the group. In particular the Persian Gulf War of 1990–1 reduced revenues for the airline business as a whole. Increasingly, Branson relied upon joint ventures to finance new business development. The period from 1990 to 1992 was one of major change for the Virgin group. During that time, Branson forged several important joint venture agreements with other companies. The partnering arrangements were primarily in the retailing area and included one with Marui, a leading Japanese retailer, and another with W. H. Smith, a prominent UK retail chain. Branson and his Virgin group have long relied on the joint venture as an important strategic tool for expanding into new businesses. In 1998, the company's various arrangements with partners continue to play a critical role in Virgin's overall strategy.

By now, the airline had come to dominate Branson's business interest and imagination. As the capital-hungry Virgin Atlantic needed more money, Branson would have to let go of other parts of his empire. In March 1992 Branson sold his most profitable and successful business, Virgin Music, the world's biggest independent record label, to Thorn EMI for 560 million pounds (close to $1.0 billion). Virgin Music's tangible assets had a balance sheet value of only 3 million pounds. The sale marked a dramatic shift in focus for Virgin away from its core entertainment business towards airlines and travel, and provided the capital to support new business ventures.

In the meantime, Branson's long-standing rivalry with British Airways took a nasty turn. Evidence emerged that British Airways had pursued a "dirty tricks" campaign against Virgin. This included breaking into Virgin's computer system, diverting Virgin customers to BA flights, and spreading rumors about Virgin's financial state. These allegations promoted furious denials from the BA chairman Lord King and criticism of both Branson and Virgin. The outcome was a UK court case which resulted in BA paying $1.5 million dollars in damages to Branson and Virgin. Branson has also litigated against BA in the US. The episode greatly damaged BA's reputation as "the world's favorite airline" and prompted Lord King's early retirement.

Virgin Atlantic's long-running war against BA later shifted to opposing the BA–American Airlines alliance. Although a drain on Branson's time and energy, these continuing battles did little to constrain the Virgin group's business development. Indeed, the second half of the 1990s saw extremely rapid diversification with entry into an extraordinary range of markets. New ventures included entry into financial services (Virgin Direct), the successful bid to operate passenger rail services in Britain's newly privatized rail system, the start-up of a European budget airline (Virgin Express), plus a host of smaller ventures ranging from bridal shops to cola drinks to Internet services.

Table 13.1 summarizes the principal steps in the development of the Virgin group of companies.

THE VIRGIN GROUP OF COMPANIES IN 1998

The Virgin group was not a single corporate entity. The Virgin companies comprised some 20 holding companies (most of which were entirely financial and legal entities, the majority registered in the British Virgin Islands) and close to 200 operating companies, most of which were based within Britain. They were owned by Branson, both individually and through a series of Channel Islands-located trusts, the beneficiaries of which were Branson and his family. The linkage between the companies was the common use of the Virgin name and trademark, Branson's role as shareholder (both directly and indirectly through the trusts), Branson's role as chairman of the companies, and Branson's management role, which was primarily in publicity, public and government relations, and appointing senior executives. The Virgin empire comprised those companies which were wholly or majority owned by Branson and those in which Branson held a minority equity stake. Figure 13.1 shows the major operating companies and the holding companies that owned them.

The core of the Virgin empire was the travel business, its best known and most profitable segment (with approximately $145 million in profits for 1996). The airline

TABLE 13.1
The history of Virgin

1968	First issue of *Student* magazine, January 26.
1970	Start of Virgin mail order operation.
1971	First Virgin record shop opens in Oxford Street, London.
1972	Virgin recording studio opens at The Manor near Oxford, England.
1973	Virgin record label launched with Mike Oldfield's "Tubular Bells."
1977	Virgin Records signs the Sex Pistols.
1978	Virgin opens The Venue night club in London.
1980–2	Virgin Records expands overseas. Signs Phil Collins and Boy George/Culture Club.
1983	Virgin Vision (forerunner of Virgin Communications) formed to distribute films and videos and to operate in television and radio broadcasting. Vanson Developments formed as real estate development company. Virgin Games (computer games software publisher) launched. Virgin Group's combined pre-tax profit climbs to £2.0 million on turnover of just under £50 million.
1984	Virgin Atlantic Airways and Virgin Cargo launched. First hotel investment (Deya, Mallorca). Virgin Vision launches *The Music Channel*, a 24-hour satellite-delivered music station and releases its first feature film *1984* with Richard Burton and John Hurt.
1985	Private placement of 7% Convertible Stock completed with 25 English and Scottish institutions. Virgin wins Business Enterprise Award for company of the year. Virgin Vision extends film and video distribution internationally. Virgin Holidays formed.
1986	Virgin Group, comprising the Music, Retail & Property, and Communications divisions, floated on London Stock Exchange. 35% of equity sold to 87,000 shareholders. Airline, clubs, holidays, and aviation services remain part of the privately owned Voyager Group.
1987	Virgin Records subsidiaries in US and Japan launched. British Satellite Broadcasting (Virgin a minority partner) awarded satellite broadcasting license. (Virgin sells its shareholding in 1988.) Virgin acquires Mastertronics Group, which distributed Sega video games in Europe. Virgin Airship & Balloon Company launched to provide aerial marketing services.
1988	Recording studios opened in Barnes, London. New international record label, Virgin, launched. Virgin Broadcasting formed to further develop Virgin's radio and TV interests. Virgin Hotels formed. Virgin Megastores opened in Sydney, Paris, and Glasgow. Branson takes Virgin private with 248 million pound bid for outstanding shares.
1989	Virgin Music Group sells 25% stake to Fujisankei Communications for $150 million. Virgin Vision (video distribution) sold to MCEG of Los Angeles for $83 million.
1990	Virgin Retail Group and Marui form joint venture company to operate Megastores in Japan. Virgin Lightships formed to develop helium airships for advertising.

TABLE 13.1 *Continued*

1991	W. H. Allen plc acquired. Merged with Virgin Books to form Virgin Publishing. Sale of Virgin Mastertronic to Sega. Remaining part of the business becomes Virgin Games. Virgin Retail Group forms 50:50 joint venture with W. H. Smith to develop UK retail business.
1992	Sale of Virgin Music Group to Thorn EMI plc. Joint venture with Blockbuster to own and develop Megastores in Europe, Australia and US. UK Radio Authority grants Virgin Communications and TV-AM plc the license for Britain's first national commercial rock station (Virgin 1215AM goes on the air in April 1993). Virgin acquires Euro-Magnetic Products, a specialist in the personal computer consumable market. Vintage Airtours established to fly Orlando–Florida Keys in vintage DC-3s.
1993	Virgin Games floated as Virgin Interactive Entertainment plc with Hasbro and Blockbuster taking minority equity stakes. Virgin Euromagnetics launches a range of personal computers.
1994	Virgin Cola Company formed as joint venture with Cott Corp. Agreement with W. Grant to launch Virgin Vodka. Virgin acquires Our Price retail music chain, owned 75% by W. H. Smith, 25% by Virgin. Virgin Retail Group forms joint ventures to develop megastores in Hong Kong and S. Korea. Virgin City Jet service launched between Dublin and London City Airport.
1995	Virgin Direct Personal Financial Service is launched as a joint venture with Norwich Union (whose stake is later acquired by Australian Mutual Provident). Acquisition of MGM Cinemas, UK's biggest movie theater chain, to create Virgin Cinemas.
1996	Virgin Travel Group acquires Euro-Belgian Airlines to form Virgin Express. V2 record label and music publishing company formed. London & Continental Railways (in which Virgin is a major shareholder) wins a £3bn. contract to build the Channel Tunnel Rail Link and operate Eurostar rail services.
1997	Virgin Rail wins bid to operate the InterCity West Coast and is awarded the 15-year rail franchise. Virgin Net, an Internet service provider, formed with CableTel. Branson acquires a 15% stake in the London Broncos rugby league team. Victory Corporation, a joint venture with Rory McCarthy, launches the Virgin Clothing and Virgin Vie toiletry products. Majority share in Virgin Radio sold to Chris Evans' Ginger Media Group. Virgin Bride, a chain of wedding retailers, formed. Virgin One telephone bank account and "one-stop integrated financial service" launched in collaboration with Royal Bank of Scotland.
1998	Virgin Entertainment acquires W. H. Smith's 75% stake in Virgin/Our Price. Virgin Cola launched in the US.

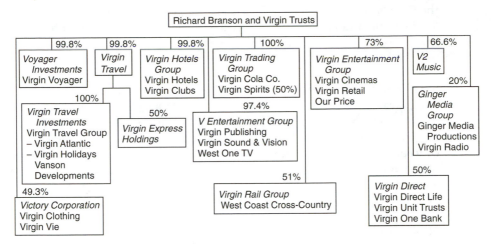

Figure 13.1 The Virgin companies

Source: *Financial Times*, August 13, 1998, p. 25.

business was the only segment of Virgin's diversified organization directly managed by Richard Branson (he was the Chief Executive Officer).

Virgin Atlantic

Although launched as a cut-price airline in 1984, Virgin Atlantic's success was based upon targeting the lucrative business traveler segment of the North Atlantic market with superior and innovative customer service. The airline has offered business travelers amenities not even offered to first-class passengers on other airlines. Virgin provided state-of-the-art reclining seats, in-flight massages, hair stylists, aromatherapists, and motorcycle and limo home-pick-up service. In 1998 it began a luxury boat service up the Thames from Heathrow to the City of London to allow executives and financiers to avoid traffic jams. In coach, Virgin was the first to provide passenger-controlled personal video screens in every seat-back. In-flight entertainment has included clowns, London buskers, even Richard Branson serving drinks while dressed as a female flight attendant. The inaugural transatlantic flight was still remembered fondly by travel writers who took the journey to New York. Bands played music in the aisles, Miss World danced with passengers, butlers handed out caviar, brandy, and cigars. Branson's father, who was along for the ride, commented, "When I die, I hope heaven is like this: 35,000 feet up, endless champagne and surrounded by pretty women."[7] What Virgin did was to recreate the mystique of air travel through mixing unique in-flight luxuries with circus side-show.

The airline won numerous awards for its customer service and became one of the most profitable of the world's smaller airlines. Its success in the North Atlantic market encouraged it to extend its routes to the Far East (Tokyo and Hong Kong) and the Caribbean. It continued to be a leader in passenger amenities. Describing plans for the future Branson explained, "In first class, we're planning to introduce private bedrooms, 12 per plane, and yes, showers and Jacuzzis, we'll have the first legitimate mile-high club. If you can do it on ships and trains, why not on planes?"[8]

A constant theme of Virgin Atlantic's development was its war against the major airlines and against BA in particular. This involved Branson in one of his favorite roles: casting his plucky Virgin upstart as David against the corporate Goliaths of traditional big business. In terms of establishing Virgin Atlantic as a virtuous under-dog, British Airways played almost perfectly into Branson's hands, first, in its poorly concealed "dirty tricks" campaign and, second, in its pursuit of transatlantic domi-nance through the alliance with American Airlines. Opposition to the AA–BA alliance was time-consuming for Branson, involving testimony in front of the US Congress, media interviews, and extensive lobbying. However, it provided Branson and Virgin Atlantic with a huge amount of exposure, and further established Virgin as representing entrepreneurship and the spirit of competition.

Although Virgin Atlantic thrived in a period when few major airlines were prof-itable, the airline business was a high-fixed-cost business in a cyclical market. Virgin Atlantic lost money for three straight years at the beginning of the 1990s and faced increasing competitive pressure in the future. If the AA–BA alliance went ahead, this would mean not only an exceptionally powerful competitor, but also the reallo-cation of some precious landing slots at Heathrow to other US airlines. The risk of increased transatlantic competition could hit Virgin Atlantic's bottom line seriously. Not only was profitability highly sensitive to load factors, but business fares between the US and London were 25 percent higher than fares between the US and other European gateways. Virgin Atlantic earned most of its profits from flying business customers between London and the US.

Yet, by 1998, Virgin Atlantic showed no signs of succumbing to these various threats. Virgin Travel, which comprised Virgin Atlantic and Virgin Holidays, saw a 40 percent increase in profit in 1997–98 as compared with 1996–97, and was opti-mistic about 1998–99. Revenues and profits for Virgin Travel were as follows:

	Year to April 1997	Year to April 1998
Sales (millions of pounds)	785.0	942.3
Profits (millions of pounds)	64.7	89.5

Virgin Cargo

Air freight business was an important complement to Virgin Atlantic's passenger service. While planning the launch of Virgin Atlantic, Branson asked New York "Air Freight Godfather" Angelo Pusateri to join him on Branson's London houseboat to discuss the start-up of a Virgin Airlines cargo service. "It was sort of strange," remembered Pusateri. "He was a very relaxed guy, continually scribbling in this big notebook. He said he was putting together an airline and it was going to be fun. He told us, 'I don't know much about cargo, but I know it's important to our revenue package, and I'd like you guys to build an air freight operation for us. Go forth and develop.' Anyone who could lay out a plan of this size without a single typed piece of paper – I was impressed."[9] Based at the then underutilized Newark airport, Virgin Cargo grew to handle over 77,000 metric tons of volume in 1997. Another 10 percent increase was expected for 1998. The company managed freight operations for other carriers such as Lufthansa, America West, and Midwest Express. Pusateri was chief executive of Virgin Aviation Services, the parent company to Virgin Cargo and other smaller Virgin aviation companies. The Virgin management style based upon initiative, entrepreneurship, and a high level of autonomy worked well in the air cargo business. Managers were encouraged to tailor products to customer needs, price service aggressively, and take risks. When a federal regulation required US law enforcement agencies to discard outdated, but still effective bullet-proof vests, Pusateri had the vests collected and shipped free of charge to London's metropolitan police force: "The bobbies get piece of mind, English taxpayers don't pay a quid, and Virgin gets some great PR."

Virgin Holidays

A much smaller component of Virgin Travel was Virgin Holidays, a tour operator which offered combined air travel and accommodation packages for British holiday-makers. It specialized in offering vacations to the US, but also to South Africa, Asia, and the Mediterranean. Unlike the more high-profile companies within the Virgin group, Virgin Holidays attracted little publicity – although its dispute with the Greek government over the proposed construction of a resort on the island of Kaminia provided some unwelcome attention.

Virgin Hotels

Virgin Hotels owned a collection of 39 hotel properties in the UK, Ireland, France, Italy, Spain, and the US. Included in the properties was Branson's Caribbean island, which was a favorite relaxation spot for him, but which Virgin also rented out for over $8,000 per day.

Virgin Express

In April 1996, Branson purchased Euro-Belgian Airlines SA, a short-haul carrier based in Brussels servicing destinations throughout Europe. He quickly changed the name of the airline to Virgin Express plc. The company floated 49 percent of its stock on the Brussels and NASDAQ stock markets. Virgin Express took advantage of the liberalization of the European aviation market to expand its range of both scheduled and charter services. Virgin Express moved into profit in 1997, but in competing with low-cost airlines such as EasyJet and the new BA subsidiary, GO, was hampered by a high cost base resulting from its Belgium location. In July 1998, Virgin Express announced its intention to move its company's registration to Ireland, where it would benefit from lower corporate taxation and lower employment taxes. Its operational base would remain Brussels. One question over the airline was the extent to which a Belgium-based, low-cost airline whose routes did not link with those of Virgin Atlantic could benefit from its links with Virgin Atlantic. Central to the Virgin Express strategy was the idea that a low-cost, economy-priced airline could also deliver a superior customer experience: "Smiles don't cost anything," said Branson.[10]

Virgin Rail

Virgin's biggest, and potentially riskiest, diversification of the 1990s was its entry into rail travel. Early in 1996, Virgin Rail was formed to bid for operating franchises in the partitioned and privatized British Rail system. By 1997 Virgin Rail operated two rail companies: Virgin Cross-Country with train services between the South West, Midlands, and Wales, with Birmingham as a hub; and Virgin West Coast with services between London and Glasgow. In addition, Virgin was one of the six investors in London and Continental Railway (LCR), which was responsible for running the Eurostar train service between London and Paris through the Channel Tunnel and building a high-speed rail linkage between London and the Channel Tunnel.

To promote awareness of the Virgin brand, Branson had all of the trains painted in Virgin's cardinal red. Virgin Rail was profitable to mid-1998, but with government operating subsidies due to decline to zero by 2001, future profitability was not assured. In addition Virgin Rail faced substantial investment demands. In order to maintain the quality of the service and attract new customers to the rail lines, experts suggest that Virgin will need to invest 1.2 billion pounds in new high-speed tilting trains and other equipment. The additional investment was not forthcoming from the various venture capitalists who had backed Virgin Rail, hence Branson sold 49 percent of the company to Stagecoach, a large operator of buses and trains in Britain, for 158 million pounds. Branson, as always, expressed optimism about the future of Virgin Rail. On top of the investment needs of Virgin Rail, LCR's proposed high-speed line from London to the Channel Tunnel was a multi-billion pound project for which finance seemed unforthcoming.

In the meantime, Virgin Rail was subject to increasing customer dissatisfaction and low performance grades from the rail regulator, who identified poor punctuality by both the Cross-Country and West Coast services. Although Virgin Rail invested heavily in a new reservation system, overall customer satisfaction with Virgin's rail services appeared to be low, even compared with other British rail companies.

The rail ventures represented a highly vulnerable area of business for Branson. Not only were they a potential cash flow drain, but the risks to the Virgin brand were substantial. The opportunities for innovative differentiation appeared to be few, and it was notable that rail transport was an area where privatization was unpopular among the British public.

Virgin Entertainment Group

The Virgin Entertainment Group was the parent company for both Virgin Cinema Group Ltd. and Virgin Retail Group Ltd. Although the two sides of the business were operated independently, increased linkages between the two seemed likely in the future.

Virgin Retail Group

Virgin Retail Group included the highly popular Virgin Megastores, with 122 locations around the world. The Megastores sold music, music accessories, electronic equipment, clothing, and concert tickets, among other items. It was noted that the Megastore in Paris received more visitors than either the Eiffel Tower or the Louvre.[11] The Virgin Megastores did not form a single integrated business but were operated as separate businesses with different business partners in different countries. Thus, in Japan, Virgin Megastores were a joint venture with Marui, a Japanese department store. The arrangement permitted Virgin to expand into Japan while avoiding the prohibitive real estate costs associated with prime retail space in Tokyo and other cities. The first Virgin Megastore in Japan opened in the basement of one of Marui's department stores in Northern Tokyo.

The other major retail business was the Virgin/Our Price music retailing chain, 75 percent of which had been sold to the book and newspaper retailer W. H. Smith in 1991. In 1998, Branson bought out the W. H. Smith shareholding for 145 million pounds, partly to prevent the retailer from being acquired by a third party.[12]

Despite the success of the Virgin stores as leading retailers of recorded music, the format has not developed into a "category killer" in the same way as Home Depot in home improvement supplies, Wal-Mart in discount retailing, IKEA in home furnishings, or The Gap in casual clothing. Retailing revenues totaled about 750 million pounds in 1997. But margins in the business were slim, with operating profits amounting to only about 2.2 percent of sales. "Music retailers are vulnerable because their margins are low, so it would not take much of a shift in trade towards the Internet to devastate their profits," noted George Wallace, a retail consultant with Management Horizons Europe.[13] A key problem of the chain was inconsistent performance between countries and between stores. Virgin Entertainment promised to rationalize the unprofitable European Megastores, closing loss-making stores and pulling out of Spain and Norway completely.

Virgin Cinemas

Virgin Cinemas owned and managed 120 movie theaters in Britain and Ireland, making it the largest British cinema chain.

Lately, Branson has focused his retail efforts on the creation of large entertainment centers that include Megastores along with restaurants and movie cinemas. Branson hoped this strategy would counter the threat from various home-based entertainment media. Referring to the massive array of computer games, interactive and satellite television, and Internet services that have invaded homes around the world, Branson stated, "We must make it worth their while to leave their homes to shop, because in the not-too-distant future there's not going to be any reason for them to do so. If we are going to get people out of their homes and into a retail environment, they have to be entertained" [14]

Virgin Trading Group Limited

Virgin Trading Group, a wholly owned Virgin subsidiary, comprised Branson's beverage start-ups. The first of these was Virgin Spirits, a joint venture with Scottish whisky distiller William Grant. The only product, Virgin Vodka, failed to establish itself in the market, and Virgin Spirits was wound up in March 1998.

The Virgin Cola Company was a joint venture with the Canadian soft drink company Cott & Company, the world's largest supplier of retailer own-brand soda drinks. Virgin Cola was first introduced in the UK in 1994. In the UK, Virgin Cola was priced below Coke and Pepsi. It achieved some success in breaking into the pub and restaurant trade, and at its peak is believed to have attained a market share of close to 8 percent. However, after its initial success, its sales were on a steady downhill slide. The result was that, after a small operating profit in 1996, Virgin Cola incurred heavy losses thought to be around five million pounds on a revenue of 30 million pounds last year. Early in 1998, Branson bought out the 50 percent of Virgin Cola owned by Cott Corporation, which was unwilling to lose more money on the venture.

The US launch took place in the spring of 1998, backed with a $25 million marketing budget. Branson's goals for the cola in the US were characteristically ambitious. He stated the launch's goal was "to make absolutely certain it gets the best start it can, with the hope of driving Coke out of the States."[15] In the US, successful soft drink marketing depended on a broad distribution strategy, as exemplified by the vast bottling and distribution enterprises of both Coke and Pepsi. Virgin faced the challenge of trying to stake out a niche position in an industry where large-scale distribution, advertising, and promotion were key. With the end of the partnership with Cott, it was unclear how Virgin Cola would be bottled and distributed in the United States.

While the publicity over the "Pammy" cola bottle gave Virgin Cola substantial media coverage and a certain notoriety, it is unclear whether publicity would translate into sales. Although Virgin was used to playing the "giant-killer" in markets dominated by giant corporations, the US soft drink market, estimated at about $53 billion, was almost 75 percent owned by Coke and Pepsi. Coke recently launched its Surge brand with a $100 million advertising budget. Sizing up his chances against two premier American brands, Branson stated, "If we take on Coca-Cola and fail, at least we tried. I think the Virgin name would be enhanced for trying." While giving Coke considerable respect for its marketing capabilities, Branson chose to attack Pepsi more fiercely. "I am still convinced we can rival the Pepsi brand," stated Branson.[16] Further, Virgin Cola's Managing Director, Nick Kirkbride, stated, "Coke is in a phenomenally strong position, but Virgin is a brand which is much stronger than Pepsi."[17] Observers remained skeptical, noting that Virgin's past success were based upon offering a superior product. Virgin Cola was not a demonstrably superior product to Coke or Pepsi, nor were Coca-Cola and PepsiCo the lumbering mono-liths that Virgin could easily run rings around.

Virgin Direct

The Virgin Direct financial services group was launched in the UK in March 1995. It was a joint venture between Virgin, which owned 49.9 percent and Australian Mutual Provident Society. Virgin Direct offered retirement plans called "PEPs" (personal equity plans), life insurance, and other financial services. It was organized into three units, Virgin Direct Life, which offered life insurance and retirement plans, Virgin Unit Trusts Managers, which managed mutual funds, and the Virgin One Bank. It direct marketed several index-linked mutual funds ("unit trusts") that demonstrated lower management costs and better performance than almost all actively managed mutual funds. Mutual fund management and marketing grew to become the major part of Virgin Direct's business, having gone from nothing to 1.5 billion pounds under management in three years. In 1998, Virgin Direct had some 250,000 customers.

While index funds similar to Virgin Direct's had been on the market for several years, Virgin appeared to have found its niche in marketing and promoting its funds, while its partner provided money management capabilities. Referring to the mutual fund and retirement planning business, Branson stated, "The existing funds were not properly promoted. I thought I could set up a business and bring new customers into an area they did not know anything about." Putting his money where his mouth is, Branson launched the first fund by investing $15 million of his own money.

In October 1997, Virgin Direct announced its plan to launch *One* – a single account that would allow customers to borrow and save from the same account. A joint venture between Virgin Direct and The Royal Bank of Scotland, the One account provided telephone transactions for all Virgin Direct customers who were homeowners. Explaining Virgin's entry into banking, Branson stated, "Virgin only goes into new businesses where we believe we can do a better job for the customer than existing suppliers."[18]

Virgin's rapid growth in the financial services industry was the result not just of innovative marketing but also of price-cutting. The result was to trigger aggressive price competition in the mutual fund business. The combination of start-up costs, heavy marketing expenses from rapid expansion, low fees, and slim margins meant that, despite its success in the market, Virgin Direct had not by early 1998 reached profitability. Its pre-tax loss was close to 20 million pounds in 1997.

Victory Corporation

Victory Corporation was Virgin's clothing and cosmetics company, which was floated as a start-up company on London's Alternative Investment Market in 1996. The two parts of the company were:

- Virgin Vie, a cosmetics and toiletries company which designed and marketed its own range of products (intended to expand to about 1,000 separate products) to be sold through 3,000 consultants and 100 UK stores, as well as an international launch. By mid-1998, the venture was going badly, with the planned store openings canceled after the pilot stores failed to achieve target sales.
- Virgin Clothing Company, a designer and marketer of men's clothing that sold through UK fashion retailers and through its Internet site, www.virgin-clothing.com. The company's advertisements showed a scruffy Richard Branson with the caption, "Giorgio designs. Ralph designs. Calvin designs. Don't worry, Richard doesn't." The clothing range did not sell well. Launches of new ranges were behind schedule because of the need to redesign.

Since flotation, Victory Corporation's share price declined from 55 pence to under 20 pence, reflecting the dismal profit performance – the company turned in operating losses of eight million pounds for 1997. Finance director, Stephen Murphy, said that a key lesson for Virgin from the Victory Corporation experience was the danger of floating start-up companies: "Thrusting a start-up company into the public arena on day one is not a good thing to do. Because of the public company perspective, we did not grasp control in the way we should have done."[19]

Other Virgin Enterprises

These include:

- Virgin Euromagnetics: A distributor of computer and audio media such as diskettes and cassettes.
- V2: A new music label launched in November 1996 brought Virgin back into its once-core business of music publishing, though not under the Virgin name since that record label was owned by EMI.
- Virgin Radio: An AM/FM radio station supported by an interactive web site (www.virginradio.com) that was successful in gaining audience, but not in achieving profitability. In October 1997, Chris Evans, one of Britain's most successful broadcasters, joined Virgin Radio to host the Virgin Radio Breakfast Show. In December, through his company Ginger Productions, Chris Evans bought a majority share in Virgin Radio, leaving Branson with a 20 percent stake in the combined company, Ginger Media Group.
- Virgin Digital Studios: A multimedia and Internet production facility in England.
- Virgin Bride: One of Branson's latest ventures, which he launched by wearing a $10,000 bridal gown. It's unclear in which subsidiary this division was to be placed. Again, this was a market where Branson saw incumbent firms doing a mediocre job and where he saw the potential for Virgin to capture substantial share of the many pounds spent on wedding dresses, wedding event planning, and honeymoon trips.

- Virgin Cafes: A group of urban gathering places with restaurants and bars.
- Virgin Net: An Internet service provider which offered low-cost Internet access, while providing a range of proprietary content and links with Virgin's other businesses. The company was a joint venture with CableTel.
- Mates: A line of condoms sold through pharmacies and vending machines.

FINANCIAL STRUCTURE AND PERFORMANCE

Financial reporting by the Virgin companies was fragmented, difficult to locate, and awkward to consolidate because of lack of public information and different financial years. The data pieced together by the *Economist* and the *Financial Times* was the closest to an aggregated profit statement for the group (see Table 13.2 and Figure 13.2). Despite the limited information available, it was apparent that, in terms of accounting profitability, cash flow, and economic value added (EVA), the profit performance of the Virgin group as a whole was far from stellar during the period 1995–97. Branson and Virgin executives have dismissed the analysis by both newspapers, claiming that accounting profits are poor indicators of the value and performance of the Virgin companies. Since most of the companies are privately held, there was little outside pressure to report increased accounting profit each year. Its goal was value creation in the long term. The *Financial Times* reported, "Mr. Branson's preferred yardstick is cash flow. He recently gave an upbeat account of the group's financial performance in which he claimed that Virgin companies collectively generate 150 billion pounds of cash a year. 'We are in the strongest position we have ever been in,' he said."[20]

In terms of financial structure, the primary feature of the group was the stand-alone financing of each company. The near-failure of the group during the 1990–2 recession resulted in substantial changes in financial structure. The *Financial Times* reported:

In 1991, Mr. Branson's companies had gross debts of more than $400 million, most of which were personally guaranteed by him, or subject to cross-guarantees within the group. This left Virgin highly vulnerable, ensuring that if bad debts occurred in one part of the group, they had the potential to swiftly infect the rest.

Nowadays, Mr. Branson's interests are more conservatively structured. Each is separately financed, often with outside investors taking much of the risk. Lenders to Virgin companies have no recourse to Mr. Branson's assets or those of any other part of the group.

"After the sale of Virgin Records, I took the decision that I never wanted to be in a position where I have to sell a company again," said Mr. Branson.

Virgin's strategy of outside finance was designed to avoid the reliance on bank borrows that almost unseated the group in the last recession. But as Virgin Atlantic has grown organically, and Virgin Entertainment by acquisition, both have financed expansion mainly through borrowed money.

Capitalizing aircraft leases as debt, Virgin Travel, which owns Virgin Atlantic, had net borrowings of about 500 million pounds last year and a debt equity of about 4:1. Although high gearing is not uncommon in the airline industry, BA's debt/equity ratio is by comparison about 145%. Virgin Atlantic is continuing to expand rapidly.

TABLE 13.2

The profit performance of the Virgin group of companies, 1997[a] (£ million)

	EBIT[b]	Net cash flow	EVA[c]
Virgin Travel Group	51.5	37.9	32.5
Virgin Express	6.9	9.0	0.5
Virgin Retail UK (excl. Our Price)	−7.9	0.5	−16.7
Virgin Our Price	12.6	−1.4	2.5
Virgin Cinema	6.9	−11.5	−5.3
Virgin Hotels	−2.7	1.3	−6.7
Virgin Rail	12.6	7.5	12.1
V Entertainment	−8.1	−0.7	−10.6
V2 Music	−15.4	−16.2	−15.8
Virgin Direct	−19.9	−24.8	−18.6
Virgin Cola	−0.3	0.9	−0.4
Virgin Spirits	−1.9	−1.6	−1.5
Victory Corporation	−8.2	−9.0	−10.3

[a] The profit data are for the latest financial year, typically for the financial year ended closest to the end of December 1997.
[b] EBIT is earnings before interest and tax.
[c] EVA is operating profit before interest and after tax, less the weighted average cost of capital multiplied by capital employed.

Source: *Financial Times*, August 13, 1998, p. 25.

> Virgin Entertainment has borrowings of more than 300 million pounds following the 145 million pound acquisition of Virgin Our Price, which was funded entirely by debt. Of this, 100 million pounds is an expensive bridging facility, which must be repaid in the near future. The group hopes to refinance the company through a high-idled bond issue in the autumn.[21]

While Branson had become more financially conservative than he was ten years ago, it was apparent that most of the Virgin companies possessed narrow equity bases and were heavily reliant upon bank borrowing. The *Financial Times* analysis showed interest coverage to be low. This raised the question of the ability of the Virgin companies to service debt if a downturn in the general economy reduced the operating cash flows of the companies. The *Financial Times* pointed to the cyclical nature and high fixed costs of the airline business. While North Atlantic traffic remained strong, the routes to Hong Kong and Tokyo had been hit by the financial problems of the Far East. The retail side, which was heavily dependent on sales of recorded music, was vulnerable both to recession and to increased direct sales, especially through the Internet.

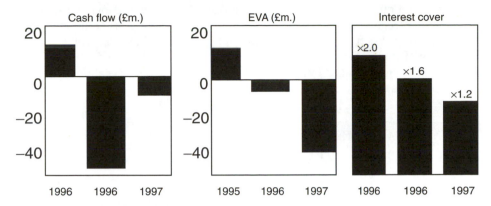

Figure 13.2 Financial performance of the Virgin Group
Source: *Financial Times*, August 13, 1998, p. 24.

The rapid diversification of the 1990s, together with the cash demands of the railroad companies, retailing, and financial services, encouraged Branson to look increasingly to outside equity financing. This has resulted in Branson attracting investment by venture capital funds, joint venture partners, and initial public offerings. Of the 13 businesses that formed the bulk of Virgin's operations, only three were wholly owned by Branson and his interests: Virgin Atlantic, Virgin Hotels, and the V Entertainment Group. The others all had substantial outside interests:

■ Virgin Rail was half-owned by Stagecoach.
■ Virgin Direct was half-owned by Australian Mutual Provident, with its direct banking venture with The Royal Bank of Scotland.
■ Virgin Retail had different partners and investors. These included Blockbuster and Marui.
■ Virgin Trading drinks ventures were with William Grant and Cotts.
■ Victory Corporation, the fashion and toiletries companies, was pioneered by entrepreneur and investor Rory McCarthy. In addition outside investors owned 25 percent of the equity. McCarthy also held one-third of V2 Music.
■ Virgin Express was a publicly traded company.
■ Apart from the joint venture partners and public stockholders, there were also a number of private investors – often major equity and venture capital funds.

A central role for Branson was his ability to attract outside investors through his high profile, personality, and network of connections. Typically, by offering the Virgin brand and his own celebrity status to promote new ventures, Branson was able to negotiate some very attractive deals. For example, Branson put up only 2,000 pounds initially for minority stakes in Virgin Clothing and Virgin Vie. The attractiveness of Virgin to The Royal Bank of Scotland and Australian Mutual was that it permitted these companies to develop a novel approach to marketing and distribution using one of the best-known and highly regarded personalities in Britain, and without putting their own names at risk. The Virgin name together with the image and entrepreneurial drive of Branson were also major considerations in encouraging Stagecoach to acquire a major stake in Virgin Rail. Branson's willingness to extend the Virgin brand to a wide range of new enterprises, many of them with minor equity stakes by Virgin, has stimulated the observation that Virgin was increasingly a brand-franchising operation.

ORGANIZATIONAL STRUCTURE AND CORPORATE CULTURE

As noted earlier, the Virgin group was an unusual organization. It comprised a loose alliance of companies linked primarily by the Virgin trademark and Branson's role as shareholder, chairman, and public relations supremo. The group's financial and legal structure was partly a reflection of Branson's unconventional ideas about business and his wariness of the financial community. To some extent, the intricate structure of offshore-owned private companies was a deliberate attempt by Branson to cloak the Virgin empire in a thick veil of secrecy. This was apparent from the use of "bearer shares" by several of the Virgin holding companies through which minority shareholders (venture capitalists and other investors) could not be identified. However, there was more to the Virgin structure than opaqueness and tax efficiency. Branson viewed the loosely knit structure as consistent with his vision of people-orientated capitalism:

> We're structured as if we are 150 small companies. Each has to stand on its own two feet, as if they are their own companies. Employees have a stake in their success. They feel – and are – crucial to their company because they are one-in-fifty or one-in-a-hundred instead of one-in-tens-of-thousands. They indeed are all under the Virgin umbrella, but they are generally not subsidiaries. I'm over them to see if one company can't help another, but otherwise they are independent. Some people like the idea of growing fiefdoms – companies that brag about sales of over $5 billion a year – but there is no logical reason to think that there is anything good about huge companies. History in fact shows the opposite. Those huge corporations with tentacles and divisions and departments become unwieldy, slow growing, stagnant. Some chairmen want them like that so that one division's loss can make up for another's profit, but we'd rather have a lot of exciting companies that are all making profits – as are all of ours.

The Virgin group has been likened both to a Japanese-style *keiretsu* and to a franchising operation. The reality, according to *Management Today*, was somewhere between the two. Although each company was nominally independent, there was some form of corporate organization. Branson's London residence in Holland Park acted as an improvised corporate office where a small core of Branson advisers and senior executives spent time. These include:

■ Will Whitehorn, originally Branson's press spokesman and head of PR, but widely regarded as Branson's second-in-command. Whitehorn was viewed as a loyal lieutenant and a sounding-board for Branson.

- Rowan Gormley was managing director of Virgin Direct. In addition Gormley, an ex-Arthur Andersen accountant, played an important role advising on corporate development.
- Brad Rosser was Branson's head of new business development. An accounting and finance major from Australia with an MBA from Cornell, he was previously employed by Australian entrepreneur Alan Bond and by McKinsey & Company. He subjected new business proposals to rigorous criteria as to whether they fit the Virgin business model: "The products must be innovative, challenge authority, offer value for money, be of good quality, and the market must be growing."
- Simon Burke joined Virgin after working as an accountant for Binder Hamlyn and Coopers & Lybrand to manage the buyback of the Virgin outstanding shares. Burke headed Virgin's entertainment group, and was highly regarded for his work in turning around Virgin's retail operations.
- Jim Campbell headed Virgin Radio until its sale to Chris Evans. He had a strong marketing background and was Pepsi Cola's youngest marketing manager in the US. He had worked with Branson since 1986, initially in the communications division.
- Michael Herriot at 55 was one of the eldest of Branson's top management team. He was hired from Grand Metropolitan in 1989 to head up Virgin Hotels.
- Rory McCarthy was business partner, friend, and soul-mate of Branson. Having set the world hang-gliding altitude record as well as starting up a string of companies, he had similar drives as Branson. His McCarthy Corporation held 33 percent of V2 and 50 percent of Virgin Helicopters.
- Jonathan Ornstein was the chairman of Virgin Express. He was a veteran of the aggressively competitive US aviation market, where he had been a turnaround chief at West Air, Mesa, and Continental's shuttle operations. He was hired by Branson in 1995.
- Simon Glasgow was selected by Branson to launch the Virgin Clothing range. A former IBM salesman, he started his own sports attire retailing chain.
- Gordon McCallum was a recent hire of Branson's who acted as group strategy director and was formerly a McKinsey & Company consultant.
- Roy Gardiner was a former Laker manager who was executive director, flight operations for Virgin Atlantic. Together with David Tait, director of overseas operations, Paul Griffiths, commercial director, Nigel Primrose, finance director, Steve Ridgeway, customer services director, and Frances Farrow, corporate services director, the group formed the Virgin Atlantic senior management team often referred to as "the six-pack."[22]

A key feature of the Virgin group was the roles which senior executives played and the way in which they interacted. Although their formal positions were as executives of the individual operating companies, a number were long-time Branson associates who participated more widely in the management of the group. For instance, while Frances Farrow headed up corporate services at Virgin Atlantic, her experience with a City law firm meant that she acted as legal adviser to the Virgin group as a whole. Thus, although the Virgin group had no corporate structure, Branson and his senior executives and advisers did, in effect, form a team which guided strategy, new business development, and overall financial control.

A key aspect of this informal integration and control was the Virgin culture. This was defined almost entirely by Branson's own values and management style. It reflected his eccentricity, sense of fun, disrespect for hierarchy and formal authority, commitment to employees and consumers, and belief in hard work and individual responsibility. The group provided an environment in which talented, ambitious people were motivated to do their best and strive for a higher level of performance. While the working environment was informal, anti-corporate, and defined by the pop culture of its era, expectations were high. Branson expected a high level of commitment, the acceptance of personal responsibility, and long hours of work when needed. Financial rewards for most employees were typically modest, but fringe benefits include social activities, company-sponsored weekend getaways, and impromptu parties.

Although seemingly chaotic, with an absence of formal structure and control systems, the business acumen of the Virgin group should not be underestimated – British Airways made that error. The Virgin group possessed considerable financial and managerial talent, and what Virgin lacked in formal structure was made up for by a strong culture and close personal ties. The Virgin organizational structure was virtually flat, offering short lines of communication and flexible response capability. Employees were given a great deal of responsibility and freedom in order to stimulate idea generation, initiative, commitment, and fun. The lack of a corporate headquarters and the small size of most of the Virgin operating companies was intended to foster teamwork and a strong entrepreneurial spirit.

BRANSON'S CHARACTER AND BUSINESS PHILOSOPHY

As the creator of Virgin and its unique corporate culture, and the primary promoter of its image and entrepreneurial spirit, Richard Branson was synonymous with Virgin. Robert Dick referred to Virgin as a "counter-cultural enterprise" and to Branson as a "hippie entrepreneur." To many of his generation he embodied the spirit of "New Britain." In a country where business leaders were members of "The Establishment" and upholders of the existing social structure, Branson was seen as a revolutionary. Despite a privileged family background (his father was a lawyer and Richard attended a private boarding school), Branson had the ability to transcend the social classes which traditionally divided British society and segmented consumer markets. As such, he was part of a movement in British culture and society that has sought to escape the Old Britain of fading empire, class antagonism, Victorian values, and stiff-upper-lip hypocrisy. In the recreation of British culture and society, Branson could be grouped with pop musicians such as the Beatles, new-age entrepreneurs such as Anita Roddick, politicians like Margaret Thatcher and Tony Blair, and radicals within the Royal Family such as Princess Diana.

His informality and disrespect for convention were central to his way of business. Branson's woolly sweaters, beard, windswept hair, and toothy grin were practically a trademark of the Virgin companies. His dislike of office buildings and the usual symbols of corporate success was reflected in the absence of a corporate head office and his willingness to do business from his family homes – the Manor in Oxfordshire, a Maida Vale houseboat, and later his Holland Park house.

His lack of a clear distinction between work and his social and family life is reflected in the fact that his cousins, aunts, childhood friends, and dinner-party acquaintances were all drawn into business relationships with him. Although his second wife showed no interest in his business activities, his former wife was involved in a hotel development project in which Branson was a partner. His approach to his business relationships was that work should be fun and his employees should gain both pleasure and sense of fulfillment from their role in creating enterprises. Branson has experienced few problems in paying quite modest salaries to the great majority of Virgin employees. According to Robert Dick:

> Much of the operating style was established not so much by design but the exigencies of the time when Virgin was getting started. It has proved to be a successful model that Branson can replicate. His philosophy is to immerse himself in a new venture until he understands the ins and outs of the business, and then hand it over to a good managing director and financial controller, who are given a stake in it, and are then expected to make the company take off. He knows that expansion through the creation of additional discrete legal entities not only protects the Virgin group, but also gives people a sense of involvement and loyalty, particularly if he trusts them with full authority and offers minority share holdings to the managers of subsidiaries. He is proud of the fact that Virgin has produced a considerable number of millionaires. He has said that he does not want his best people to leave the company to start a venture outside. He prefers to make millionaires within.

His use of joint ventures was an extension of this model reinforced by his dealings with the Japanese. Branson was impressed by the Japanese approach to business, admiring their commitment to the long term and the way they took time to build a business through organic growth rather than acquisition. (Branson's only major acquisition was his rail service company. Prior to that Branson had been proud of the fact that he had made only two significant acquisitions: Rushes Video, for 6 million pounds some years ago, and the forerunner to Virgin Express.) He saw similarities in the Japanese *keiretsu* system (multiple companies interlocking through managerial and equity linkages in a collaborative network) and the structure he created at Virgin, with around 200 mostly small companies, which combined "small is beautiful" with "strength through unity." He explained this and other business maxims that he believed to be necessary for success in a speech to the Institute of Directors in 1993. "Staff first, then customers and shareholders" should be the chairman's priority if the goal is better performance. "Shape the business around the people," "Build don't buy," "Be best, not biggest," "Pioneer, don't follow the leader," "Capture every fleeting idea," and "Drive for change" were other guiding principles in the Branson philosophy.

Branson's values of innocence, innovation, and irreverence for authority were apparent in his choice of new ventures. He drew heavily on the ideas of others within his organization and was prepared to invest in new start-ups even in markets that were dominated by long-established incumbents. His business ventures, just like his sporting exploits, reflected a "just live life" attitude and a "bigger the challenge, greater the fun" belief. In identifying opportunity he was particularly keen to iden- tify markets where the conservatism and lack of imagination of incumbent firms meant that they were failing to create value for customers. Branson entered markets with a "new" and "anti-establishment attitude" that sought to offer customers a better alternative. An example of this was Virgin's entry into financial services. Into a business that was long regarded as conservative and stuffy, Branson hoped to bring "a breath of fresh air."

At the same time, the affection of the British public towards Branson reflected the fact that Branson was a traditionalist as well as a radical. Branson's values and his sense of fair-play were consistent with many traditional values that defined the British character. His competitive battles against huge corporations like British Airways and Coca Cola link well with the English heroes who have battled against tyranny and evil: King Arthur, Robin Hood, and St. George. His fights against British Airways' dirty-tricks campaign, and his resisting unethical practices in competing for the franchise to run the National Lottery, resonate well with the British sense of fair play. Even his willingness to appear in outlandish attire reflected a British propen- sity for ludicrous dressing-up whether at fancy-dress parties, morris dancing, or the House of Lords.

MARKETING

The Virgin brand was the group's greatest single asset. What the brand name com- municated and how it enhanced the products to which it was applied was complex. It had connotations of value for money, but also linked with concepts of style and broader social values, too. Most importantly, the brand was not associated with any specific products or markets – it allowed Virgin to cross product and market bound- aries more easily than almost any other brand name. While Marks & Spencer was successful in extending its St. Michael brand from clothing to food, Ralph Lauren extended his brand from clothing to cosmetics, toiletries, and accessories, and Harley-Davidson applied its brand to clothing, toiletries, cigarettes, and cafes, no company had extended its brand to so diverse a range of products and services as airlines, railroads, cosmetics, financial services, music, and soft drinks.

Much of the brand value could be attributed to Richard Branson and his persona and style. The values and characteristics that the Virgin brand communicated are inseparable from Richard Branson the entrepreneur, joker, fair-playing Brit, and challenger of giants. The differentiation that the Virgin brand offered was linked to the innovation and offbeat marketing approach that characterized the different Virgin start-ups. A key aspect of Branson's business enterprises was the difference in competitive approach between Virgin and the established market leaders in the sectors where it competed. Thus the difference between Virgin Atlantic and BA, between Virgin Cola and Coke, and between Virgin Direct and the leading banks was not just the characteristics of the product offered, it was also about the companies and how they related to their customers. As Virgin moved increasingly into international markets, the ability of the Virgin brand to attract consumers was less obvious. If the appeal of Virgin was the humor, style, fun, and irreverence that Richard Branson epitomized, Virgin had to consider how well this image could cross the boundaries of national culture. Although Branson was well known in Europe and North America, in many respects he was a quintessentially British character who was a product of time and place.

With the rapid diversification of the 1990s, and the significant number of start-ups that had achieved neither profitability nor significant market penetration, the group was considering the extent to which the Virgin brand had become overextended. Critics suggested that Virgin's brand stretching had damaged the goodwill associated with the Virgin name and compromised the core values it was founded on. Although still popular, Branson, too, might be waning in market appeal. Was there a risk that, having seen Branson as flight attendant, Branson in a wedding dress, Branson with successive prime ministers, and Branson attempting to fly around the world in a hot-air balloon, the public was beginning to tire of his exploits? A report by *Marketing News* noted:

> Virgin is curbing its expansion into packaged goods to redirect investment towards its "core" activities, including its troubled rail business. The move comes close to an admission that the group has bitten off more than it can chew.
>
> Virgin corporate affairs director Will Whitehorn says: "We don't plan to extend the brand much further." Observers see the Virgin strategy shift as an admission that some brand extensions, such as its forays into cola and vodka, have not been as successful as it hoped, and that others, such as its massive commitment to railways, are eating up both capital and senior management time. "We are not going to see a Virgin motorbike or Virgin motor car," says Whitehorn. "And I don't think you will see many more consumer goods products in the next few years. The cosmetics and clothing companies are going to be our last big moves in fmcg." [Fast-Moving Consumer Goods]
>
> Its clothes brand is scheduled to be launched in the autumn, having been previously delayed. But the group has flouted conventional marketing wisdom over the past 15 years by extending its brand over a host of businesses from airlines to cola, to PEPs and trains.
>
> Virgin has identified a number of "core businesses" where it wants to see growth: Virgin Atlantic; Virgin Express (Virgin's low-cost European airline); its cinema business through expansion in the US; its Virgin Megastores, especially in South America; and its rail business.
>
> "We are going to consolidate around these core areas," says Whitehorn, "because we have a lot to do with them." But in an apparent contradictory move, Whitehorn also says Virgin will "look at telecoms" in relation to entertainment, retailing and media opportunities.[23]

Applying the Virgin name to rail services was criticized by a number of marketing experts. The Virgin name had traditionally been identified with dynamic start-up business, not the renaming of a former public sector monopoly.

LOOKING AHEAD

As the world economy continues to deteriorate during 1998, several of Branson's inner circle of key executives see the need for changes within the Virgin group. The most immediate threats are on the financial front, where the investment needs of the capital-intensive businesses such as rail services and airlines, and losses in several start-up businesses, impose heavy cash flow needs. Virgin went through a cash crunch in the last recession, and Branson is anxious not to relive the experience. The financial foundations of the group could be improved in several ways. One would be to launch more of the Virgin companies on to the stock market. Virgin Travel (the parent of Virgin Atlantic) appears the obvious choice. However, current stock market conditions are unfavorable and, in any event, Branson does not relish the obligations and limitations of becoming the chairman of a publicly listed company.

There are also fundamental strategic questions about the Virgin group. What kind of enterprise is Virgin? Is it a brand management and franchising company, an incubator of start-up businesses, a vehicle for Richard Branson's personal ambitions, or a novel form of conglomerate? Is Virgin one business or a loose federation of many, independent businesses?

Whatever the identity and rationale of the Virgin group, it is not apparent that the existing structure or organization fits any of these categories. If Virgin is a brand-franchising organization, then the critical role for the Virgin group is to develop and protect the brand and maximize the licensing revenues from its use by other companies. Clearly Branson would need to play a role in promoting the brand, but it is not necessary that he should have any strategic, operating, or ownership role in the companies using the brand.

If Virgin is to be an incubator of new start-ups, then there needs to be a more systematic approach to evaluating new business opportunities and monitoring their progress and development.

If Virgin is a conglomerate, then does this imply a stronger corporate role? What kind of strategic planning and financial control are needed to ensure that value is not being dissipated? And can Virgin really perform across so wide a range of businesses?

Whichever path Virgin follows, it appears that some changes would be needed in organization in terms of managing inter-company linkages. Although Branson liked to maintain that the different companies were independent and "stood on their own two feet," the reality was somewhat different. Some companies were big-time cash generators, others were heavy loss makers. At present, financial relationships between the companies were ad hoc, and Branson was proud of the fact that no consolidated financial statements were prepared, even for internal management purposes. Also, to the extent that the brand was a common resource, how could it be best protected? The potential for bad management in one operating company (say, Virgin Rail or Virgin Clothing) to inflict serious damage on the Virgin brand was a serious issue.

Although Virgin had continued to spawn new businesses at a frantic rate, some moves towards greater business focus appeared to be gaining ground within Virgin.

According to Corporate Affairs Director Will Whitehorn, Virgin was focusing increasingly around select "core businesses" in which it wanted to see a great deal of growth – in particular, airlines, cinemas and retailing, and the new railway business. Consolidation was apparent in the merging of the retailing and cinemas businesses into the Virgin Entertainment Group. In addition, the desire to establish better control over the Virgin brand had encouraged the buying-out of several joint venture partners.

As always, the future of the Virgin group could not be considered without taking account of Branson himself. What kind of role did he anticipate now that he was approaching his half-century? If Branson was to become less active as chief entrepreneur, public relations director, and strategic architect for the Virgin companies, who or what would take his place?

NOTES

1. *Washington Post*, March 26, 1998.
2. "Behind Branson," *Economist*, February 21, 1998, pp. 63–6.
3. Michael Harrison, "Is Branson's honeymoon finally over?" *The Independent*, London, February 21, 1998, p. 3.
4. Richard Branson, letter to the *Economist*.
5. It is well known that Branson is one of Britain's richest individuals, with a net worth exceeding $1 billion. Branson also spent a night in Dover police cells when arrested for excise duty offenses after he sold through his Virgin store a batch of Virgin records intended for export to Belgium. The case was settled out of court.
6. Robert Dick, "Branson's Virgin: the coming of age of a counter-cultural enterprise," Insead, Fontainbleau, 1995.
7. *Worldpaper*, April 1997.
8. *Forbes*, February 24, 1997.
9. *Journal of Commerce*, January 26, 1998.
10. *Forbes*, February 24, 1997.
11. "Can he keep it up?" *Sunday Telegraph*, January 11, 1998, p. 33.
12. James Doran, "Branson plans 135m buyback of Virgin stores," *Scotland on Sunday*, March 22, 1998, p. 1.
13. "The future for Virgin," *Financial Times*, August 13, 1998, pp. 24–5.
14. Adam Sandler, "Branson rallies behind artists' rights," *Daily Variety*, March 16, 1998, p. 5.
15. Peter Robison, "Briton hopes beverage will conquer Coke's monopoly" *Bloomberg News*, December 14, 1997.
16. Roland Gribben, "Branson hits back at cash crisis claims, Virgin entrepreneur denies that rail arm leaves business empire barely profitable," *The Daily Telegraph*, February 21, 1998, p. 27.
17. "Virgin fans the cola war flames – again," *Financial Times*, February 19, 1998, p. 22.
18. http://www.virgin.com
19. "The Future for Virgin," *Financial Times*, August 13, 1998, pp. 24–5.
20. Ibid.
21. Ibid.
22. Chris Blackhurst, "At the court of King Richard," *Management Today*, May 1998, pp. 40–5.
23. Alan Mitchell, "Virgin in fmcg U-turn," *Marketing News*, April 17, 1997.

CHAPTER FOURTEEN

IMASCO LIMITED: THE ROY ROGERS ACQUISITION

Kent E. Neupert prepared this case under the supervision of Professor Joseph N. Fry solely to provide material for class discussion. The authors do not intend to illustrate either effective or ineffective handling of a managerial situation. The authors may have disguised certain names and other identifying information to protect confidentiality.

In January 1990, Purdy Crawford, the chairman, president and CEO of Imasco Limited, was reviewing an acquisition proposal from one of Imasco's operating companies, Hardee's Food Systems, Inc. (Hardee's) to purchase the Roy Rogers restaurant chain. Bill Prather, Hardee's CEO, was coming to Montreal the following day to present the proposal to the Imasco board. Prather thought the acquisition would permit Hardee's to expand rapidly into markets where they had very little presence. While Crawford was inclined to support Prather's proposal, he wanted to carefully weigh its broader impact for Imasco as a whole. The probable price of more than $390 million represented a substantial commitment of funds, at a time when growth in the U.S. fast food business was slowing.

IMASCO BACKGROUND

Imasco was a diversified Canadian public corporation with consolidated revenues of $5.7 billion in 1989 and net profits of $366 million.[1] Imasco's founding and largest

TABLE 14.1
Imasco operating highlights ($ million unless otherwise noted)

	1989	1988	1987	1986	1985
System-wide sales	14,715.6	13,836.5	12,951.5	11,132.2	8,371.8
Revenues	5,724.7	6,000.6	5,924.4	5,596.6	5,110.2
Operating earnings	692.0	636.7	578.4	455.6	464.1
Total assets	5,378.0	5,310.2	5,656.6	5,505.5	2,905.7
Earnings before extraordinary items	366.1	314.3	282.7	226.4	261.6
EPS before extraordinary items ($)	2.87	2.51	2.24	1.92	2.40
DVDS/share ($)	1.12	1.04	0.96	0.84	0.72

shareholder was B.A.T Industries (B.A.T), which had maintained a relatively constant 40% equity ownership over the years. B.A.T was a very large diversified British company with roots, like Imasco, in the tobacco business. The balance of Imasco shares were widely held.

In 1990, Imasco's operations were focused on four major operating companies, "the four legs of the table," as Crawford referred to them. The companies were: Imperial Tobacco, Canada's largest manufacturer and distributor of cigarettes; CT Financial, the holding company for Canada Trust, a major Canadian retail financial services business; Imasco Drug Retailing Group, made up of Shoppers Drug Mart in Canada and Peoples Drug Stores in the U.S.; and Hardee's Food Systems, Inc. in the U.S. A fifth, smaller company was The UCS Group, Canada's leading small space specialty retailer. Highlights of Imasco's operations for the years 1985–89 are shown in Table 14.1.

IMASCO DIVERSIFICATION ACTIVITIES

Imasco Limited was created in 1969 as a corporate entity to encompass and oversee the tobacco, food and distribution businesses of Imperial Tobacco Limited, and to manage a program of further diversification. The aim was to build a broadly based corporation that would rely less on the tobacco business and be better received in the stock market.

Paul Paré was the first president, chairman and CEO of Imasco, and the person with prime responsibility for its diversification program up to his retirement from the chairmanship in 1987. Paré's 38-year career began in the legal department of Imperial Tobacco and led to senior positions in the marketing areas. He became President and CEO in 1969 and Chairman in 1979. Except for a two-year stint with the Department of National Defence, his career was always in the tobacco industry. Paré's approach to diversification in the early years had been a conservative one. He preferred to make a number of relatively small investments, and build or divest the positions as experience dictated.

Crawford, Paré's successor, pictured the first ten years of diversification as a process of experimentation and learning. He described the evolution of thought and action: "Imperial's first attempt at diversification had been through vertical integration." Crawford explained: "Although it appeared logical that if Imperial bought a tinfoil company and made foil wrap themselves there were economies to be realized, we quickly learned that making cigarettes and making tinfoil are two different things." Imperial knew little about the highly specialized tinfoil business, and also discovered that "the competition didn't like the idea of buying tinfoil from us."

Upon reflection, management determined that they were "in the business of converting and marketing agricultural products." Crawford recounted: "It made sense then that the next acquisition was a winery. Unfortunately, we failed to take into consideration provincial liquor regulations which made it impossible to operate at a sufficient scale to be profitable."

Management then broadened its perspective and decided that they were best at marketing. This led to acquisitions that "embodied exciting new marketing concepts," such as two sporting goods companies, Collegiate and Arlington, and a discount bottler and retailer of soft drinks called POP Shoppes. These investments were held for several years, but they failed to live up to their promise and were subsequently sold off. Other acquisitions, in food processing and distribution, for example, were quite successful, but not on a scale of importance to Imasco. These were later divested when Imasco refocused its efforts.

For the most part, these early diversification moves involved the acquisition of several small companies, and subsequent restructuring of them into a larger enterprise. Most of these acquisitions were then later divested. For example, Imasco's three food companies, which were sold in the late 1970s and early 1980s, were originally ten different companies. Amco Vending, sold in 1977, was built up from eight separate vending companies across Canada. Other businesses which were grown and later sold included wines, drycleaning, and video tape services.

With time, Paré's team built an understanding of its capabilities, sharpened its sense of mission, and focused its acquisition criteria. The mission was to "create shareholder value as a leading North American consumer products and services company." Based on their learning, the criteria for acquisitions were formalized. Imasco would acquire companies that (1) were well positioned in the consumer goods and services sector of the economy; (2) had a capable management team in place, or were able to be smoothly integrated into an existing operating division; (3) had above average growth potential, and were capable of making a meaningful and immediate contribution to profits; and (4) were North American based, preferably in Canada. Crawford noted that "perhaps the most important end result of approximately ten years of experimentation was that we developed a clear vision of what the company was and was not."

As Imasco became more focused and confident of its skills, the acquisitions became less frequent and larger in size, and the diversification from tobacco more significant. Imasco's acquisitions and net investments are given in Exhibit 14.1. The

EXHIBIT 14.1:

Imasco acquisitions: distinguishable eras in acquisition size, with acquisition cost (if available)

Acquisition	Acquisition price (company location)
1963–77	
Canada Foils	not available
Growers Wine	not available
Simtel and Editel	not available
S&W Foods	$18.4 million (Canadian)
Uddo & Taormina (Progresso)	$32.5 million (Canadian)
Pasquale Brothers (Unico)	$4 million (Canadian)
Grissol	$12.2 million (Canadian)
Collegiate	$1.4 million (Canadian)
Arlington Sports	not available
Top Drug Mart and Top Value Discount	not available
Tinderbox	$1.4 million (US)
POP Shoppes investment	$10.5 million (Canadian)
Canada Northwest Land Ltd. investment	not available
Hardee's Food Systems investment—Includes Imperial Tobacco Limited acquisitions	$15 million (US)
1978–86	
Shoppers Drug Mart (Koffler's)	$66.6 million (Canadian)
Further Hardee's investment	$15 million (Canadian)
Hardee's totally acquired	$76 million (US)
Burger Chef	$44 million (US)
Peoples Drug Stores	$398 million (Canadian)
Rea & Derick Drug Stores	$114 million (Canadian)
Genstar	$2.4 billion (Canadian)

most significant events of the 1980s are described below in the review of the present-day Imasco operating companies. The net result of 20 years of diversification was that Imasco increased its revenues tenfold and its earnings twentyfold. Moreover, its reliance on tobacco for corporate earnings went from 100% in 1970 to 48% in 1989. A twenty year review of Imasco performance is given in Exhibit 14.2.

Corporate Management

While Imasco's diversification policy was directed from the central office, its operations were not centralized. The corporate management structure was decentralized

EXHIBIT 14.2:
20-year financials: Imasco Ltd. and tobacco business ($ million unless noted)

Year	Imasco Ltd.				Tobacco Business			Imasco Ltd.		
	Total revenues	Operating earnings	Net earnings before extraordinary items	Earnings per common share ($)[d,e]	Tobacco operating earnings/total operating earnings (%)	Tobacco revenue	Tobacco operating earnings	Stock price high ($)[f]	Stock price low ($)[f]	Annual dividend[e] per common share ($)
1970[a]	582.2	37.3	15.7	0.20	88	435.2	32.7	16.13	12.00	0.10
1971[a]	569.6	40.6	17.7	0.22	88	418.0	35.9	20.50	15.25	0.125
1972[a]	625.6	48.1	22.2	0.28	84	430.4	40.4	28.38	19.00	0.1375
1973[a]	717.1	56.0	28.0	0.36	81	446.9	45.4	34.75	25.75	0.15
1975[c]	1,030.3	78.5	36.8	0.47	79	610.5	62.0	33.25	18.75	0.19375
1976[b]	941.2	74.9	36.5	0.47	81	560.1	60.7	32.00	26.00	0.1625
1977[b]	1,031.6	74.7	34.9	0.45	81	605.4	60.9	27.25	20.63	0.169
1978[b]	1,049.4	84.2	43.1	0.55	81	655.0	68.3	31.63	24.00	0.18
1979[b]	1,161.5	114.8	56.4	0.70	69	741.4	78.8	40.75	29.75	0.205
1980[b]	1,150.5	132.1	68.2	0.83	75	826.7	99.1	47.25	38.25	0.25
1981[b]	1,423.7	168.8	89.6	1.07	73	952.9	123.2	38.25	21.25	0.30
1982[b]	2,190.7	247.0	124.2	1.39	63	1,120.2	156.0	44.50	29.50	0.35
1983[b]	2,713.9	300.3	156.8	1.73	61	1,242.9	182.3	37.50	18.00	0.40
1984[b]	2,873.2	339.6	194.2	2.03	60	1,358.9	205.2	36.25	29.88	0.50
1985[b]	4,353.2	432.0	234.1	2.25	52	1,451.1	224.0	28.25	17.38	0.645
1986[b]	5,325.1	465.9	261.7	2.40	53	1,769.8	246.0	35.00	22.63	0.75
1987[a]	5,924.4	578.4	282.7	2.24	48	1,926.0	279.1	46.00	24.25	0.96
1988[a]	6,000.6	636.7	314.3	2.51	48	2,018.1	308.0	29.50	23.75	1.04
1989[a]	5,724.7	692.0	366.1	2.87	48	2,385.6	334.0	40.50	27.63	1.12

[a] January–December fiscal year.
[b] April–March fiscal year.
[c] Reflects 15-month period from January 1974 to March 1975.
[d] Before extraordinary items.
[e] Prior to 1980, adjusted to reflect three stock splits; after 1980, 2 for 1 stock splits July 1980, November 1982, and March 1985.
[f] Not adjusted for stock splits.

Source: Imasco Limited.

and rather flat. Only 50 people staffed the head office in Montreal. The various companies, with operations across Canada and most of the U.S., were encouraged to aggressively pursue the development of their businesses and related trademarks. Management believed that "combining the experience and expertise that flow from the individual operating companies creates a unique opportunity to add value to all of its [Imasco's] operations and assets." Accordingly, Imasco saw its greatest strengths as the high degree of autonomy, and clear lines of authority and responsibility, which existed between Imasco's head office (the Imasco Centre) and the operating companies. While each company's CEO operated with the widest possible autonomy, they also contributed to the development of the annual and five-year plans, and "to furthering Imasco's overall growth objectives." The role of the Imasco Centre was to guide Imasco's overall growth without interfering with the operating companies. The 1988 business plan stipulated that "the role of the Imasco Centre is to be a source of excellence in management dedicated to achieving overall corporate objectives, and supporting Imasco's operating companies in the fulfilment of their respective missions and objectives."

It was very important to Imasco that any acquisition be friendly. While it was not formally stipulated in the acquisition criteria, it was evident in Imasco's actions, such as the aborted acquisition of Canadian Tire in 1983.

In June of that year, Imasco initiated an attempted acquisition of Canadian Tire, but later withdrew the offer. Imasco had outlined a proposal to the members of the Billes family, majority shareholders in Canadian Tire, and the management of Canadian Tire in which Imasco would purchase as many of Canadian Tire's outstanding common and Class "A" shares as would be tendered. Imasco stipulated the offer was conditional on family and management support. Imasco expected the cost of the acquisition to be about $1.13 billion.

Several days later, Paré issued a press release in which he stated:

> We at Imasco are obviously disappointed with the reaction of the senior management group at Canadian Tire to purchase all of the outstanding shares of the company. We stated at the outset that we were seeking both the support of the major voting shareholders and the endorsement of management. It now appears that such support and endorsement are not forthcoming. In light of this and in view of the announcement made . . . by the trustees of the John W. Billes estate, we have concluded that one or more of the conditions to our offer will not be satisfied. Therefore, we do not propose to proceed with our previously announced offer.

In explaining Imasco's rationale for withdrawing the offer, Paré continued:

> Throughout the negotiations, we have been keenly aware of the essential ingredients that have made Canadian Tire one of the retail success stories in Canada. These ingredients include the able leadership of the management group, the unique relationship between management and the associate-dealers, and the employee profit-sharing and share-ownership plans. As we have mentioned on several occasions, it was our intention to preserve these relationships and the formulas that have so obviously contributed to the success of the Canadian Tire organization.

TABLE 14.2
Imperial Tobacco operating summary ($ million unless otherwise noted)

	1989	1988	1987	1986	1985
Revenues	2,385.6	2,018.1	1,926.0	1,754.6	1,701.8
Revenues, net of sales and excise taxes	896.2	862.0	816.2	712.0	757.5
Operating earnings	334.0	308.0	279.1	208.1	243.7
Operating margins (%)	37.3	35.7	34.2	29.2	32.2
Market share–domestic (%)	57.9	56.2	54.4	51.5	52.6
Capital employed[a]	558.1	496.4	513.9	594.6[b]	587.0[b]

[a] Capital employed of each consolidated segment consists of directly identifiable assets at net book value, less current liabilities, excluding income taxes payable and bank and other debt. Corporate assets and corporate current liabilities are also excluded.
[b] Reflects fiscal year ending March 31.

OPERATING COMPANIES

Imperial Tobacco

Imperial Tobacco was the largest tobacco enterprise in Canada, with operations ranging from leaf tobacco buying and processing, to the manufacture and distribution of a broad range of tobacco products. The manufacture and sale of cigarettes constituted the largest segment of its business, representing 89.4% of Imperial Tobacco's revenues in 1989. Highlights of Imperial Tobacco's operations for the years 1985–89 are shown in Table 14.2.

Over the years, Imperial had concentrated on building its market share in Canada from a low of 36% in 1970 to 57.9% in 1989. Revenues in 1989 reached an all time high of almost $2.4 billion, in spite of a 4% decline in unit sales to 27.5 billion cigarettes. The market share gains had been achieved by focusing on the strength of Imperial Tobacco's trademarks, particularly the continued growth of its two leading Canadian brands, Player's and du Maurier. Together these two brands held 47.4% of the market in 1989.

Imperial Tobacco had production and packaging facilities in Montreal and Joliette, Quebec, and Guelph, Ontario, and leaf processing facilities in Joliette and LaSalle, Quebec, and Aylmer, Ontario. Imperial continually modernized its production facilities to the point that management claimed them to be "the most technologically advanced in the tobacco industry in Canada." The distribution and promotion of Imperial Tobacco's products to wholesalers and retailers was carried out through a nationwide sales staff operating out of the sales offices and distribution centers in St. Johns, Moncton, Montreal, Toronto, Winnipeg, Calgary and Vancouver.

TABLE 14.3
Investments in Imasco Enterprises, Inc. ($ million)

	1989	1988	1987[a]
Equity in net earnings of Imasco Enterprises	152.5	142.1	126.5
Investment in Imasco Enterprises	2,700.2	2,655.4	2,613.5

[a] Financial information is shown beginning with 1987 to reflect the acquisition of Canada Trust in 1986.

Imasco Enterprises (Including Canada Trust)

Imasco Enterprises, Inc. (IEI) was wholly owned through Imasco Limited and three of its other companies, making it an indirect wholly owned subsidiary. In 1986, Imasco announced its intention to acquire all of the outstanding common shares of Genstar Corporation (Genstar) through IEI. At the time, Imasco's primary objective was to gain entry into the financial services sector by assuming Genstar's 98% ownership position in Canada Trust. Genstar had purchased Canada Trust in 1985 for $1.2 billion dollars and merged it with Canada Permanent Mortgage Corporation, which Genstar had purchased in 1981. This merger created Canada's seventh largest financial institution with $50 billion in assets under administration.

Once acquired, Imasco intended to sell off all of Genstar's non-financial assets. Within the year, all of the shares were acquired at a cost of approximately $2.6 billion. This was the first acquisition orchestrated by Crawford.

In addition to Canada Trust, Genstar had holdings in an assortment of other businesses. Most of these, such as the cement and related operations, Genstar Container Corporation, and Seaspan International, were sold off. The cost of those assets retained, including Canada Trust, was about $2.4 billion, of which all but $150 million was attributed to the Canada Trust holding. The balance of the amount was accounted for by a variety of assets which included Genstar Development Company, Genstar Mortgage Corporation, a one-third limited partnership in Sutter Hill Ventures, a portfolio of other venture capital investments, and certain other assets and liabilities. Genstar Development Company was involved in land development in primary Canadian metropolitan areas, such as Vancouver, Calgary, Edmonton, Winnipeg, Toronto and Ottawa. U.S.-based Sutter Hill Ventures had capital investments in over 43 different companies. Most of these investments were in the areas of medical research, biotechnology, communications and computer hardware and software. Highlights of investments in IEI are shown in Table 14.3.

CT Financial was the holding company for the Canada Trust group of companies. In 1989, Canada Trust was Canada's second largest trust and loan company, and a major residential real estate broker. The principal businesses of Canada Trust were financial intermediary services, such as deposit services, credit card services,

TABLE 14.4
Operating performance data for CT Financial ($ million unless otherwise noted)

	1989	1988	1987[a]
Assets under administration	74,096.0	67,401.0	60,626.0
Corporate assets	32,666.0	29,219.2	25,514.8
Deposits	30,403.0	27,319.5	23,859.0
Loans	24,201.1	22,661.7	19,679.3
Net earnings attributed to common shares	240.2	232.0	201.0
Return on common shareholders' average equity (%)	17.3	19.0	19.4

[a] Financial information is shown beginning with 1987 to reflect the acquisition of Canada Trust in 1986.

mortgage lending, consumer lending, corporate and commercial lending, and investments. It also offered trust services, real estate services and real estate development. Canada Trust operated 331 financial services branches, 22 personal and pension trust services offices, and 275 company operated and franchised real estate offices. Total assets under the administration of Canada Trust at the end of 1989 were $74.1 billion, comprised of $32.7 billion in corporate assets, and $41.4 billion in assets administered for estate, trust and agency accounts. Total personal deposits were estimated to be the fourth largest among Canadian financial institutions. The return of common shareholders' average equity was 17.3% compared with an average of 7.7% for Canada's six largest banks. Highlights of CT Financial operations are shown in Table 14.4.

Imasco Drug Retailing

Shoppers Drug Mart
Shoppers Drug Mart provided a wide range of marketing and management services to a group of 633 associated retail drug stores located throughout Canada, operating under the trademarks Shoppers Drug Mart (585 stores), and Pharmaprix in Quebec (48 stores). The Shoppers Drug Mart stores also included the extended concepts of Shoppers Drug Mart Food Baskets and Shoppers Drug Mart Home Health Care Centres.

In 1989, Shoppers Drug Mart was the largest drug store group in Canada with about 33% of the retail drug store market. In system-wide sales, it ranked first and fifth among all drug store groups in Canada and North America, respectively. In the past, competition had come primarily from regional chains and independent drug stores, but food stores with drug departments represented a growing challenge. During 1989, management had emphasized strengthening the productivity and

TABLE 14.5
Shoppers Drug Mart operating summary ($ million unless otherwise noted)

	1989	1988	1987	1986	1985
System-wide sales	2,597.7	2,355.6	2,073.4	1,775.0	1,522.3
Revenues	136.2	114.9	95.7	86.6	73.4
Operating earnings	70.6	57.1	51.3	48.9	42.5
Operating margins (%)	51.8	49.7	53.6	56.5	57.9
Average sales per store	4.1	4.2	4.1	3.9	3.6
Number of stores	633	613	586	543	431
Capital expenditures	24.0	28.0	27.6	23.3	16.4
Capital employed[a]	204.1	209.8	194.2	117.9	106.8[b]
Depreciation	26.6	20.6	17.9	13.0	11.8

[a] Capital employed of each consolidated segment consists of directly identifiable assets at net book value, less current liabilities, excluding income taxes payable and bank and other debt. Corporate assets and corporate current liabilities are also excluded.
[b] Reflects fiscal year ending March 31.

profitability of existing stores, particularly the former Super X Drugs and Howie's stores, recently converted to Shoppers Drug Mart stores.

The Shoppers Drug Mart operating division utilized licensing and franchise agreements. Under the licensing arrangement, each Shoppers Drug Mart was owned and operated by a licensed pharmacist, called an Associate. In Quebec, Pharmaprix stores used a franchise system. In return for an annual fee, each Associate of a Shoppers Drug Mart store and Franchisee of a Pharmaprix store had access to a variety of services, such as store design, merchandising techniques, financial analysis, training, advertising and marketing. Highlights of Shoppers Drug Mart operations are shown in Table 14.5.

Peoples Drug Stores

Peoples Drug Stores, Incorporated (Peoples) operated 490 company owned drug stores in the U.S. during 1989. The stores were primarily operated from leased premises under the trade names Peoples Drug Stores, Health Mart, and Rea and Derick. Imasco had built the Peoples operating division from several acquired drug store chains in six eastern U.S. states and the District of Columbia.

After a disappointing performance in 1986, Peoples began a comprehensive plan to revitalize the chain and focus on areas of market strength. Earnings steadily improved, with operating earnings of $8.0 million in 1989, compared with operating losses of $8.3 million in 1988 and $22.5 million in 1987. The turnaround involved restructuring, including the divestment of Peoples' Reed, Lane, Midwest, Bud's Deep Discount, and other smaller divisions. During 1989, a total of 326 drug stores were sold, 21 were closed, and 13 opened for a net decrease of 334 stores. At

TABLE 14.6
Peoples Drug Stores operating summary ($ million unless otherwise noted)

	1989	1988	1987	1986	1985
Revenues	1,207.2	1,841.6	1,850.2	1,922.5	1,737.3
Operating earnings	8.0	(8.3)	(22.5)	0.1	52.5
Operating margins (%)	0.7	(0.5)	(1.2)	—	3.0
Average sales per store (US$ million)	2.1	1.8	1.7	1.7	1.5
Number of stores	490	829	819	830	824
Capital expenditures	12.4	41.9	29.1	32.7	58.5
Capital employed[a]	369.4	523.5	703.6	819.5[b]	653.5[b]

[a] Capital employed of each consolidated segment consists of directly identifiable assets at net book value, less current liabilities, excluding income taxes payable and bank and other debt. Corporate assets and corporate current liabilities are also excluded.
[b] Reflects fiscal year ending March 31.

the beginning of 1990, only five Bud's stores remained to be sold. The result was a concentration on Peoples' strongest markets, primarily the District of Columbia, Maryland, Virginia, West Virginia and Pennsylvania. The highlights of Peoples operations are shown in Table 14.6.

The UCS Group

In 1989, The UCS Group operated 531 stores in Canada from leased premises. The stores carried a wide variety of everyday convenience items, including newspapers and magazines, cigarettes and smokers accessories, confectionery, snack foods, gifts and souvenir selections. The retail outlets were all company-operated, and included UCS newsstands in shopping centers, commercial office towers, airports, hotels, and other high consumer traffic locations. The UCS group operated 531 stores in five divisions: Woolco/Woolworth, Specialty Stores, Hotel/Airport, Den for Men/AuMasculin, and Tax and Duty Free. Highlights of The UCS Group operations are shown in Table 14.7.

Hardee's Food Systems

Imasco's move to make a major investment in a U.S.-based company arose in part from the greater opportunity offered by the U.S. economy for potential acquisitions of an interesting nature and scale, and in part from the constraints on Canadian acquisitions posed by the Foreign Investment Review Act (FIRA). The purpose of FIRA was to review certain forms of foreign investment in Canada, particularly controlling acquisitions of Canadian business enterprises, and diversifications of

TABLE 14.7
The UCS Group operating summary ($ million unless otherwise noted)

	1989	1988	1987	1986	1985
Revenues	286.1	256.6	235.3	206.0	187.8
Operating earnings	8.3	7.5	6.7	6.6	5.5
Operating margins (%)	2.9	2.9	2.9	3.2	2.9
Average sales per store ($000)	543	489	461	432	410
Average sales per sq.ft. ($)	790	718	675	651	629
Number of stores	531	525	524	494	460
Capital employed (est.)[a]	41.4	45.6	40.7	37.6[b]	57.2[b]

[a] Capital employed of each consolidated segment consists of directly identifiable assets at net book value, less current liabilities, excluding income taxes payable and bank and other debt. Corporate assets and corporate current liabilities are also excluded.

[b] Reflects fiscal year ending March 31.

existing foreign controlled firms into unrelated businesses. For several years, Imasco came under the control of FIRA due to B.A.T's 40% ownership of Imasco. In later years, however, Imasco was re-classified as a Canadian owned enterprise.

Imasco's involvement with Hardee's and the U.S. restaurant business developed slowly. Imasco first became acquainted with Hardee's in 1969 when its pension fund manager was on holiday in South Carolina. The manager and his family were so fond of the Hardee's hamburgers that upon returning to Montreal, he investigated Hardee's as a possible pension fund investment. The following year, Imasco made a relatively small investment in Hardee's.

Later, when Hardee's was looking for expansion capital, it approached Imasco. In March 1977, Imasco invested $18.2 million in convertible preferred shares which, if converted, would give Imasco a 25% position in Hardee's. Between March 1980 and January 1981, Imasco converted their preferred shares and purchased the outstanding common shares at a cost of $114.1 million. At this time, Hardee's was the seventh largest hamburger restaurant chain in the U.S. Later, Imasco made additional investments in Hardee's to facilitate growth and acquisition.

By 1989, Hardee's Food Systems, Inc. (Hardee's) was the third largest hamburger restaurant chain in the U.S., as measured by system-wide sales and average unit sales volume. In number of outlets, it ranked fourth. With its head office in Rocky Mount, North Carolina, Hardee's restaurant operations consisted of 3,298 restaurants, of which 1,086 were company-operated and 2,212 were licensed. Of these restaurants, 3,257 were located in 39 states and the District of Columbia in the U.S., and 41 were located in nine other countries in the Middle East, Central America, and Southeast Asia. Average annual unit sales for 1989 were $1,060,300, compared with $1,058,000 in 1988. Highlights of Hardee's operations are shown in Table 14.8.

TABLE 14.8
Hardee's operating summary ($ million unless otherwise noted)

	1989	1988	1987	1986	1985
System-wide sales	4,146.7	4,058.9[a]	4,059.1	3,721.6	3,248.4
Revenues	1,786.5	1,756.9	1,801.7	1,642.0	1,457.0
Operating earnings	118.6	130.3	137.3	129.0	117.1
Operating margins (%)	6.6	7.4	7.6	7.9	8.0
Average sales per restaurant (US$000)	922	920	877	837	801
Capital expenditures	155.3	209.9	217.0	135.6	99.9
Depreciation	78.9	78.0	75.5	63.0	53.4
Restaurants company owned	1,086	1,070	995	893	876
Restaurants franchised	2,212	2,081	1,962	1,818	1,662
Total restaurants	3,298	3,151	2,957	2,711	2,538
Capital employed[b]	618.3	587.7[a]	777.5	668.1[c]	555.4[c]

[a] Includes sale and leaseback of properties.

[b] Capital employed of each consolidated segment consists of directly identifiable assets at net book value, less current liabilities, excluding income taxes payable and bank and other debt. Corporate assets and corporate current liabilities are also excluded.

[c] Reflects fiscal year ending March 31.

Hardee's had encouraged multi-unit development by licensees. In some cases, Hardee's granted exclusive territorial development rights to licensees on the condition that minimum numbers of new licensed restaurants in the area be opened within specific periods of time. As of December 31, 1989, Hardee's had license agreements with 234 licensee groups operating 2,205 restaurants. The ten largest of these licensees operated 1,213 restaurants, representing 55% of the licensed restaurants in the chain, and the two largest operated 738 licensed restaurants, or approximately 33% of the licensed restaurants.

Hardee's restaurants were limited-menu, quick-service family restaurants, and featured moderately priced items for all meals. These products were principally hamburgers, roast beef, chicken, turkey club, ham and cheese and fish sandwiches, breakfast biscuits, frankfurters, french fries, salads, turnovers, cookies, ice cream, and assorted beverages for both take-out and on-premise consumption. Recent additions to the Hardee's menu included a grilled chicken sandwich, Crispy Curl fries, and pancakes. These new products followed a series of initiatives taken in 1988, which included being the first hamburger chain to switch to all vegetable cooking oil in order to lower fat and cholesterol levels in fried products. Hardee's also introduced more salads and more desserts to the menu.

Fast Food Merchandisers, Inc. (FFM) was an operating division of Hardee's that furnished restaurants with food and paper products through its food processing and distribution operations. All company-operated Hardee's restaurants purchased their food and paper products from FFM. Although licensees were not obligated to purchase from FFM, approximately 75% of Hardee's licensees purchased some or all of their requirements from FFM. FFM operated three food processing plants and eleven distribution centers. FFM also sold products to other food service and supermarket accounts.

THE PROPOSED ROY ROGERS ACQUISITION

The U.S. Food Service Industry

Over the past twenty years, Americans spent a rising portion of their food dollars at restaurants. More two-income families, fewer women as full-time homemakers and a decline in the number of children to feed made dining out increasingly popular. In 1989, U.S. consumers spent $167 billion at 400,000 restaurants.[2] This excluded an estimated $61 billion spent at other food and beverage outlets, such as employee cafeterias, hospitals, ice-cream stands and taverns. Although sales growth for the restaurant industry outpaced the economy in recent years, industry analysts noted indications of outlet saturation. In 1989, franchise restaurant chains expected to have U.S. sales of $70.4 billion, up 7.4% from the year before. However, on a per unit basis, 1989 sales for franchise chain units averaged $737,000, up only 4.3% from the previous year. Analysts pointed out that this rise corresponded to increases in menu prices.

Quick service or "fast food" restaurants had led industry growth for several decades, and were expected to do so over the near term. However, industry analysts cautioned that, as the average age of the American consumers increased, a shift away from fast food restaurants toward mid-scale restaurants might occur. Increased emphasis on take-out service and home delivery would help to maintain momentum, but analysts expected that fast food sales and new unit growth would not be up to the 6.6% compound annual rate from 1985 to 1989. McDonald's 8,000 U.S. outlets had sales of $12 billion, or about 7% of total U.S. restaurant spending. Chains that emphasized hamburgers, hot dogs, or roast beef were the largest part of the U.S. franchise restaurant industry, with 1989 sales of $33.8 billion from 36,206 outlets. McDonald's U.S. market share in the segment was about 36.1%, followed by Burger King (19.2%), Hardee's (9.9%), and Wendy's (8.5%).

Nature of Operations

The large hamburger chains generated revenues from three sources: (1) the operation of company owned restaurants; (2) franchising, which encompassed royalties and initial fees from licensees operating under the trade name; and (3) commissary, consisting of food processing and the distribution of food, restaurant supplies and equipment essential to the operation of the company and franchised outlets. Profitable operation of company-owned restaurant operations called for high unit sales volume and tight control of operating margins.

Franchising had been the major chains' initial growth strategy. This enabled them to increase revenues, establish a competitive position, and achieve the scale necessary for efficient commissary and marketing operations. In 1989, there were 90,000 franchise operations accounting for 40% of U.S. restaurant operations. In 1989, McDonald's operating profit from franchising ($1.2 billion) substantially exceeded its profit from company operated restaurants ($822 million).

It was often the case that in a franchising relationship, the cost of the land, building and equipment was the responsibility of the franchisee. The franchisee also paid a royalty, typically 3–6% of sales, and was charged 1–5% of sales for common advertising expenses. In return, the franchisee got brand name recognition, training and marketing support. However, some of the larger chains had taken an alternate approach by owning the land and the building. Not only did such an approach provide lease revenue but it also allowed the company to maintain some control over the franchisee's facilities.

Competition

Fast food restaurants competed with at-home eating, other restaurant types, and each other. To build and maintain unit volumes, top chains developed strategies to differentiate themselves by target market, style of operation, menu and promotional approach, among other methods.

McDonald's

McDonald's was the leader of the fast food restaurant business. The chain began in the early 1950s in California. The McDonald brothers discovered that a combination of assembly line procedures, product standardization and high volume made it possible to offer exceptional value, providing consistent quality food at a reasonable price. The potential of their concept was recognized by Ray Kroc, a paper cup and milkshake mixer salesman. He acquired the operations, and provided the leadership for the formation and subsequent growth of the McDonald's corporation.

McDonald's had traditionally targeted children, teens and young families, and focused its menu of products around hamburgers and french fries. Scale, experience and simplified operating procedures permitted McDonald's to operate at significantly lower costs than its competitors. In the late 1970s, the company broadened its target market to follow demographic shifts and increase unit volumes. The menu was expanded to include breakfast line and chicken items, and the hours of operation were increased. The emphasis on simplicity and efficiency was maintained, and the company continued its rigorous dedication to quality, service and cleanliness. This strategy was supported by the largest promotional budget in the industry. McDonald's typical arrangement with franchisees was that it owned the property, which the franchisee then leased. Highlights of McDonald's operations are shown in Table 14.9.

Burger King

Burger King had been a subsidiary of Pillsbury until December 1988, when Grand Metropolitan PLC acquired Pillsbury and its holdings, which included Burger King. Burger King's traditional target market had been the 25–39 age group, but it was

TABLE 14.9
McDonald's operating summary (US$ million unless otherwise noted)

	1989	1988	1987
Revenues	6,142.0	5,566.3	4,893.5
Depreciation	364.0	324.0	278.9
Operating income	1,459.0	1,283.7	1,161.9
Operating profit margin (%)	23.7	23.1	23.7
Interest expense	332.0	266.8	224.8
Pretax income	1,157.0	1,046.5	958.8
Net income	727.0	645.9	596.5
Net income margin (%)	11.8	11.6	12.2
Earnings per share (US$)	1.95	1.72	1.45
Dividend per share (US$)	0.30	0.27	0.24
Market price year end (US$)	34.50	24.06	22.00
Price/earnings ratio	17.7	14.0	15.2
Shareholders' equity	3,549.0	3,412.8	2,916.7
Total common shares outstanding (million)	362	375	378

Source: Worldscope 1990.

trying to improve its appeal to the family trade. The key element of Burger King's competitive strategy had been to offer more product choice than McDonald's. Burger King's food preparation system was centered around a hamburger that could be dressed to customer specifications, with onions, lettuce, tomato, etc. Burger King had had been the first hamburger chain to diversify significantly into additional hot sandwich items, but this had resulted in somewhat longer service times and higher food preparation costs.

In 1989, Burger King's profits were $48.2 million, down 49% from the previous two years. Its market share was 19.2%, down from 19.9% in 1987. Average unit sales in 1989 were $1.05 million. Burger King had had four different CEOs during the past ten years, and was having problems with its marketing program, changing advertising campaigns five times in two years. Additionally, Burger King had experienced problems with its franchisees prior to the acquisition by Grand Metropolitan, but these were beginning to subside with the ownership change.

Wendy's
Wendy's also targeted the young adult market. Like Burger King, it provided food prepared to specification, and had broadened its initial emphasis on hamburgers to cover a variety of items, including chili and a self-service buffet and salad bar. In 1989, Wendy's 3,490 restaurants' had average unit sales of $.79 million. This was an increase from $.76 million and $.74 million in 1988 and 1987, respectively. Highlights of Wendy's operations are shown in Table 14.10.

TABLE 14.10
Wendy's operating summary (US$ million unless otherwise noted)

	1989	1988	1987
Revenues	1,069.7	1,045.9	1,051.1
Depreciation	56.4	57.3	55.4
Operating income	51.3	44.0	0.1
Operating profit margin (%)	4.8	4.2	NIL
Interest expense	22.3	16.9	24.2
Pretax income	36.9	43.8	(12.8)
Net income	30.4	28.5	4.5
Net income margin (%)	2.8	2.7	0.4
Earnings per share (US$)	0.25	0.30	0.04
Dividend per share (US$)	0.24	0.24	0.24
Market price year end (US$)	4.63	5.75	5.63
Price/earnings ratio	18.5	19.2	140.6
Shareholder equity	428.9	419.6	412.2
Total common shares outstanding (million)	96	96	96

Source: Worldscope 1990.

Hardee's

Hardee's was the third largest hamburger-based fast food chain in the U.S., in terms of total sales and unit sales volume; and fourth in outlets. Approximately 30% of Hardee's sales were at breakfast, and it was a leader in the breakfast trade. The other major sales category was hamburgers, with 34% of sales.

The demographic profile of Hardee's customers was skewed slightly to males. Children and 25- to 34-year-olds were two groups that had been targeted for higher penetration. The introduction of ice cream in 1987 had spurred a 98% increase in visits by children under 13. Packaged salads and the broadening of menu selections were expected to help attract 25- to 34-year-olds.

Hardee's management was highly regarded in the food service industry for taking a very shaky firm in 1972–73 and turning it into a good performer. In 1979, Hardee's was cited by *Restaurant Business* magazine as a prime example of a corporate turnaround. In 1981, Jack Laughery, Hardee's CEO through the turnaround period, was awarded the Food Manufacturer's Association gold plate award for exemplary involvement in the food service industry. In 1990, Laughery was Hardee's Chairman, and Bill Prather was the President and CEO.

Hardee's Acquisition of Burger Chef

In 1981, Hardee's was relatively small in the industry, and decided it had to expand quickly just to keep pace with its larger competitors. Competition had intensified, and the ability to support heavy fixed promotional costs became increasingly critical. Hardee's viewed an acquisition as a way to build a stronger market share base to support an increased television campaign.

Burger Chef, acquired by General Foods in 1968, had 1981 sales of $391 million. General Foods had nurtured it into a profitable regional chain. However, due to management changes at General Foods and the acquisition of the Oscar Meyer company, Burger Chef was no longer important to General Foods' future plans.

Imasco and Hardee's saw this as an opportunity. The Burger Chef chain was made up of about 250 company units and 450 franchised units, located primarily in the states of Michigan, Ohio, Indiana, Iowa and Kentucky. Most of the locations complemented Hardee's markets. Imasco purchased Burger Chef in 1981 for $51.8 million. During the next three years, they converted the sites to Hardee's at a cost of about $80,000 per unit. The acquisition of Burger Chef created two more market areas for Hardee's overnight. By 1986, the stores in these areas were, and still are, the most profitable in the entire Hardee's system. Similarly, in 1972, Hardee's had expanded their market base by acquiring Sandy's Systems, a fast food chain of about 200 restaurants, for $5.7 million.

The Roy Rogers Opportunity

The Roy Rogers restaurant chain was owned by the Marriott Corporation (Marriott), and was located in the northeastern U.S. In Baltimore, Washington, D.C., Philadelphia and New York, it was second only to McDonald's in number of locations. Roy Rogers restaurants were well known for fresh fried chicken and roast beef sandwiches. In 1989, Roy Rogers system-wide sales[3] were $713 million, up from the previous year's $661 million. In 1988, revenues were $431 million, up from $399 million in 1987. Operating earnings in 1988 were $43.7 million, up from $38 million the year before. The chain had 660 units, up from 610 the previous year, with average annual unit sales of $1,081,000.

Marriott was a leader in the hotel lodging industry and had extensive restaurant holdings. In 1988, Marriott began to refocus on lodging. As a result, it had reevaluated its other holdings, among these the Roy Rogers chain. In 1988, Marriott had talked to Hardee's about the possible sale of Roy Rogers. However, Marriott was not yet committed to selling the chain and the two companies were unable to agree on a sale price. In late 1989, Marriott announced it was again interested in selling Roy Rogers.

Prather contacted Marriott about the details. Marriott was offering to sell 648 of its Roy Rogers units, of which 363 were company owned and 285 were franchised. These units were in attractive market locations that would not otherwise be available. However, Marriott wanted to retain several sites located on various turnpikes and interstate highways. Additionally, Marriott had a 14-point contract to which any purchaser had to agree. The contract addressed such things as Marriott's concern for Roy Rogers franchisees and indemnification against future litigation.

Prather saw this as the opportunity he had been waiting for and began putting together an acquisition proposal. Before he could make a serious offer to Marriott, he had to first get the approval of Crawford and the Imasco board. While preparing the proposal, Prather had reflected on what it was like to work in the Imasco organization. He had built his career in the food service industry, coming up through the ranks, starting as an assistant store manager. Until 1986, he had been the Number Three man at Burger King, Vice President in charge of World Operations. Prather had spent 14 years with the company, when it was owned by Pillsbury. Pillsbury, a highly centralized company, had required that any expenditures over $1 million had to be authorized by the head office. He thought how much this contrasted with Imasco. For him, Imasco was "like a breath of fresh air," a decentralized organization in the best sense. He had a great working relationship with Crawford and the others at the Centre, in contact by phone every couple weeks or as required. There was easy and open access with no surprises.

Prather had received preliminary approval from Crawford to proceed with the negotiations. Marriott had structured the Roy Rogers sale in two rounds. In the first round, all those parties who were interested in the chain were interviewed, "much like a job interview," Prather recalled. It was during this first round that Marriott expressed their concerns for their franchisees, and assessed the capabilities and sincerity of those interested in buying the chain. To Prather, "the first round was a screening process just to get into the game."

Prather made it through the first round, but there were three or four other interested groups still in the running. During the next round, the terms of the sale would be negotiated. Although the rumored price had initially been $390 million, Prather thought that it might be more. Prather felt he could convince Marriott that Hardee's offered the best means of exit, given Marriott's concern for the franchisees, and that a solid offer of $420 million would convince them to sell Roy Rogers to Hardee's.

Prather figured conversion to Hardee's outlets would cost $80,000 to $115,000 per unit, depending on local conditions. He weighed this against the average "from scratch" start-up cost of $1.2 million per site. Additionally, Roy Rogers' menu, which included their popular fresh fried chicken, would complement Hardee's current menu. However, he was not sure it would be an "easy sell" in Montreal. Imasco's 40%-shareholder, B.A.T, was in the midst of fighting off a takeover bid from Sir James Goldsmith (see Appendix). Prather knew that Crawford and the board would be concerned about Goldsmith's run at B.A.T, but the Roy Rogers deal was just what he needed to solidify Hardee's number three industry position.

APPENDIX
IMASCO LIMITED, 1990

In the summer of 1989, Sir James Goldsmith formed a syndicate of investors under the name of Hoylake Investments Limited to mount a takeover attempt on B.A.T, Imasco's largest shareholder. Goldsmith's argument was that B.A.T was being valued by the market at less than the sum of its parts, and that the true value would only be realized by the "unbundling" of B.A.T. The stakes in the bid were enormous – it was estimated that Hoylake and its partners would have to put up over $25 billion to carry through on the transaction. Hoylake's intentions with respect to the block of Imasco's shares that B.A.T owned were unknown. Imasco's position was that, while it was an "interested observer," it was not directly involved in the proceedings and would only monitor developments related to the offer. While the specifics of Goldsmith's case are not pertinent here, the general arguments are. These are given below as excerpts from Goldsmith's letter to B.A.T shareholders dated August 8, 1989.

The key questions

The case for this bid must rest on the answer to simple questions. Has the existing management placed B.A.T in a position to compete successfully? Are the subsidiaries growing healthily, or are they failing relative to their competitors? Have shareholders' funds been invested in a wise and progressive way which adds value to the shares of the company? Is the conglomerate structure able to provide strength and innovation over the longer term to its diversified subsidiaries? In short, is B.A.T in a state to compete in the modern world and to face the future with confidence? Or has it been managed in a way which could lead to progressive senescence and decay? That is the crux of the argument.

Conglomeration – B.A.T's failure

It is our case that B.A.T's management has sought size rather than quality or value; it has used shareholders' funds to acquire totally unconnected businesses, about which it knew little, and which are being damaged by having been brought under the control of B.A.T's bureaucratic yoke.

The cause of failure

Before presenting the case in factual detail, I would like to explain why such a state of affairs can occur. It is not that the men in charge are malevolent. Not at all. No doubt they are serious administrators. The problem originates from their belief that tobacco was a declining business, and that the company should diversify into other industries. This logic sounded compelling. The flaw was that B.A.T's management knew something about tobacco, but little about the businesses of the companies that it was acquiring. Also there exists a very natural conflict of interest between management and shareholders. Management wishes its company to be big. The bigger it is, the greater the respect, power and honours that flow to management. Shareholders, on the other hand, want value. They do not seek size for the sake of size. They want growth to be the result of excellence, and thereby to improve the short and long term value of their investment. Some conglomerates have performed well under the leadership of their founders. But that ceases when the flame of the founder is replaced by the dead hand of the corporate bureaucrat. That is why great conglomerates often have been well advised to de-conglomerate before they retire.

Purpose of the offer

1. We intend to reverse B.A.T's strategy. Instead of accumulating miscellaneous companies within B.A.T, we intend to release them and, as described below, return the proceeds to you.
2. We would concentrate B.A.T's attention on running its core business, tobacco. That is the process which we have described as "unbundling."

Consequences

Of course, you will be concerned to know the consequences for the companies being released, and for those who work within them. Will those companies suffer? Will jobs be sacrificed? Would their future be jeopardised, for example, by a reduction in the level of investment in research, development and capital equipment? That is what you may have been led to believe. The reality is the opposite. Instead of vegetating within B.A.T, those companies would either return to independence, or they would join more homogeneous companies. Such companies have the skills which would contribute to future development, and a true mutuality of interest would result. This would lead to increased opportunity for employees, greater long-term investment, productivity and growth. The real danger to employees is that they should remain trapped within B.A.T, and condemned to slow but progressive relative decline. Ultimately that would lead to employee hardship, despite the benevolent intentions of existing management.

Conclusion

To summarize, the flawed architecture of the tobacco-based conglomerates was exposed, first with the acquisition of Imperial Group by Hanson in 1986, and late last year when the management and directors of RJR/Nabisco recognized that shareholder values could only be properly realized by a sale of the company.

Size is often a protection against change, but these same basic structural defects have now been revealed, and the logic of unbundling B.A.T has become inescapable.

NOTES

1. All dollar figures are stated in Canadian dollars unless otherwise noted.
2. Industry figures in U.S. dollars.
3. System-wide sales reflect retail sales figures of both company-owned and franchisee stores. Revenues reflect retail sales of only company-owned stores, in addition to royalties received from franchisees.

CHAPTER FIFTEEN

SEAGRAM AND MCA

In early March 1995, Edgar Bronfman, Jr., the 39-year-old president and chief executive of Seagram Company Ltd. (Seagram), was flying from Osaka to New York. He had just concluded a round of meetings with the senior management team of Matsushita Electric Industrial Company Ltd. (Matsushita). The meetings were held to discuss Seagram's possible acquisition of MCA Inc. (MCA), the entertainment company. Matsushita, the largest consumer electric manufacturer in the world, had acquired MCA in 1990 for $6.59 billion (all $ figures refer to US dollars). Matsushita was clearly interested in selling a portion or possibly all of MCA.

At the meetings, designed as get-acquainted sessions, the two sides agreed to negotiate exclusively for a possible sale. Although the meetings had gone well, Bronfman had some major reservations. An acquisition of MCA could cost as much as $9 billion. To finance the acquisition, Seagram would have to sell some or possibly all of its stake in E. I. du Pont de Nemours & Co. (Du Pont). This investment was worth an estimated $9–10 billion at current market prices. Because equity income from these shares was equal to more than forty percent of Seagram's 1995 income, a sale of the Du Pont shares could result in an adverse reaction from Seagram shareholders. Although Bronfman saw huge potential in the entertainment industry, he was concerned that besides cash Seagram would bring little to the acquisition of MCA in terms of entertainment assets or management. Hollywood had a history of treating newcomers badly. Would Seagram fare any better in the unpredictable world of entertainment, where relationships in the Hollywood network were just as important as creativity, technology, and business experience?

BACKGROUND HISTORY OF SEAGRAM

In 1916 Samuel Bronfman, a Russian immigrant, bought the Bonaventure Liquor Store Company in Montreal and began selling liquor by mail order, the only way liquor could be sold legally during Canadian prohibition. In 1924 along with his brother Allan, Bronfman opened a distillery and named his company Distiller's Corporation. In 1928 he purchased Joseph E. Seagram and Sons Ltd. and changed the name of his company to Distillers Corporation-Seagram Limited.

During the 1920s and after Canadian prohibition ended, Bronfman established a lucrative business smuggling whiskey to the dry United States. Anticipating that U.S. prohibition would soon end, Bronfman began stockpiling whiskey. In 1933 when prohibition ended, Bronfman had the world's largest supply of aged rye and sour mash whiskey. He then purchased three U.S. distillers to add to his Canadian operations.

During the 1930s and 1940s, the company expanded its product line. Seagram's 7 Crown whiskey was introduced to honor the Canadian visit of King George VI and Queen Elizabeth and Crown Royal was developed in 1939. In 1942 distilleries in the West Indies were purchased and after World War II, several acquisitions were made: Mumm and Perrier-Jouet (champagne), Barton & Guestier and Augier Frères (wine), and Chivas Brothers (scotch).

In 1959 Edgar Bronfman succeeded his father as president. The company diversified into many new businesses, including Texas gas fields and Israeli supermarkets. In the late 1960s, Seagram bought, and then sold, 5% of the MGM film studio. Bronfman produced several Broadway plays during this period. In 1980, after a battle with Du Pont to acquire the oil and gas company Conoco, Seagram ended up with a 20.2% share in Du Pont. Additional shares of Du Pont were acquired through open market purchase, bringing Seagram's ownership to 24.2%. In 1988 Seagram acquired Martell, the cognac firm, for $850 million and 28 times earnings. Tropicana, a manufacturer of fruit juices, was acquired for $1.2 billion. In 1991 Seagram was realigned into spirits and non-spirits groups and began purchasing shares in Time Warner, the huge entertainment and media company. Seagram eventually spent $2 billion to acquire a 14.95% stake, leading Time Warner to adopt a poison pill anti-takeover device to prevent Seagram from increasing its ownership.

Seagram Operations in 1995

In 1995 Seagram was the second largest distiller in the world after Grand Metropolitan. The Seagram Spirits and Wine Group produced, marketed, and distributed more than 230 brands of distilled spirits and 195 brands of wines, champagnes, ports and sherries. Spirits and wine were produced and bottled by the group at facilities located in 22 countries in North America, South America, Europe, Asia, and Australia. Subsidiaries and affiliates marketed products in 36 countries, while the company's brands were sold through independent distributors in virtually all other markets in which spirits and wine were sold. Some of Seagram's best known brand names, such as Chivas Regal Premium Scotch Whisky, Martell Cognac and Mumm Champagne, were sold throughout the world, while others were produced primarily for sale in specific markets. In addition to marketing company-owned brands, the firm distributed spirits and wine produced by others. In late 1993 V&S Vin & Sprit of Sweden awarded Seagram global marketing rights to Absolut Vodka, the best selling premium vodka in the United States.

The Tropicana unit produced and marketed one of the leading brands of orange juice in the world. Tropicana pioneered not-from-concentrate orange juice in the United States with Tropicana Pure Premium Orange Juice. Tropicana offered a number of other juices not made from concentrate plus several brands of juices made from concentrate and frozen concentrate juices.

Seagram was actively looking for expansion opportunities around the world. For example, in 1993 Seagram became the only company to receive approval from the Indian government to establish a wholly owned subsidiary to produce and market a range of spirits, wines and juice beverages.

The financial results of the recent diversifications were mixed (see Exhibits 15.1 and 15.2 for Seagram financial statements and Exhibit 15.3 for product segment information). The financing costs on the Time Warner shares exceeded the dividends and the share value was stuck at $2 billion. In 1994 Seagram offered to invest a further $1 billion in Time Warner but this offer was rejected by Time Warner management. Estimated annual earnings for Tropicana were less than $100 million and senior executive turnover was very high.

The New CEO

The Bronfman family continued to play a major managerial and ownership role in Seagram. The descendants of Samuel Bronfman and trusts established for their benefit controlled 36.4% of the company. In 1994 38-year-old Edgar Bronfman, Jr. became president and CEO of Seagram. Bronfman had spearheaded the Martell, Tropicana, and Time Warner acquisitions. Edgar Sr. remained as chairman.

When he was 16, Edgar Bronfman, Jr. left his family in New York to board with movie producer David Puttnam in London. In his early twenties, Bronfman worked in Hollywood, producing several movies and a play. He was also involved in song-writing; Dionne Warwick and Ashford and Simpson are among the artists who recorded songs co-authored by Bronfman (under the pseudonym Junior Miles). Although he joined the family business in 1982, Bronfman maintained close ties with the people he had met in Hollywood. Later, he became friends with David Geffen, chairman of Geffen Records, and Michael Ovitz, influential Hollywood talent agent (Ovitz' father was a Seagram distributor). At Bronfman's recent wedding, guests had included actor Michael Douglas, entertainment industry executive Barry Diller, and Michael Ovitz.

EXHIBIT 15.1:
Seagram income statements (US$000,000 unless otherwise noted)

Year ending 01/31:	1995	1994	1993	1992	1991
Sales & other income	6,399	6,038	6,101	6,345	6,127
Cost of sales	–3,654	–3,451	–3,535	–3,794	–3,632
Net sales	**2,745**	**2,587**	**2,566**	**2,551**	**2,495**
Selling, general & administrative expenses	–2,020	–1,833	–1,804	–1,791	–1,787
Operating income	**725**	**754**	**762**	**760**	**708**
Gain on divestitures	0	0	0	201	0
Dividend income	318	295	286	276	266
Interest expense	–396	–339	–326	–334	–338
Income before income taxes & unremitted earnings	**647**	**710**	**722**	**903**	**636**
Provision for income taxes	–189	–171	–176	–229	–160
Income from beverage operations & dividends	**458**	**539**	**546**	**674**	**476**
Equity in unremitted DuPont earnings	353	–160	–72	53	280
Net income under Canadian GAAP	**811**	**379**	**474**	**727**	**756**
Cumulative effect of accounting changes, Seagram	0	0	–195	0	0
Cumulative effect of accounting changes, DuPont	0	0	–1,179	0	0
Cumulative effect of accounting changes for US GAAP	–75	0	0	0	0
Net income under US GAAP	**736**	**379**	**–900**	**727**	**756**
Average number of shares outstanding (000,000)	372	373	376	378	376
Net income per share under US GAAP (US$)	**1.98**	**1.02**	**–2.38**	**1.92**	**2.01**

Source: Seagram Annual Report.

EXHIBIT 15.2:
Seagram balance sheets (US$000,000)

	1995	1994	1993	1992	1991
Assets					
Cash and short-term investments at cost	157	131	116	266	131
Receivables	1,328	1,170	1,135	1,250	1,064
Beverages	2,398	2,234	2,341	2,562	2,507
Materials & supplies	121	116	106	114	127
Prepaid expenses	172	143	138	135	141
Total current assets	**4,176**	**3,794**	**3,836**	**4,327**	**3,970**
Common stock of E.I. du Pont de Nemours and Co.	3,670	3,154	3,315	4,566	4,504
Common stock of Time Warner Inc.	2,043	1,769	0	0	0
Property, plant and equipment, at cost	2,125	1,969	1,875	1,832	1,775
Less: Accumulated depreciation	−858	−749	−660	−618	−566
Net property, plant & equipment	**1,267**	**1,220**	**1,215**	**1,214**	**1,209**
Excess of cost over fair value of assets acq.	1,547	1,520	1,511	1,526	1,558
Sundry assets	253	261	227	243	236
Total assets	**12,956**	**11,718**	**10,104**	**11,876**	**11,477**
Liabilities					
Short-term borrowings & indebtedness	2,475	1,844	851	568	1,752
Payables and accrued liabilities	1,423	1,011	1,023	1,116	1,122
Income and other taxes	193	141	129	212	170
Indebtedness payable within one year	0	0	0	0	86
Total current liabilities	**4,091**	**2,996**	**2,003**	**1,896**	**3,130**
Long-term indebtedness	2,841	3,053	2,559	3,013	2,038
Deferred income taxes and other credits	515	668	612	484	357
Common shares	638	617	595	583	444
Cumulative gain on equity securities	−85	46	0	0	0
Cumulative currency translation adjustments	−359	−479	−369	−87	−13
Retained earnings	5,315	4,817	4,704	5,987	5,521
Total shareholders' equity	**5,509**	**5,001**	**4,930**	**6,483**	**5,952**
Total liabilities & stockholders' equity	**12,956**	**11,718**	**10,104**	**11,876**	**11,477**

Source: Seagram Annual Report.

MATSUSHITA ELECTRIC INDUSTRIAL AND THE PURCHASE OF MCA

In 1918 Konsuke Matsushita, a 23-year-old grade-school dropout and inspector for the Osaka Electric Light Company, invested ¥100 to start production of electric

EXHIBIT 15.3:
1994 Seagram segmented information (%)

	Sales	Operating income
By region:		
United States	43	14
Europe	36	55
Canada	2	20
Other countries	19	11
Total	100	100
By product category:		
Spirits and wine	75	
Fruit juices, coolers and mixers	25	
Total	100	

Source: *Hoover's Handbook of World Business, 1995–1996.*

sockets in his home.[1] Matsushita Electric Industrial (Matsushita) grew by developing inexpensive lamps, batteries, radios, and motors in the 1920s and 1930s. In 1953 Matsushita began producing televisions, refrigerators, and washing machines. This was followed by stereos, tape recorders, and air conditioners in 1959; and color TVs, dishwashers, and electric ovens in 1960. Manufactured under the National, Panasonic, and Technics names, the company's products were usually not leading edge but were manufactured efficiently in huge quantities at low prices.

By the late 1960s, Matsushita produced 5,000 products and sold them in Japan in more than 25,000 company-owned retail outlets. Matsushita's transition from a predominantly Japanese company to a global giant can be largely attributed to the firm's success with the videocassette recorder (VCR). After a fierce battle with Sony, Matsushita's VHS format became the accepted VCR standard in the late 1970s. In 1980 Matsushita's international sales grew by 52% and in 1981, by 35%.

Although Matsushita was the largest consumer electric company in the world, the firm had earned the nickname Maneshita, or copycat, for its practice of introducing products only after its competitors created a market for them.[2] Traditionally very conservative, the firm was said to be run by bureaucrats, not innovators. In surveys of Japanese businessmen and consumers, Matsushita had fallen from the top of preeminent Japanese firms. Matsushita's main rival, Sony (which acquired Columbia Pictures in 1989 for $3.5 billion), was usually ranked first or second. In addition, Japanese customers were starting to switch from Matsushita retail stores to lower-priced discount outlets.

To move beyond consumer electric products, Matsushita began investing in areas such as semiconductors, industrial robots, high definition TV, and computers. In 1989 Matsushita senior managers began a series of meetings with talent agent Michael Ovitz about a possible acquisition in the entertainment industry. These meetings culminated in Matsushita's acquisition of MCA for $6.59 billion in November 1990.

MCA History

MCA was founded in 1924 as Music Corp. of America by Jules Stein, a Chicago ophthalmologist who had worked his way through medical school by organizing bands to play one-night stands. In 1936 he hired Lew Wasserman, a Cleveland theater usher and former publicity director for a local nightclub. Wasserman became president in 1946. By 1937, when the company moved to Hollywood, MCA was managing talent for radio, TV and motion pictures. In 1952 MCA began producing television shows when the Screen Actors Guild and its president and MCA client, Ronald Reagan, gave the firm a waiver from the rule prohibiting talent agencies from producing television shows. In 1959 MCA purchased Universal Studios, and in 1961 purchased Universal Pictures and its parent, Decca Records. Universal would subsequently release some of the top-grossing movies of all time, including *Jaws*, *E.T.*, and the *Indiana Jones* series. In 1964 MCA created its Universal Studios tour business. In 1986 MCA acquired a 42% stake in Cineplex Odeon, a large movie theater chain and in 1990 acquired Geffen Records from David Geffen for $545 million in stock. This made David Geffen MCA's largest shareholder prior to the Matsushita acquisition.

MCA began searching for a partner or a buyer in the mid-1980s. The decision to sell the company was driven by concerns that MCA needed greater access to investment capital. With three major movie studios – Warner Bros., 20th Century Fox, and Columbia – owned by large media conglomerates, MCA risked losing future business opportunities to its richer competitors. In particular, MCA's international presence lagged that of its rivals. The takeover by Matsushita, the largest acquisition of an American firm by a Japanese firm, seemed ideal from both sides. Prior to making the acquisition, Matsushita had $10 billion in cash. According to MCA Chairman, Lew Wasserman, the acquisition by Matsushita would provide MCA with many opportunities for expansion, especially in the global arena.[3] David Geffen indicated that "this [MCA] will be the most acquisition-minded company in the world."[4]

While there were questions about the cultural fit between conservative, bureaucratic Matsushita and Hollywood, analysts generally agreed that Matsushita acquired MCA for a bargain price, perhaps as much as 25% lower than recent valuations. For Matsushita, the strategic benefits of the acquisition seemed clear. The deal would combine MCA's entertainment "software" – movies, music, and TV shows – with Matsushita's wide range of "hardware" – TVs, VCRs, CD players, etc. There was much talk about the synergy that would allow Matsushita to revolutionize the marketing of new technologies such as high definition TV and laser disc players. The acquisition would also counter rival Sony's push into new product areas.

In negotiating the sale, both Lew Wasserman and president Sidney Sheinberg agreed to five-year employment contracts. No significant changes in MCA personnel or policies were planned and Matsushita's president, Akio Tanii, pledged never to interfere with the creative independence of MCA.

EXHIBIT 15.4:
Matsushita financial information (Yen 000,000 unless otherwise noted)

Year ending 03/31:	1994	1993	1992	1991
Income statement information				
Net sales	6,623,586	7,055,868	7,449,933	6,599,306
Cost of sales	4,573,964	4,831,572	5,068,877	4,393,502
Gross profit	2,049,622	2,224,296	2,381,056	2,205,804
Selling, general and administrative expenses	1,876,016	1,988,466	1,997,784	1,733,214
Operating profit	173,606	235,830	383,272	472,590
Interest & dividend income	79,832	118,310	170,915	266,634
Interest expenses	99,790	133,363	177,324	161,371
Income taxes	99,878	128,388	193,784	304,994
Net income	24,493	37,295	133,904	258,914
Net income per common share (¥)	11.67	17.66	61.13	117.12
Balance sheet information				
Total current assets	4,073,697	4,349,559	4,440,439	4,402,929
Net property	1,395,454	1,499,568	1,496,507	1,158,252
Total assets	8,192,632	8,754,979	9,019,707	8,761,143
Total current liabilities	2,578,737	2,962,571	3,262,876	3,177,287
Total noncurrent liabilities	1,767,266	1,708,579	1,565,646	1,513,057
Stockholders' equity	3,288,945	3,406,303	3,495,867	3,434,747

Source: Matsushita Annual Report.

MCA and Matsushita Fours Years Later

Not long after the acquisition, Japan's "bubble" economy burst, hitting Matsushita especially hard. Through 1993 and 1994, Matsushita sales and profits dropped substantially (see Exhibit 15.4 for Matsushita financial information and Exhibit 15.5 for product segment information). It was expected that 1995 results would show a slight improvement. Because of the poor results, Matsushita's president and architect of the MCA acquisition was ousted. The new president, Yoichi Morishita, was pushing a "revitalization" strategy focused on electrical consumer goods. For these and other reasons, Matsushita was unable to support MCA's expansion goals. Matsushita vetoed MCA's 1992 proposed acquisition of Virgin Records and 1994 plans to join with ITT to bid for CBS.[5] The predicted seamless blending of Matsushita hardware and MCA software was not happening.

Cultural clashes added to the problems. Matsushita executives spoke little or no English, rarely visited the United States, and had little contact with MCA managers other than to turn down requests for funds.[6] These clashes boiled over in October 1994. MCA Chairman Wasserman, now 81 and the industry's most revered elder statesman, told Matsushita that he would resign when his contract expired at the

EXHIBIT 15.5:
Matsushita sales (%)

By product category:	
Communications and industrial equipment	25
Video equipment	20
Home appliances	13
Electronic components	12
Entertainment	9
Audio equipment	8
Batteries & appliances	5
Other products	8
Total	100
By region:	
Japan	68
Other countries	32
Total	100

Source: Hoover's Handbook of World Business, 1995–1996.

end of 1995 unless MCA was granted more management control and sufficient capital to compete with the other movie studios. Sidney Sheinberg indicated that he would also leave. There were rumors that as many as 100 MCA employees might defect, along with Wasserman and Sheinberg.[7] In addition, film director Steven Spielberg, one of the most successful directors in history, said that he would stop working for MCA if Sheinberg left.[8] Sheinberg was a close friend and mentor of Spielberg, having given Spielberg his first directing job. In the previous year Spielberg had released *Jurassic Park*, the biggest grossing film in history at that time, and the Academy Award winning *Schindler's List*, both with Universal Pictures.

Spielberg's formation of a new entertainment company with former Disney Studio chief Jeffrey Katzenberg and David Geffen was of further concern to Matsushita. The equity in the new company, Dreamworks, would be split equally between the three founders, who together had an estimated net worth of more than $2 billion. Both Wasserman and Sheinberg endorsed the plans for the new company, although there were many unanswered questions. The films made by Dreamworks would have to be distributed through one of the established studios, such as Universal. According to one report, Spielberg sent a letter to Matsushita executives indicating an interest in an MCA distribution deal only if Sheinberg and Wasserman remained with MCA.[9] If the company were to produce records, David Geffen's potential role raised a further question for Matsushita. Geffen was chairman of MCA's Geffen Record division and in 1994 the division was having its most successful year. If Geffen left MCA and started a new label, top MCA recording artists and executives might follow him.

Wasserman and Sheinberg's concerns were reported publicly in the *Wall Street Journal*, the *Los Angeles Times*, and other newspapers. Matsushita executives reacted

EXHIBIT 15.6:
MCA income statement for the year ended December 31, 1994 (US$ millions)

Revenues:	
Filmed Entertainment	$3,313
Music Entertainment	1,293
Recreation	440
Publishing and Other	525
Total Revenue	$5,571
Earnings before interest, tax, depreciation, and amortization:	
Filmed Entertainment	$ 176
Music Entertainment	192
Recreation	128
Publishing and Other	37
Total Earnings	$ 533

Source: company document.

with surprise at the MCA managers' public announcement of their unhappiness with Matsushita. Matsushita president, Yoichi Morishita, was quoted: "I am surprised at the report in the U.S. as it is a bolt from the blue"[10] and "the relationship with MCA remains unchanged . . . at this moment we have no plan to sell MCA."[11] On October 18, 1994, Matsushita executives met with Wasserman and Sheinberg in a meeting that ended acrimoniously and left both sides frustrated.[12] In December, Matsushita hired Michael Ovitz and the New York investment banking firm of Allen & Co. to explore alternatives for MCA. In January 1995 in Osaka, Ovitz and several associates from his firm, Creative Artists Associates, met for eight hours with Matsushita's senior management team.

MCA OPERATIONS AND PERFORMANCE IN 1995

MCA had 1994 revenues of $5.6 billion and an operating profit of $533 million from four primary businesses (Exhibit 15.6): movies and television ($3.3 billion in revenue), music ($1.3 billion), theme parks ($440 million), publishing, software, and other businesses ($525 million).

In recent years, MCA's movie business, Universal Pictures, had been highly dependent on movies produced and/or directed by Steven Spielberg, to the extent that MCA had been called the "House of Steven." These movies had made Spielberg immensely wealthy; his typical deal involved taking 15% of the revenue of every film he made. Other than the Spielberg movies, Universal had created few recent hits. Universal was also in the process of making *Waterworld*, a film that, at a cost of $175 million, was on its way to becoming the most expensive of all time. Universal also controlled a library of more than 3,000 films, including classics such as *Psycho* and *To Kill a Mockingbird*. The value of these films was uncertain. If MCA could strike a deal with a broadcast or cable TV network, the value could increase substantially.

The MCA television business produced series such as *Northern Exposure* and *Murder She Wrote*. The business had produced few new hits in recent years and was rumored to be poorly managed. The business also owned 50% of the shares in the cable networks USA Network and the Sci-Fi Channel.

MCA's Music Entertainment Group, the smallest of the six leading music conglomerates, had an estimated profit of $220 million and was growing at more than 10% annually.[13] MCA's largest music label was Geffen Records, which had sales of $500 million and estimated profits of $90 million. Geffen Records had a reputation as one of the best in the business at discovering new talent. Among its biggest sellers in 1994 were bands such as Counting Crows and Nirvana. Geffen Records was also the label for veteran acts such as Peter Gabriel, Aerosmith, and the Eagles. In 1994 the president of Geffen Records signed a long-term agreement to run the company after David Geffen's contract expired in April 1995. MCA also owned a concert division and the 6,000-seat Universal Amphitheatre. The estimated market value for the music division ranged from $2.3 to $3 billion.

The Recreation Division owned Universal Studios Hollywood and 50% of Universal Studios Florida. Both parks included major TV and film production facilities. Although highly profitable, both parks would require upgrades in the coming years. In February 1995 MCA submitted a plan to municipal authorities for a $3 billion development at the Hollywood park that would include expansion of the theme park, new film production facilities, and new shops, restaurants and resort hotels. In the Florida park, a *Jurassic Park* ride was under development that could cost several hundred million dollars.

The Publishing and Software Group included two publishing houses, Putnam and Berkeley, and published books by bestselling authors Dean Koontz and Tom Clancy. The Universal Interactive unit distributed multimedia and video games. MCA owned 42% of Cineplex Odeon, a Canadian firm with 2,800 movie screens and revenues of about $350 million. The Bronfman family was also involved as a minority shareholder in Cineplex Odeon. Finally, MCA owned Spencer Gifts, a retail gift store chain with more than 500 outlets.

THE ENTERTAINMENT INDUSTRY

Since the early 1990s, annual growth in entertainment industry revenues in the United States had averaged about 10%. In contrast, expenditures on food, clothing, and autos had grown much more slowly. Two key sectors of the entertainment industry were movies and music.

Movies

Besides MCA, the film industry was dominated by six other major studios and had been for 50 years. Warner Bros. was owned by Time Warner, in which Seagram had a major stake. In recent years, Warner Bros. had realized the highest U.S. market share among the major studios. Warner Bros.' television unit was the largest TV show producer and the firm was moving aggressively into merchandising to take advantage of its animated characters such as Bugs Bunny and the Road Runner. In addition to its movie and television business, Time Warner was involved in periodical and book publishing, music, and cable TV operations. Because of its major acquisitions, Time Warner was burdened by about $15 billion in debt and had lost money in the past few years.

Walt Disney Studios, the most financially sound of the major studios, was divided into three units: Walt Disney Motion Pictures Group, which produced live action movies; Walt Disney Television and Telecommunications Group, which handled TV, home video and new technology; and the Feature Animation Group, which developed Disney's animated feature films. In recent years, Disney was the leading studio in terms of the number of new film releases and had a string of highly successful animated films, including *The Lion King*, the most successful film in Disney's 73-year history. With the success of this film and others (*Aladdin*, *Beauty and the Beast*, and *Little Mermaid*), Disney was recharging its theme parks, consumer products, television and video divisions with fresh characters. Although with limited success to date, Disney was building music and publishing divisions and was committed to capitalizing on the strength of the Disney name. Overall, the Disney Co. (movies, television, theme parks, etc.) had experienced tremendous growth over the past decade, growing from $1.7 billion in revenue to more than $10 billion.

Paramount Studios was acquired by Viacom in 1994 for $10 billion. Viacom, a diversified entertainment company, owned television and radio stations, cable TV operations, the publisher Simon and Schuster, MTV, and Blockbuster Video. One of Paramount's strongest assets was its *Star Trek* franchise, which had generated a reported $1.3 billion for the studio in combined revenues from films, syndication rights and merchandising. Paramount produced the 1994 box office winner *Forrest Gump*, which generated more than $300 million.

Sony Pictures Entertainment, and its studios Columbia Pictures and Tri-Star Pictures, was owned by Sony Corp. Sony Pictures was reeling from box office failures, executive turnover, and according to industry insiders, a succession of bad creative and financial decisions. Sony had recently taken a $3.2 billion charge for writeoffs at its Columbia and Tri-Star Studios and was reportedly seeking an investor to buy at least 25% of the business.

Twentieth Century Fox was a division of Rupert Murdoch's News Corp. More than the other studios, Fox was aggressively trying to become integrated into the worldwide media network. Fox had formed several international distribution joint ventures and was planning its first overseas production facility in Sydney, Australia. News Corp.'s global operations included the Hong Kong-based satellite network Star TV covering much of Asia; the London-based satellite service British Sky Broadcasting covering Britain; the Los Angeles-based cable channel El Canal Fox servicing 18 countries in Latin America; and the Fox network in the U.S.

MGM/United Artists was owned by the French bank Crédit Lyonnais. The studio had lost money annually since 1987 and was on it third management team since being acquired by Crédit Lyonnais in 1992. In 1995 the latest management team appeared to be making progress in getting the studio back to profitability.

In 1994 sales of movie tickets in the United States were $5.4 billion, an increase of 4.7% from 1993. The major studios released 185 films in 1994, compared with 161 in 1993. The average film cost $34 million to produce and $16 million to market, a 15% jump over the previous year. Top box office draws such as Sylvester Stallone and Arnold Schwarzenegger were able to earn $20 million a film. In addition to rising costs, the movie business was well known for attracting outsiders who went on to suffer huge losses. For example, in the 1970s the San Francisco financial services firm Transamerica bought United Artists. Faced with huge writeoffs after the most expensive film fiasco up to that point, *Heaven's Gate*, Transamerica sold the studio to Metro-Goldwyn-Mayer (MGM), which was controlled by financier Kirk Kerkorian. Italian financier Giancarlo Parretti purchased MGM from Kerkorian, after Kerkorian had little success in the film business. After MGM suffered major losses under Parretti, Crédit Lyonnais foreclosed on Parretti and took over MGM. Crédit Lyonnais was forced to remove $800 million in bank debt from MGM's books in early 1994 and provided an additional $400 million credit line. The Japanese firm Pioneer Electronics was expected to write off its $60 million investment in the independent film studio Carolco Pictures.

An area of very positive growth for the film studios was overseas sales and distribution. For example, international revenue at The Walt Disney Co. was 17 times greater in 1994 than in 1984. There was a huge and growing international market for American films, to the extent that several European countries decided to restrict the market share of American films. To illustrate the kind of deal the studios were involved in, MCA was one of the overseas distributors for the movie *True Lies*, a film produced and released in the United States by Twentieth Century Fox. *True Lies* grossed $145 million in the United States. Because Twentieth Century Fox wanted to spread its risk, MCA was distributing *True Lies* in various countries, including Australia, Brazil, Mexico, and South Korea. The gross in MCA's territory was estimated to be $115 million, with MCA spending about $20 million on marketing.[14] As another example, Warner Bros. in 1994 signed a movie distribution deal with China's exclusive film import agency, China Film Distribution, Exhibition, Export & Import Corp. The films were to be dubbed in Mandarin. Also in 1994, Turner Broadcasting's TNT Network announced that it would introduce a 24-hour movie channel in Asia. The program was to be beamed from a China satellite and dubbed initially in Mandarin and Thai.

Music

Like the film industry, the recorded music industry was also dominated by a small number of large companies. MCA's music business, with a 1994 market share of

10.7%, was the smallest of the six major distributors. The other major firms were: WEA, owned by Time Warner, 21.1% share; Sony, 15.2%; Bertelsmann, 12.9%; PolyGram, owned by Philips Electronics, 12.9%; and Thorn EMI, 11.2%. Independent distributors had a 16% market share.[15]

Music differed from films in several respects. Most important, the average album cost a few hundred thousand dollars to produce, which allowed a music company to produce several hundred titles a year and spread its risk. In contrast, the major movie companies released an average of 26 films each in 1994. Movie companies had to wait years to see a revenue stream; music companies could start making money within months of recording. Unlike movie stars, few recording artists could command multi-million dollar fees and when they did, it was usually spread over several projects. Because music fans tended to be loyal, once an artist became established there was a fairly predictable sales base with each new album. For some records, sales never seemed to end. Pink Floyd's *Dark Side of the Moon* spent a record 741 weeks on Billboard's Top 200 after its release in 1973 and sold more than 500,000 copies in 1994. *The Eagles Greatest Hits: 1971–75* sold 662,000 copies in 1994 and outsold all but 119 of the more than 5,000 new releases.[16]

The movie and music industries also differed when it came to developing new artists. Movie-goers tended to be loyal to their favorite stars and as a result, the studios were reluctant to use lesser-known actors and actresses in their films. Nevertheless, success was never guaranteed, even when the most well-known stars, directors, and screenwriters were involved. In contrast, the music business relied heavily on new artists. Each year, dozens of new music acts had successful records. Although about 85% of all acts signed never made money for the music companies, the other 15% plus sales of previously released records more than made up for the losses. New acts could be huge moneymakers for the music companies because of their low costs and because of the high profit margins for bestselling records. When a record sold in the millions, manufacturing costs became pennies per unit. At this point, operating margins could be as high as $7 per unit.

At many of the large entertainment conglomerates, including MCA, the music business was more profitable and consistent than the film business. For example, Time Warner's film division in 1994 generated $565 million in operating income on $5 billion in revenue. Its music business did much better, earning $720 million on revenue of $4 billion.[17] In 1994 Sony's music unit earned $550 million on $4.5 billion in revenue.

Recorded music sales in the United States were estimated at $11 billion for 1994, up nearly 20% from 1993. Worldwide music sales were about $30 billion, with the highest annual sales increases in emerging markets such as Hungary, Poland, and Brazil. A recent trend in the global music business was the linkages between the record companies and music videos. Music video broadcasting, pioneered by Viacom's MTV, reached 60 million homes in the United States. MTV International reached 250 million homes in 67 countries. A competing channel in Europe, Viva, was partially owned by Thorn EMI, Sony, Warner Germany, and PolyGram. In early 1995 Bertelsmann, Thorn EMI, Sony Pictures, and Warner Music Group joined as equity partners in an Asian music video channel. MTV Mandarin, a partnership between MTV and PolyGram, was set to launch in April 1995 in Asia. This was the first MTV channel to have an outside partner. In 1994, when Warner, Sony Pictures, Thorn EMI, PolyGram, and Ticketmaster announced plans to start a rival U.S. service to MTV, Viacom Chairman Sumner Redstone threatened an antitrust suit and declared that Viacom and MTV would compete with its suppliers and start a record company.

SEAGRAM AND MCA

Seagram's Chief Financial Officer, Stephan Banner, had worked as a mergers and acquisitions lawyer in New York prior to joining Seagram. As a mergers lawyer, Banner had worked on Matsushita's acquisition of MCA. In January 1995 Banner talked with a lower-level Matsushita executive and indicated that Seagram might be interested in acquiring MCA.[18] For the next month, Seagram executives debated the pros and cons of the possible acquisition. The main attraction of MCA was the opportunity to become a controlling shareholder of one of the major firms in the entertainment industry. If the industry was able to continue its international expansion and if the merging of entertainment, telecommunications, and computers happened as many analysts predicted, the rewards for those in the "software" side of entertainment could be enormous. The downside was the high risk nature of the business and Seagram's lack of entertainment industry experience.

On March 6 in Osaka, Bronfman met with Matsushita president Morishita and other senior executives to discuss the possible purchase. At the meeting, the two sides agreed to negotiate exclusively for a possible sale. For Seagram, an exclusive negotiation would preclude the deal from turning into an auction. For Matsushita, the company would be spared public embarrassment if the deal fell through. At this point, MCA's Wasserman and Sheinberg were not involved in the discussions and were not even aware they were going on.

The meetings had gone well and Bronfman was convinced that Matsushita was genuinely interested in selling all or a majority of MCA. He knew that he would have to come back to Matsushita with a firm offer fairly quickly or risk losing the exclusive negotiation privilege. He also knew there would be some heated debate with his father and other Seagram board members. In particular, selling the Du Pont shares would surely be a very contentious issue. Reports that Seagram was interested in selling the Du Pont shares had surfaced publicly in June 1994 at a meeting between financial analysts and Seagram management (including Edgar Bronfman). There was speculation that Seagram would sell the shares if they hit a price of $80–$85. Although Seagram, when asked about the Du Pont shares, did not say it planned to sell the stock, it did not deny the possibility either. According to a Seagram spokeswoman, "We're not looking to sell the Du Pont stock. You never say never – this is our position now."[19] By January 1995, and before the first discussions with MCA, discussions with Du Pont about selling the shares back to Du Pont were under way.

EXHIBIT 15.7:
Du Pont financial information (US$000,000,000 unless otherwise noted)

Income statement year ended 12/31:	1994	1993	1992	1991
Total sales	40.26	37.84	38.35	39.52
Cost of goods sold	21.98	21.40	21.86	22.52
Selling, general & administrative expenses	2.88	3.31	3.74	3.58
Depreciation	2.98	2.83	2.66	2.64
Research and development	1.01	1.13	1.28	1.30
Restructuring charges	−1.42	−1.84	−0.48	
Total expenses	35.88	36.88	36.54	36.71
Income before taxes	4.38	0.96	1.81	2.82
Net income	2.73	0.56	−3.93	1.40
Earnings per share (US$)	4.00	0.82	−5.82	2.09
Balance sheet:				
Total current assets	11.11	10.90	12.23	11.32
Total assets	36.89	37.05	38.87	36.56
Long-term debt	6.38	6.53	7.19	6.46
Shareholders' equity	12.82	11.23	11.77	16.74
Employees (number)	107,000	107,000	124,916	132,578

Source: Du Pont Annual Report.

Du Pont

Du Pont was the largest chemical company in the United States, with revenue of $40 billion in 1994, and the fourth largest in the world (Exhibit 15.7). Du Pont was founded in 1802 as a manufacturer of gunpowder by a French immigrant, E. I. du Pont de Nemours. Over the years, Du Pont had invented many products, such as neoprene, nylon, Teflon, Orlon, and Dacron, and diversified into many areas. In 1995 Du Pont had five major divisions: chemicals (fluorochemicals, specialty chemicals, pigments), fibers (textiles, flooring, nonwovens, nylon, polyester, lycra), polymers (films, finishes, elastomers), petroleum (Conoco – exploration, production, refining, marketing, petrochemicals), and diversified businesses (agricultural herbicides and insecticides; medical products, printing and publishing materials). The largest unit was Conoco with $17.2 billion in sales and $1.1 billion in operating profit. Fibers, which accounted for $6.8 billion in sales and more than $1 billion in profit, was growing rapidly. The polymers division was also doing well, with sales of $6.5 billion and profit of more than $1 billion.

In 1991 Du Pont initiated a major reengineering effort. Since then, Du Pont had cut 37,000 employees, sold $1.8 billion in assets, and eliminated more than $2 billion in annual expenses. Operating margins increased from 5.4% in 1992 to 8%. In 1994 Du Pont had the highest earnings in its history and net cash flow (operating cash flow after dividends and capital expenditures) was $1.6 billion and was projected to be $2 billion for the next two years. International sales increased from 39.8% in 1989 to 47% in 1994. Du Pont was actively looking for new projects and acquisition targets in the Asia-Pacific region. In early 1994 Du Pont was evaluating more than 30 projects in China alone.

After dropping below $30 in 1989, Du Pont shares were trading at about $60. Seagram owned 164 million Du Pont shares which, at a market value of $60 each, were worth $9.8 billion. Seagram had acquired the shares for $3.28 billion.

BRONFMAN'S DECISION

Selling the Du Pont stake would have an enormous impact on Seagram's bottom line and cash flow. In 1995 Seagram reported equity in unremitted Du Pont earnings of $353 million (Exhibit 15.1). Seagram also received $318 million in dividends from Du Pont. MCA's earnings would make up some of the impact of the lost Du Pont earnings and dividends but not all. For the next few years it looked as if the Du Pont shares would provide a steady source of income and cash flow for Seagram. However, Bronfman saw some problems with Du Pont's business lines. Most were cyclical, highly capital-intensive, and fraught with potential environmental problems. Although Seagram had three positions on the 15-member Du Pont board of directors, Seagram had only minimal control over Du Pont strategy. MCA represented an opportunity to acquire a controlling interest in one of the largest entertainment companies in the world. As well, Bronfman felt that Seagram management would be comfortable with MCA because its businesses were customer-driven and moving toward global expansion. Bronfman now had to decide if MCA was the right opportunity for Seagram.

NOTES

1. Robert W. Lightfoot and Christopher A. Bartlett, *Philips and Matsushita: A Portrait of Two Evolving Companies*, Harvard Business School Case #388-144.
2. *Wall Street Journal*, November 26, 1990, A1.
3. *Wall Street Journal*, November 28, 1990, A3.
4. *Wall Street Journal*, November 28, 1990, A3.
5. *Los Angeles Times*, April 10, 1995, A12.
6. *Wall Street Journal*, April 10, 1995, A8.
7. *Wall Street Journal*, April 10, 1995, A14.
8. *Wall Street Journal*, November 18, 1994, A11
9. *Los Angeles Times*, April 8, 1995, D8.
10. *Wall Street Journal*, October 14, 1994, A5.
11. *Wall Street Journal*, October 17, 1994, A5.
12. *Los Angeles Times*, April 10, 1995, A12.
13. *New York Times*, April 10, 1994, D8.
14. *Wall Street Journal*, November 22, 1994, B1.
15. *New York Times*, April 10, 1995, D8.
16. *Los Angeles Times*, April 10, 1995, F1.
17. *New York Times*, April 10, 1995, D8.
18. *Los Angeles Times*, April 10, 1995, A12.
19. *Financial Post*, June 10, 1994, Section 1, 3.

CHAPTER SIXTEEN

GENERAL ELECTRIC: THE JACK WELCH ERA, 1981–1998

Robert M. Grant prepared this case solely to provide material for class discussion. The author does not intend to illustrate either the effective or ineffective handling of a management situation. The author may have disguised certain names or other identifying information to protect confidentiality.

The General Electric (GE) that Jack Welch inherited in 1981 was widely regarded as one of the world's most successful business enterprises. It was, and still is, the only company to have remained a member of the Dow Jones 30 share industrial index since the index was first created.

GE was founded in 1892 from the merger of Thomas Edison's Electric Light Company with the Thomas Houston company. Its business was tied to the exploitation of Edison's patents relating to electricity generation and distribution, light bulbs, and electric motors.

During the twentieth century it became not only the biggest and most diversified industrial corporation in America, but "a model of management – a laboratory studied by business schools and raided by other companies seeking skilled executives."[1]

Under Reg Jones, Welch's predecessor as CEO, GE created an organizational structure and strategic planning system that were to become the model for diversified companies throughout the world. Table 16.A1 at the end of this chapter summarizes the main events of GE's 106-year corporate history.

Jack Welch's contribution as CEO was to dismantle much of this organizational structure and the management systems associated with it. In its place Welch created a corporation intended to mesh the strengths of enormous size and diversity with the agility and entrepreneurial drive of a series of small enterprises. In the process, Welch reformulated GE's business portfolio, pioneered global expansion, and pushed GE to unprecedented levels of profitability and shareholder return.

After 16 years of Welch's leadership and with Welch two years away from the mandatory retirement age of 65, the only question remaining for GE employees and the army of GE-watchers in securities companies, business schools, and consulting companies was: "What next?"

JACK WELCH

Welch attributes his personality and his management style to the values and beliefs that were shaped during his upbringing in Massachusetts.

> I was an only child. My parents were about 40 when they had me, and they had been trying for 16 years. My father was a railroad conductor, a good man, hard working, passive . . . [My mother] always felt I could do anything. It was my mother who trained me, taught me the facts of life. She wanted me to be independent. Control your own destiny – she always had that idea. Saw reality. No mincing words. Whenever I got out of line, she would whack me one, but always positive, always constructive, always uplifting. And I was just nuts about her.

One of Welch's high-school classmates described him as "a nice, regular guy, but always very competitive, relentless, and argumentative." A college classmate said, "The desire to win was in his eyes. He was always looking one step ahead." Another classmate said, "He hated losing – even in touch football," and another said, "Jack wasn't blessed with a lot of grace or athletic ability. He trounced people by trying harder." One of Welch's most remembered comments was, "We're still friends?"

His management style is also drawn from his years playing ice-hockey. "Hockey is the kind of game where people bang you up against the boards and then go out and have a drink with you after," he said. Using "constructive conflict," Welch often forced managers to defend their views, even if that meant getting into shouting-match arguments. "Jack will chase you around the room, throwing arguments and objections at you," said one executive. "Then you fight back until he lets you do what you want, and it's clear you'll do everything you can to make it work."

Welch completed a Ph.D. in chemical engineering at the University of Illinois in the record time of three years. In 1960 he joined GE Plastics. In 1968, at only 33 years of age, Jack Welch became the youngest general manager at any GE division. Earnings at GE Plastics increased at a compound rate of 34 percent under Welch, and at 37 he was asked to head up the Components and Materials Group, which added GE Medical Systems to his responsibilities.

Welch was not even included in the original list of candidates expected to succeed Reginald Jones as CEO, so his selection was a surprise to many. Welch was widely viewed as a maverick and a renegade. In contrast, Jones had developed GE's reputation for stability, sound management, and predictable earnings increases. However, Jones later explained that he was looking for someone to take GE to the next level – someone who could effect change.

In 1977, Jones reorganized the company into six sectors and appointed one of six potential CEOs to each one. Welch was put in charge of Consumer Products and Services. His experience with corporate headquarters in Fairfield, Connecticut came as a shock to him. He was astonished at the byzantine nature of GE's bureaucracy. In his view, corporate staff was interfering too much in line activities – requiring presentations, demanding reports – but doing little to create or sell more products. He felt that this led line people to waste their time playing political games with corporate staff in the hope that they would receive some benefit. He cringed as he recalled the $30,000 the light bulb business had spent to produce a film to support its capital appropriations request to corporate for a new piece of equipment.

The field was further narrowed to three in 1979: Welch was one of three vice chairmen appointed by Jones. In December 1980, Welch was unanimously chosen CEO by the Board of Directors. The news surprised outsiders and made many GE employees nervous. John T. Cornell, a Paine Webber analyst, reported: "The word inside the company is that he's chomping at the bit to go crazy once he takes over." The *Wall Street Journal* observed that GE was "replacing a legend with a live wire."

From the outset Welch's goals for GE were lofty. In April 1981, as the 45-year-old chairman and chief executive officer of General Electric, he described his vision for GE:

> A decade from now I would like General Electric to be perceived as a unique, high-spirited, entrepreneurial enterprise . . . a company known around the world for its unmatched level of excellence. I want General Electric to be the most profitable, highly diversified company on earth, with world-quality leadership in every one of its product lines.

RECONFIGURING THE BUSINESS PORTFOLIO

If Jones's tenure as CEO of GE had been characterized by the development of a sophisticated system of strategic planning, Welch's was dominated by his desire to turn GE into a performance-driven organization. Rather than develop a clearly articulated corporate strategy, Welch preferred to establish an objective that could be relevant to everyone in the company. His goal was to create a company that was to be "better than the best," the simplest indicator of which was for each of GE's businesses to be number one or number two within their global markets. This set a challenge to each business-level chief executive, and defined Welch's own agenda: "My biggest challenge will be to put enough money on the right gambles and no money on the wrong ones. But I don't want to sprinkle money over everything."

To assist in this task of focusing GE and to help conceptualize GE in a way that could be communicated to others, Welch formulated a view of GE as three areas of business. These comprised: core businesses, whose strategic focus was to be "reinvestment in productivity and quality," high-technology businesses, which were to "stay on the leading edge," and service businesses with a mandate to grow by "adding outstanding people who often can create new ventures and by making contiguous acquisitions." Figure 16.1 shows Welch's three-circle framework. According to Welch, "We have our hands on a simple, understandable strategy for where we are, where we are not, where we can't find a solution, and where we have to disengage. We have to get used to the idea that disengaging does not mean bad people or bad management – it's a bad situation and we cannot tie up good resources, good dollars, chasing it." Only the 15 businesses that dominated their markets would be

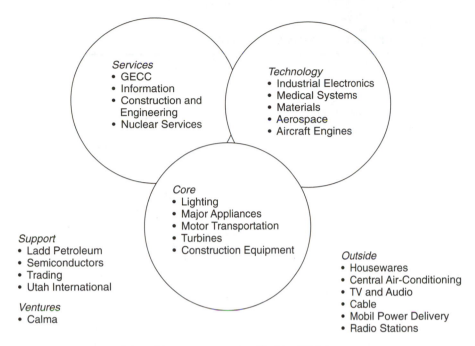

Services
- GECC
- Information
- Construction and Engineering
- Nuclear Services

Technology
- Industrial Electronics
- Medical Systems
- Materials
- Aerospace
- Aircraft Engines

Core
- Lighting
- Major Appliances
- Motor Transportation
- Turbines
- Construction Equipment

Support
- Ladd Petroleum
- Semiconductors
- Trading
- Utah International

Ventures
- Calma

Outside
- Housewares
- Central Air-Conditioning
- TV and Audio
- Cable
- Mobil Power Delivery
- Radio Stations

Figure 16.1 GE's portfolio of businesses as classified by Welch

placed in a circle; businesses that either did not fit these three areas or did not meet the criterion of being number one or two in their respective markets were identified as potential divestments. The result was a series of acquisitions and disposals (see Table 16.1).

DELAYERING AND DESTAFFING

The changes in the portfolio transformed the product-market face of GE, with a much bigger emphasis on service businesses. However, Welch's main work was in revitalizing the management systems and management style of GE. To achieve this changes in structure were needed. In December 1985, Welch announced a major organizational change eliminating the sector level, reallocating responsibilities, and reorganizing management. The leaders of GE's 13 businesses were required to report directly to the CEO. The office of the CEO was expanded, and a Corporate Executive Council (CEC) was created to provide a forum for the leaders of GE's 13 businesses and the chief corporate officers. Led by Welch, the CEC met twice a quarter to discuss common issues and promote collaboration. Figures 16.2 and 16.3 show GE's organization structure in 1980 and 1994.

TABLE 16.1
GE's acquisitions and disposals 1981–1992

	Acquisitions	Disposals
1981	Calma Corp. (CAD/CAM) Intersil (semiconductors) Structural Dynamics Research (48%)	
1982		Pathfinder Mines Mining products business Central air-conditioning business
1983	AMIC Corp. (mortgage insurance) Reuter-Stakes (instruments)	Utah International Housewares business 10 broadcasting stations Family Financial Services
1984	Employers Reinsurance Corp.	GE Cablevision
1985		Australian Coal Properties
1986	RCA Kidder Peabody	
1987	CGR (medical diagnostic imaging) Navistar Financial Canada Gelco Corp. (auto leasing)	Consumer electronics business NBC radio networks battery and nuclear waste businesses
1988	Montgomery Ward Credit Corp. Roper Corp. (appliances) Borg-Warner chemicals	RCA Global Communications semiconductor business
1989	Tungsram (Hungarian lighting co.)	
1990	leasing companies Travelers Mortgage Services	Ladd Petroleum
1991	Financial News Network EMI Thorn light source business Bank of New York Chase Manhattan's leasing business Itel Corp.	Columbia Home Video
1992		GE Aerospace & GE Government Services merged with Martin Marietta

The elimination of the sectors was one element of a broader process of delaying in which Welch sought to eliminate layers of hierarchy and push decision-making down to the operating units.

We are now down in some businesses to four layers from the top to the bottom. That's the ultimate objective. We used to have things like department managers, section managers, subsection managers, units managers, supervisors. We are driving those titles out

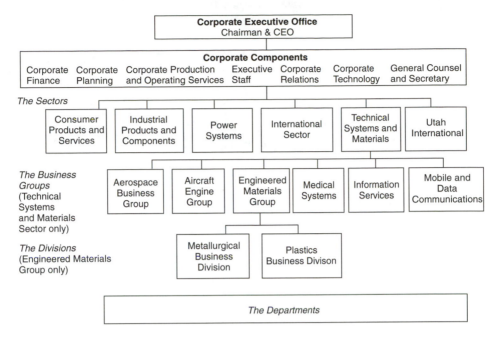

Figure 16.2 GE's organization structure, 1980
Source: *General Electric: Strategic Position – 1981*, HBS Case # 381-174.

. . . We used to go from the CEO to sectors to groups to businesses. We now go from the CEO . . . to businesses. Nothing else. There is nothing else there. Zero.

When you take out layers, you change the exposure of the managers who remain. They sit right in the sun. Some of them blotch immediately – they can't stand the exposure of leadership. I firmly believe that an overburdened, overstretched executive is the best executive, because he or she doesn't have time to meddle, to deal in trivia, or to bother people. Remember the theory that a manager should have no more than six or seven direct reports? I say the right number is closer to 10 or 15. This way you have no choice but to let people flex their muscles, to let them grow and mature.[2]

Welch also sought staff reductions in corporate functions. His goal was to "turn their role 180° from checker, inquisitor and authority figure to facilitator, helper and supporter of the businesses. . . . Ideas, initiatives and decisions could now move quickly. Often at the speed of sound – voices – where once they were muffled and garbled by the gauntlet of approvals and staff reviews."[3]

The combination of divestment, delayering, and staff reductions resulted in large reductions in employment. Between 1980 and 1990, GE's employment fell from 402,000 to 298,000. Moreover, where job growth occurred, it was primarily overseas. One implication was a huge reduction in the number of unionized employees at GE. In 1980 over 70 percent of GE's workforce was unionized, by 1988 35 percent were union members.

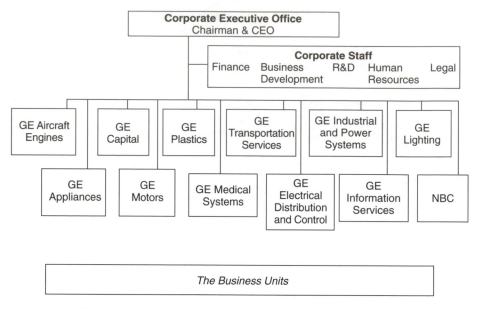

Figure 16.3 GE's organization structure, 1994

Source: Noel Tichy and Stratford Sherman, *Control Your Destiny or Someone Else Will*, New York: HarperBusiness, 1994.

By the mid-1980s, Welch had earned the nickname "Neutron Jack" – the building remained, but the people had gone.

STRATEGIC PLANNING

The changes in GE's structure were aimed at creating a more flexible and responsive corporation. This goal also necessitated changes in GE's highly developed management systems. In particular, Welch led a major overhaul of GE's much celebrated and widely emulated strategic planning system. The framework of an annual planning cycle was retained, but the staff-led, document-driven process was replaced by a less formal, more personal process. Instead of the big planning reports, Welch asked each business head to prepare a slim "playbook" that summarized the key strategic issues that the business faced, and how it intended to address them. This document provided the basis for a half-day, shirtsleeves review in mid-summer when Welch and key corporate officers would engage in discussion and debate with the top management team of each businesses. On the 1986 meetings, Welch commented:

> We asked the 14 business leaders to present reports on the competitive dynamics in their businesses. How did we do it? We had them each prepare one-page answers to five ques-

tions: What are your market dynamics globally today, and where are they going over the next several years? What actions have your competitors taken in the last three years to upset those global dynamics? What have you done in the last three years to affect these dynamics? What are the most dangerous things your competitor could do in the next three days to upset those dynamics? What are the most effective things you could do to bring your desired impact on those dynamics?

Five simple charts. After those initial reviews, which we update regularly, we could assume that everyone at the top knew the plays and had the same playbook. It doesn't take a genius. Fourteen businesses each with a playbook of five charts. So when Larry Bossidy is with a potential partner in Europe, or I'm with a company in the Far East, we're always there with a competitive understanding based upon our playbooks. We know exactly what makes sense, we don't need a big staff to do endless analysis. That means we should be able to act with speed.

FINANCIAL PLANNING AND CONTROL

Supporting GE's strategic planning system was a sophisticated financial budgeting system which centered around the annual budget. Budget preparation began in July and involved extensive negotiation between the operating units, the intervening groups and sectors, and the corporate headquarters. Once the budget was set, managers were locked in to meet it "at all costs" regardless of changes in the marketplace. It was generally agreed that the system had undesirable consequences, such as gaming to set low targets, and cutting long-term development to meet short-term targets. Because managers were locked in to figures established 18 months before, the budgeting system often inhibited adjustment to external changes and gave little information of management performance.

Welch's commitment to a performance-driven organization meant that financial targets were of critical importance. However, the key was to create shareholder value rather than accounting profits per se. In addition it was essential that the system should permit the performance of divisional and business unit managers to be assessed. Two changes were made. First, the controller's office prepared a set of financial objectives for each operating unit in order to reflect more realistically each unit's prospects and to reduce gamesmanship in target-setting. Second, the budgets (now called operating plans) were subject to revision as economic or competitive conditions changed. Thus, line managers could propose changes to the plans once the original assumptions on which they had been based could be shown to have changed. Performance evaluation was then made against the revised targets.

Central to the changes in financial control was the idea that performance was not about "making the budget." It was about raising performance expectations to be "as good as possible":

Shun the incremental and go for the leap. Most bureaucracies – and ours is no exception – unfortunately think in incremental terms rather than in terms of fundamental change. They think incrementally primarily because they think internally. Changing the culture – opening it up to the quantum change – means constantly asking not how fast am I going, how well am I doing versus how well I did a year or two before, but rather, how fast and how well am I doing versus the world outside. Are we moving faster, are we doing better against that external standard?

"Stretch," emphasized Welch, "means using dreams to set business targets – with no real idea of how to get there . . . We certainly didn't have a clue how we were going to get to 10 inventory turns [a year] when we set that target. But we're getting there, and as soon as we become sure we can do it – it's time for another stretch."[4]

The primary task of the businesses, emphasized Welch, was to produce earnings. As a guideline, Welch proposed that GE's earnings should grow at between one-and-a-half and two times the growth of GDP.

INCENTIVES

The key to GE's long-term development and performance was the development of its management talent. GE had a well-developed system of management appraisal and development which Welch retained. He believed giving managers greater profit-and-loss responsibility earlier in their careers would be conducive to an even greater flourishing of managerial talent. Welch gave greater emphasis to internal growth through new business development; however, the key output of these new ventures was managers rather than profits:

> The ventures are far less important than the product of the processes, which are the people. By having high visibility on these people – each having their own P&L statement, their own game, competing against the world – we get a chance to look at how they perform. They can blow it and they lose a little money, it doesn't matter. We get a feel for who they are and what they can manage. We get far more out of the people end of ventures than we do out of the earnings end.[5]

Creating a performance-driven organization also required the right incentives. Welch believed in giving more recognition to individual contributors and higher rewards to those who produced superior results.

> A flat reward system is a big anchor to incrementalism. We want to give big rewards to those who do things but without going for the scalps of those who reach for the big win but fail. Punishing failure assures that no one dares.

Welch redesigned the bonus system to reach deep into middle management. The bonuses became much more discriminating. The typical 10 percent to 15 percent bonuses for senior managers were replaced by 30 percent to 40 percent bonuses for far fewer managers. In addition, stock options were extended from the top echelon of management to a much wider range of managerial and technical employees. By 1996, Welch was able to report that the number of employees receiving stock options had increased from 400 in the early 1980s to 22,000 by the end of 1995: "Today, stock option compensation, based on total GE performance, is far more significant than the salary or bonus growth associated with the performance of any individual unit or business. This aligns the interests of the individual, the Company, and the share owner behind powerful, on-company results."[6]

WELCH'S MANAGEMENT PHILOSOPHY: SPEED, SIMPLICITY, SELF-CONFIDENCE

The changes in GE's strategic planning system were part of a wider change in the principles and systems through which GE was to be managed. Welch explained his ideas in an interview with *Harvard Business Review*:

> Good business leaders create a vision, articulate the vision, passionately own the vision, and relentlessly drive it to completion. Above all else, though, good leaders are open. They go up, down, and around their organization to reach people. They don't stick to the established channels. They're informal. They're straight with people. They make a religion out of being accessible. They never get bored telling their story.
>
> Real communication takes countless hours of eyeball to eyeball, back and forth. It means more listening than talking. It's not pronouncements on a videotape; it's not announcements in a newspaper. It is human beings coming to see and accept things through a constant interactive process aimed at consensus. And it must be absolutely relentless. That's a real challenge for us. There's still not enough candor in this company.
>
> I mean facing reality, seeing the world as it is rather than as you wish it were. We've seen over and over again that businesses facing market downturns, tougher competition, and more demanding customers inevitably make forecasts that are much too optimistic. This means they don't take advantage of the opportunities change usually offers. Change in the marketplace isn't something to fear; it's an enormous opportunity to shuffle the deck, to replay the game. Candid managers – leaders – don't get paralyzed about the "fragility" of the organization. They tell people the truth. That doesn't scare them because they realize their people know the truth anyway.
>
> We've had managers at GE who couldn't change, who kept telling us to leave them alone. They wanted to sit back, to keep things the way they were. And that's just what they did – until they and most of their staffs had to go. That's the lousy part of this job. . . . The point is, what determines our destiny is not the hand you're dealt; it's how you play the hand. And the best way to play your hand is to face reality – see the world the way it is – and act accordingly.
>
> For a large organization to be effective, it must be simple. For a large organization to be simple, its people must have self-confidence and intellectual self-assurance. Insecure managers create complexity. Frightened, nervous managers use thick, convoluted planning books and busy slides filled with everything they've known since childhood. Real leaders don't need clutter. People must have the self-confidence to be clear, precise, to be sure that every person in their organization – highest to lowest – understands what the business is trying to achieve. But it's not easy. You can't believe how hard it is for people to be simple, how much they fear being simple. They worry that if they're simple, people will think they're simpleminded. In reality, of course, it's just the reverse. Clear, tough-minded people are the most simple.
>
> Simple doesn't mean easy, especially as you try to move this approach down through the organization. When you take out layers, you change the exposure of the managers who remain. They sit right in the sun. Some of them blotch immediately; they can't stand the exposure of leadership.

By the end of the 1980s, Welch's ideas about management were summarized in the slogan "Speed, Simplicity, Self-Confidence":

> We found in the 1980s that becoming faster is tied to becoming simpler. Our businesses, with tens of thousands of employees, will not respond to visions that have sub-paragraphs and footnotes. If we're not simple, we can't be fast . . . and if we're not fast, we can't win. Simplicity, to an engineer, means clean, functional winning designs, no bells or whistles. In marketing, it might manifest itself as clear, unencumbered proposals. For manufacturing people, it would produce a logical process that makes sense to every individual on the line. And on an individual, interpersonal level, it would take the form of plain-speaking directness, honesty.
>
> But just as surely as speed flows from simplicity, simplicity is grounded in self-confidence. Self-confidence does not grow in someone who is just another appendage on the bureaucracy; whose authority rests on little more than a title. People who are freed from the confines of their box on the organization chart, whose status rests on real-world achievement – those are the people who develop the self-confidence to be simple, to share every bit of information available to them, to listen to those above, below and around them and then move boldly.
>
> But a company can't distribute self-confidence. What it can do – what we must do – is to give each of our people an opportunity to win, to contribute, and hence earn self-confidence themselves. They don't get that opportunity, they can't taste winning if they spend their days wandering in the muck of a self-absorbed bureaucracy.
>
> Speed . . . simplicity . . . self-confidence. We have it in increasing measure. We know where it comes from . . . and we have plans to increase it in the 1990s.[7]

Work-Out

To communicate his message and provide an example of the style of open, direct management he believed in, Welch was a frequent visitor to GE's Management Development Institute at Crotonville, New York. With each class of GE managers, he conducted an open discussion session to explain his vision and, equally importantly, to engage in a no-holds-barred give-and-take question and debate session about GE. After a particularly outspoken session in late 1988, Welch and Jim Baughman, Director of Management Development, were impressed with the energy and power for change that such sessions generated. During their helicopter ride from Crotonville to GE headquarters in Fairfield, they wondered if the type of interaction which took place that day could not be replicated across the company in some kind of process in which all employees could participate. Before the helicopter landed, they had outlined a new initiative which they termed "Work-Out."

The idea was to create a forum where a cross-section of employees could speak their minds about the management of their business without the fear of retribution by their superiors. More importantly, it was to be a place to get immediate action on their recommendations. In January 1989, Welch announced the new idea at the company's annual meeting of its top 500 executives. Although introduced as "a fluid and adaptable concept – not a program," it was equally clear to all in attendance that Work-Out was not optional.

While each business approached Work-Out in its own way, some common structural and procedural characteristics gradually emerged. Typically, the sessions assembled a cross-section of 50 to 100 of the business's employees for meetings that ran for two or three days. In an environment that Welch likened to an old New England town meeting, the group would be asked to openly and honestly review the management process and practices in their part of the operation. Initially they focused on unproductive or bureaucratic behaviors which had limited their personal effectiveness. At the end of each Work-Out, the group's manager returned to hear the findings and recommendations, and could either accept or reject them on the spot, or appoint a team to report back with more data by a given date.

As the concept was rolled out in GE, Welch commented on his expectations:

> Work-Out has a practical and an intellectual goal. The practical objective is to get rid of thousands of bad habits accumulated since the creation of General Electric. . . . The second thing we want to achieve, the intellectual part, begins by putting the leaders of each business in front of 100 or so of their people, eight to ten times a year, to let them hear what their people think. Work-Out will expose the leaders to the vibrations of their business – opinions, feelings, emotions, resentments, not abstract theories of organization and management. Ultimately, we're talking about redefining the relationship between boss and subordinate.
>
> These Work-Out sessions, create all kinds of personal dynamics. Some people go and hide. Some emerge as forceful advocates. As people meet over and over, though, more of them will develop the courage to speak out. The norm will become the person who says, "Damn it, we're not doing it. Let's get on with doing it. This process will create more fulfilling and rewarding jobs. The quality of work life will improve dramatically."[8]

The Work-Out sessions quickly evolved from their focus on removing bureaucratic practices ("low-hanging fruit" as it was called) to more complicated and sensitive issues involving cross-functional processes or shared responsibilities. By getting a business's real operating teams together to work jointly on improving product flaws, yield rates or quality levels, Work-Out sessions produced some impressive results. Eventually, Work-Outs began involving customers and suppliers in discussions about how to improve external processes and relationships.

In the first two years of its implementation, more than 2,000 Work-Out sessions had been conducted throughout GE and over 90 percent of the suggestions had been acted on. Welch expected the process to continue throughout the 1990s at a rate of over 700 sessions annually. "If you get ideas from those closest to the work, and let them keep pouring them out, you must keep getting better and better practices. Productivity grows," Welch said.

> At a Workout session at a GE silicone plastics plant in Waterford, N.Y. for example, participants brought up the plant's centralized quality control system, set up when the facility was built 40 years ago and never reorganized as the plant expanded over the years. The antiquated system forced workers to use a jerry-built system of pneumatic tubes and motorized carts to move product samples from factory floor to the distant lab – rather than testing them on the spot.
>
> "It was almost like out of the Dark Age," Welch says. "So right there we agreed to break up this lab and move it out."

"You start with things like the filing systems and 'Hey, why do we have all those reports?' " says Jeff Bunten, an operations manager in St. Louis who has been through two workouts. "The next step in the process is to focus on the customer . . ."

Some divisions have adapted Work Out to the budgeting process . . . a session held by NBC Sports knocked nearly $1 million out of the cost of televising professional football games. And others are inviting customers and suppliers to join the process. . . . "It allows us to bring a group of buyers from Sears to spend three days with us on what we are we doing wrong serving Sears, how we can serve them better," Welch said.[9]

Not everyone was enthusiastic about Work-Out. Some managers complained that Work-Out sessions encouraged employees to question, challenge, and second-guess them, undermining their authority. And as work was eliminated and people were laid off, even initially enthusiastic salaried and hourly workers became increasingly concerned. Said Norm Mitchell, a once-supportive union leader, "I'm not as comfortable today as I was yesterday."

THE BOUNDARY-LESS ORGANIZATION

As the changes to GE's systems, behaviors, and attitudes penetrated further and further into the organization, Welch turned increasingly to the need to create strength from GE's tremendous product and geographical diversity.

A "best practices" project which originated with a study of 25 companies that had sustained a faster productivity growth than GE over the previous decade led to a program of discussions and visits to identify and analyze leading-edge management practices. The study teams brought back a variety of new ideas: asset management from Digital, product development from Honda, quality improvement from Hewlett-Packard, and customer service from American Express.

If learning could be transferred across companies, the scope for transferring learning within GE must be huge. By 1990, Welch was developing the vision of a new GE organization that would be a truly "boundary-less" company. His boundary-less company was one in which both external barriers and internal barriers became blurred:

In a boundary-less company, suppliers aren't outsiders. They are drawn closer and become trusted partners in the total business process. Customers' vision of their needs and the company's view become identical and every effort of every man and woman in the company is focused on satisfying those needs.

The boundary-less company blurs the divisions between internal functions; it recognizes no distinctions between "domestic" and "foreign" operations; and it ignores or erases group labels such as "management," "salaried," and "hourly" which get in the way of people working together.[10]

Boundary-lessness required changes in incentives, attitudes, and behaviors that would permit GE to achieve "integrated diversity – the ability to transfer the best ideas, most developed knowledge and most valuable people freely and easily across GE's 13 businesses." For example:

Two years ago, one of our people spotted a truly innovative method of compressing product cycle times in an appliance company in New Zealand. After testing it successfully in our Canadian affiliate, we transferred the methodology to our largest appliance complex in Louisville, KY. It has revolutionized processes, reduced cycle times, increased our customer responsiveness, and reduced our inventory levels by hundreds of millions of dollars. Teams from all of our manufacturing businesses are now living in Louisville so we can spread the New Zealand-to-Montreal-to-Louisville learning to every business in GE.[11]

THE LATE 1990s: SERVICES, GLOBALIZATION, QUALITY

By the late 1990s, Welch's priorities for driving "GE's Growth Engine" were focused around three major themes: expansion in services, taking advantage of international opportunities, and the pursuit of "Six Sigma" quality.

Financial Services

By 1997, Welch's conceptualizing of the GE business portfolio had evolved from a three-circle to a two-circle model. The 1996 Annual Report described GE's financial model thus:

> On the one side is a group of 11 large businesses, virtually all #1 or #2 in their marketplaces, that consistently improve operating margins, earnings and cash flow and support the triple-A debt rating of the parent company. GE's triple A, in turn, supports a huge diverse, global financial services enterprise, also rated triple A. The uniqueness of this model lies in its consistency. The operating businesses in the model grow their revenues, operating margins and working capital turns, while the 27 businesses that make up the financial services arm grow earnings at consistent double-digit rates.[12]

During the 1990s GE Capital Services was the most profitable and rapidly growing part of the GE empire. In 1997 its operating profit amounted to $4.4 billion, compared to $10.6 billion for the rest of GE.

International Growth

Together with financial services, the central feature of GE's earnings growth in the 1990s had been global expansion. Welch summed up his attitude towards international growth and his reactions to the economic problems in Asia in the 1997 Annual Report:

> We've been down this road before. In the early 1980s, we experienced a United States mired in recession, hand-wringing from the pundits and dirges being sung over American manufacturing. We didn't buy this dismal scenario; instead, we invested in both a widespread restructuring and in new businesses. . . .

To us, Europe looked a lot like the United States in the 1980s, and in need of the same remedies: restructuring, spin-offs, and the like. So, while many were "writing-off" Europe, we invested heavily, buying new companies and expanding our existing presence. Following the restructuring of its industrial and financial structure, as well as a dose of the powerful export medicine of a devalued currency, Europe is now recovering, and "GE Europe" is now a $20.6 billion operation. Our revenues have more than doubled from 1994 to 1997; net income has tripled to more than $1.5 billion; and growth is accelerating as the European recovery progresses. . . .

Mexico in the mid 1990s was a similar story: dislocation, uncertainty and turbulence. Reacting to the peso crisis of 1995 and its aftermath, GE moved, acquiring 10 companies and investing more than $1 billion in new and existing operations. The result was revenue growth of 60% and a doubling of earnings in the two years following the crisis.

Today we are determined, and poised, to do the same thing in Asia we have done in the United States, Europe and Mexico: invest in the future.

Six Sigma

If Work-Out was the primary vehicle for driving large-scale corporate change at GE during the late 1980s and early 1990s, Welch views GE's Six Sigma program as the primary driver of organizational change and performance improvement from 1998 into the next millennium.

Unlike many of Welch's other initiatives, there is nothing new about Six Sigma quality initiatives. They were pioneered by Motorola during the 1980s. Six Sigma is a disciplined methodology that focuses on moving every process that touches a company's customers toward near-perfect quality. Working on five basic activities – defining, measuring, analyzing, improving, and then controlling processes – Six Sigma focuses on improving customers' productivity and reducing their capital outlays while decreasing GE's costs, increasing its own productivity, and accelerating returns on investment. GE has jumped aboard this productivity train and hopes to realize over $800 million in net savings in 1998, thus increasing its returns on capital, equity, and sales and, in turn, strengthening its overall financial resource which it utilizes to make the investments in global and business opportunities.

Welch views Six Sigma as the next "soul-transforming cultural initiative" after Work-Out in creating a learning environment within GE:

> Six Sigma has spread like wildfire across the Company and it is transforming everything we do . . . Today, in the uncountable meetings across GE – both organized and in-the-hall – the gates are open to the largest flood of innovative ideas in world business. These ideas are generated, improved upon and shared by 350 business segments – or, as we think about them, 350 business laboratories. Today, these ideas center on spreading Six Sigma "best practices" across our business operations . . .
>
> - Medical systems described how Six Sigma designs produced a 10-fold increase in the life of CT scanner x-ray tubes . . .
> - Superabrasives – our industrial diamonds business – described how Six Sigma quadruples its return on investments by improving yields . . .
> - Our railcar leasing business described a 62% reduction in turnaround time at its repair shops . . .[13]

TABLE 16.2
GE's performance under Jack Welch

	1997	1996	1995	1994	1993	1992
Revenues ($bn.)	90.8	79.2	70.0	60.1	55.7	53.0
Earnings from continuing operations ($bn.)	8.2	7.3	6.6	5.9	4.2	4.1
Net earnings ($bn.)	8.2	7.3	6.6	4.7	4.3	4.7
Return on av. shareholders' equity	25.0%	24.0%	23.5%	18.1%	17.5%	20.9%
Total assets ($bn.)	304.0	272.4	228.0	194.5	251.5	192.9
Long-term borrowings ($bn.)	46.6	49.2	51.0	37.0	28.2	25.3
Employees at year end ('000)						
United States	165	155	150	156	157	168
Other countries	111	84	72	60	59	58
Discontinued operations	n.a.	n.a.	n.a.	5	6	42
Total employees	276	239	222	221	222	268
	1991	1990	1989	1988	1987	1986
Revenues ($bn.)	51.3	49.7	54.6	50.1	48.2	42.0
Earnings from continuing operations ($bn.)	3.9	3.9	3.9	3.4	2.1	2.5
Net earnings ($bn.)	2.6	4.3	3.9	3.4	2.9	2.5
Return on av. shareholders' equity	12.2%	20.2%	20.0%	19.4%	18.5%	17.3%
Total assets ($bn.)	166.5	152.0	128.3	110.9	95.4	84.8
Long-term borrowings ($bn.)	22.6	20.9	16.1	15.1	12.5	10.0
Employees at year end ('000)						
United States	173	183	243	255	277	302
Other countries	62	62	49	43	45	71
Discontinued operations	49	53	n.a.	n.a.	n.a.	n.a.
Total employees	284	298	292	298	322	373
	1985	1984	1983	1982	1981	
Revenues ($bn.)	28.3	27.3	26.8	26.5	27.2	
Earnings from continuing operations ($bn.)	2.3	n.a.	n.a.	n.a.	n.a.	
Net earnings ($bn.)	2.3	2.3	2.0	1.8	1.7	
Return on av. shareholders' equity	17.6%	19.1%	18.9%	18.8%	19.1%	
Total assets ($bn.)	26.4	24.7	23.3	21.6	20.9	
Long-term borrowings ($bn.)	0.8	0.8	0.9	1.0	1.1	
Employees at year end ('000)						
United States	236	248	246	n.a.	n.a.	
Other countries	68	82	94	n.a.	n.a.	
Discontinued operations	n.a.	n.a.	n.a.	n.a.	n.a.	
Total employees	304	330	340	367	404	

n.a. = not available.

Source: General Electric Annual Reports.

TABLE 16.3
Relative performance under GE's different CEOs

Ranking by profitability	CEO	Av. annual pretax ROE
1	Wilson, 1940–9	46.72%
2	Cordiner, 1950–63	40.49%
3	Jones, 1973–80	29.70%
4	**Welch, 1981–**	**27.81%**
5	Borch, 1964–72	27.52%
6	Coffin, 1915–21	14.52%
7	Swope/Young, 1922–39	12.63%

The dates given for each CEO are for the financial years that correspond most closely to each CEO's tenure.

TOWARD A POST-WELCH GE

Among the financial community, practicing managers, and business school academics, Welch's tenure at the head of GE was regarded as one of the most remarkable eras of corporate leadership in history. In terms of both financial performance and management innovation, Welch was widely compared with Alfred Sloan, the architect of General Motors.

By mid-1998, Welch had reached his last two years as chairman and CEO of GE. There was no doubt as to the impact that Welch had had on the organization. This was not simply a matter of financial performance (see Tables 16.2 and 16.3); everything about the management of GE reflected his ideas, his values, and his personality. It was difficult to envisage a GE led by anyone other than Welch. His refusal to make any comment whatsoever on management succession only fueled discussion both inside and outside GE of who would be the heir to Welch's mantle, and how on earth anyone could step into his shoes.

Questions about succession inevitably turned to questions concerning the future of GE. In an era of corporate refocusing, GE was unique in American business in demonstrating that a century-old conglomerate could outperform the focused giants of the new technology-based industrial sectors. But, if this success-against-the-odds was a tribute to the ideas and the driving personality of Jack Welch, what kind of future could GE expect under his successor? Already, forecasts were being made that GE would spin off its Capital Services subsidiary. Could this signal the ultimate breakup of GE in the same way that other once-successful conglomerates such as ITT and Hanson had broken up?

TABLE 16.A1
General Electric's history

Leadership	Company events	Product introductions	Financial highlights
1879–1889. Thomas Edison. Envisioned a company that would "light a nation."	1879. Edison Electric Light Company founded. 1886. Manufacturing moved to Schenectady "Works."	1880. First incandescent light bulbs sold commercially.	
1890–1922. Charles A. Coffin. Broadened Edison's vision to include any and all electrical technologies in GE's domain.	1892. Merger with Thomson Houston formed the General Electric company. 1905. GE controlled 97% of US lamp business.	1905. GE's first electric toaster, the Model X2. 1905. Commercial electric refrigerators introduced.	1892. Rev. $11.7m, NI $2.9m, 4,000 employees. 1900. Rev. $28.8m, NI $6.9m, 12,000 employees. 1910. Rev. $71.5m, NI $10.9m, 36,200 employees.
1922–39. Owen D. Young/ Gerald Swope. Broad diversification of the number of products manufactured by GE.	1919. Organized the Radio Corporation of America. 1925. Formation of Plastics Department. 1926. The GE X-Ray Corporation founded 1927. GE Contracts Corporation began to finance purchase of refrigerators. 1932. RCA separated from GE.	1932. The tree-way lamp was developed for multi-level illumination. 1932. First GE Dishwashers were marketed.	1930. Rev. $376.2m, NI $60.5m, 78,400 employees.

TABLE 16.A1 *Continued*

Leadership	Company events	Product introductions	Financial highlights
1939–50. Philipp Reed/ Charles Wilson. GE greatly expanded its defense-related business.	1939. GE Radio and TV department was formed.	1942. GE built and tested first US jet engine.	1940. Rev. $411.9m, NI $56.2m, 76,300 employees.
1950–63. Ralph J. Cordiner. Sent GE on a path to take advantage of new markets that opened after WW II.	1950. Changed to decentralized organizational structure. Each operating department given P&L responsibility.	1954. First industrial installations of numerical controls for machine tools.	1955. Rev. $2,234m, NI $179.7m, 206,000 employees.
1963–72. Fred J. Borch. Identified 9 growth sectors in US economy and GE decided to become leader by entering all of them.	1968. McKinsey study led to establishment of GE's SBU organization structure. 1970. Exit from computers.	1968. First commercial order for GE airplane engines.	1965. Rev. $6,213m, NI $355m, 333,000 employees.
1972–81. Reginald H. Jones. Implemented SBU structure and new strategic planning system. Linked strategic planning with annual budget process.	1971. New $30 million medical systems complex built in Waukesha, WI. 1976. Utah International acquired.	1976. A CT scanner developed by the medical systems division.	1970. Rev $8,762m, NI $328m, 396,600 employees. 1980. Rev. $24,959m, NI$1,514m, 402,000 employees.
1981–present. John F. Welch, Jr. During early 1980s key issues were:	1981. Downsizing/delayering: between 1981 and 1988 approximately 100,000	1981. USS Ohio designed at GE's atomic power laboratory.	1982. Rev. $26,500m, NI $1,817m, 367,000 employees.

- Rethinking the business portfolio – businesses that were not either # 1 or # 2 in their markets would have to be fixed, closed, or sold.
- Cost-cutting.

positions eliminated. Many layers of management removed.

1984. Sale of Utah Int. and Housewares

1983. Rev. $26,797m, NI $2,024m, 340,000 employees.

1983. Introduces Signa Magnetic Resonance (MR) Technology for medical diagnostic imaging.

Mid-1980s–1990. Welch focuses upon removing bureaucracy, rethinking corporate systems, and changing the culture.

1988. Welch outlines "The GE Growth Engine."

1989. Work-Out inaugurated.

Acquires RCA, Kidder Peabody, and Montgomery Ward Credit Corporation.

1985. Sectors removed. Each business reports directly to the CEO.

1987. Consumer electronics business swapped with Thompson SA of France for CGR medical diagnostics.

1988. Semiconductor business sold.

1985. Rev. $32,624m, NI $2,277m, 299,000 employees.

1987. Rev. $48,158m, NI $2,915m, 322,000 employees.

1989. Rev. $54,547m, NI $3,893m, 292,000 employees.

1985. GE ships the first Dash 8 computer-controlled locomotives.

1986. Ford Taurus contains 7 lbs. of GE plastics.

1987. GE selected by NASA to produce major portions of its planned space station.

1989. Introduced new line of RCA major appliances.

1989. CNBC cable-TV network launched by NBC.

1990s. Focus on growth, the boundary-less corporation, and quality management.

1991. Welch promotes "boundary-less" behavior and "integrated diversity."

1992–7. Emphasis on globalization.

1997. Six Sigma program launched.

1991. NBC acquired FNN.

1992. GE Aerospace merged with Martin Marietta.

1993. Tungsram (Hungary) acquired.

1995. GECS acquires banks, consumer finance cos., and reinsurance cos.

1996. GECS acquires leading and equipment financing companies worldwide.

1997. Greenwich/UNC jet service co. acquired.

1991. Rev. $60,236m, NI $4,435m, 284,000 employees.

1993. Rev. $70,028m, NI $4,315m, 222,000 employees.

1995. Rev. $70,028m, NI $6,573m, 222,000 employees.

1997. Rev. $90,840m, NI $8,203m, 276,000 employees.

1991. NBC launches around-the-clock news channel.

1992. 9F gas turbine introduced.

1995. PACE automated credit evaluation system introduced.

1996. MSNBC launched, 6000HP locomotive introduced.

Notes

1. "Can Jack Welch reinvent GE?" *Business Week*, June 29, 1986, pp. 40–5.
2. Noel Tichy and Ram Charan, "Speed, simplicity, and self confidence: an interview with Jack Welch," *Harvard Business Review*, September/October 1989.
3. "GE 1984," HBS Case No. 385–315.
4. GE Annual Report, 1993, p. 5.
5. Welch interview, *Harvard Business Review*.
6. GE Annual Report, 1995, p. 4.
7. Jack Welch, address to 1989 shareholders' meeting.
8. Welch interview, *Harvard Business Review*.
9. Mark Potts, "Towards a boundaryless firm at General Electric," in R. M. Kanter, B. A. Stein, and T. D. Jick, *The Challenge of Organizational Change*, New York: Free Press, 1992.
10. GE Annual Report, 1990.
11. Ibid.
12. GE Annual Report, 1996, p. 2.
13. GE Annual Report, 1997, pp. 3–4.

CHAPTER SEVENTEEN

AES Corporation: Rewriting the Rules of Management

Robert M. Grant prepared this case solely to provide material for class discussion. The author does not intend to illustrate either the effective or ineffective handling of a management situation. The author may have disguised certain names or other identifying information to protect confidentiality. Matt Carlson, Diana Cortes, Tom Cuggino, Christian Jepsen, and Mark Rutherford helped prepare the case.

God made us all a certain way. We're all creative, capable of making decisions, trustworthy, able to learn, and perhaps most important, fallible. We all want to be part of a community and to use our skills to make a difference in the world.
Dennis Bakke, CEO, AES

We broke all the rules. No overtime. No bosses. No time records. No shift schedules. No assigned responsibilities. No administration. And guess what? It worked!
Oscar Prieto, AES manager and director of Light Servicios de Electricidade, Brazil

October 1998

August and September 1998 were nervous months for AES's shareholders. As "global financial contagion" spread from Southeast Asia to Russia and Latin America, AES's share price felt the shock waves. With operations in China, Pakistan, Kazakhstan, Georgia, Hungary, Argentina, Brazil, the Dominican Republic, El Salvador, and Mexico (as well as the US, Canada, the UK, and Australia), AES appeared to have focused its overseas investment on countries most vulnerable to financial meltdown. After reaching a peak of $56.50 in June 1998, by early September AES's share price was down to $24.

By October, investors were able to breathe a sigh of relief. The inclusion of AES within the S&P 500 had resulted in a surge of buying from mutual funds, and the quarterly financial results reported on October 22 confirmed that AES's growth trend was intact: revenues were 71 percent higher than the year-ago period, earnings were 58 percent higher. Announcing the results, AES's founders, Roger Sant and Dennis Bakke, expressed satisfaction with the present and confidence in the future. "The fundamentals of our business continue to remain strong. Our plants ran well and we are making significant progress with the distribution companies that we acquired during the last few years. All of these accomplishments have been achieved during a quarter in which economic conditions were difficult around the world," commented President and CEO Bakke. "I continue to be amazed by the ability of AES people to find new opportunities and overcome difficulties in existing businesses. The global restructuring of the electric sector has not slowed down. This restructuring provides us with the chance to expand our businesses with acquisitions and greenfield plants," added Chairman Sant.

Not everyone was so sanguine about AES's future prospects. AES was like no other company within its industry. It was committed to social responsibility and providing fun for employees. Its principles were reflected in a management system which the *Wall Street Journal* referred to as "empowerment gone mad."[1] Its unique organization was referred to by Board Member Robert Waterman (of *In Search of Excellence* fame) as an "adhocracy." There were no staff functions or corporate departments; almost all traditional management functions were devolved to workers at the plant level. The system had worked well. It had encouraged amazing loyalty, commitment, and initiative from employees, remarkable entrepreneurial drive at all levels of the company, and unmatched levels of operational efficiency.

But AES was no longer an entrepreneurial start-up company. By October 1998 it owned more than 100 power plants and employed 11,000 people in 23 countries of the world. In a decade and a half it had gone from a single-plant operator to the world's largest independent power producer (IPP). The diversity of the company had also increased: from one plant in Texas, it now spanned the globe; it had expanded from coal-fired into gas-fired and hydro plants; from being a power production specialist, it was now into power distribution. It seemed that growing scale and scope would inevitably place increasing strains on AES's ad hoc style of management.

Its management principles and style were rooted in the personal beliefs of its two founders and in traditional American values of equality of opportunity, openness, and individualism. As AES became increasingly global with major operations in traditional Islamic societies such as Pakistan, socialist systems such as China, and the oligarchic societies of Latin America, would it need to adapt its carefully nurtured management system? And for how much longer would the remarkable partnership of Sant and Bakke continue to guide the company? By 1998, Roger Sant was 68 years old, and as chairman of the World Wildlife Fund and head of a foundation dealing with issues of population and the environment, he was likely to play a smaller and smaller role in AES's future.

Finally, the market itself was changing. AES was a product of deregulation. It had been founded to take advantage of public utility deregulation in the US, and its international expansion had been driven by opportunities made available by privatization and liberalization. While the stream of privatization was continuing, the level of competition in the industry had increased substantially. The world power-generation industry had been recognized as a growth sector by many companies. Competitors for electricity supply contacts included IPPs such as AES, traditional utilities such as Electricité de France, Duke Power, Entergy, and British Energy, gas companies such as Enron and British Gas, the oil majors such as Amoco, Exxon, and Mobil, and a range of other players. Moreover, the structure of the industry was in flux. Could AES survive and prosper as an IPP, or would it be at a disadvantage to competitors which were backward integrated (such as the oil and gas producers), or forward integrated (such as the electricity utilities)?

AES'S ORIGINS AND DEVELOPMENT

In January 1982, Roger Sant and Dennis Bakke founded Applied Energy Systems based in Arlington, Virginia. Their purpose was to take advantage of a 1978 Public Utility Regulatory Policy Act (PURPA) that required utilities to purchase power from independent energy producers. Sant and Bakke believed they could build a business in a niche segment of the enormous power-generation industry.

At first glance, Sant and Bakke seemed a rather unlikely pair to start what has become a large international energy company. Although both held Harvard MBAs, their experience was primarily public sector. Sant headed the Ford Administration's energy conservation efforts and Bakke served as a chief aide. Following government service, they moved on to the Mellon Institute's Energy Productivity Center, where they spent several years researching various techniques for energy conservation. The highlight of their career at Mellon was the publication of a book entitled *Creating Abundance: America's Least-Cost Strategy*. It was during this time that the pair came up with the idea of starting their own company.

Sant and Bakke had a very difficult time raising money at first, because nobody took them very seriously. According to Bakke, "[we] had the worst possible background for raising money . . . first government and then academic experience. It looked to investors like a combination of inefficiency and ivory tower."[2] However, Sant and Bakke had one key advantage: as a result of their involvement in drafting PURPA, they were among the first to recognize the opportunity for independent generators to produce power at much lower costs than the established utilities.

Sant and Bakke raised $1.3 million from private investors and began looking for deep-pocketed partners. From 1981 to 1985 Sant and Bakke sought alliances with Arco, IBM, and Bechtel to name but a few. In 1985, the founders decided to go it alone and built their first power plant adjacent to an oil refinery in Houston, Texas, using petroleum coke (essentially a waste product) for fuel. Because AES agreed to link the price of the electricity generated to the price of natural gas (which subsequently fell sharply), the plant was not profitable. However, the second and third plants that AES built "weren't disastrous, and four, five and six turned out to be superb. By 1989 it was clear that we had reached viability."[3]

In 1991, AES went public. With a stronger equity base it was ready to look at opportunities overseas. Because of the rapid growth in electricity demand in many emerging markets, inadequate generating capacity, and the trend towards privatization, Sant estimated that over 70 percent of AES's opportunities lay outside the US. The fast-growing Asian markets for electricity, especially the huge potential markets of India and China, were especially attractive. In the early 1990s AES inaugurated its international strategy by acquiring two plants in Northern Ireland and one in Argentina. International expansion involved participating in the auctioning of state-owned electricity companies by governments, and bidding for long-term power supply contracts from governments which were opening the generating end of their electricity industries to competition. During the mid-1990s, AES's biggest new investments in power generation were in Kazakhstan and China. The 1996 acquisition of Light Servicios de Electricidade, Brazil was a major strategic departure for AES: this was its first entry into the distribution end of the power business. Overseas expansion was primarily through the acquisition of existing power-generating facilities rather than building new plants. A similar transition was occurring in the US. Changes in utility regulations at the state level resulted in some utilities selling off their generating facilities – AES was among the most prominent bidders for these facilities.

During 1998, AES continued to expand both at home and overseas:

- In January, AES acquired the CLESA electricity distribution company in El Salvador for $96.5 million.
- Also in January, AES won a bid to supply electricity from a 360 MW plant in Haripur, Bangladesh. This was followed in June by a further power supply agreement in Bangladesh, with AES acquiring and operating the 450 MW Meghnaghat power station.
- In April, AES affiliate Light Servicios acquired the electricity distribution company serving São Paulo, Brazil.
- In May, AES purchased three generating stations from Southern California Edison.
- In May, AES acquired 90 percent of Edelap, an electricity distribution company in Buenos Aires, Argentina.
- In June, AES raised $173 million to finance the construction of a 484 MW gas-fired power station in Merida, Mexico.
- In August, AES acquired six coal-fired power stations from New York State Electricity and Gas Corporation for $950 million.
- In October, AES acquired 49 percent of the 420 MW Orissa Power Generation Corporation from the Orissa state government in eastern India.
- Also in October, AES announced that it had won a bid to acquire a 75 percent interest in Telasi, the electricity distribution company of Tbilisi, Georgia, for approximately $25.5 million.

Tables 17.1a–c show AES's plants and distribution facilities in 1998. AES also owns and operates the Lyukobanya coal mine in Hungary, which has an output of approximately 1 million tonnes per year of brown coal and is the sole supplier for AES Borsod.

TABLE 17.1a
AES's generating plants in operation

Company	Location	Fuel	Capacity (MW)	AES interest (%)
AES Deepwater	TX, US	Pet coke	143	100
AES Beaver Valley	PA, US	Coal	125	80
AES Placerita	CA, US	Gas	120	100
AES Thames	CT, US	Coal	181	100
AES Shady Point	OK, US	Coal	320	100
AES Hawaii	HI, US	Coal	180	100
Kilroot	N. Ireland	Coal/oil	520	47
Belfast West	N. Ireland	Coal	240	47
AES San Nicolás	Argentina	Coal/oil/gas	650	69
AES Cabra Corral	Argentina	Hydro	102	98
AES El Tunal	Argentina	Hydro	10	98
AES Xiangci-Cili	China	Hydro	26	51
Medway	England	Gas	688	25
AES Sarmiento	Argentina	Gas	33	98
AES Ullum	Argentina	Hydro	45	98
Fontes Nova-Light	Brazil	Hydro	144	14
Ilha dos Pombos-Light	Brazil	Hydro	164	14
Nilo Pecanha-Light	Brazil	Hydro	180	14
Pereira Passos-Light	Brazil	Hydro	100	14
AES Borsod	Hungary	Coal	171	96
AES Tisza II	Hungary	Oil/gas	860	96
AES Tiszapalkonya	Hungary	Coal	250	96
AES Ekibastuz	Kazakhstan	Coal	4,000	70
AES Wuxi	China	Oil	63	55
Wuhu	China	Coal	250	25
Yangchun	China	Oil	15	25
AES Indian Queens	England	Oil	140	100
AES Los Mina	Dom. Republic	Oil	235	100
CEMIG (35 plants)	Brazil	Various	5,068	9
Chengdu Lotus City	China	Gas	48	35
AES Kingston	Canada	Gas	110	50
AES Jiaozou	China	Coal	250	70
AES Hefei	China	Oil	76	70
AES Ust-Kamenogorsk	Kazakhstan	Hydro	332	85
AES Shulbinsk	Kazakhstan	Hydro	702	85
AES Ust-Kamenogorsk	Kazakhstan	CHP	240	85
AES Leninogorsk	Kazakhstan	CHP	50	85
AES Sogrinsk	Kazakhstan	CHP	50	85
AES Semipalatinsk	Kazakhstan	CHP	10	85
AES Lal Pir	Pakistan	Oil	351	90
PakGen	Pakistan	Oil	344	90
AES Quebrada	Argentina	Hydro	45	100
AES Alamitos	CA, US	Gas	2,083	100
AES Redondo Beach	CA, US	Gas	1,310	100
AES Huntington Beach	CA, US	Gas	563	100
Total			21,787	

TABLE 17.1b
AES's generating plants under construction, 1998

Company	Location	Fuel	Capacity (MW)	AES interest (%)
AES Elsta	Netherlands	Gas	405	50
AES Hefei	China	Oil	39	70
AES Fuling Aixi	China	Coal	50	70
Miranda—CEMIG	Brazil	Hydro	390	9
Igarapava—CEMIG	Brazil	Hydro	210	1
AES Barry	Wales, UK	Gas	230	100
AES Warrior Run	MD, US	Coal	180	100
AES Mt. Stuart	Australia	Kerosene	288	100
Yangcheng	China	Coal	2,100	25
AES Merida III	Mexico	Gas	484	55
AES Uruguaiana	Brazil	Gas	600	100
AES Parana	Argentina	Gas	830	67
Total			5,806	

TABLE 17.1c
AES's Distribution companies, 1998

Company	Location	Customers (millions)	Network (km)	Sales (GWH)	AES interest (%)
Cemig	Brazil	4.1	274,000	32,179	13
Light	Brazil	2.7	174,500	19,981	14
AES Eden	Argentina	0.3	15,300	3,572	60
AES Edes	Argentina	0.1	4,600	1,182	60
AES Sul	Brazil	0.8	29,000	5,772	91
AES CLESA	El Salvador	0.2	5,771	561	64
Eletropaulo	Brazil	4.3	34,789	—	10
AES Edelap	Argentina	0.3	2,000	—	90

PERFORMANCE

AES's financial and operating performance during the 1990s has placed it among the top-performing firms not only in its sector, but across the stock market as a whole. As a result, AES has been prominent among *Fortune* and *Washington Post* lists of companies with fastest growing and best returns to shareholders. In the three years to April 1998, returns to shareholders averaged 80 percent a year.

This performance is surprising to many observers, including many within the company, since profitability and shareholder returns are not the primary yardsticks through which AES monitors and assesses its own performance. AES's assessment of its progress over time focuses upon four measures:

- Shared values – How did we do in having an organization that is fun, that is fair, that acts with integrity, and that is socially responsible?
- Plant operations – How safe, clean, reliable, and cost-effective were our facilities?
- Assets – What changes occurred in our assets, including AES people, during the year? This intends to measure the company's project development and construction progress as an indicator of future earnings potential.
- Sales backlog – What happened to our backlog of contract revenues during the year?

In terms of setting performance targets for the future, these tend to be a mixture of efficiency, employee satisfaction, community development, project development, and growth objectives. The company's goals for 1998 were stated in "Our Wish List" published in the 1997 Annual Report. These included:

- Continuing progress in adapting to and living the AES principles and values.
- Creating the most fun workplace since the beginning of the industrial revolution, and eliminating hourly payment systems.
- Adding 10 to 15 new businesses to the AES portfolio.
- Engineering a breakthrough in slow development businesses such as Ib Valley (India), Puerto Rico, and Nile Power (Uganda).
- Maintaining 100 new business ideas in the development pipeline.
- Making our 1998 budgeted net income and cash flow.

Operationally, AES plants have performed among the best in their industry. AES's US plants operate at around 95 percent capacity, compared to an industry average of 83 percent. AES's West Belfast power station achieved 95 percent availability in 1997, remarkable for a 43-year-old facility.

Not all of AES's efforts have been successful. As already noted, its first power station was unprofitable from the start. In 1992, AES flirted with disaster when its Shady Point generating facility in Oklahoma was discovered to have been discharging polluted water and to have falsified the samples it provided to the Environmental Protection Agency. In the same year, AES was forced to abandon its rebuilding of a power plant at Cedar Bay, Florida following a dispute with state officials and the local community. These events caused AES's share price to fall by half.[4]

The February 1997 acquisition of Destec's international generation assets also appears to have been disappointing in terms of projected returns. Destec's assets included power plants in Australia, the Dominican Republic, Canada, Netherlands, and the UK.

Tables 17.2 and 17.3 summarize some key indicators of AES's performance during 1991–7.

STRATEGY

In a submission to the Securities and Exchange Commission, AES described its strategy as follows:

TABLE 17.2
AES's performance in the 1990s

	1997	1996	1995	1994	1993	1992	1991
Revenue ($ million)	1,411	835	679	533	519	401	334
Net income ($ million)	188	125	107	98	71	56	43
Earnings per share ($)	1.11	0.81	0.71	0.66	0.49	0.40	0.33
Assets ($ million)	8,909	3,622	2,341	1,915	1,687	1,552	1,440
Sales backlog ($ billion)	155	80	41	43	27	n.a.	n.a
Equity generating capacity (MW)	4,569	3,357	2,127	1,470	1,469	1,248	711
Return on average equity (%)	16.3	19.7	22.6	28.3	29.2	35.1	48.6

Sources: Annual Reports, UBS Securities Equity Research.

TABLE 17.3
AES's performance during January–September 1998 and 1997 ($ million, except where noted)

	9 months of 1998	9 months of 1997	Change
Revenues	1,752	880	+99%
Cost of sales and services	1,182	576	+105%
SGA expenses	42	25	+58%
Operating income	516	256	+98%
Interest expense (net)	299	126	+138%
Net income	217	129	+68%
Earnings per share ($)	1.22	0.79	+56%

Source: AES press release, October 22, 1998, www.aesc.com

The Company's strategy in helping meet the world's need for electricity is to participate in competitive power markets as they develop either by greenfield development or by acquiring and operating existing facilities or distribution systems in these markets. The Company generally operates electric generating facilities that utilize natural gas, coal, oil, hydro power, or combinations thereof. In addition, the Company participates in the electric power distribution and retail supply businesses in certain limited instances, and will continue to review opportunities in such markets in the future.

Other elements of the Company's strategy include:

- Supplying energy to customers at the lowest cost possible, taking into account factors such as reliability and environmental performance;
- Constructing or acquiring projects of a relatively large size (generally larger than 100 MW);
- When available, entering into power sales contracts with electric utilities or other customers with significant credit strength; and
- Participating in electric power distribution and retail supply markets that grant concessions with long-term pricing arrangements.

The Company also strives for operating excellence as a key element of its strategy, which it believes it accomplishes by minimizing organizational layers and maximizing company-wide participation in decision-making. AES has attempted to create an operating environment that results in safe, clean and reliable electricity generation. Because of this emphasis, the Company prefers to operate all facilities which it develops or acquires; however, there can be no assurance that the Company will have operating control of all of its facilities.

Where possible, AES attempts to sell electricity under long-term power sales contracts. The Company attempts, whenever possible, to structure the revenue provisions of such power sales contracts such that changes in the cost components of a facility (primarily fuel costs) correspond, as effectively as possible, to changes in the revenue components of the contract. The Company also attempts to provide fuel for its operating plants generally under long-term supply agreements, either through contractual arrangements with third parties or, in some instances, through acquisition of a dependable source of fuel.

As electricity markets become more competitive, it may be more difficult for AES (and other power generation companies) to obtain long-term power sales contracts. In markets where long-term contracts are not available, AES will pursue methods to hedge costs and revenues to provide as much assurance as possible of a project's profitability. In these situations, AES might choose to purchase a project with a partial hedge or with no hedge, with the strategy that its diverse portfolio of projects provides some hedge to the increased volatility of the project's earnings and cash flow. Additionally, AES may choose not to participate in these markets.

The Company attempts to finance each domestic and foreign plant primarily under loan agreements and related documents which, except as noted below, require the loans to be repaid solely from the project's revenues and provide that the repayment of the loans (and interest thereon) is secured solely by the capital stock, physical assets, contracts and/or cash flow of that plant subsidiary or affiliate. This type of financing is generally referred to as "project financing." The lenders under these project financing structures cannot look to AES or its other projects for repayment, unless such entity explicitly agrees to undertake liability. AES has explicitly agreed to undertake certain limited obligations and contingent liabilities, most of which by their terms will only be effective or will be terminated upon the occurrence of future events. In certain circumstances, the Company may incur indebtedness which is recourse to the company or to more than one project.[5]

VALUES AND PRINCIPLES

AES's unique organization and management systems are the direct result of the values upon which the company was established and continue to define every aspect of its management. These values reflect the personal beliefs of the two founders, Sant and Bakke. Both men were brought up in strongly-religious families: Bakke as a Baptist, Sant a Mormon. Bakke was raised on a farm in Washington State. From the age of five he had worked in the fields and by the time he was 18 he had built up a herd of 29 beef cattle. Bakke's attitude to enterprise and material possessions was strongly influenced by ideas of Christian stewardship, which emphasized responsibility, building for the future, and sharing good fortune with others. Sant attended Brigham Young University and spent two years as a missionary with Native

Americans in Wisconsin. As he grew older, Sant became less committed to the Church and increasingly active in the environmental movement.

From the outset, both men viewed AES as an opportunity for them to pursue their values and effect a fundamental change in business practices. The goals of AES are enshrined in its "core values":

- Integrity – AES strives to act with integrity, or "wholeness." The company seeks to honor its commitments. The goal is that the things AES people say and do in all parts of the company should fit together with truth and consistency.
- Fairness – AES wants to treat fairly its people, its customers, its suppliers, its stockholders, and the governments and communities in which it operates. Defining what is fair is often difficult, but the company believes it is helpful to routinely question the relative fairness of alternative courses of action.
- Fun – AES desires that people employed by the company and those people with whom the company interacts have fun in their work. AES's goal has been to create and maintain an environment in which each person can flourish in the use of his or her gifts and skills and thereby enjoy the time spent at AES.
- Social Responsibility – The Company believes that it has a responsibility to be involved in projects that provide social benefits, such as lower costs to customers, a high degree of safety and reliability, and a cleaner environment.

Sant and Bakke recognize that these values cannot easily be reconciled with the concept of a shareholder-focused, profit-maximizing corporation, and both leaders have made it very clear where their priorities lie:

Where do profits fit? Profits . . . are not any corporation's main goal. Profits are to a corporation much like breathing is to life. Breathing is not the goal, but without breath, life ends. Similarly, without turning a profit, a corporation too, will cease to exist . . . At AES we strive not to make profits the ultimate driver of the corporation. My desire is that the principles to which we strive would take preeminence.[6]

AES's commitment to its values, at the expense of shareholder gain where necessary, is indicated by the proviso which AES inserts in all of its prospectuses for new security offers which identifies AES's values as a source of investor risk:

The Company seeks to adhere to these principles, not as a means to achieve economic success, but because adherence is a worthwhile goal in and of itself. However, if the Company perceives a conflict between these principles and profits, the Company will try to adhere to its principles – even though doing so might result in dominated or forgone opportunities or financial benefits.

The AES principles and the way they are implemented reflect a set of assumptions about human nature. Sant and Bakke believe in the ultimate goodness of people. Hence, within organizations, people can and should be trusted to exercise responsibility, and at the same time should be held accountable. Critical to the ability to motivate people is the innate desire of people to make a contribution to society. Hence, for an organization to be effective and to harness human effort and ingenuity, the organization must be committed to a wider social purpose. These views are at variance with many of the assumptions upon which many traditional management systems and techniques are based. In the 1997 Letter to Shareholders Bakke emphasizes: "[t]he people in AES are not principally economic resources. We are not tools of the corporation. Rather we hope the corporation is structured to help individuals make a difference in the world that they could not otherwise make."[7] One way in which AES seeks to implement its principles is through annual surveys, both company-wide and at each location, designed to measure how well its people are doing in supporting these principles. AES noted that, "These surveys are perhaps most useful in revealing failures, and helping to deal with those failures." Dennis Bakke has commented that he devotes more attention to studying the annual employee surveys than the annual financial statements.

Organizational Structure and Management Systems

AES's organizational structure and management systems manifest the company's values and principles. AES describes the key features of its organization in its statement of values:

> In order to create a fun working environment for its people and implement its strategy of operational excellence, AES has adopted decentralized organizational principles and practices. For example, AES works to minimize the number of supervisory layers in its organization. Most of the Company's plants operate without shift supervisors. The project subsidiaries are responsible for all major facility-specific business functions, including financing and capital expenditures. Criteria for hiring new AES people include a person's willingness to accept responsibility and AES's principles as well as a person's experience and expertise. Every AES person has been encouraged to participate in strategic planning and new plant design for the Company. The Company has generally organized itself into multi-skilled teams to develop projects, rather than forming "staff" groups (such as a human resources department or an engineering staff) to carry out specialized functions.
>
> Many people have asked us about our team structure and how it works. To begin with, there is no one person in charge of teams and there is no Human Resources department. Teams are the basis of our structure, and they encompass the four values of our company. They are fluid; many people are members of more than one team at one time. A team is somewhat autonomous; all decisions about a project are made within that team, with final say granted to that team. Decisions are made not from the top-down, but from the bottom-up. Furthermore, responsibility is pushed to the lowest level possible, encouraging everyone to be part of a decision. As a result, each team member views the project in terms of a whole. Colleagues and team members must trust each other to follow through to the best of their ability.
>
> Because people are what make up AES, we have decided not to resort to an organizational model. Instead, we give you the following comments from AES people regarding

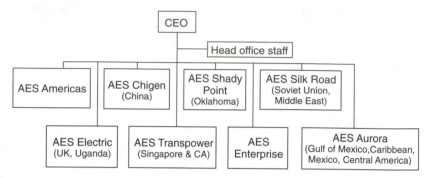

Figure 17.1 AES's divisional structure

teamwork. In general, AES teams work extremely well in both achieving a common goal and having fun while doing so. The following ideas provide insight on what makes teams work well and what can stimulate true and productive teamwork.

"Teams imply friendship; not only the ability but the desire to work together. Starting with the wonderful example set by the original AES team, Roger and Dennis, working together in small groups has been a natural way to get big things done while preserving the dignity of each person." Tom Tribone

"There are two reasons why teams are successful at AES: the type of people we have here and the environment in which they work. People at AES tend to be independent and thrive in a loose environment where roles and responsibilities are not always clearly defined. The environment at AES is one where responsibility is pushed down to the lowest level possible, encouraging everyone to take ownership for not only their piece of the project, but for the project in its entirety." Michael Cranna

This is not to say that AES lacks formal structure altogether. The most striking feature of its organization is the few layers of hierarchy: there are only three organizational layers between the front-line employees and the CEO. AES is divided into eight regional organizations or "Groups." These groups comprise the different plants, each of which is headed by a plant manager. Within each plant there are typically seven areas or "families," each of which is headed by a superintendent. Figure 17.1 shows the structure.

No Functional Departments

The company does not have a legal, human resources, or any other department. Decisions in such matters are made by teams at the plant level, which often times have little or no experience in those decision areas. A few years ago, CFO Barry Sharp estimated that the company had raised $3.5 billion to finance ten new power plants. But, he added, he was personally responsible for raising only $300 million of that sum. The rest was secured by decentralized, empowered teams. When AES raised 200 million pounds sterling (about $350 million) to finance a joint venture in Northern Ireland, two control room operators led the team that raised the funds.[8] The same goes for other aspects of the finance function. Treasury management is also decentralized to the individual plant level, where it is performed by teams of non-specialists:

> His hands still blackened from coal he has just unloaded from a barge, Jeff Hatch picks up the phone and calls his favorite broker. "What kind of rate can you give me for $10 million at 30 days?" he asks the agent, who handles Treasury bills. "Only 6.09? But I just got a 6.13 quote from Chase."
>
> In another room, Joe Oddo is working on J.P. Morgan & Co. "6.15 at 30 days?" confirms Oddo, a maintenance technician at AES Corp.'s power plant here. "I'll get right back to you."
>
> Members of an ad hoc team that manage a $33 million plant investment fund, Messrs. Oddo and Hatch quickly confer with their associates, then close the deal. "It's like playing Monopoly," Mr. Oddo says as he heads off to fix a leaky valve in the boiler room, "Only the money's real."[9]

Similarly, there is no human resources department. At the corporate level there are no staff specialists dealing with salary ranges, or annual review procedures, or personnel policies, or contract negotiations with unions. There is a person whose responsibility is to track 401k retirement plan benefits and send out the necessary reports, but that's about it at the corporate level. Everything else is devolved to the individual divisions, and within these it is the teams within each plant which handle almost all the human resource functions.

The company operates without any written policies or procedures. Issues such as hiring practices, leave periods, and promotion criteria, which in more conventional companies would be spelled out in a "Policies and Procedures" handbook, are left at the employees' discretion. When trying to find out how much time she could take off after the birth of her daughter, a Project Director for AES Puerto Rico discovered that the company did not have a policy about maternity leave. After investigating what other "AES people" had done, she decided to do what made sense for both herself and the business requirements of the project. In the end she decided to take three months, but she made herself available at critical points in the project's execution.[10]

Virtually all human resource decisions are made at plant level, and within the plant, decisional-making authority is among the different teams. For example:

- ■ Recruiting – The recruiting process is done at the plant level, without any support or guidelines from corporate headquarters. AES people at all levels are committed to the hiring process, and everyone can participate in it. The process generally involves an initial résumé review, and a phone interview followed by a group interview. Interviews usually do not include technical questions. Instead, they focus on characteristics that help determine how the candidate will fit with the company's culture and values. There is little importance given to the candidates' educational background or experience, as greater emphasis is placed on the candidates' desire to learn, contribute, and grow, as well as their personal values and self-motivation.

- Training and development – In line with corporate values, AES employees are empowered to make decisions about their own development. Training is mostly done on-the-job, through open communication channels and embedded advice-seeking practices. However, AES people are free to take outside classes and they are reimbursed for them, as long as the courses are work-related.
- Career paths – Regarding development, there are no established career paths. Rather, the company encourages flexibility, which is a necessary requirement in such a dynamic industry. Because one of the company's shared values is to "have fun," employees are encouraged to move within the company if they feel their current assignment is "boring." Job vacancies are always posted and promotion decisions are made at an area superintendent's meeting.
- Compensation and benefits – AES does not have a set salary schedule for any given job, and salaries are determined based on what others are being paid inside and outside the company. Raises are given every year and superintendents usually determine them in an annual meeting. Most AES people put their retirement savings in company stock, and the company matches up to 5 percent of the person's salary in the retirement plan.

This emphasis on multi-functionalism is central to AES's concept of making work fun. The key is to make people's work fulfilling by continually providing challenge and learning experiences. Moreover, argues Bakke, specialization does not promote efficiency or better decision-making: "As soon as you have a specialist who's very good, then everyone else quits thinking," Bakke says. "The better that person is, the worse it is for the organization. The information goes through the specialist, so all the education is to the person who knows the most."[11]

Moreover, AES relies heavily on outside expertise. A key aspect of the system of empowerment is that individuals and teams are encouraged to seek out the best advice available, whether it is within the company or outside. In relation to finance, while AES's financial management and project management teams lack great depth in financial expertise, they draw upon the knowledge of bankers and financiers. In any event, Bakke's view is that most management expertise, whether functionally specialized or general management skill, is not inherently difficult. Motivation, attitude, and a willingness to learn are more important determinants of ultimate performance.

The "Honeycomb"

AES refers to its organizational structure as a "honeycomb." The idea is that each plant comprises a number of small, flexible, self-managed teams who are able to operate cooperatively and efficiently without any centralized direction. At the basis of this structure is the belief that organizations do not need to be managed. Thinking, motivated people can manage themselves and undertake the communication and mutual adjustment needed to coordinate complex tasks. According to Dennis

Bakke, the key to effective decentralization is keeping the basic units of organization small:

> I think of AES as a conglomeration of small communities. And I don't think there's any company in the world that's so big that you can't organize this way. Even a plant with 400 people can be broken down into smaller groups. It's a small enough community that there is the ability to have an accountability structure within it, you know, a social structure as opposed to a military structure. We will break down the Kazakhstan plant into four units. How can we stay small and be big? By breaking the organization into groups with chief operating officers.[12]

The principle of self-organization imposes a very different role on managers from the conventional management model. Indeed, the term "manager" is seldom heard within AES; it is at odds with the principle of letting people decide for themselves. The example comes from the top. "The most difficult thing for me as CEO," confided Bakke, "is not to make decisions." If individuals are to develop, they must be given responsibility and allowed to learn:

> "[T]he modern manager is supposed to ask his people for advice and then make a decision. But at AES, each decision is made by a person and a team. Their job is to get advice from me and from anybody else they think it's necessary to get advice from. And then they make the decision. We do that even with the budget. We make very few decisions here," indicating the headquarters office. "We affirm decisions."[13]

Sant has made similar observations:

> If Dennis and I had to lead everything, we couldn't have grown as much as we have. People would bring deals for us to approve and we would have a huge bottleneck. We've shifted to giving advice rather than giving approval. And we've moved ahead much faster than we would have otherwise."[14]

One consequence of this approach is the small size of AES's corporate headquarters. At any point of time there may be between 40 and 60 AES employees at the Arlington office, but in terms of actual corporate staff, these number only about 30.

In terms of performance, one of the most important advantages of the AES system is that it permits speed in decision-making, preparing bids, and completing projects. AES abounds with a folk history of teams and individuals given huge responsibilities or thrust into unique and unexpected situations. Consider the following:

- Oscar Prieto, a chemical engineer with two years' experience with AES, was visiting AES headquarters in May 1996 when he was asked by Thomas Tribone to join a meeting: "I've got 14 people from France and some guys from Houston coming to talk about buying a business in Rio de Janeiro. We've only got two AES people. Could one of you show up?" The meeting with Electricité de France and Houston Light & Power concerned a possible joint bid for one of Brazil's largest utilities, which was being privatized. Within a month,

Tribone was on his way to Paris to negotiate an agreement with Electricité de France. The deal was concluded, and by 1997 Tribone had moved to Rio to become one of the utility's four directors and a key player in a succession of deals in which AES acquired a string of power plants and distribution facilities in Brazil and Argentina.[15]

- The development of the $404 million Warrior Run power plant in Cumberland, Maryland was undertaken by an AES team of ten people who handled all the work necessary leading up to the plant's groundbreaking in October 1995. They secured 36 different permit approvals involving about 24 regulatory agencies and arranged financing that involved tax-exempt bonds and ten lenders. Within the industry, such a project would typically involve well over a hundred employees.

- Scott Gardner joined AES in 1992 right after graduating from Dartmouth College. Gardner joined a team developing a $200 million cogeneration plant in San Francisco. "It involved a lot of work and few people to do it," he says. "I took on tasks that ranged from designing a water system to negotiating with the community to buying and selling pollution credits." Gardner also helped lead a bid for a $225 million cogeneration plant in Vancouver, British Columbia. When a comparable deal emerged in Australia, Gardner volunteered for that assignment. Two weeks later, he was on his way to Brisbane. "My task was to understand an unfamiliar regional power system, develop a design for the plant, and prepare a financial and technical bid document – all in six weeks," he says. When Gardner's proposal made the final round of competition, his division manager had him negotiate the terms of the $75 million deal. "The stress was incredible, but I was having fun," he says. His bid won. "I held a press conference and was interviewed by local TV stations," says Gardner, who has since left AES to attend business school. "I had to pinch myself to be sure this was happening."[16]

- Paul Burdick, a mechanical engineer, had only been at AES briefly when he was asked to purchase $1 billion in coal. "I'd never negotiated anything before, save for a used car," he said. Burdick spent three weeks asking questions of people both within and outside of the company on how to accomplish the task. At AES, he says, "You're given a lot of leeway and a lot of rope. You can use it to climb or you can hang yourself."[17]

- Ann Murtlow, a chemical engineer with no experience in pollution abatement, was given the job of buying air-pollution credits. She had already purchased the option to buy $1 million in credits when she discovered that the option she had bought was for the wrong kind of credit and useless to AES.

The Relationship with Employees

The AES principles and its concept of the honeycomb organization imply a different type of relationship between employed and the corporation than characterizes most companies. To begin with, the absence of functional specialists and the ideas about self-organization require a tremendous amount of information-sharing. According to the company, employees are given full access to the company's operating and financial information. Because of the extent of employee access to information that would normally be confidential at other companies, AES lists all its employees as "insiders" in its submissions to the SEC.

One of AES's current crusades is to eliminate the distinction between salaried and hourly paid employees and to put all employees on a salaried basis. The 1997 Annual Report states that its goal for 1998 will be to continue eliminating hourly payment systems. The Annual Report notes that the number of AES employees compensated hourly had decreased from 90 percent to 50 percent over the past two years. At AES, a belief that every person can "be a business person" requires a "salaried approach" to compensation. However, this task has been stymied by Federal health and safety legislation which perpetuates staff/worker distinctions by specific regulations governing the hours and working conditions of manual workers. Bakke's attempts to interest the Secretary of Labor and President Clinton in what Bakke regards as an anachronistic hangover from the industrial revolution have met with little Federal response so far.

The primacy that AES accords its "people," as the company refers to its employees, is emphasized by its listing of every employee's name in the back of the AES Annual Report.

AES and the Environment

AES's deep commitment to the environment extends well beyond Chairman Sant's personal involvement in environmentalist issues and his active roles in the World Wildlife Fund and as a member of the Environmental Defense Fund. Because building and operating power plants is not one of the world's most environmentally friendly endeavors, AES tries to compensate for the emissions it generates. When the company constructed a coal-fired plant in Montville, Connecticut, it calculated that it would generate 15 million tons of carbon dioxide over its estimated life of 40 years. The company then captured national attention when it announced that it would plant 52 million trees in Guatemala to offset the Connecticut's plant carbon dioxide emissions. According to AES Executive Vice-President Robert F. Hemphill: "Making electric power historically has had a relatively high level of environmental assault. We are not planting trees as part of our strategy to make us a more valuable company, we're doing it because we think it's a responsible thing to do." AES's average company-wide emission levels are 40–60 percent of permitted rates. These actions are of course in line with one of the company's four core values: social responsibility.[18]

Emphasis on responsibility to the environment and to local communities is viewed as integral to the efficient running of power plants. Professor Jeff Pfeffer of Stanford Business School describes a visit to the Thames, Connecticut power plant:

A visitor to the plant is immediately struck by its cleanliness, and the people who work in the plant are proud of its appearance. The walls of the plant exterior are very light colored (off-white), so that any dirt would be immediately visible. The color of the walls was intentionally chosen to encourage respect for the physical environment and cleanliness. The place where the coal is unloaded from the barges that bring it up the Connecticut River is also immaculate. The coal handling system is covered to avoid excess dust or debris getting into the surroundings and the loading dock and surrounding area is swept by a mechanical sweeper after the once a week delivery. There is no smell of sulfur in the air, and in fact, no odor at all. The attitude to cleanliness extends inside the plant as well. For example, there are two lunch rooms, both have stoves, microwave oven, cooktops, refrigerator, and dishwasher which makes them more than a typical plant eating area. Quite elaborate meals are cooked there. Both lunch rooms are clean with no dirty dishes sitting around. The cabinetry is of excellent quality and appearance as are the appliances. The turbine rooms are also immaculate.[19]

The Challenge of a Multicultural AES

As more and more of AES's business becomes located outside the US, and non-US citizens far outnumber US citizens among AES's employees, an increasingly important challenge is to retain AES's culture as the company grows. The company acknowledges that even the stated value of having fun is difficult to accomplish with so many people with many different backgrounds. Currently, the most prevalent languages within the company are Russian, Hungarian, and Portuguese, with fewer than 8 percent of AES people being native English speakers. The principles of equality, teamwork, empowerment, and individual initiative are also likely to be more difficult to implement in traditional Islamic societies such as Pakistan, and countries with a socialist heritage such as China and Kazakhstan.

Nevertheless, AES remains committed to its principles not just for its US, but for its worldwide operations. Bakke firmly believes that the AES principles are universal and are not culturally specific either to the US or to the West in general. AES's experience so far is that its own corporate culture can be transplanted in many different national cultures. The challenges presented in running one of the world's biggest (and once one of the most dilapidated) coal-fired power stations in Kazakhstan, and turning around heavily bureaucratized, former state-owned utilities in South America have provided remarkable test-cases in AES's ability to export its company culture. The results have often been amazing. Even though AES has been unable to eliminate the distinction between salaried and hourly paid employees within the US, in England, Argentina, and Pakistan it has moved to an all-salary workforce.

Instilling the AES culture into the 100-year-old Light Servicios de Electricidade involved, first, a generous severance package to cut the workforce by half, second, the careful selection of young, motivated, engineers and supervisors to take key positions as facility supervisors, and finally, the devolving of decision-making power to them. At Light's Santa Branca facility, Oscar Prieto chose Carlos Baldi, a 34-year-old engineer, to lead the plant. "I knew he was the right person," says Prieto, "He was young, eager to do more." After agreeing to shared goals and expectations – zero accidents, thrifty construction budgets – Prieto turned Santa Branca and a $35 million upgrading project over to Baldi. After a short while, Baldi was managing in the same way with his project and team leaders.[20]

THE INDUSTRY OUTLOOK

AES is a product of deregulation in the electricity-generating industry. Its ability to grow its business so quickly is a result of the global trend of electricity market restructuring, which has created significant new business opportunities for independent power generation. The trend is away from government-owned electricity systems toward deregulated, competitive market structures. Many countries have rewritten their laws and regulations to allow foreign investment and private ownership of electricity generation, transmission, or distribution systems. Some countries have privatized or are in the process of privatizing their electricity systems by selling all or part of such systems to private investors. The demand has been for new, more efficiently operated electric-generating capacity – and it is this demand that companies like AES have been able to meet so effectively.

AES's continued growth is dependent upon a continued opening of power markets to competition both in the US and overseas. The Public Utility Regulatory Policies Act of 1978 provides exemptions to IPPs from regulation as public utilities and requires utilities to purchase electricity from IPPs. Further Federal deregulation of the industry might involve repealing PURPA and more of the legislation relating to the regulation of public utilities (The Public Utility Holding Company Act of 1935).

In the meantime, electric utility deregulation is proceeding at the state level. As a result a number of utilities are selling off their generating assets, while others are seeking to expand through acquiring generating assets outside of their own states. Competition has begun in the supply of electricity to many commercial and industrial customers. The result has been increased opportunities to acquire existing generating assets.

Overseas, the trend towards deregulation and privatization continues. Throughout much of the world, electricity generation is undertaken by publicly owned utilities. Considerable opportunities remain for IPPs like AES to acquire existing generating assets in tender sales by national authorities, and to supply electricity distribution utilities through building new power plants.

While growth opportunities in the global power business continue to emerge, competition for these opportunities is intensifying. As well as start-up companies such as AES, many companies have diversified into the power business. These include gas companies such as Enron, Columbia Gas Systems, and British Gas, oil companies such as Exxon, Mobil, BP-Amoco, Shell, and Arco, engineering and construction companies such as Bechtel, and equipment suppliers such as GE and ABB. Moreover, many nationally focused electricity utilities have expanded internationally. Long-established global players such as the Southern Company and Electricité de France are being joined by new international venturers such as Scottish Power. The different companies bring with them different resources and capabilities. For example, the oil and gas companies such as Enron, BP-Amoco, Shell, and Mobil not only have huge financial resources, they also own gas reserves and have the incentive to add value to these reserves by forward integrating into power production.

The concern is that this increased competition will put downward pressure on the prices contained in new power sales agreements and upward pressure on the acquisition prices for existing assets through competitive bidding practices. If electricity prices within the US are deregulated, and prices are set by market forces within a restructured US electric utility industry, increased competition may result in lower prices and less profit for US electricity sellers.

There is also the likelihood that IPPs will face greater risks. Falling electricity prices and uncertainty as to the future structure of the industry are inhibiting United States utilities from entering into long-term power purchase contracts. The tendency for more and more electricity to be sold on a spot basis or on short-term contracts has been encouraged by the development of a commodity market for power spot and futures contracts in electricity. This development has been pioneered by Enron in particular. Until now, IPPs within the US have been guaranteed a market for their electricity. However, in a more fully deregulated market they are likely to face greater competition and greater risk. The IPPs are the least vertically integrated players in the industry. While the traditional utilities are vertically integrated from power generation through transmission to electricity marketing and distribution, and the oil and gas companies are backward integrated into fuel supplies, the IPPs have traditionally been involved only in the generation of power. As a result, IPPs like AES are particularly vulnerable to market risks: they are dependent upon the market for their fuel suppliers and the market for their sales. The risks over the prices and availability of input supply and output demand have been managed by the IPPs through long-term contracts. Long-term supply contracts for electricity are typically matched with long-term purchasing contracts for fuel.

Outside of the US, the power-generation business is subject to additional risk factors. These include political risks, foreign exchange risks, risks arising from currency repatriation restrictions and currency inconvertibility, and risks relating to the ability to complete new projects on time and within budget. Not all of these risks can be hedged against or insured against. The uncertainty of the legal environment in some countries can also limit a power producer's ability to protect its rights under contractual agreements. The global financial uncertainties of 1997–8 have increased the levels of risk associated with doing business in most of the regions of the world where opportunities for new power supply contracts exist, such as Latin America, the former Soviet Union, South and East Asia. During 1998, these additional risks were becoming evident in the availability of financing for power projects in the emerging market countries. Investment in power stations tends to be project finance, where the financing loans are secured on the cash flows and asset values of the particular project and there is no recourse to the company. The risks involved in such finance often mean that government guarantees are required.

THE FUTURE

AES's unique organizational structure, management systems, and corporate culture had served it well. Although unorthodox, not only in the power industry, but in the corporate sector generally, the AES approach had shown itself to be highly effective both in the efficient operation of power stations and in supporting the entrepreneurial capabilities required for winning power supply contracts all over the world.

Since 1992, when its first overseas plants went on line (in Northern Ireland), AES has acquired a greater depth of experience in bidding for power contracts and operating power plants in more countries of the world than any other power company. Moreover, because of its very low rate of employee turnover and open internal communication, it has been very effective in retaining this expertise and sharing it internally.

But the industry and AES itself continue to change. On the external front, overseas opportunities are likely to continue. The critical issue is whether increased competition will make it difficult for AES to obtain contracts with the kinds of returns which it considers commensurate with the level of risk it undertakes. In particular, companies like Mobil and GE with their huge internally generated cash flows and synergies between their power businesses and their other business interests may be willing and able to take on power contracts at prices which are unattractive to AES. Internally, the greatest concern was whether a S&P 500 company with $10 billion in assets and 11,000 employees (over 30,000 including affiliates) operating in 23 countries could retain a family culture where a set of principles substitutes for formal management systems and procedures.

NOTES

1. "A power producer is intent on giving power to its people," *Wall Street Journal*, July 3, 1995, p. A1.
2. "Arlington's AES Corp. leads a battery of US energy companies overseas," *Washington Post*, May 22, 1995.
3. "The principles behind its power," *Washington Post*, November 2, 1998, p. F12.
4. An account of this period is found in "AES Honeycomb A" (HBS Case 9-395-132) and "AES Honeycomb B" (HBS Case 9-395-122).
5. AES, 10K Report, 1997, www.aesc.com.
6. Dennis W. Bakke, "Erecting a grid for ethical power," *The Marketplace*, May/June 1996, p. 5.
7. Annual Letter, *1997 AES Corporation Annual Report*.
8. Alex Markels, "Power to people," *Fast Company*, 13 (March 1998), p. 155.
9. "A power producer," *Wall Street Journal*.
10. Jeffrey Pfeffer, "Human resources at the AES Corporation: the case of the missing department," Graduate School of Business, Stanford University, 1997, p. 14.
11. "A power producer," *Wall Street Journal*.
12. Pfeffer, "Human resources at the AES Corporation."
13. "The power of a team: Arlington's AES Corporation," *The Washington Post*, February 12, 1996, p. F12.
14. Markels, "Power to people," p. 160.
15. Ibid. 156.
16. Ibid. 157.
17. "A power producer," *Wall Street Journal*.
18. "Power plant builder tries to reenergize environmental image," *The Washington Post*, July 6, 1992, p. F1.
19. Pfeffer, "Human resources at the AES Corporation," pp. 6–7.
20. Markels, "Power to people," p. 164.

INDEX